In Mozart's
FOOTSTEPS

A HA'PENNY
PRESS BOOK

Paragon House

NEW YORK

In Mozart's
FOOTSTEPS

Harrison

James

Wignall

First edition, 1991
Published in the United States by

Paragon House
90 Fifth Avenue
New York, NY 10011

Library of Congress Cataloging-in-Publication Data

Wignall, Harrison James.
  In Mozart's footsteps / by Harrison James Wignall.
    p.   cm.
  "A Ha'penny Press book."
  Includes bibliographical references.
  ISBN 1-55778-494-9 : $21.95
  1. Mozart, Wolfgang Amadeus, 1756–1791—Homes and haunts. 2. Europe—Description
and travel—1971-   —Guide-books.   I. Title.
ML410.M9W58   1991   91-3059
780'.92—dc20   CIP
                                                                        MN

Book Design by Barbara M. Bachman

Photographs appearing on pages 7, 49, 53, 55, 159, 193, 231, 285, 297, 309, 315, 319, and 323
by Harrison James Wignall.

Manufactured in the United States of America
10 9 8 7 6 5 4 3 2

—For Beatrice Mary Gradwell Wignall

E Beatrice . . .
Io ritornai dalla santissim'onda
Rifatto sì, come piante novelle
Rinnovellate di novella fronda,
Puro e disposto a salire alle stelle.

DANTE, LA DIVINA COMMEDIA

And Beatrice . . .
I returned from the most holy waters
Renewed indeed, like new plants
Whose foliage shines with new life,
Pure and ready to climb to the stars.

DANTE, THE DIVINE COMEDY

Contents

ENGLAND

FRANCE

GERMANY

ITALY

NETHERLANDS

SWITZERLAND

Introduction

THERE is no better way to understand Mozart and his music than to follow in his footsteps, to see the churches and public buildings that he visited, the houses in which he lodged, the palaces, concert halls and salons in which he performed. Several of these sites now have become Mozart museums; others are important buildings in European cultural history; still others are humble inns or flats. Small or large, all bear the traces of Mozart's presence; all are richly evocative of the persona of the young man who became the best-loved and "most universal composer in the history of Western music." The universal appeal of Mozart's music is tied to his compelling travel experiences, which began when he was five years old, and continued to the very last year of his life. In fact, one third of his lifetime Mozart spent traveling.[1]

As the supreme child prodigy of the eighteenth century and later as a mature composer, Mozart toured nine countries and visited or passed through over two hundred European cities. Among these are the major cities familiar to every European traveler—Paris, Rome, London, Venice, Amsterdam, Florence, Vienna, Munich and Salzburg—as well as other cities of rare beauty that are often overlooked—Antwerp, Prague, Innsbruck, Brussels, Bern and Canterbury.

Some of the cities Mozart visited have remained largely intact and provide the visitor with an illuminating glimpse into the eighteenth century. Prague, where much of the film *Amadeus* was filmed, was frozen in time as a Baroque city and presents a remarkable historical picture from which to appreciate the music of Mozart. Other carefully restored "Mozart cities" that provide similarly fascinating walks into the past include Parma, Strasbourg, Utrecht, Augsburg, Potsdam, Dijon, Nancy, and Cremona. Almost every city in Europe has an old section that reflects Mozart's time, as well as prior centuries of its history. Today, retracing Mozart's journeys brings the eighteenth century to life in a very special way, and directs the traveler to many of the finest cultural resources—musical, artistic, and architectural—in the world.

The guide is arranged alphabetically by country and alphabetically by city within each country. A brief introduction to each city will relate its significance in Mozart's life and work. Within each city are listings of the sites associated with the composer, with relevant biographical details and current tourist data.

Memorial sites in cities of lesser importance to Mozart's itinerary have been included under the heading "Other Sites of Interest," at the end of the country listing. Using this guide, the visitor can readily reconstruct Mozart's stay in over seventy cities. For those who want to plan more ambitious itineraries, an appendix offers a chronological listing of Mozart's travels city by city, so that the traveler can retrace all or a part of Mozart's actual tours.

Whether used comprehensively or selectively, *In Mozart's Footsteps* is an indispensable guide to Mozart sites—the only such guide in any language. To date, published information concerning Mozart memorial sites has been frequently outdated, incomplete, and inaccurate. This guide is a collection of exhaustive research from archives all over Europe and from the author's own visits to most of the sites listed here. Based on the latest biographical, historical, and tourist information, this book contains numerous new details that were previously unknown in the Mozart literature. *In Mozart's Footsteps* is an invaluable resource for the music-loving traveler, as well as for the armchair Mozartian.

N o t e s

1 Cf. Eibl, *Chronik eines Lebens,* 90.

Author's Preface

TWO YEARS ago when Maury Solomon of Ha'penny Press commissioned me to write *In Mozart's Footsteps*, I quickly discovered that there were problematic areas in the current state of research and documentation regarding Mozart's travels. The Mozart literature was frequently as much as fifty years out-of-date. The present state of numerous sites was unclear, and the literature had astonishing gaps when it came to such basic biographical questions as where events took place. To confront these problems, I traveled to over fifty-five cities in Mozart's itinerary of over two hundred cities and collaborated extensively with the archivists of each town.

The result was a surprising amount of new information, and numerous corrections of previously published work. This new information is the basis of this book.

Throughout my research, I found that many Mozart sites or their addresses no longer exist yet continue to be cited in even the most recent Mozart literature. Furthermore, many important sites have been cited incorrectly or overlooked completely. Many of these edifices are in a fine state of preservation, and though ignored by the present Mozart literature, were often known to archivists outside of the area of Mozart studies. Still others were found either in published works or unpublished documents by myself or by archivists in response to my queries. For example, I located for the first time, with their help, the sites of many inns where Mozart and his family stayed. This can be useful as Mozart and his family generally stayed in the center of cities, close to the homes of important nobility and theaters, and most of their activities took place within a radius from their lodgings, restricted by the very length of their stay.

My study is related to that of the late Mozart scholar Joseph Heinz Eibl, whose annotations to the Bauer/Deutsch/Eibl edition of the Mozart letters encompass the literature of Mozart sites with encyclopedic thoroughness. The frequent communications by Eibl to various European archives and libraries greatly extended the scope of information contained in the numerous published articles. The Eibl annotations to the Bauer/Deutsch/Eibl edition of the Mozart letters, and the articles from which much of his information derived, provided the foundation for my study; I then proceeded to update the information through new correspondence with archivists, in great detail, as my research was limited to sites. The Eibl notes are an extremely valuable resource, and the dates used in my book are based on Eibl's useful *Chronik eines Lebens*.

Throughout this work I have used my own translations, as the Emily Anderson translation of the Mozart letters is often outmoded and inaccurate. However, for the general traveler or Mozart enthusiast acquainted with English, hers remains a helpful source.

When Mozart's music is cited, there are references to the Köchel catalogue. This invaluable work attempts a complete chronological listing of Mozart's *oeuvre*; it has been revised numerous times, and will undoubtedly be revised many more times in the future. In general, a single number indicates that the Köchel number in the sixth edition is identical to that of the first edition. Where two numbers are cited, they refer to Köchel 1 and Köchel 6 respectively (i.e. K. 365/316a). Occasionally, where three numbers appear, they refer to the first, third, and sixth editions of the Kochel catalogues, respectively.

I omitted a few cities for which the information was insufficent. However, all the cities Mozart visited appear in the general chronology of Mozart's travels at the end of the book.

Over seventy cities are treated in this book in great detail. During my travels, at times I found that Mozart sites had been replaced by massive, twentieth-century concrete buildings. To help the reader gauge the relative importance of the sites, I have used the following rating scale throughout:

★ ★ ★ *of great interest*
★ ★ *very worthwhile*
★ *worth a visit*
(*no stars*) *of historical interest*

The sites within each city have been arranged in a practical itinerary so that in cities such as Paris and London travelers will not have to retrace their steps across the city to get from one site to another. To recreate a broad picture of each city as it appeared in the eighteenth century, I have also included here sites of interest and important contemporary monuments which are not directly connected with Mozart.

It is hoped that this book will provide an important glimpse into Mozart's life and travels as well as contribute clarity and accuracy to the current state of Mozart studies.

—HARRISON JAMES WIGNALL

Mozart's Family at a Glance

LEOPOLD MOZART (1719–1787)

Leopold, the father of Mozart, was a native of Augsburg and moved to Salzburg to study at the Benedictine University. In Salzburg, he found a position as violinist for the Archbishop of Salzburg, and a wife, Maria Anna Pertl. They married in 1747, and in 1756 (the year of Mozart's birth) his renowned treatise on playing the violin was published. After realizing the gifts of his two children (and particularly those of Mozart), he dedicated himself to their education and development, traveling to present them to the greatest courts in Europe.

MARIA ANNA MOZART (1720–1778)

Mozart's mother was born Anna Maria Pertl in St. Gilgen. After her marriage to Leopold, the attractive couple had a total of seven children, of which only Mozart and his sister lived. Although she was not fond of traveling, Maria Anna accompanied Mozart to Paris in 1778 (as Leopold was not granted leave), where she died on 3 July 1778.

MARIA ANNA MOZART (1751–1829)

"Nannerl," Mozart's sister, was a talented prodigy on the keyboard. Her father, Leopold, a superb educator with a keen eye for business, took her and her young brother, Mozart, to numerous courts throughout Europe to display their musical abilities. Mozart's gifts, however, soon began to overshadow those of his sister. Nannerl was fashionable, attractive, and had highly refined manners; she later married a magistrate, Baron Johann von Berchtold zu Sonnenburg, and moved to St. Gilgen, where she lived in the same house in which her mother was born. Like Leopold, she did not approve of Mozart's choice of a wife, Constanze. After her husband's death in 1801, she moved back to Salzburg, where she gave clavier lessons. When the Novellos visited her in 1829, she was almost blind and living in poverty.

CONSTANZE MOZART (1762–1842)

In 1782, Mozart married Constanze Weber, several years after her sister, Aloisia, rejected his suit. Although they had a successful, loving marriage, Constanze was criticized for her inability to help Mozart manage his finances. Only two of their six children reached adulthood, Karl Thomas and Franz Xaver. After Mozart's death, Constanze married Georg Nissen, who wrote a biography of Mozart.

Austria

Baden (bei Wein), Innsbruck,
Lambach Abbey, Linz,
Melk, Salzburg, Vienna

Other Sites of Interest:

St. Gilgen

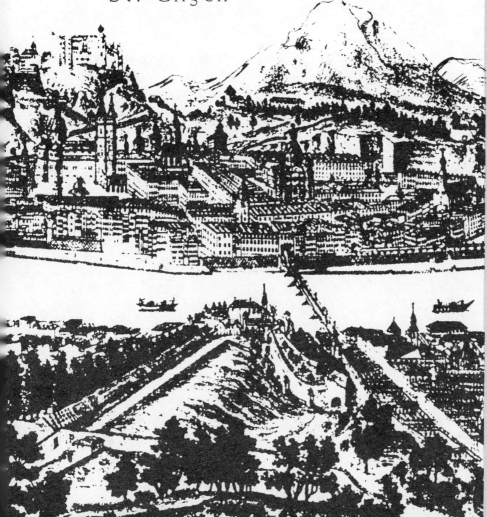

ozart in Baden (bei Wien)

Dates

21–23 August 1773 ▪ **Beginning June 1784**
About 15–18 August 1789 ▪ **June 1790** ▪ **June 1791**
15 October 1791

Mozart and his family first visited Baden in 1773; it was a visit that left Leopold Mozart favorably impressed.

In 1789, Mozart was concerned about his wife Constanze's failing health, and sent her here for a "cure," visiting her in August. Mozart was experiencing financial difficulties and asking for loans from Puchberg, a wealthy merchant, who was his fellow Freemason and creditor in his later years. Mozart was content that he could contribute to his wife's recuperation, but was concerned that she not make herself "so cheap." In 1790, Mozart complained of feeling seriously ill; Constanze's health again required visits to Baden, where Mozart visited her for short visits. Again, in 1791, he sent Constanze to Baden, with Karl, their son; Mozart visited her several times in June and July.

Music

Motet "Ave verum corpus," K. 618, written 17 June 1791 for Anton Stoll in Baden.

Baden Sites

★★ ST. STEPHAN'S PARISH CHURCH (PFARRKIRCHE ST. STEPHAN). Pfarrplatz. Here, on 13 June 1790, a Mass by Mozart (probably K. 317) was performed; on 10 July 1791, Mozart directed "Ave verum corpus," and his *Missa brevis*, K. 275/272b was performed. "Ave verum corpus," K. 618, written while Mozart was in Baden, was dedicated to Anton Stoll, schoolteacher and choir director in Baden, who directed it on the Feast of Corpus Christi. Commemorative plaque citing Mozart's dedication to Stoll.

SITE OF HOUSE "ZUM BLUMENSTOCK." Renngasse 4. At the end of May 1791, Mozart wrote to Anton Stoll, asking him to find an apartment for Constanze. Stoll found a ground floor apartment in the house of Johann Grundgeyer, the house "Flower Stalk" ("Zum Blumenstock"). To work undisturbed on "Ave verum corpus," Mozart rented a small apartment over Constanze's later in June, in the courtyard.[1] Nothing remains of the original building; a modern medical treatment center (**Bauernkrankenkasse**) occupies the site today.[2] Commemorative plaque.

SITE OF THE ANTONSBAD. Near Renngasse 4. Here, at the baths near the apartment that Mozart rented in 1791, Constanze took the waters during her visits to Baden. Mozart emphasized his fear that she would fall leaving the bath, which would have been serious during her pregnancy. In his letter of 8 October 1791, he noted, "As I write, no doubt you will be having a good swim." Nothing remains of the original building; the modern medical center, **Bauernkrankenkasse** occupies the site.[3]

SITE OF THE BADEN THEATER. Theaterplatz. Mozart, in June 1791, wrote to Anton Stoll at Baden, and asked whether the theater at Baden had opened yet. The original theater was demolished, and a new theater was erected by Joseph Kornhäusel in 1812. Later, in 1908, the present **Jubilaeumsstadttheater** was constructed on the same site.[4]

SITE OF THE CASINO. Hauptplatz 15. In Baden, a casino was located which was frequented by Constanze and Mozart together, as well as by Constanze when she was alone. Dancing took place here, and Mozart tried to dissuade Constanze from going to the casino on several occasions, as he didn't approve of the company. The edifice, built by Philipp Otto about 1750, later became the Hotel Stadt Wien; nothing remains of the original building. The **Badener Sparkasse** occupies the site today.[5]

[★ CHARACTERISTIC SIGHTS OF BADEN]. During the visit of Mozart and his father to Baden in 21–23 August 1773, and during Mozart and Constanze's numerous visits from 1789–91, they toured the town at leisure. Leopold noted in 1773, "Baden is a tiny little town. There are a great many baths, all much like those at Gastein, except that here they are built more comfortably." A fire in 1812 destroyed the entire center of the city; as a result, there are no buildings from the time of Mozart's visit, except for the **Pfarrkirche**. However, the most famous Biedermeier architects reconstructed the city after 1812 with the substantial help of the Austrian nobility and the imperial family, who spent their summer holidays in Baden from 1791–1834.[6] Antonio Salieri, Mozart's rival, stayed in Baden from 1786–1823, at the Hotel Sauerhof, which was constructed by Joseph Kornhäusel.[7]

[★ ★ MEMORIAL MUSEUM]. Rathausgasse 10. To commemorate Mozart and Beethoven, the famous guests of Baden, a small museum has been created in this building, one of the oldest in Baden. Beethoven stayed here three times during 1821–23; he wrote parts of the *Missa solemnis* in 1821, worked on the overture to the "Consecration of the House" in 1822, and finished the Ninth Symphony here in 1823. Open 1 May to 15 October 9–11 AM and 3–5 PM; closed Thursday; 16 October to 30 April, Tuesday and Saturday 3–5 PM; Thursday 9–11 AM; admission charge.[8]

Baden. Water-color by L. Janscha. Graphische Sammlung Albertina, Vienna.

N o t e s

1 Bauer/Deutsch/Eibl, *Mozart Briefe*, VI, zu 1153/17.
2 Communicated by Dr. A. Pfann, Baden Tourist Board.
3 Communicated by Dr. A. Pfann, Baden Tourist Board.
4 Communicated by Dr. A. Pfann, Baden Tourist Board.
5 Communicated by Dr. A. Pfann, Baden Tourist Board.
6 Communicated by Dr. A. Pfann, Baden Tourist Board.
7 Communicated by Dr. A. Pfann, Baden Tourist Board.
8 Michelin, *Austria*, 51.

Mozart in Innsbruck

Dates

15–19 December 1769 ▪ 25/26 March 1771 ▪ 14/15 August 1771 ▪ 14
December 1771 ▪ 25–27 October 1772 ▪ About 12 March 1773

For each of the three trips that Mozart and his father made to Italy, they stopped in Innsbruck, after leaving Salzburg, and on the return journey. The most significant trip was the first, in 1769, when Count Spaur put his coach at their disposal, and Mozart played a concert at the home of Count Künigl. Upon returning from Italy, Leopold wrote on 25 March 1771 that they arrived with "strong wind, snow and dreadful cold."

They stopped in Innsbruck *en route* to Italy for the second time, and again passed through on the way back to Salzburg. During the third Italian sojourn, Leopold and Mozart took an excursion to Halle, where Mozart played the organ in the Damenstift. Upon leaving Milan for the third time, they again passed through Innsbruck.

Innsbruck Sites

★ ★ "GOLDEN EAGLE" INN ("ZUM GOLDENEN ADLER"). Herzog-Friedrich-Strasse 6. On their way to Italy for the third time, Mozart and his father arrived in Innsbruck at 10 PM on 25 October 1772 and lodged here in the Golden Eagle Inn, which was at the post stop. Again, when returning, Leopold had his wife send mail here, as he was planning to stay here again when he arrived, around 12 March 1773. The inn, founded in 1390, has had many distinguished guests: Goethe, Heinrich Heine, King Gustav III of Sweden, and Emperor Joseph II (who traveled incognito as the Count of Falkenstein on 29 July 1777, after a secret visit to his sister Marie Antoinette in France). The inn has been refurbished inside, yet maintains architectural features of the past such as brick vaulting, "Goethe's room," (somewhat preserved as it was during Goethe's stay), and antique oil-on-wood paintings. The exterior features fine Tirol architecture, with a weathered, ornamentally painted facade.

★ ★ "WHITE CROSS" INN ("ZUM WEISSEN KREUZ"). Herzog-Friedrich-Strasse 31. *En route* to Italy for the first time, Leopold and Wolfgang arrived on 15 December 1769 at 5:30 PM, and lodged here in the White Cross Inn, which dates from 1465. The fine shield outside, with a white cross surrounded by grapevines, was constructed in 1665. All rooms have undergone modern renovation, with architectural features often maintained. Several restaurant rooms are in a rustic style. Outside there is a commemorative plaque about the stay of the thirteen-year-old Mozart, and his concert at Count Künigl's.

Innsbruck. Inn, "The Golden Eagle."

★ ★ PALAIS OF COUNT KÜNIGL. Maria-Theresien-Strasse 38. On their way to Italy for the first time, Mozart and Leopold notified Count Johann Spaur that they had arrived, and soon received a note from Count Leopold Franz Künigl, the vice-president of the provincial government, inviting them to a concert at his home the next evening, 17 December 1769, at 5 PM. Mozart played a "very beautiful concerto" at sight, and Leopold wrote his wife that they were "as usual, received with all honors." Leopold received twelve ducats as an honorarium. The building, which has been altered since the time of Mozart, has been attributed to Johann Martin Gumpp the Elder and is presently Palais Trapp,[1] in the private ownership of the Trapp family; *the interior cannot be visited*. However, the splendid ornate portal, leading to a courtyard renovated in the old style, is of interest. The public may visit the inner courtyard and the entrance to the stairway.[2]

★ ★ PALAIS OF COUNT SPAUR. Maria-Theresien-Strasse 29.[3] Upon arriving in Innsbruck on 16 December 1769, Leopold had himself announced to his countryman Johann Nepomuk Spaur, who was Governor of the Tirol. Leopold wrote that Count Spaur sent his servant immediately and later sent his coach to their lodging at 2 PM. His wife then "received them graciously," and Count Spaur left his coach at their disposal. Spaur also brought them home from the concert at the *palais* of Count Künigl, where Mozart had played a concerto at sight. The present building, probably originally made up of three houses, was built together (three stories high) when it was inhabited by Count Johann Nepomuk Spaur; in 1921 it was reconstructed by Welzenbach, with the facade completely redone, and the interior extensively renewed.[4]

[★ ★ ★ CHARACTERISTIC SIGHTS OF INNSBRUCK]. Many of the sights of Innsbruck from the time of the Mozarts' visits are still splendidly preserved, including the Golden Roof (**Goldenes Dachl**), finished in 1500, which represents the power and wealth of the Hapsburgs. St. Anne's Column (**Annasäule**) of 1706, recalls the retreat of troops from Bavaria during the War of the Spanish Succession. In addition, the Renaissance Belfry (**Stadtturm**), and the Triumphal Arch (**Triumphpforte**) of 1765 are noteworthy. The massive, sober **Hofburg**, finished in 1770, is painted in "Maria Theresa yellow"; it was the site of the death of Maria Theresa's husband during celebrations in 1765. Inside can be found the sumptuously decorated Giant's Hall (**Riesensaal**) with a ceiling dating from 1776 (after Mozart's last visit to Innsbruck). The Court Church (**Hofkirche**), built 1533–63, contains the Renaissance Mausoleum to Emperor Maximilian I and the splendid Silver Chapel. The Cathedral of St. James (**Dom zu St. Jakob**) has superb Baroque decoration by the Asam brothers dating from 1722. Finally, the Wilton Abbey, dating back to 1126, was an important institution; the Church (**Stiftskirche**) and the Rococo Basilica (which was a frequent pilgrimage site) are also of interest.[5]

★ ★ EXCURSION TO THE LADIES' ABBEY IN HALLE (FORMER DAMENSTIFT HALL IN TIROL). Stiftsplatz; Kloster Schulgasse Nr. 2. On 26 October 1772, on the way to Italy for the third time, Leopold and Wolfgang made an afternoon excursion to this abbey, located about seven miles from Innsbruck. Leopold was interested in walking around the Royal Abbey, and Countess Marianne Lodron showed them all around. In the abbey, founded for noble ladies by Archduke Ferdinand II in 1566, Mozart played the organ in the abbey church (**Stiftskirche**). Several years after the secularization ordered by Emperor Joseph II in 1783, the organ was moved to Fügen, where it is found today, although not in a completely preserved state.[6] The medieval Upper Town has many picturesque facades, including the sixteenth-century Town Hall and the fifteenth-century Parish Church. The sober, classical Ladies' Abbey, however, provides a marked contrast. The facade of the former **Damenstift** Church (today a convent for the Sisters of the Heart of Jesus) is Baroque, with a fine Renaissance doorway.[7] Although the building is essentially the same as in 1722, nothing from the eighteenth-century inventory is preserved in the present convent; as the order of the nuns is contemplative, *the convent is not open to the public*, and concerts are never given in the church.[8]

N o t e s

1 The citation in the *Österreichische Kunsttopographie* XXXVIII/I. Part, p. 406, indicates that Count Leopold Künigl inhabited the present Palais Trapp in 1769 (compare M. Krapf, *Die Baumeister Gumpp*, p. 309). Communicated by Dr. Christian Fornwagner, Tiroler Landesarchiv.

2 Communicated by Dr. Christian Fornwagner, Tiroler Landesarchiv.

3 This site, which has been overlooked in the Mozart literature, has been located in the published architectural history of Innsbruck by Dr. Christian Fornwagner, Tiroler Landesarchiv, in response to my queries. It has not been possible to locate the homes of Kassian Jgnaz Freiherr von Enzenberg, Herr von Kalckhammer or Baron Cristani, as there are no indications of houses or apartments cited for them in 1769; communicated by Dr. Christian Fornwagner, Tiroler Landesarchiv.

4 *Österreichische Kunsttopographie*, Band XXXVIII, I. Teil, 337.

5 Michelin, *Austria*, 80.

6 Communicated by Dr. Caramelle, Landeskonservator für Tirol.

7 Michelin, op. cit. 87–9.

8 Communicated by Dr. Caramelle, Landeskonservator für Tirol.

 ozart in Lambach Abbey

Dates

12 September 1767 · 4 January 1769
25 September 1773 · 28 October 1783

The Mozart family stayed several times in the hospitable Lambach Abbey, on the way to and from Vienna. They lunched in the monastery on 12 September 1767, on the way to Vienna for the marriage festivities of Archduchess Josepha to the King of Naples; returning to Salzburg from Vienna, they stopped here around 4 January 1769. Mozart and his father again stopped in the Lambach Abbey on 25 September 1773.

Later in life, Mozart and his wife had a pleasant reception here; on 28 October 1783, returning to Vienna after a stay in Salzburg which included the performance of Mozart's C minor Mass, they arrived at the abbey "just in time" for Mozart to accompany the *Agnus Dei* on the organ. Shortly after, he performed on the clavichord. Leopold Mozart dedicated fifteen symphonies to the abbey.

Music

The "Old Lambach" Symphony, K. Anh. 221/45a, and another Symphony in G, known only through the copy here ("New Lambach" Symphony, G16), have presented a problem of attribution, as to which was by Mozart, and which by Leopold.[1] However, the newly discovered parts of the "Old Lambach" Symphony were bought by the Munich Staatsbibliothek 1982, and clearly indicate that it is by Mozart.[2]

Lambach Abbey Sites

★ ★ LAMBACH ABBEY AND CHURCH (STIFTSKIRCHE). This abbey, so rich in associations with Mozart's music, was founded in 1056, and remodeled in the present form in the seventeenth century. Recently uncovered and restored Romanesque wall paintings are located in the west chancel. The fine portal by Auer, decorated with marble columns and statues, is from 1693.[3] The frescoes can be seen only during tours (which last an hour) 9–11 AM (10–11 AM Sunday) and 2:30–5 PM; admission charge.

Lambach Monastery. Engraving by Johann Ziegler, later 18th century. Österreichische Nationalbibliothek.

N o t e s

1 The "Old Lambach" Symphony, K. Anh. 221/45a, was believed to be by Mozart, until 1964, when Anna Amalie Abert, based on style analysis, speculated that the copyist mixed the two inscriptions, and that it was written by Leopold. She believed, instead, the Symphony in G ("New Lambach" Symphony), known only through the copy here, was by Mozart. See, for example, Bauer/Deutsch/Eibl, *Mozart Briefe*, VI, zu 766/7.

2 Cf. Zaslaw, *Mozart's Symphonies*, for a review of the problem.

3 Michelin, *Austria*, 100–01.

Mozart in Linz

26 September 1762–4 October 1762 ▪ 2 January 1763 ▪ 12 September 1767
About 24 September 1773 ▪ 30 October 1783 to the end of November 1783
About 8 November 1790

The Mozart family stopped several times in Linz, on the way to or from Vienna. The first trip was to play before Maria Theresa in Vienna, at which time they stopped here to play a public concert on 1 October 1762. They again stopped in Linz on 2 January 1763 on the way back to Salzburg. Mozart and his family again stopped in Linz, on the way to the festivities in Vienna surrounding the marriage of Archduchess Josepha to the King of Naples. (This ended in tragedy when the bride died of smallpox.)

Leopold and Mozart made a brief trip to Vienna after the third Italian journey (perhaps with the hopes of an appointment at the Viennese Imperial Court), stopping in Linz on the way back to Salzburg.

Of the visits made by Mozart to Linz, the most important was the end of October to the end of November 1783 when, returning with Constanze from Salzburg to Vienna, he stayed with Count Johann Thun-Hohenstein and composed a symphony in the "breakneck speed" of four days, which was then performed in Linz.

Music

Symphony, K. 425 ("Linz"), composed October-November 1783; performed 4 November 1783.

Mozart wrote an introduction (K. 444/425a) to a symphony by Michael Haydn, probably at the beginning of November 1783 in Linz.

In addition, based on a study of watermarks, paper types, and stave rulings, Alan Tyson has suggested that one of Mozart's most renowned piano sonatas, K. 333/315c in B flat, was written in Linz and/or Vienna, possibly making this a "Linz" sonata.

Linz Sites

★ ★ "TRINITY" INN (GASTHOF "ZUR DREIFALTIGKEIT"). Hofgasse 14. On 26 September 1762, the Mozart family, on the way to Vienna for the first time, arrived in Linz in the afternoon and stayed in this inn. They were well served by the "two unmarried daughters" who continued to run the inn after the death of their father, Wolfgang Kiener. Leopold wrote, "They love my children so much, they do everything that is in their power [for us]. My children, by the way, amaze everyone." The concert by the children in Linz was, most likely, either in this inn, or in the **Landhaus.**[1] Today the building houses the Café Centrum. The edifice was first mentioned in documents in 1595; it served as an inn since 1660.[2] Commemorative plaque.

★ ★ THUN PALACE. Altstadt 17–Klostergasse 20 (on Minoritenplatz). On their arrival on 30 October 1783, Mozart and his wife were met by the son of "old Count Thun." He explained that his father, Count Joseph Anton Thun-Hohenstein, had been waiting eagerly for fourteen days for Mozart's arrival. They stayed here in the house of the Count, who, like Mozart, was a Freemason, for about a month, until around 28 September 1783. Mozart wrote, "I can not say enough about how we are showered with kindness in this house." It was here that Mozart, as he had not brought any symphonies along, wrote the "Linz" Symphony, K. 425, at "breakneck" speed, in four days. The Renaissance building, dating from the sixteenth century, has a portal and facade which were renewed in the Baroque period. Today it is modernized, maintaining many

Linz. Engraving by Johann Ziegler after a drawing by Ferdinand Runk. Stadtmuseum, Linz.

original features such as vaulted ceilings. It houses the Tourist Information office and private apartments. There is a fine three-story courtyard with arcades inside the palace. Commemorative plaque.

★ "BLACK RAM" INN (GASTHOF "ZUM SCHWARZEN BOCK"). Altstadt 22. In April 1785, after a long visit with his son in Vienna, Leopold Mozart came to Linz with his pupil Heinrich Marchand, and they stayed a pleasant week in this inn across from Count Thun. They slept here, as the sons of the Count were all home, and all his rooms were being used. However, Leopold wrote to Nannerl on 30 April 1785, "We are at table and in society the whole day at the Count's; even breakfast is brought over here each day." There was a large party at the Thun Palace on 29 April 1785, and Leopold's pupil Marchand gave a successful concert in Linz. The building was damaged in WW II, but was rebuilt in 1956–58 as it had been. Although a modern inn of a different name is presently located in the building, the "Black Ram" shield by Peter Dimmel can still be seen.[3] Klostergasse today has many small historic buildings intact; 10 Altstadt, which is the former **Kremsmünsterer Stiftshaus**, dating from 1710, has bound Tuscan pillars.[4]

[★ ★ ★ MINORITE CHURCH (MINORITENKIRCHE)]. Although Mozart did not mention this extraordinary Gothic church, part of a monastery founded in the thirteenth century by the Minorite Brothers (Franciscans) and redone in Rococo style (1753–59), it is unlikely that he and Constanze would have overlooked it. Living immediately across the street for about a month, they would most likely have attended Mass here. The high altarpiece by Altomonte (the "Annunciation") over a red-veined marble Baroque altar (1724), and the six side altars are noteworthy. Open Monday–Saturday 8–11 AM; Sunday 8 AM–Noon (July/August 8 AM–4 PM).

★ ★ LANDHAUS. 39 Promenade (entrance also on Minoritenplatz). The Mozart children gave a public concert on 1 October 1762, attended by the wife of Count Leopold Schlick and also Count Karl Hieronymus Pálffy (who proceeded to Vienna, describing the amazing talent of the children). The concert took place either here in the "Hall of Stone" (**Steineren Saal**), or in the "Trinity" Inn.[5] The Renaissance complex (1564–71), which today houses the provincial government, has an exceptional marble portal in Renaissance style on Minoritenplatz. The inner court, lined with arcades, has a Planet Fountain (1582) which commemorates Kepler, the astronomer and mathematician, who taught at Linz College from 1612 to 1626, located at that time here in the *Landhaus*. The renovated "Hall of Stone," where concerts are often held, has a fine Renaissance doorway of red Untersberg marble (1570). Although government offices are found in the complex, permission may be asked to see it: Ask the porter daily 7 AM–6:30 PM (closed Saturday and Sunday).

★ SITE OF THE LINZ THEATER. 37 Promenade (presently **Amt der Land-esregierung**). Mozart, visiting Linz with his wife, presented an academy here on 4 November 1783, during which the "Linz" Symphony, K. 425, was performed, and probably Michael Haydn's symphony, for which Mozart wrote an introduction, K. 444/425a.[6] Although the theater in which Mozart performed no longer exists, the present Linz Theater (**Landestheater**), adjacent to the site, has a splendid facade dating from 1803.

[★ ★ BISHOP'S RESIDENCE (BISCHOFSHOF)]. Herrenstrasse 19–Bischofstrasse 8. Count Ernst Johann Herberstein, who had traveled with the Mozarts by boat from Passau to Linz, and who spread the word of the prodigious Mozart children in Vienna in 1762, was appointed Bishop of Linz by Emperor Joseph II and was required to make his entry into the city on foot. Leopold Mozart, during his visit to Linz with his pupil Heinrich Marchand, again met with the "bent, limping" Count Herberstein, exchanging recollections.[7] Although Leopold talked with the new bishop at Count Thun's, this residence of the bishop is also worthy of note; the massive structure, built 1721–26 after plans of F. M. Pruckmayr, is regarded as the most monumental edifice of the eighteenth century in Linz.[8] The portal has bound Tuscan pillars surmounted by the coat-of-arms of the bishop.[9]

★ ★ HOME OF LAMBACH PRELATE. Landstrasse 28. On their way to Vienna for the festivities surrounding the marriage of Archduchess Josepha to the King of Naples, the entire Mozart family and their servant Bernhard arrived in Linz on 12 September 1767. Leopold immediately notified the Prelate of Lambach Monastery, Amand Schikmayr, of their arrival, and they were invited here to lunch the next day; at such occasions, Mozart and his sister usually performed. The imposing edifice belonged to the abbey from 1636–1825.[10] Still to be seen are the round arched portal and the arcaded court with Roman-Tuscan pillars from 1672. The northern part of the court is from 1750, while the southern part was probably built by Gangl in 1764, at the same time as the garden house; the third floor (American: fourth floor) was added in 1863. Since 1825, the building has been occupied by private owners.[11]

SITE OF THE "GREEN TREE" INN (GASTHOF "ZUM GRÜNEN BAUM"). Bethlehemstrasse 4–6.[12] *En route* to Vienna, the Mozart family lodged in this inn on 12 September 1767, near the home of the Lambach Prelate. The structure was demolished in 1962/3 for the construction of the department store, **Passage-Kaufhaus**.[13] Nearby, at Bethlehemstrasse 7 is the **Stadtmuseum Nordico**, originally a suburban house for the monastery of Kremsmünster, built 1607–10 by Silva and used by the Jesuits until 1786 as a training center. In the main hall of the **Stadtmuseum** are frescoes by Mazza; the building today houses archeological exhibits and the city's history museum.[14]

[★ ★ CHARACTERISTIC SIGHTS OF LINZ]. Numerous sights from the time of the Mozarts' visits are preserved. The Cathedral (**Alter Dom**), designed by Carlone and built 1669–78, has enormous carved choir stalls from the old monastery church of Garsten and a dramatic altar. The organ by Krismann is from the monastery of Engelszell; Anton Bruckner was organist here. The Ursuline Church (**Ursulinerkirche**), built 1736–72, has a massive Baroque altar of brown-veined marble and gilded wood. The Weighing House (**Waaghaus**) was bought in 1525 by the municipality. Dating back as far as 799 is the Castle (**Linzer Schloss**), which was rebuilt in 1477 by Emperor Frederick III and about 1600 by Emperor Rudolf II. St. Martin's Church (**Martinskirche**) is the oldest church in Austria maintained in its original state. The Carmelite Church (**Karmeliterkirche**), 1674–1726, is modeled after St. Joseph's Church in Prague. In addition, the Seminar Church (**Seminarkirche**) was built 1718–25 to plans by Hildebrandt, and the Parish Church (**Stadtpfarrkirche**) was originally a Romanesque basilica from 1286. It was rebuilt in Baroque style in 1648. Finally, the white marble Pillar of the Holy Trinity (**Dreifaltigkeitssäule**) dates from 1723, and the Town Hall (**Altes Rathaus**) has a Gothic octagonal corner turret from 1513 with a lunar clock; it was extended with a Baroque facade in 1658, with the present facade dating from 1824.

N o t e s

1 Bauer/Deutsch/Eibl, *Mozart Briefe*, V, zu 32/9.
2 Communicated by Hans Zöttl, Café Centrum.
3 Communicated by Dr. Fritz Mayrhofer, Director, Linz Archives.
4 Communicated by Dr. Fritz Mayrhofer, Director, Linz Archives.
5 Bauer/Deutsch/Eibl, op cit. V, zu 32/9.
6 Bauer/Deutsch/Eibl, op cit. VI, zu 766/22.
7 Schenk, *Mozart and His Times*, 359.
8 Communicated by Dr. Fritz Mayrhofer, Director, Linz Archives.
9 Communicated by Dr. Fritz Mayrhofer, Director, Linz Archives.
10 Bauer/Deutsch/Eibl, op cit. V, zu 116/8.
11 Communicated by Dr. Fritz Mayrhofer, Director, Linz Archives.
12 Communicated by Dr. Fritz Mayrhofer, Director, Linz Archives.
13 Communicated by Dr. Fritz Mayrhofer, Director, Linz Archives.
14 Bauer/Deutsch/Eibl, op cit. V, zu 116/8.

Mozart in Melk

Dates

14 September 1767 ▪ 28/29 December 1768

The Mozart family made at least two visits to the spectacular monastery of Melk. In September 1767, at the beginning of the second trip to Vienna, Leopold decided to play a little joke on the organist, by not announcing whom they were, and seeing if the organist would recognize them (which suggests that they had made a previous visit).

They again visited on the way back from their second trip to Vienna, on the occasion of the marriage of Archduchess Josepha to the King of Naples, which ended in tragedy, when the 16-year-old bride died during a smallpox epidemic. During this visit, the Mozart family was invited to the table of the Abbot Urban Hauer.

Melk Sites

★ ★ ★ BENEDICTINE ABBEY AND CHURCH (STIFTSKIRCHE). The Mozart family arrived at the monastery of Melk on 14 September 1767. Leopold planned a little scheme by which he would not give their identities until Mozart had played on the organ, to see if the organist could "recognize him, or, better, guess" who he was. Immediately afterwards, however, the family returned to their coach and traveled on toward Salzburg. Someone who heard Mozart at this time was Abbé Maximilian Stadler, then a young novice, who is known for having finished various works by Mozart after Mozart's death.[1] Returning from Vienna, the Mozarts stayed in Melk on 28 December 1768, at which time Mozart again played the organ.

The Abbey, on the site of a Roman stronghold, was constructed from a castle which Leopold III gave to the Benedictines in the eleventh century. It was designed by Prandtauer, under Abbot Dietmayr, and built in 1702–49. The Emperors' Gallery (**Kaisergang**), with paintings of Austrian kings and regents, including Empress Maria Theresa and her husband, Francis of Lorraine, and the Marble Hall (**Marmorsaal**) in red-brown marble stucco are of interest. The renowned Library (**Bibliothek**), with about 80,000 books and 2,000 manuscripts, has a frescoed ceiling by Paul Troger. Finally, the church, with a massive octagonal dome and two symmetrical towers, is a masterpiece of Baroque architecture: marble decoration, sumptuous stucco ornament in red-brown, grey, orange, and gold, and frescoes by Rottmayr and Troger work together to create a harmonious ensemble.[2] The organ which Mozart played, by the Viennese builder Sonnholz, no longer exists; it was a victim of early twentieth-century modernization.[3] Guided tours (about an hour) are given 15 March–30 April and 1 October–Palm Sunday from 9 AM–Noon and 1–4 PM (–5 PM 1 May–30 September); the remainder of the year only at 11 AM and 3 PM; admission charge.

Melk. Benedictine Abbey. Engraving by Lorenz Janscha after Johann Ziegler.

N o t e s

1 Bauer/Deutsch/Eibl, *Mozart Briefe*, V, zu 116/13.
2 Michelin, *Austria*, 109.
3 Bauer/Deutsch/Eibl, op. cit., V, zu 116/14–15.

Mozart in Salzburg

Dates

27 January 1756–12 January 1762 (*beginning 12 January the first trip to Munich*) • beginning of February 1762–18 September 1762 (*beginning 18 September the first trip to Vienna*) • 5 January 1763–9 June 1763 (*beginning 9 June the "Great Western" trip, including Paris and London*) • 29 November 1766–11 September 1767 (*beginning 11 September the second trip to Vienna*) • 5 January 1769–13 December 1769 (*beginning 13 December the first trip to Italy*) • 28 March 1771–13 August 1771 (*beginning 13 August the second trip to Italy*) • 15 December 1771–24 October 1772 (*beginning 24 October the third trip to Italy*) • 13 March 1773–14 July 1773 (*beginning 14 July the third trip to Vienna*) • 26 September 1773–6 December 1774 (*beginning 6 December the second trip to Munich*) • 7 March 1775–23 September 1777 (*beginning 23 September the trip to Paris*) • mid-January 1779–5 November 1780 (*beginning 5 November the trip to Munich and Vienna, with Mozart's subsequent residence in Vienna*) • end of July 1783–end of November 1783

Salzburg, whose numerous churches, palaces, and squares reflect a progressive, "enlightened" architecture, is set within spectacular natural surroundings. In addition to being the native city of Mozart, it was also the scene of bitter disappointments for both Mozart and his father. Amid the musical politics, however, Mozart always had a group of determined supporters, who lobbied for his interests in the court of Prince Archbishop Hieronymus Colloredo, whose preference for Italian musicians and musical taste was in keeping with the aesthetic of the period.

Mozart, either with his family, or with his father alone, however, made frequent trips away from Salzburg; each time, upon returning, the musical provincialism of the city seems to have weighed more heavily. In 1781, after an altercation with the Prince Archbishop (whose court was visiting Vienna), Mozart made a final break and remained in Vienna, where he spent the rest of his life, visiting Salzburg only once again, in 1783, with his wife, Constanze.

M u s i c

For a detailed listing of Mozart's music written in or for Salzburg, see *The New Grove Mozart,* by Stanley Sadie; in addition, numerous compositions are cited in the following descriptions of Mozart sites in Salzburg.

Salzburg Sites

★ ★ ★ MIRABELL CASTLE AND GARDENS (SCHLOSS MIRABELL). When Mozart and his mother left Salzburg in September 1777, on the first leg of their trip to Paris, they were near the town of Schinn, when a fat merchant, Herr von Krimmel, came up and recognized Mozart; Mozart immediately responded that he had seen him "at a concert in Mirabell," a year earlier. In addition, Mozart wrote numerous divertimenti for oboes, horns and bassoons, which were probably to be played as **Tafelmusik** (table music) at the Archbishop's meals in the Mirabell[1]; these include K. 213, K. 240, K. 252/240a, and K. 270. Mozart also composed numerous pieces of "final music" for the end of the academic year, which were performed in front of the palace, before a procession to the college. There is little left of this summer residence of the Prince Archbishop where such musical events took place in the time of Mozart, most probably with Mozart's participation. It was built in the seventeenth century and remodeled in the eighteenth century by Hildebrandt. It burned in 1818.[2] The impressive staircase, however, remains from the period, and has been splendidly restored. The gardens, which have some exceptional vistas, were designed by Fischer von Erlach in the early eighteenth century; pools, arbors, and numerous sculptures ornament the spacious formal landscape. Concerts are given three times a week 8–10:30 PM.

★ LODRON PRIMOGENITUR PALACE. Dreifaltigkeitsgasse 17–19. Mozart often played here for Countess Maria Lodron, for whom (along with her two daughters, Aloisia and Josepha) he composed the Divertimenti, K. 247 (with March, K. 248) and K. 287/271h, and the concerto for three claviers, K. 242. Count Ernst Londron had two palaces, the Primogenitur and Secondogenitur.[3] The Countess, along with other nobles, played an important role in supporting the return of the young Mozart to Salzburg from Paris. During Mozart's stay in Paris, Leopold wrote him describing an amateur orchestra that met in Count Lodron's hall every Sunday afternoon, with Leopold "keeping the second violins in order," Nannerl playing clavier, and including Abbé Bullinger and members of the Robinig, Andretter, and Lodron families. Today the building (with an arcade which was added later) houses the Music Conservatory (**Hochschule für Musik**). The interior burned in 1818 and is no longer interesting; the facade, which remains from the period, however, is noteworthy.

★ LORETO CHURCH (LORETTO FRAUENKLOSTER). Paris-Lodron-Strasse 6. On several occasions during their "Great Western" trip of 1763–66, Leopold wrote to his landlord, Lorenz Hagenauer, to have Masses said here. It was one of the Mozart's favorite churches. The magnificently dressed ivory statuette of the Christ Child of Loreto, with a cross, a crown, and a sceptre, was venerated by Salzburg families since the mid-seventeenth century.[4]

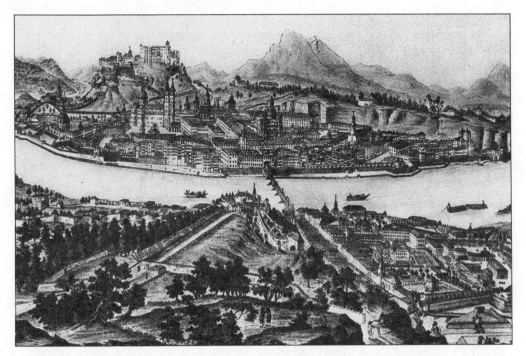

Salzburg. Engraving by Anton Amon, after a drawing by Franz von Naumann, end of 18th century.

★ ★ ★ "DANCING MASTER'S" HOUSE (TANZMEISTERSAAL). Makart-platz 8. In 1773 (probably in late March, after the third Italian journey), the Mozart family moved into this eight-room house on the (former) Hannibalplatz; Mozart lived here until his departure for Munich and Vienna in 1780. Nannerl also lived here with her father until her marriage in 1785, and Leopold remained until his death in 1787. The house, which was rebuilt after 1944, is one of the oldest on the square. Various "dancing masters" had lived here; the name dates back at least to 1617. It is full of rich musical associations with Mozart's Salzburg years. Works composed in this period include the "little G minor" Symphony, K. 183/173db, and numerous other symphonies; Mozart's first piano concerto, K. 175, was written while Mozart lived here, as well as other piano concertos, K. 238, K. 242 (three-piano), K. 246, K. 271 ("Jeunehomme"), and K. 365/31ba (two-piano). In addition, the Symphonie Concertante, K. 364/320d, the Bassoon Concerto, K. 191/186e, the Oboe Concerto, K. 271/k (314/285d), and the violin concertos, K. 207, 211, 216, 218, and 219, all date from this period. The operatic works, *Il ré pastore, La finta giardiniera* (for Munich), and *Zaide* had their beginnings during this period, as did numerous

Masses and church sonatas. The Mozarts also gave private concerts here, such as that on 15 August 1777, with the singer Josepha Duschek from Prague, when Mozart and Nannerl also played four-hand music. Two rooms are today used for cultural events; in July and August, chamber music recitals are held here. Plans are underway to relocate the adjacent building and to reconstruct the edifice according to its original appearance from the time of Mozart. Open 10 AM–4 PM (June–September); 10 AM–5 PM (October–May); closed Sundays; admission charge; performance on historic instruments (July–August) 11 AM, Noon, and 3 PM (September 11 AM only).

★ ★ TRINITY CHURCH (DREIFALTIGKEITSKIRCHE). Here, in this church so near to the Mozarts' home, Michael Haydn was organist, and Nannerl often attended early morning Mass. The church was built 1694–99 by Fischer von Erlach; the remarkable oval dome, the Baroque interior, and the fine frescoes by Rottmayr are all of interest.[5]

★ ★ ST. SEBASTIAN'S CEMETERY (FRIEDHOF ST. SEBASTIEN). Linzer Gasse 41. Buried here are Leopold Mozart, Mozart's grandmother, Eva Rosina Pertl, Nannerl's first daughter, Jeannette von Berchtold zu Sonnenburg, Constanze Mozart and her second husband, the biographer Georg Nissen. The Mausoleum of Archbishop Wolf Dietrich (d. 1617) is also found here. Friends of Mozart buried here include the Robinig family; however, Count Karl Arco, renowned for "the kick in the ass" that he gave Mozart in Vienna in 1781 after Mozart asked to be released from Archbishop Colloredo's service, is also buried here. The graves of the Mozart family are marked by memorial plaques.

★ MOZARTEUM. Schwartzstrasse. This library, the most important Mozart archive in the world, has holdings of almost 35,000 volumes. In addition, a large number of Mozart's original letters and autographed scores are found here. Derived from two earlier organizations, which date from 1841 and 1870 respectively, the Internationale Stiftung Mozarteum was founded in 1880, and since has actively promoted music festivals, scholarly conferences, publications and performances. The building dates from 1910 to 1914; the **Grosser Saal** of the Mozarteum is one of the main concert halls in Salzburg. Guided tours, beginning at 11:15 AM, include the "Magic Flute" Cottage (see next entry), and the "Dancing Master's" House.

★ ★ MAGIC FLUTE COTTAGE. In the "Bastion Garden" behind the Mozarteum. This cottage, which originally stood in the garden of the **Theater auf der Wieden** in Vienna, has rich associations with Mozart's composition of *The Magic Flute* in 1791. In 1873, it was moved to Salzburg, and was originally located first in the Zwerglgarten, and then on the Kapuzinerberg; however, so many admirers of Mozart took souvenirs of the shingles that it had to be relocated here in 1950, after an extensive restoration. It can only be seen as part of the 11:15 AM tour of the Mozarteum.

Salzburg. Mozart's Birthplace, Hagenauerplatz. Unsigned drawing after a 19th century engraving.

★ ★ ★ MOZART'S BIRTHPLACE (MOZARTS GEBURTSHAUS). Getreidegasse 9. On 27 January 1756, Mozart was born here in the house of Johann Lorenz Hagenauer, who was both landlord and friend to the Mozart family. Here, where Nannerl had also been born in 1751, Leopold and his wife, Anna Maria Pertl, lived on the second floor (American: third floor) from 1747 to 1773. Many of Mozart's early works were written during this period, such as the Andante, K. 1a, and other pieces for clavier (some of which became movements to later sonatas for clavier and violin); *Die Schuldigkeit des ersten Gebots*; *Apollo et Hyacinthus*, the "Father Dominicus" Mass, K. 66; *La Betulia liberata*, and *Il sogno di Scipione*; in addition, numerous symphonies (for example, K. 128–34), church sonatas (K. 67–9/41h, i, k); divertimenti, and miscellaneous works date from this period. Deeds to the house date back to the early fifteenth century; since 1880 it has been a Mozart museum directed by the Mozarteum, with exhibits of autographs, letters, portraits, memorabilia, and original instruments, such as Mozart's tiny violin of his childhood, his "Hammerflügel," and his clavichord. The Getreidegasse is fascinating for the numerous wrought-iron signs and characteristic facades. Open October–May 9 AM–6 PM; June and September 9 AM–7 PM; July and August 9 AM–8 PM; admission charge. At 11 AM there are performances on historical instruments.

★ RESIDENCE OF CONSTANZE MOZART. Alter Markt 11. This was one of the three dwellings of Constanze Mozart, after her relocation to Salzburg. Inside the door, there is a pink marble commemorative plaque.

★ CITY HOUSE OF SIGISMUND HAFFNER. Sigmund-Haffner-Gasse 6. Sigismund Haffner was a wealthy Salzburg banker and mayor for whose family two Mozart works were written: the "Haffner" Serenade, K. 250/248b, and the "Haffner" Symphony, K. 385. The serenade was written after Haffner's death for the wedding of his daughter Elizabeth, and was also later played as open-air street music.[6] Mozart wrote the symphony in Vienna in 1782, for the ennoblement of Sigismund Haffner in Salzburg; it was first orchestrated as a serenade (with a march and additional minuet), and later four movements were reworked as a symphony with flutes and clarinets. In addition to the city house and business which was located here, Haffner also owned a summer house on Loretogasse (which no longer exists), where Mozart's "Haffner" Serenade was performed for the wedding. The marble portal of the city house, with a round painting of the Virgin and Child, is still preserved today.

★ LAST HOME OF NANNERL MOZART. Sigmund-Haffner-Gasse 12. Mozart's sister moved here after the death of her husband in St. Gilgen and lived there until her death on 19 October 1829. She gave clavier lessons at this house and was visited by many admirers of Mozart, including Vincent and Mary Novello, who came with a monetary gift from England in 1829. They found Nannerl almost blind, feeble, and living in poverty. There is presently a **Bierhaus** in the building; also there is a plaque remembering Erich Schenk, the important Mozart biographer, who was born here.

★ ROBINIG HOUSE. Sigmund-Haffner-Gasse 14. Mozart's Divertimento, K. 334/320b (with a particularly well-known minuet and rondo) is believed to have been written for these long-standing friends of the Mozart family. They also owned the beautiful Rococo house outside Salzburg (the **Robinighof** at Robinigstrasse 35 in Schallmoos) where several visits by Mozart are documented. In addition to their iron shop in the Getreidegasse, the family owned this house (#14 on the former Kirchgasse). Today, on the ground floor two shops are located; the remainder of the building is privately owned.[6]

★ ★ FRANCISCAN CHURCH (FRANZISKANERKIRCHE). Franziskanergasse 5. On several occasions, such as in a letter of 9 July 1765 from London, Leopold asked his landlord, Lorenz Hagenauer, to have Masses said for his family in this **Pfarrkirche**, or parish church, one of the favorite Salzburg churches of the Mozarts. The church, with a Romanesque nave, and a late-Gothic chancel, was consecrated in 1223.[8] There is also a "rosary" of seventeenth-century chapels, and a dramatic high altar from 1709 by Fischer von Erlach. During music festivals, Mozart Masses and church sonatas are performed here.

★ ★ OLD AULA THEATER OF THE OLD UNIVERSITY (AULA ACCADEMICA). Now part of the University Library[9]; Universitätsplatz. One of Mozart's earliest operatic works, the "school opera" in Latin, *Apollo et Hyacinthus*, was performed here, on the stage across from the Aula on 13 May 1767.

That same evening, Mozart performed at the keyboard for the assembled professors. The Old University (founded 1622, closed 1810) was restored in 1962. In addition, other works were written by Mozart as graduation music (*Finalmusik*) on 6 and 8 August 1769 (probably the Serenade, K. 100/62a and the Cassation K. 63), 12 August 1773 ("Antretter" Serenade, K. 185/167a) and 9 and 23 August 1775 (probably the Serenade, K. 204/213a). On the University Square (**Kollegienplatz**; today **Universitätsplatz**), at 9 PM on 24 September 1779, Mozart's "Haffner" Serenade, K. 250/248b, and a March, K. 249, were performed. In the Collegiate Church, Mozart's *Missa brevis*, K. 65/61a, was first performed on 5 February 1769. The church, built 1696–1707 by Fischer von Erlach, has fine altar paintings by J. M. Rottmayr.

★ ★ ARCHBISHOP'S RESIDENCE (RESIDENZ). Residenzplatz 1. The Prince Archbishops of Salzburg, who lived on the site since the twelfth century, initiated this edifice in 1595 (with the exception of the northwest wing, which dates from the late eighteenth century).[10] Several of Mozart's works had their first performances in the **Residenz**, such as *Il ré pastore* on 23 April 1775. In addition, in the Knights' Room (Rittersaal), the oratorio, *Die Schuldigkeit des ersten Gebotes* (of which only Act I was by Mozart) was premiered on 12 March 1767; his opera, *La finta semplice* was performed on 1 May 1769, and *Il sogno di Scipione* in May 1772. The Knights' Room is one of the main concert halls in Salzburg. In addition, on 29 March 1767, Mozart and his sister probably participated in a concert and an "unbelievably refined, and costly dinner" in the Emperor Room (**Kaisersaal**) to honor the brother of Colloredo, the future archbishop of Salzburg. On 2 and 4 September 1780, Mozart played at court, and on 3 September 1780, Mozart played a concerto for two claviers (an arrangement of K. 242) with Nannerl, and a four-hand sonata, K. 381/123a. The edifice offers a painting gallery, and 15 state rooms with eighteenth-century stucco decoration.[11] Forty-minute tours 10 AM–5 PM (July–August); 10 AM, 11 AM, 2 PM and 3 PM Monday–Friday (September–July); 10 AM and 11 AM Saturday, Sunday, and holidays (September–July); admission charge.

★ ★ CATHEDRAL (DOM). Domplatz. Mozart and his sister were baptized here in the Romanesque baptismal font, and both Mozart and his father worked here as violinists in the Archbishop's orchestra. From 1779 to 1781, Mozart was court organist in the cathedral, where many of his compositions were first performed; for example, most of the one-movement church sonatas (organ and strings). On 17 April 1767, a Passion cantata by the young Mozart, K. 42/35a (supposedly written during a week in which Mozart was "locked up," to prove to the Archbishop that he, in fact, wrote it), is believed to have been performed here. On 31 March 1776, Mozart's Litany, K. 243, was performed here, and on 7 April 1776, his Mass, K. 262/246a. The Dom, built 1614–55, reflects the Baroque over the vestiges of the Italian Renaissance; the marble, stucco, and paintings are noteworthy, as is the crypt (remodeled from the ruins of the Romanesque cathedral).[12] Open 6 AM–7 PM (summer); 6 AM–5 PM (winter).

Salzburg Cathedral. Etching by Karl Schneeweis, later 18th century.

★ ANTRETTER HOUSE. Mozartplatz 4. Two works by Mozart have the name Antretter associated with them, the Divertimento, K. 205/173a/167A and the Serenade, K. 185/167a. The Serenade was commissioned in 1773 by Judas Thaddeus von Antretter as graduation music of the students of logic. Musical finales were common for the closing academic year ceremonies of the logic students and the physicians; traditionally music for the prince was first performed, followed by a parade of the professors; in addition, a march was played for the entrance and exit of the students. Today, there are numerous lawyers' offices in the building, as well as the Department of Musicology (**Institut für Musikwissenschaft**) of Salzburg University. The arched portal and the iron door with Rococo ornaments are of interest; in addition, in the second courtyard there is a fine chapel, dating from 1592.

★ MOZART MONUMENT (MOZART-DENKMAL). Mozartplatz. This monument, cast in brass to a model by the Munich sculptor, L. von Schwanthaler, was unveiled on 4 September 1842, after the death of Constanze, at a music festival in which both of Mozart's sons participated.

★ RESIDENCE OF CONSTANZE MOZART. Mozartplatz 8. After the death of Mozart, Constanze, who relocated to Salzburg from Vienna, lived here. There is a commemorative plaque citing Constanze and her husband Georg Nissen, who wrote a biography of Mozart. The building, which has a simple, elegant facade, today houses government education offices (**Amt der Landesregierung Schul und Bildungswesen**).

★ ★ ★ ST. PETER'S CHURCH AND MONASTERY (STIFTSKIRCHE ST. PETER). St.-Peter-Hof. On 15 October 1769, Mozart's Mass, written for Father Dominicus Hagenauer, a close friend of Mozart and his family, was performed in this church. Many years later, during Mozart's visit to Salzburg from Vienna with Constanze, his C minor Mass, K. 427/417a was most likely first performed here on 26 October 1783 under Mozart's direction, with his wife singing one of the two soprano parts, and the participation of the musicians of the entire court. The interior, with fine paintings and Baroque decoration, features pale green, contrasted by white walls; the elaborately gilded grille is also noteworthy.[13] The monastery complex, remarkably restored, is fascinating; a wine cellar (*Weinkeller*) is built into the vaulted cliffs. In the churchyard, Nannerl is buried. In addition, Mozart's friend and colleague, Michael Haydn, for whom he wrote the two duets for viola and violin (K. 423 and 424), is buried here. Entering the church, in the first chapel on the right (up the incline), the memorial plaques can be found, set in the pavement. A slide show about Michael Haydn is presented daily (except Wednesday) 10 AM–Noon and 2:30–4:30 PM (July–September); admission charge.

[★ ★ ★ CHARACTERISTIC SIGHTS OF SALZBURG]. Hohensalzburg, with a castle begun in 1077, and considerably refurbished and extended in the following centuries, is interesting for the panorama; there is a museum as well. Of interest also is the late-Gothic Benedictine Nonnberg Convent, which has a splendid altarpiece. Nearby, at Nonnberggasse 12, is one of the three dwellings of Constanze, after her relocation to Salzburg. The massive Horse Trough (*Pferdeschwemme*), built around 1700, has a fine sculpture group and frescoes. Finally, Judengasse, in the former Jewish ghetto, is noteworthy for its many characteristic wrought iron signs.[14]

Salzburg Concerts and Musical Events

SALZBURG MOZART FESTIVAL. This annual music festival, commencing in January, features solo and chamber recitals by world-class artists, alternating with orchestral concerts by the Vienna Philharmonic. For information, call the Tourist Office, Makartplatz 9.

SALZBURG FESTIVAL. A major annual music festival, held each July and August. The festival was founded in 1922, and was originally dedicated almost exclusively to Mozart's music. Today the repertory is wide-ranging; however, it still features performances of Mozart operas.

MARIONETTE THEATER. Schwarzstrasse 24. This remarkable theater presents Mozart's theatrical works, including early and rarely performed operas, in first-rate performances (with recorded music, as is common for marionette opera).

Excursion to
Maria Plain

★ ★ MARIA PLAIN PILGRIMAGE CHURCH (WALLFAHRTSKIRCHE MARIA PLAIN). Plainbergweg. The small oil painting of the Virgin with Jesus sleeping, found in this church, has been the object of veneration since 1632; however, the so-called "Coronation" Mass, K. 317, was not written for the coronation ceremony, but was written for performance in the cathedral, in 1779. Mozart probably wrote his Masses, K. 192/186f and 194/186h for the Maria Plain basilica. The church figures prominently in both religious life in Salzburg and in the life of the Mozarts: Leopold wrote to his landlord, Lorenz Hagenauer, on 3 October 1762 to have his wife "arrange for four Masses to be said on our behalf" here. In addition, when Mozart and Constanze visited Salzburg from Vienna, Nannerl wrote in her notebook that they took two coaches at 6 AM on 2 August 1783 (to attend Mass here). The church was designed by G. Dario, and built 1671–74; the interior, with pulpit, organ, and chancel screen, reflects an ornate Rococo style from the seventeenth century.[15] It can be reached by public transportation; by foot, it takes about 1-1/2 hours.

N o t e s

1 Kenyon, *Mozart in Salzburg*, 121.
2 Michelin, *Austria*, 134.
3 The Lodron Sekundogeniturpalais is still located at Mirabellplatz 8, but it is not authentic from the time of Mozart. Today it houses a hotel (Austrotel). Communicated by Dr. Johanna Senigl, Librarian, Mozarteum.
4 "A middle-class apartment typical in Salzburg during Mozart's lifetime," brochure from Mozart's Geburtshaus, [nd].
5 Michelin, ibid.
6 Kenyon, op. cit., 120.
7 Communicated by Dr. Johanna Senigl, Librarian, Mozarteum.
8 Michelin, *Austria*, 133.
9 The new Aula Accademia is situated on another place, and is used today as a concert hall. Communicated by Dr. Johanna Senigl, Librarian, Mozarteum.
10 Michelin, Ibid.
11 Michelin, Ibid.
12 Michelin, op. cit. 131.
13 Michelin, op. cit. 133.
14 Michelin, op. cit. 134.
15 Michelin, op. cit. 135.

Mozart in Vienna

Dates

6 October 1762–11 December 1762 (*excursion to Pressburg*) ▪ 24 December 1762–31 December 1762 ▪ 15 September 1767–23 October 1767 (*Mozart contracts smallpox in Olmütz*) ▪ 10 January 1768–about 27 December 1768 ▪ 16 July 1773–about 24 September 1773 ▪ 16 March 1780–5 December 1791 (*Mozart's permanent residence in Vienna*)

During the first trip of the Mozart family to Vienna, the children were received twice at court by Maria Theresa and Emperor Francis I; in addition, they were invited to visit Pressburg (Bratislava) by Baron L. Amadé and the Counts of Pálffy.

After the extensive "Great Western" trip of 1763–66, Mozart and his family again traveled to Vienna, for the wedding festivities of a daughter of Maria Theresa. However, the bride-to-be died of smallpox, and Leopold took his family away from the city, to Brünn (Brno) and Olmütz (Olomouc), where Mozart and his sister nevertheless contracted smallpox. Upon returning to Vienna, Mozart wrote the opera buffa *La finta semplice*, which, due to intrigues, was not produced. *Bastien und Bastienne* was, however, produced privately, and Mozart also wrote a Mass for the dedication of the Waisenhauskirche.

After the three Italian trips, Mozart and his father again visited Vienna, where Empress Maria Theresa received them but did not offer Mozart a position. Mozart's six string quartets, K. 168–73, date from this visit.

After Mozart's break with Archbishop Colloredo in 1781, he moved permanently to Vienna; here he married Constanze Weber (before his father's blessing arrived). His career as a pianist and composer was highly successful for several years. Despite such masterworks as *The Marriage of Figaro, Cosí fan tutte, The Magic Flute*, and the extensive corpus of instrumental music, the later Vienna years were marred by a less enthusiastic public, and by debts which Mozart found increasingly difficult to pay. At a time when it seemed that his career was beginning an upswing, Mozart died (probably of rheumatic fever) at the age of 35.

M u s i c

During Mozart's ten years in Vienna (1781–91), he produced an enormous number of works, which represent the masterpieces of his late style. For a useful listing of Mozart's Vienna works, see Sadie, *The New Grove Mozart*, pp. 174–220; in addition, many of Mozart's works are cited in the following text.

Vienna Sites

★ ★ ★ SCHÖNBRUNN PALACE. 13th District; Schönbrunner Schloss-Strasse. During their first trip to Vienna, Mozart and his sister played here from 3–6 PM on 13 October 1762, where they were received "extraordinarily graciously." Emperor Francis I had Mozart play with a covered keyboard, and then with one finger, and the six-year-old Mozart sprang on the lap of Empress Maria Theresa and "kissed her soundly." When Mozart slipped on the polished floors (as the young princes and princesses were showing him the apartments of Maria Theresa), Marie Antoinette, the future queen of France, came to his aid.[1] Again on 21 October 1762, they played, after which time Mozart contracted scarlet

Vienna. Kärntnerthor Theater. Unsigned engraving. Historisches Museum, Vienna.

fever. Much later, on 7 November 1781, Mozart attended the celebration performance of Gluck's *Alceste*, held in the Schlosstheater (which has recently undergone an impressive restoration). In addition, Mozart's *The Impresario* was performed on 7 February 1786 opposite an opera by Salieri in the orangerie of the palace (part of which still exists, but is closed to the public). While it is frequently said that Mozart and his sister performed in the mirrored room (**Spiegelsaal**), this is not known definitively; the "*Rosen*" room is also a possibility. The palace was begun in 1696 by Fischer von Erlach, and essentially completed by 1713. Open for tours in English 1 May to 30 September 9 AM–Noon and 1–5 PM (–4 PM during the other months); admission charge.

[★ ★ ★ CHURCH OF ST. CHARLES (KARLSKIRCHE)]. 4th District; Karlsplatz. On 4 November 1762, after Mozart recovered from an attack of scarlet fever, Leopold took him here and they walked in the **Glacis** (the plains surrounding the city walls which have been replaced by the Ringstrasse) in the Josefstadt district. This church, the most important Baroque church in Vienna, was begun by Fischer von Erlach from 1716 to 1722 following a vow by Emperor Charles VI during the plague of 1713, and was finished by Charles's son Joseph Emmanuel from 1723 to 1739. The important cupola with frescoes by Rottmayr, the stucco decoration, and the painting by Ricci over the magnificent pink marble altar are of great interest.[2]

1st District: City Center

SITE OF THE KÄRTNERTOR THEATER. 1st District; Philharmonikerstrasse 4 (behind the Opera House approximately where the Hotel Sacher is now located). This important theater was the location for three **Tonkünstler-Societät** academies in which Mozart performed as pianist: On 3 April 1781, a symphony of Mozart's was performed, and he played piano variations (probably K. 354/299a), although the Archbishop Colloredo had initially refused him permission to perform; he performed with his pupil Josepha Auernhammer on 3 November 1782, and with the violinist Regina Strinasacchi on 29 April 1784 (playing the Sonata for clavier and violin, K. 454, with only a shorthand piano part).[3] The Society presented concerts, usually with oratorios, for the benefit of widows and orphans of musicians. Works by Mozart performed in these concerts were the cantata *Davidde penitente*, K. 469, the Clarinet Quintet, K. 581, and, very possibly, the Symphony in G minor, K. 550, in the second version with clarinets.[4] Mozart's Adagio and Rondo for glass harmonica, flute, oboe, viola, and cello, K. 617, was also performed here on 19 August 1791 by Marianne

Kirchgässner. The theater has been demolished; the present opera house was built 1861–69 adjacent to the site.

SITE OF THE PALACE OF THE RUSSIAN AMBASSADOR GALITSIN (GOLICYN). 1st District; Krugerstrasse 10–Walfischgasse 9.[5] Mozart and his sister performed in March 1768 at the palace of his important patron, Prince Dimitri Galitsin, who lived at 1074 Krugerstrasse (previously 1046) in the "Blue Sable" House. On 17 March 1781, before Mozart's altercation with Archbishop Colloredo, he and other musicians of the Archbishop performed here. Again, he played a house concert here on 4 December 1782, and gave at least five concerts here in 1784 (26 February and 4, 11, 18, and 25 March). The palace, containing 11 major rooms run by about 20 trained staff and more than 20 servants, was furnished with more than 250 fine paintings and etchings.[6] The house ("**Zum blauen Säbel**"), and the adjacent "White Lily" house ("**Zur weissen Lilie**") were replaced with the fine Empire edifice, the Erdödy Palace, which was demolished in 1965.[7]

Vienna. Michaelerplatz, with Burg Theater in background. Engraving by Carl Postol, 1810.

SITE OF THE MEHLGRUBE. 1st District; Neuer Markt 5 (Kärntnerstrasse 22). The inn "Zur Mehlgrube" was the location of the casino where amateur concerts were given by Martin since 1781. On 11 January 1783, Mozart gave an academy during which Aloisia Lange sang the recitative and rondo, K. 416. The Piano Concerto in D minor, K. 466 (which Mozart finished a day earlier) was first performed here, in the presence of Mozart's father, during a subscription concert on 11 February 1785, and further concerts were given on 18 and 25

February, and on 4, 11 and 18 March 1785.[8] Today the Hotel Ambassador stands on the site.

★ ★ ROOMS OF IGNAZ JAHN. 1st District; Himmelpfortgasse 6. Here, Mozart directed the Pastorale from the first of his four Handel arrangements, *Acis and Galatea*, for Baron van Swieten in November 1788, for his own benefit.[9] In addition, on 4 March 1791 Mozart made his last public appearance, playing the Piano Concerto in B flat, K. 595. After Mozart's death, the premiere of his *Requiem* was performed here on 2 January 1793, directed by Gottfried van Swieten, to benefit Constanze.[10] In this patrician house, built in 1720, the style of J. L. von Hildebrandt is apparent; reconstruction took place at the end of the nineteenth century, with construction of the upper floor first in 1953.[11] Today Café Frauenhuber is found in the building, the facade of which is almost unchanged from the time of Mozart. Commemorative plaque; open Monday–Friday 8 AM–11 PM; Saturdays 8 AM–4 PM; closed Sundays. Also on this street was the "Mausoleum" with automated clocks and devices, erected by Count Joseph Deym, a modeler in wax, for whom Mozart wrote an Adagio and Allegro, K. 594, and probably two other works for mechanical organ, K. 608 and K. 616. The name of the street derives from the "Gate of Heaven" monastery which was located in this area, abolished by Joseph II.

SITE OF MOZART'S LAST RESIDENCE. 1st District; Rauhensteingasse 8. On 30 September 1790, while Mozart was in Frankfurt, Constanze and their son Karl moved here, to the first floor (American: second floor). Here Mozart wrote his last Piano Concerto in B flat, K. 595, the Clarinet Concerto, K. 622, the (unfinished) *Requiem*, K. 626, as well as a string of Minuets and Contredanses. In addition, *The Magic Flute* originated during this period. Their sixth child, Franz Xavier (who had a career as a concert pianist), was born here 26 July 1791. The building where Mozart sang the *Requiem* on his deathbed with his friends Franz Hofer, Benedikt Schacks, and Franz Gerls, and where he died at 1:05 AM on 5 December 1791, has been demolished. Today there is a large department store, **Warenhaus Steffl**, with an ugly bust of Mozart crowded into an unworthy corner of the fifth floor sports department.

SITE OF THE SCHMALECKER HOUSE. 1st District; Weihburggasse 3. On 15 September 1767, upon arriving in Vienna during their second trip to the capital, the Mozarts lodged in the "Cirivolt" House, with the goldsmith Schmalecker, who lived on the second floor (American: third floor). The city was in the midst of a smallpox epidemic, and the family was not informed when the oldest son of Schmalecker came down with the disease. After the death of Maria Theresa's daughter, the 16-year-old bride-to-be Josepha, Mozart wrote a duet here for two sopranos, K. Anh. 24a/43a (unfinished). After two other children of the goldsmith came down with smallpox, Leopold took Mozart, leaving his wife and daughter and a servant here, and moved from the house, probably to the home of the physician Laugier. Despite the family's flight to Olmütz via Brünn, both children contracted smallpox; each later recovered. At Weihburggasse 3 today, the Empress Elisabeth Hotel is found, with a plaque in the foyer commemorating the stays of Wagner, Liszt, and Grieg.

★ ★ DEUTSCHRITTERORDENSHAUS. 1st District; Singerstrasse 7. Archbishop Colloredo was staying here in the Palace of the Teutonic Order, when Mozart, who had been called from Munich, arrived at 9 AM on 16 March 1781. Still exhausted from the trip, he had to perform at 4 PM for 20 people of the "greatest nobility." On 8 April 1781, for a concert for Prince Rudolph Colloredo, Mozart composed an aria (K. 374) for Ceccarelli, a violin rondo (K. 373) and a violin sonata (K. 379/373a) for Brunetti; for the sonata, composed here from 11–12 PM the previous night, he wrote out only the violin part and played the piano part from memory. On 8 June 1781, after two confrontations with the Archbishop, the famous break took place, during which Mozart left with a kick of the foot in his rear by Count Arco. After the first courtyard, there is a beautiful courtyard to the left, with ancient sculpture incorporated into the walls. Open Monday–Friday 8 AM–Noon. The Gothic church of St. Elizabeth at Singerstrasse 7, and the Treasury of the Order of Teutonic Knights, are also of interest. Treasury open 10 AM–Noon and 3–5 PM; closed Monday, Thursday, Sunday, and holiday afternoons; admission charge.

★ ★ ★ MOZART RESIDENCE: *"FIGARO* HOUSE." 1st District; Domgasse 5–Schulerstrasse 8; first floor (American: second floor). It is astonishing to reflect on the masterpieces Mozart wrote during the time he lived here with Constanze, from 29 September 1784 to 24 April 1787, including the Piano Concertos in B flat "Paradi(e)s," K. 456; F, K. 459; D minor, K. 466; C, K. 467; E flat, K. 482; C minor, K. 491; A, K. 488; and C, K. 503; several "Haydn" Quartets (including the "Hunt" and the "Dissonant"); *The Impresario; The Marriage of Figaro;* the Horn Concerto in E flat, K. 495; Recitative and Aria, K. 512; and the Piano Quartet in G minor, K. 478. Important occasions took place here, such as the performance of the "Haydn" Quartets by Mozart and his father in 1785, in the presence of Haydn who said to Leopold, ". . . your son is the greatest composer that I know in person or by name," and the visit of the 16-year-old Beethoven from 7–20 April 1787 to study with Mozart. The building, constructed in the seventeenth century, has an authentic facade which is charming and unimposing. The present museum (with no original furniture, but several period pieces) has a superb pink *faux-marbre* room and a collection of eighteenth-century engravings of Vienna, as well as scores and documents. Commemorative plaque. Open 10 AM–12:15 PM and 1–4 PM; closed Monday; admission charge except Friday morning.

★ ★ ★ ST. STEPHEN'S CATHEDRAL. 1st District; Stephansplatz. The monumental Romanesque-Gothic edifice, built partly 1147–1511, figured prominently in Mozart's life. His marriage to Constanze on 4 August 1782 took place here, with Leopold's blessing arriving only afterward. In 1791, Mozart's request to become Kapellmeister of the Cathedral upon the death of Hoffman was granted; however, Mozart's death on 5 December 1791 prevented him from succeeding to this position. The day after his death, a funeral service took place to the left of the main entrance, in a small chapel beneath the **Heidenturm**, and the coffin with Mozart's body was placed on a bier in the Crucifix Chapel (which can only be entered from outside, and which forms the entrance to the crypt), before being taken to St. Marx Cemetery.[12] Constanze was ill, and at the end of her pregnancy, and did not attend the service. At the staircase leading to the crypt, there is a commemorative plaque. Works of art from many periods are found in the Cathedral including a splendid sixteenth-century carved stone pulpit with busts of the four Fathers of the Church, the carved wood Wiener Neustadt altarpiece, and the red marble sepulcher of Frederick III. Open daily 7 AM–10 PM.

SITE OF THE "WHITE OX" INN ("ZUM WEISSEN OCHSEN"). 1st District; Postgasse 15, Fleischmarkt 20. On their first arrival in Vienna, on 6 October 1762, the Mozarts probably lodged in this inn, until the middle of October.[13] Two interesting houses of the period today include the sixteenth-century edifice at Fleischmarkt 9 (House "Zur Mariahilf") with a facade from 1700, and the house from 1718 at Fleischmarkt 15, where the painter, Moritz von Schwind, was born in 1804.[14]

[★ ★ GRIECHENBEISL]. Fleischmarkt 11. This edifice has the oldest remaining inn in Vienna, dating from 1450. The signature of Mozart on one of the walls is regarded as authentic. Open 10 AM–1 AM.

SITE OF THE MASONIC MEETING HALL IN THE HOME OF BARON MOSER. 1st District; Landskrongasse 6.[15] This meeting place, with a "dark chamber," several smaller rooms, a library and a large meeting hall with 105 white chairs along walls which were "painted in the Corinthian manner with figures and hieroglyphs," had been used by several Masonic lodges since 1782.[16] After Mozart's lodge, "Beneficence," was amalgamated with the "Three Fires" and "Crowned Hope," into "New-Crowned Hope" (in response to an edict in 1785 by Joseph II and subsequent ordinances concerning police supervision of lodges), Baron Moser's house apparently became the principal Viennese lodge temple.[17] The painting in the Vienna **Historisches Museum** is now believed to represent this meeting hall with Prince Nicolaus Esterházy officiating, and Mozart present.[18] Mozart was initiated into "Beneficence" on 14 December 1784 and wrote numerous works for the functions of lodges, including the richly orchestrated "Masonic Funeral Music," K. 477/479a, performed in the lodge "Crowned Hope" on 17 November 1785, to commemorate the deaths of two brothers. On 15 December 1785, Mozart performed a piano concerto and free improvisations to benefit two musician brothers in difficulty.[19] Other works connected with Freemasonry include the song "Fellow Craft Journey," K. 468, and the cantata "Masonic Joy," K. 471. The edifice was rebuilt from the ground up in 1794; in 1945 it was destroyed.

SITE OF MOZART RESIDENCE: UNTER DEN TUCHLAUBEN. 1st District; Tuchlauben 27–corner of Schultergasse. The timing of Mozart's move to this apartment, where he and Constanze lived from the beginning of December 1787 to 17 June 1788, cannot be explained, though it has been suggested that their garden house was not suitable for the winter, particularly since Constanze was expecting a child.[20] In this apartment, Mozart's fourth child, Theresa, was born on 27 December 1787 (died 29 June 1788). Although Mozart was named Chamber Composer with a salary of 800 fl. while living here, he was still obliged to turn to Puchberg with pleas for loans. The music written here includes the Contredanses, K. 534, 535, and 535a; 6 German Dances, K. 536; an aria for Aloisia Lange, K. 538, and the Piano Concerto in D, K. 537 ("Coronation"). In addition, on 2 April 1788, Mozart published a call for a subscription to his String Quintets, in C minor, K. 406/516b, C, K. 515, and G minor, K. 516.

★ SITE OF THE "EYE OF GOD" HOUSE ("ZUM AUGE GOTTES"). 1st District; Petersplatz 8–Milchgasse 1. In early May 1781, just prior to his break with Archbishop Colloredo, Mozart moved here into the home of the Webers, on the second floor (American: third floor). Before moving out at the end of August 1781, to avoid gossip about his relationship with Constanze, Mozart wrote the first act of *The Abduction from the Seraglio*. Although the building no longer exists, the commemorative plaque which was on the original building can still be found, inside the door at the entrance on Milchgasse. Nearby is the fine ★ ★ **St. Peter's Church**, where Mozart's fourth child, Theresa, was baptized.

SITE OF MOZART RESIDENCE. 1st District; Graben 17. At the end of August 1781, Mozart moved out of the Weber house and rented a room here on the third floor (American: fourth floor), near the home of the Webers, until 23 July 1782. He continued working on *The Abduction from the Seraglio* and wrote the Wind Serenade, K. 375, which was performed here outside his window at 11 PM on 31 October 1781, by six musicians, whose performance surprised him "in the most pleasant fashion imaginable" just as he was "about to undress."

SITE OF MOZART RESIDENCE: TRATTNERHOF. 1st District; Graben 29, 29a. Mozart and Constanze lived from January 1784 to 29 September 1784 on the third floor of the Trattnerhof, a mammoth edifice with businesses, Trattner's bookshops, a concert hall, a casino, and residential quarters which accommo-dated about 600 people.[21] Trattner's second wife, Maria Theresa, was Mozart's piano pupil, and he dedicated the Fantasie and Sonata, K. 475, K. 457 to her. It was here that Mozart made his first entry into his catalog of his works (**Ver-zeichnüss**), and wrote the Piano Concertos, K. 449, K. 450, K. 451, K. 453; the Quintet for clavier and winds, K. 452; the Sonata for clavier and violin, K. 454, and Variations on "Come un' agnello." One of Mozart's two surviving children, Karl Thomas, was born here, with Johann Thomas von Trattner standing as godfather. In 1911 the building was demolished, making way for the passage-way of the same name.[22] The Column of the Plague (**Pestsäule**), constructed at the end of the seventeenth century to depict the end of the epidemic is still found on the Graben.

SITE OF MOZART RESIDENCE. 1st District; Kohlmarkt 7. In February 1783 Mozart and Constanze moved temporarily to this apartment in the "English Greeting" House from the home of Baron Wetzlar von Plankenstern. The Baron generously paid for their move and for their rent here. However, the Kohlmarkt quarters were "wretched," and on 24 April 1783, they moved to an apartment on Judenplatz. During the time he spent in this apartment, Mozart wrote a "Masquerade" (pantomine with music, K. 446/416d), which he performed dressed as Harlequin during Carnival with several friends in the half-hour intermission between dancing in the Hofburg.

★ ★ PALAIS OF COUNT COLLALTO. 1st District; Am Hof, 13. During Mozart's first visit to Vienna, on 9 October 1762, he performed in public for the first time here in the palace of Count Thomas Collalto on which occasion the singer Marianna Bianchi also performed. The palace was built in 1671; the facade was renewed 1715–25 and today has been beautifully restored. Inside are private apartments and a member of the Collalto family still lives in one apartment. Commemorative plaque. Around the building, in Schulhof, there is a fine balcony and a beautiful corner of old Vienna.

★ ★ CHURCH "AM HOF." 1st District; Am Hof. Here, in the Jesuit church adjacent to the Collalto Palais, Leopold directed his son's "Father Dominicus" Mass, K. 66, on 8 August 1773. Years later, Mozart's first child, Raimund Leopold (who died two months later) was baptized here. Built 1386–1403, the church received a Baroque facade in 1662. Some exquisite ornament can be seen over the portals of the side chapels.

SITE OF MOZART RESIDENCE. 1st District; Judenplatz 3. Here, in the former center of the Viennese Jewish community, Mozart and Constanze lived from 24 April 1783 to January 1784, in "good accommodations" on the first floor (American: second floor). According to Constanze, their son Raimund Leopold was born while Mozart was working on the D minor String Quartet (K. 421/417b), and her cries during labor were incorporated into the work (Hildesheimer suggests the octave and minor tenth leaps in the *Andante*).[23] While living here, Mozart also worked on the unfinished opera *L'oca del Cairo*, K. 422, and several operatic arias which Aloisia Lange rehearsed here with him, K. 418 and K. 419. A single commemorative plaque marks the site of the two Mozart residences in Judenplatz.

SITE OF MOZART RESIDENCE. 1st District; Judenplatz 4. Unlike Mozart's good experiences in the previous apartment in Judenplatz, the time spent in this apartment, from the beginning of 1789 to 30 September 1790 (when Constanze and Karl moved in, during Mozart's trip to Frankfurt), was marked by disillusionment and poor health for Mozart and his wife. During this period came Mozart's pleas to Puchberg for loans during Constanze's illness, the death of their fifth child, Anna Maria, after an hour, and the appearance of only one name on Mozart's subscription concert list. However, also during this time, Mozart had rehearsals in his home for *Cosí fan tutte* (with Haydn and Puchberg invited) and the string quartets, K. 575 and K. 589. In addition, the Clarinet Quintet, K. 581, was written here, and Mozart arranged Handel's *Alexander's Feast* and "Ode to St. Cecilia's Day." A single commemorative plaque marks the site of the two Mozart residences in Judenplatz.

SITE OF THE "RED SWORD" HOUSE ("ZUM ROTEN SÄBEL"). 1st District; Wipplingerstrasse 19 (on the corner of Färbergasse). Returning to Vienna from Olmütz, after Mozart and his sister contracted smallpox, the Mozarts lived here from 10 January 1768 to about 27 December 1768. Here Mozart began the opera buffa, *La finta semplice*, which was not performed in Vienna, apparently due to Affligio's intrigues. However, the Singspiel, *Bastien und Bastienne* written here, had a performance at the home of Dr. Mesmer. On 23 July 1782, after his permanent move to Vienna, Mozart lived in the same house, and arranged the "Haffner" Symphony, K. 385, for festivities in Salzburg on 29 July 1782. In December 1782, after his marriage to Constanze on 4 August 1782, they relocated nearby to Wipplingerstrasse 14. On the site today there is an unattractive modern building.

SITE OF THE HOME OF BARON WETZLAR VON PLANKENSTERN. 1st District; Wipplingerstrasse 14. Mozart and Constanze lived here in the "little Herberstein House," home of the Baron, a wealthy converted Jew who refused to take any rent for the three months they lived in his house, from December 1782 to February 1783. In this apartment, Mozart sat for the famous unfinished portrait by his brother-in-law, Joseph Lange. When the Baron took "a lady into his home," he paid for Mozart's move, and the rent of their temporary apartment on the Kohlmarkt. Later he stood as godfather for Mozart's first child, Raimund Leopold. In Baron Wetzlar's home, Mozart met an important collaborator, Lorenzo Da Ponte, who later wrote the librettos for three Mozart operas.

SITE OF THE MONASTERY OF ST. CAJETAN. 1st District; Tiefer Graben (at the corner of Tiefer Graben and Wipplingerstrasse). A luxurious monastery with a chapel on the ground floor was built 1704–07 directly adjacent to the High Bridge (*Hohen Brücke*) by the Order of the Theatines. On 7 August 1773, the feast day of St. Cajetan, Mozart and his father visited this monastery, and, when asked to play a concerto, Mozart performed a violin concerto in the choir of this church, on an instrument loaned to him by the violinist Teyber, as "the organ was no good." Later, on 11 April 1781, Mozart attended confession here, and when he mentioned to a cleric that he had once played the violin here, the man immediately recalled the name Mozart. The superb monastery, which appears in an eighteenth-century etching, was abolished in 1783 by Joseph II. The original High Bridge was replaced by two other bridges, first in 1858, and then in 1903 (with the two earlier bridges depicted on the marble surface).[24]

★ COPPERSMITH GOTTLIEB FISCHER'S HOME. 1st District; Tiefer Graben 18. Not far from the home of Dr. Bernhard, where the Mozart children played in 1762, is this house, where Mozart and his father lived from 16 July 1773 to about 24 September 1773, during their third visit to Vienna after the Italian journeys (perhaps with the hope of receiving a position at court for Mozart). Here Mozart wrote the Serenade, K. 185/167a, for von Antretter (performed as *Finalmusik* for university logic students in Salzburg) and, most likely, six string quartets (K. 168–K. 173) and several choruses to *Thamos, König in Ägypten*.[25] Commemorative plaque. There is a beautiful wrought-iron door; however, the facade, with classic windows and ornament, is in a poor state of preservation.

SITE OF THE HOME OF DR. JOHANN ANTON VON BERNHARD. 1st District; Tiefer Graben 19. On 5 November 1762, to thank Dr. Bernhard for his treatment of Mozart for "scarlet fever," the Mozart children performed a concert here.[26] The building no longer exists; only the site is of historical interest.

SITE OF THE DITSCHER HOME. 1st District; Tiefer Graben 16. During their first trip to Vienna, the Mozarts moved around the middle of October 1762 from an inn to the house of Johannes Heinrich Ditscher. Here Mozart, after performing in Schönbrunn for the Empress, developed "scarlet fever," and had to stay in bed about ten days. Leopold gave Wolfgang a notebook here as a present on his name day, 31 October 1762, with compositions by Telemann, C.P.E. Bach, and Hasse.

★ ★ HARRACH PALACE (PALAIS AUF DER FREYUNG). 1st District; Freyung 3. During their first visit to Vienna, the Mozart children played here from 4–6 PM on 20 October 1762 for Count Ferdinand Bonaventura von Harrach. The splendid monumental edifice was rebuilt by Martinelli around 1702 after a serious fire. However, it varies considerably from the time of the Mozart's visit, as it was again altered radically after 1845. The palace was seriously damaged in 1944, and rebuilt 1948–52[27]; it has just undergone a spectacular restoration of the exterior and interior. The monumental staircase, splendid parquet floors, paintings, fireplaces, and stucco decoration are of interest. Today exhibition rooms and offices are located in the building.

★ ★ PALAIS KINSKY. 1st District; Freyung 4. This edifice, which has a fine facade and staircase, was built by Hildebrandt between 1713–1716. It is the property of Prince Kinsky, and contains offices and apartments, as well as numerous splendid rooms from the eighteenth century. The smaller Palais Kinsky where the Mozart children played on 14 October 1762 was adjacent to the present palace, and no longer exists.[28] They were again invited on 27 December 1762 for a dinner given by the Countess for Field Marshal Daun. In the present Palais Kinsky, there are numerous splendid rooms, the private property of Prince Kinsky. These rooms, with an exquisite staircase and the finest ceiling painting, can sometimes be visited by asking the administrator at the entrance. The domed entrance near the courtyard, however, with elegant frieze ornament, can be seen.

SITE OF THE PALACE OF COUNT ESTERHÁZY. 1st District; Schenkenstrasse.[29] On 12 March 1783, when Mozart lived permanently in Vienna, he performed at an academy of Count Esterházy (presumably Johann Esterházy, who lived here in the Pállfy House), and played each Monday and Friday at his home in March 1784. He directed a performance of a cantata by C.P.E. Bach here in Count Esterházy's apartment on 26 February 1788 and 4 March 1788, Aloisia Lange singing, with a performance for the public on 7 March 1788.[30] Mozart's arrangement of Handel's *Acis and Galatea* was performed here in 30 December 1788, with Baron van Swieten directing, and on 6 March 1789, the first performance of Mozart's instrumentation of Handel's *Messiah* took place with a repeat performance on 7 April 1789.

SITE OF THE HOME OF MARQUESS PACHECO. 1st District; Bankgasse 4–6.[31] During the first trip of the Mozart family to Vienna, the children played on 9 November 1762 for Marquess Vincenzia Pacheco, who lived in the house of Joseph Windischgrätz.[32] On this occasion the singer Carlo Niccolini performed, and Pufendorf wrote a poem extolling Mozart's playing, hoping that he would not "go . . . like Lübeck's child, too early to the grave," a reference to Christian Heinecken, a phenomenal child prodigy who conversed on religion in French, German and Latin at the age of three, and who died at age four.[33] Today the Hungarian Embassy, which was constructed from the former Palais Strattman-Windisch-Grätz (which was built 1692–94 by Fischer von Erlach, and remodeled 1766–77 by Pacassi) and Palais Trautson (built after 1676), is on the site; the former palaces were given a unified facade in 1783–84. Although it was damaged in WW II, it has been restored and boasts a rich interior.[34]

★ ★ LIECHTENSTEIN TOWN PALACE. 1st District; Bankgasse 2.[35] At the end of January 1782, Mozart hoped for a position writing "*Harmonie*" (wind band) music for the chapel of Prince Alois Liechtenstein. The Liechtenstein Palace in the 9th District was the summer palace of the prince; this palace in town was built from 1694–1706, designed by Martinelli, and altered by de Gabrieli. It is the private property of the Princes of Liechtenstein; the interior was radically changed in 1836 and 1847.

★ ★ **PALAIS WILCZEK**. 1st District; Herrngasse 5, near Michaelsplatz. During their first visit to Vienna, the Mozarts were introduced by Countess Eleonore von Sinzendorf, who brought them to the palace of Count Johann Wilczek, where they performed on 10 October 1762. Palais Wilczek, built before 1737, has an austere facade, probably by Anton Ospel.

★ **ST. MICHAEL'S CHURCH (MICHAELERKIRCHE)**. 1st District; Michaelsplatz. Two of Mozart's six children were baptized here, both of whom died very soon afterward. The tower of the church dates from 1340, while the basic part of the church is Romanesque, with Gothic apses and chapels; the facade of 1792 is neoclassic.[36] In the adjacent "large" St. Michael's house, Mozart was supposedly tested by the most famous eighteenth-century librettist, Pietro Metastasio, in 1768, to prove that Mozart's father was not writing his compositions.[37] Metastasio is buried in the church; in addition, there is a fine fifteenth-century carved stone group, "The Mount of Olives," on the outside south wall of the church.[38] Open daily 7 AM–6 PM.

SITE OF THE BURG THEATER. 1st District; Michaelsplatz. The Burg Theater, which figured so prominently in Mozart's career, no longer exists. First performances of Mozart's operas in the Burg Theater included 16 July 1782 (*Abduction from the Seraglio*), 1 May 1786 (*Marriage of Figaro*), and 26 January 1790 (*Così fan tutte*), with the first Viennese performance of *Don Giovanni* on 7 May 1788 in the National Court Theater. Academies here in which Mozart participated include Aloisia Lange's academy on 11 March 1783 with Gluck present ("Paris" Symphony); 23 March 1783 in the presence of Emperor Joseph II ("Haffner" Symphony); Therese Teyber's academy on 30 March 1783 (Piano Concerto, K. 415/387b); Anton Stadler's academy on 23 March 1784 (Wind Serenade, K. 361/370a), and Elisabeth Distler's academy on 13 February 1785 (Piano Concerto in D minor, K. 466). Academies of the **Tonkünstler-Societät** took place on 22 and 23 December 1783 (Piano Concerto); 13 and 15 March 1785 (Cantata *Davidde Penitente*," K. 469), and 23 December 1785 (Piano Concerto in E flat, K. 482). Mozart's own academies were 1 April 1784 (two symphonies: K. 385 and "Linz" Symphony, K. 425; two Piano Concertos, K. 450 and K. 451; Quintet for Piano and Winds, K. 452), 10 March 1785 (Piano Concerto in C, K. 467), and 7 April 1786 (Piano Concerto in C minor, K. 491). When standing in the Michaelsplatz with St. Michael's Church at the left, the theater was immediately adjacent (to the right) to the convex semicircular facade of the Spanish Riding School. The site of the theater is occupied by the left concave section of the facade of the Imperial Palace on Michaelsplatz, which leads to the large entrance gate. When the Burg theater closed its doors in 1888, it was replaced by a theater of the same name built 1874–1888 on the Ringstrasse.

★ ★ ★ **IMPERIAL PALACE (HOFBURG)**. 1st District; Michaelsplatz. The concert of Mozart and his sister at 2:30 PM on 16 October 1762 for Archdukes

Ferdinand and Maximilian Franz was most likely in the Hofburg.[39] On 19 January 1768, during their second trip to Vienna, there was an audience from 2:30–4:30 PM for Mozart and his family with the Empress in the Leopold Wing, during which time Emperor Joseph II is supposed to have asked the eleven-year-old Mozart if he were interested in writing and directing an opera (stimulating Mozart to compose *La finta semplice*). During their summer trip to Vienna (probably hoping for a position at Court), Mozart and his father were received by Empress Maria Theresa here in the Hofburg on 5 August 1773, but she was "gracious, and that is all." A concert by Mozart took place here in the Fall of 1781, in the Swiss Wing, in honor of the Duke of Württemberg. The famous competition of Mozart and Clementi took place here as well, on 24 December 1781, before Emperor Joseph II and Grand-Princess Maria Feodorovna. In the **Redoutensaal** in the Hofburg Mozart and his friends performed the Carnival "Masquerade," K. 446/416d, in costume during a public masked ball on 3 March 1783. In 1787 Mozart began to receive a yearly salary of 800 florins from the court, with the sole obligation of composing numerous German dances, contredanses, Ländler and minuets for the carnival balls held in the **Redoutensaal**.[40] The ballrooms have been refurbished numerous times (in 1816, 1840, and 1930). The fifteenth-century chapel, the Imperial Treasury, and the Imperial Apartments are of great interest. Guided tours of the Imperial Apartments are 8:30 AM–Noon and 12:30–4:30 PM, Sundays 12:30–4 PM; admission charge. Guided tours of the chapel are 2:30–3:30 PM Tuesday and Thursday (except July, August and the first half of September); admission charge. Baroque/classic opera performances are sometimes given here (contact Vita-Reisen, A-1010 Wien.

★ ★ ★ AUSTRIAN NATIONAL LIBRARY. 1st District; Josefsplatz 1. Baron Gottfried van Swieten, who presented Sunday matinees at noon at which "nothing else is played except Bach and Handel," lived at the Court library (**Hofbibliothek**). Mozart performed at these matinees as early as April 1782. Van Swieten then founded a "Society of Associated Cavaliers" in 1786, which organized at least one large oratorio performance each year, some of which were held in the large hall of the court library.[41] Mozart served as conductor from 1788 and arranged four Handel works from 1788 to 1790: *Acis and Galatea, Messiah, Alexander's Feast,* and the "Ode to St. Cecilia," presumably to offset his financial difficulties. The Great Hall (**Prunksaal**) of the library in the Hofburg is a masterpiece, with frescoes by Gran in the dome and statues by the Strudel brothers. It can be visited Monday–Saturday 11 AM–Noon; (May–October during the exhibition) Monday–Saturday 10 AM–4 PM and Sundays 10 AM–1 PM; admission charge.

★ ★ PALAIS PÁLFFY. 1st District; Josefsplatz 6. Wolfgang and Nannerl performed here, at the palace of the Hungarian Court Chancellor, Count Nicolas Pálffy, on 16 October 1762, during the first visit of the Mozarts to Vienna. On 9 April 1784, after Mozart had moved permanently to Vienna, he performed at an academy of Count Leopold Pálffy. It has also been said that Mozart first played *The Marriage of Figaro* here before the premiere on 1 May 1786, for a select audience, to offset concerns of the censor. The palace, with a Renaissance facade and a classical portal, was built around 1575. After war damage, it was again restored. Today the palace serves as an Austrian culture center offering concerts from time to time, readings, films, and lectures. The interior has been reconstructed in a modern style, although several rooms remain in eighteenth-century style. The room where Mozart is said to have first played *The Marriage of Figaro* remains, including simple, elegant decoration and mirrors. *It can be viewed only during concerts*; contact the Tourist Office for concert times.

★ ★ MOZART MONUMENT. 1st District; in the gardens of the Imperial Palace (Burggarten). This convincing statue by Viktor Tilgner was unveiled on 21 April 1896 after a competition and was only transferred to this site in 1953. In front of the monument, the stone guest of *Don Giovanni* is shown; in the back, Mozart at the piano with his father playing violin and his sister singing.[42]

Outside The City Center

★ AUGARTEN. 2nd District; Obere Augartenstrasse 1. On 26 May 1782, Mozart gave a "Morning" concert here (which began at 7 or 8 AM) in a former restaurant building (about 1705) of the Imperial park with his unattractive pupil Josepha Auernhammer, who had amorous inclinations toward him. Mozart directed a symphony of his (probably K. 338) and, together they performed the Concerto for two claviers, K. 365/316a. On 18 August 1782, Mozart's *The Abduction from the Seraglio* was performed here in the composer's "*Harmonie*" (wind band) orchestration. The park was laid out 1649–50, renovated in 1712, and in 1755 it was opened to the public by Emperor Joseph II. Today the Viennese porcelain manufacturer Augarten, founded in 1718, is located in the building (which does not have even a commemorative plaque). In the nearby Augarten Palace is the home of the Vienna Boys' Choir, and is *normally not open to the public except for special concerts by prior arrangement*. This castle of the complex, in the style of Fischer von Erlach, dates from the seventeenth century. Park open 6:15 AM–5:30 PM (closing hour changes, depending on season).

SITE OF MOZART RESIDENCE. 3rd District; Hauptstrasse in Landstrasse (Vorstadt) 75 and 77. Mozart's move to this apartment, where he and Constanze stayed from 24 April 1787 to the beginning of December 1787, has been explained in terms of economic difficulties. Yet, here they had a spacious house and the use of a garden, and Mozart proceeded to work seriously on his opera commission from Prague, *Don Giovanni*.[43] In addition, he composed "A Musical Joke," K. 522, and "A Little Night Music" ("*Eine kleine Nachtmusik*") during the period that he lived in this apartment.

★ ★ ★ ST. MARX CEMETERY. 3rd District; Leberstrasse 6–8. On 6 or 7 December 1791 (the "inclement" or "unfavorable" weather during the evening, recorded by four sources, could only refer to 7 December[44]), Mozart's corpse was blessed at St. Stephan's Cathedral, and then taken to this cemetery, where it was interred in a row grave. Two of Mozart's pupils had intended to accompany the coffin three miles to the cemetery (which was not a common practice of the period), but, at the Stubentor, had to return because of bad weather and the speed of the hearse.[45] For that reason, the exact site is not known. In 1844, when Constanze returned, inquiries suggested only the third or fourth row down from the monumental cross. It has been proven, based on dental examination, that the skull recovered cannot be Mozart's. The burial was "third-class," characteristic of the economically austere reforms of Joseph II; the idea of a "pauper's burial" is a myth.[46] There is an honorary grave to Mozart: a mourning angel beside a pillar (broken in half, symbolizing Mozart's untimely and premature death). The grave is continually covered by flowers and lit candles, and wild game birds often roam the cemetery. It is a deeply moving experience. Can be reached with the streetcar #71 to Schwarzenbergplatz; open 7 AM–7 PM (Summer) and 9 AM–4 PM (Winter).

★ ★ ORPHANAGE CHURCH (WAISENHAUSKIRCHE: PFARRKIRCHE MARIA GEBURT). 3rd District; Rennweg 91. During their second extended visit to Vienna (interrupted by a trip to Olmütz, where Mozart contracted smallpox), the Mozart family was present at the laying of the foundation stone of this church, during the summer of 1768. Joseph II was also present, and inquired about the progress of Mozart's opera, *La finta semplice*. The unfinished church was dedicated on 7 December 1768, in the presence of Archbishop Migazzi and the Empress Maria Theresa with her children. For this occasion, a Mass (probably the "Waisenhaus" Mass, K. 139/47a) was directed by the twelve-year-old Mozart, as well as two lost works, an Offertory and a trumpet concerto (performed by an orphan, probably in the place of an Epistle Sonata). The church was built by Karner for the orphanage located there at the time. Inside, the main altar, "The Birth of the Virgin," is by Zoller. The church was restored 1968–69. Open Monday-Saturday 7:30–8 AM and 6:30–7 PM; Sundays 8 AM–Noon.

SITE OF THE HOUSE OF DR. MESMER. 3rd District; Landstrasse Hauptstrasse 94. After Mozart's opera *La finta semplice* did not arrive on the stage, due to intrigues, Dr. Franz Anton Mesmer presented Mozart's Singspiel *Bastien und Bastienne*, K. 50/46b, privately in September or October 1768. The performance was most likely held in a pavilion in Mesmer's garden. Dr. Mesmer was the controversial developer of "magnetism" therapy, whose name has been immortalized by the term *mesmerism* (hypnotism), and he was extremely musical: He had an agreeable tenor voice, and played cello as well as the glass harmonica, which he performed for Mozart and his father.[47] On 17, 19, and 26 July 1773, Leopold and Wolfgang again visited him after the last of the three Italian journeys, and a grand concert was held here on 18 August 1773. Mozart again renewed the acquaintance in 1781 when he arrived in Vienna.

SITE OF THE FREIHAUS THEATER. 4th District; Wiedner Hauptstrasse 10–Margaretenstrasse 10–16 to Operngasse 25; commemorative plaque. Mozart wrote a duet, K. 625/592a, for an opera in Schikaneder's theater as early as 11 September 1790. However, the most important work associated with this theater, *The Magic Flute*, K. 620, was first performed here on 30 September 1791, Mozart directing, with Josepha Weber, Mozart's sister-in-law, singing the part of the Queen of the Night.[48] Mozart brought his mother-in-law, Cäcilia Weber, his son, Karl, and Salieri and his mistress to later performances, in the last months before his death. Much of the music Mozart wrote in a garden pavilion (now in the garden of the Mozarteum in Salzburg) was here in the *Freihaus*, or "Free House," a massive complex which was the largest private house in Vienna. It was built in 1769, with additions essentially finished in 1793. The theater was opened in 1787. Demolition began in 1913 and the remaining part suffered bombing damage in 1945; at the end of the 60s, complete demolition began, (finished in the 70s).[49]

MOZART FOUNTAIN. 4th District; Mozartplatz. An unsatisfying tribute to Mozart, in the middle of an insignificant square: a fountain with a flutist and a female companion, suggestive of *The Magic Flute*.

SITE OF THE PALACE OF KAUNITZ. 6th District; Amerlingstrasse 6. The Mozart children performed in the palace of the Chancellor, Count Wenzel Anton Kaunitz-Rietberg (supposedly here at the Palais in Gumpendorf which was located here) until 9 PM on 15 October 1762, on the day that they each received a gala costume from the Empress Maria Theresa.[50] Later, in summer 1768, Mozart wrote music, with others present, to his opera *La finta semplice* in the homes of various nobles, including at the palace of Kaunitz, and he performed it here in the presence of the impresario Affligio, who was responsible for preventing the opera from being staged. In 1785, Mozart had his piano transported here on 10 April 1784 for a concert at the home of this loyal patron and influential supporter. Kaunitz bought the palace in 1754, extended it considerably in 1777, and created the park; he retired here in 1792. After WW II, the palace became the Adult Education Center (**Volkshochschule Wien-West**) and was torn down in 1971.[51]

★ ★ PALAIS AUERSPERG. 8th District; Auerspergerstrasse 1. Today Palais Weltz-Rofrano. This monumental palace was built around 1706, and was altered in 1721, and again in the nineteenth century. Mozart played here as a child on 13 October 1762, for the Prince Joseph Friedrich von Sachsen-Hildburghausen, who rented part of this palace (then called Palais Rofrano), which was the home of Countess Kinsky.[52] Much later in his life, on 13 March 1786, Mozart's directed an amateur group performing his *Idomeneo* (with several added numbers) in the private theater of Prince Johann Adam Auersperg. The interior was considerably altered at the end of the eighteenth century, and a new wing was added toward Lerchenfelder Strasse in the nineteenth century. In 1953–54, the palace, which had been damaged by bombing in WW II, was fundamentally renovated.[53] It is privately owned today; the theater can be visited during performances. In addition, there are daily waltz and polka concerts from 4–6 PM and 8–11 PM.

★ ★ CHURCH OF THE PIARIST ORDER (PIARISTENKIRCHE). 8th District; Jodok-Fink-Platz. Mozart was disappointed in the education of his son Karl, and placed him in the boarding school run by the Piarist Order. Perhaps to make a good impression, Mozart marched with the Piarist procession in June 1791, "holding a candle."[54] The church, begun in 1716 (probably to designs by J.L. von Hildebrandt), was consecrated in 1771, and forms the middle point of the structure; the Piarist School forms the left wing.[55] In the church, the fine frescoes by Maulbertsch are noteworthy.

★ ★ PALAIS LIECHTENSTEIN AND PARK. 9th District; Fürstengasse 1. Now Museum of Modern Art. During their second Viennese visit, on 23 September 1767, the Ambassador of Naples gave a ball to which the Mozarts were invited, for the festivities of the marriage of Maria Josepha, the ninth daughter of Maria Theresa, to King Ferdinand of Naples. Afterward, fireworks took place in the park of the Liechtenstein Palace. However, on 15 October 1767, the young bride died during an epidemic of smallpox, which Mozart later contracted. Much later, at the end of January 1782, Mozart hoped for a position as Kapellmeister to the wealthy Prince Alois Liechtenstein, for whom he probably wrote the Wind Serenade in C minor, K. 388/384a, in July 1782, but did not obtain the post. Martinelli designed this enormous, imposing palace, built 1698–1711. The ceiling fresco of the apotheosis of Hercules in the Center Hall is by Pozzo; the Baroque decoration as seen in the state apartment is intact. Although the Museum of Modern Art has been established here since 1979, the palace and grounds are the property of the Princes of Liechtenstein. Open Monday–Sunday 10 AM–6 PM; closed Tuesday; admission charge.

★ ★ MOZART BURIAL MONUMENT. 11th District; Central Cemetery. This imposing burial monument by Hans Gasser was unveiled at St. Marx Cemetery in 1859, and was later transferred to the present site, Group 32A/55.

SITE OF MOZART RESIDENCE: "THREE STARS" HOUSE. 18th District; Währingerstrasse 26. After difficulties with the rude landlord of the Landstrasse who insisted on being paid everything immediately, Mozart and his family moved to this apartment with a garden, from 17 June 1788 to the beginning of 1789, where he composed his last three symphonies, in E flat, G minor, and C (K. 543, K. 550, K. 551). His fourth child, Theresa, died here, and Mozart's finances were poor during the half year he lived here: He was forced to make several requests to Puchberg for financial help. To improve his financial situation, Mozart made his first of four arrangements of Handel works, *Acis and Galatea*, for Baron van Swieten's concerts. Although nothing remains of the original building, there is a commemorative plaque on the site.

Other Sites of Interest:
St. Gilgen

★ ★ BIRTHPLACE OF MOZART'S MOTHER. Ischler Strasse 15. Although Mozart never visited St. Gilgen, this memorial site has many rich associations with Mozart's family. Mozart's mother, Anna Maria Pertl, was born here on 25 December 1720. In 1784, Mozart's sister, Nannerl, married Baron Johann Berchtold zu Sonnenburg, who held the same post that had been held by her grandfather. Therefore, after her marriage and subsequent relocation to St. Gilgen, she lived in the same house that had been occupied by her mother and grandparents. The exterior is beautifully restored; the edifice is situated on a characteristic Austrian panorama. Today the building is the district court, and houses a small museum with portraits and documents relating to the Mozart family.[56]

N o t e s

1 Schenk, *Mozart and His Times*, 42.
2 Kraus, *A to Z*, 26–27.
3 Eibl, *Chronik eines Lebens*, 62.
4 Bauer/Deutsch/Eibl, *Mozart Briefe*, VI, zu 585/73, 76.
5 Before the publication of this book, the exact location of this site had been overlooked in the Mozart literature. Czeike, *Grosse Groner-Wien-Lexikon*, 461.
6 Robbins-Landon, *The Golden Years*, 113.
7 Czeike, ibid.
8 Eibl, *Chronik eines Lebens*, 64-5.
9 Eibl, op. cit., 74.
10 Bauer/Deutsch/Eibl, *Mozart Briefe*, VI, zu 1267/78–79.
11 Czeike, op. cit., 534.
12 Braunbehrens, *Mozart in Vienna*, 419.
13 Bauer/Deutsch/Eibl, op. cit., V, zu 34/18.
14 Kraus, op. cit., 74.
15 Before the publication of this book, the exact location of this site had been overlooked in the Mozart literature. Czeike, op. cit., 690. The street, Landskrongasse, is cited in Braunbehrens, op. cit., 226.
16 Braunbehrens, op. cit., 229/226.

17 Ibid., 245.
18 Robbins-Landon, *Mozart and the Masons.*
19 Braunbehrens, op. cit., 242.
20 Ibid., 116–17.
21 Ibid., 115.
22 Groner, *Wien wie es war*, 601.
23 Hildesheimer, *Mozart*, 164f.
24 Groner, op. cit., 237–38.
25 Bauer/Deutsch/Eibl, *Mozart Briefe*, V, zu 289/40 (N).
26 Ibid. V, zu 36/20 (N).
27 Czeike, *Grosse Groner-Wien-Lexikon*, 515.
28 Prior to the publication of this book, numerous staples in the Mozart literature (Eibl, *Chronik*; Bauer/ Deutsch/Eibl, *Mozart Briefe*) have erroneously cited that Mozart played in the Kinsky Palais, Freyung 4; the present palace belonged to Field Marshal Daun at the time, and only came into possession of the Kinsky family in 1790 (Czeike, op. cit., 584). The actual palace where the Mozart children played no longer exists (communicated by the Administration of the Kinsky Palace).
29 Hinteren Schenkenstrasse is today Schenkenstrasse. Groner, op. cit., 497.
30 Bauer/Deutsch/Eibl, *Mozart Briefe*, VI, zu 1083/30 (NR).
31 Prior to the publication of this book, the incorrect address of Bankgasse 7 has been cited frequently (cf. Bauer/Deutsch/Eibl, op. cit., V, zu 41/5).
32 Eibl, op. cit., 14.
33 Kupferberg, *Amadeus*, 10.
34 Czeike, op. cit., 409.
35 Prior to this publication, this Liechtenstein Town House had been overlooked by the Mozart literature.
36 Michelin, *Austria*, 166.
37 Office of Tourism, *Mozart-Promenade*, 7.
38 Michelin, ibid.
39 Bauer/Deutsch/Eibl, *Mozart Briefe*, V, zu 34/88.
40 Braunbehrens, op. cit., 317.
41 Ibid., 320.
42 Czeike, op. cit., 660.
43 Braunbehrens, op. cit., 116–17.
44 Ibid., 418.
45 Ibid., 419.
46 Ibid., 421.
47 Bauer/Deutsch/Eibl, *Mozart Briefe*, V, zu 288/34.
48 Eibl, op. cit., 84.
49 Czeike, op. cit., 483.
50 Schenk, *Mozart and His Times*, 43.
51 Czeike, op. cit., 582.
52 Bauer/Deutsch/Eibl, *Mozart Briefe*, V, zu 34/70.
53 Czeike, op. cit., 378.
54 Braunbehrens, op. cit., 370.
55 Groner, *Wien wie es war*, 439.
56 Senigl, Johanna. "W. A. Mozart and Salzburg." Salzburg: Mozarteum, 1990, 52–4.

Belgium

Antwerp, Brussels, Ghent, Leuven (Louvain)

Mozart in Antwerp

Dates

6–9 September 1765 ▪ **Beginning of May 1766**

After Mozart's illness in Lille during their "Great Western" trip of 1763–66, the Mozart family traveled to Antwerp for several days, where Leopold met the "progressive" organist, Pieter Joseph van den Bosch. They visited the stock exchange, concert hall, and theater, and Leopold wrote enthusiastically about the fine paintings of Antwerp in the churches of "black and white marble." Again, at the beginning of May 1766, on the way back to Paris, the Mozart family went through Antwerp.

Antwerp Sites

★ ST. JACOB'S CHURCH (ST. JACOBSKERK). Lange Nieuwstraat 73. Both Nannerl and Leopold mentioned this large Gothic church, and Leopold mentioned both the tomb of Rubens that is found here, and the Rubens altarpiece of the "Madonna with Saints," painted between 1626–40 and intended as Ruben's testament to the chapel. Rubens, who attended Mass here every morning, painted himself as one of the saints. Although it is not mentioned by Nannerl or Leopold, an undocumented church tradition states that Mozart played the Baroque organ here, built by Forceville in 1727, with sculptures by van der Voort from 1728. Open Monday to Saturday 9 AM–Noon and 2–5 PM; no visits on Sunday.

★ STOCK EXCHANGE (HANDELSBEURS). Borzestrasse. In addition to the "old stock exchange" in Antwerp, there is also a "new stock exchange" which dates from 1531, and is perhaps the "extremely beautiful (although died out) **Boerse**" mentioned by Leopold. The exchange, the work of Dominique de

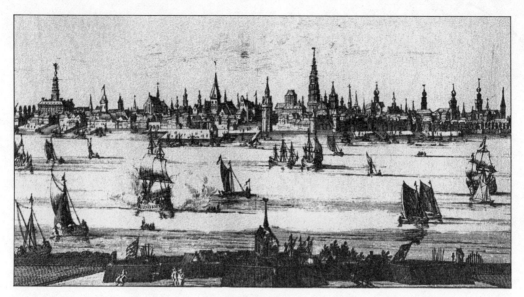

Antwerp. Engraving, published by Carel Allard, ca. 1700.

Waghemakere, was destroyed in 1858 by a fire, and was reconstructed to the original style in 1872.

★ ★ ★ ST. CHARLES'S CHURCH (ST. CAROLUS BORROMEUSKIRCHE). Hendrik Conscienceplein 12. Nannerl mentioned the Jesuit tower in her travel notes, which referred to this fabulous Jesuit church designed largely by Rubens (1614–21), with an ornate Baroque facade, set within a unique seventeenth-century courtyard. The tower mentioned by Nannerl is an unparalleled master-piece, with its ornate square base which rises to a round summit. The organ dates from around 1720 and is still used today for performances of sacred music. The altar has three massive interchangeable paintings and the dome is orna-mented with drawings by Rubens. A marvelous pulpit of carved wood depicts the Virgin Mary and life-sized angels; the Rubens chapel is dramatic and theatri-cal, composed of statues, various kinds of marble, and carved wood. In the two galleries above, paintings of the stations of the cross can be seen. Open Monday to Friday 9:30 AM–12:30 PM; Wednesday, also open from 3–5 PM; Saturday from 9:30 AM–Noon and 3–6:30 PM; Sunday from 9:30 AM–1 PM; closed Tuesday; closed to visits during religious services; admission charge.

★ ★ ★ GRAND-PLACE (GROTE MARKT). Nannerl mentioned the Town Hall, which is in the midst of this remarkable square. In the sixteenth century, the square received the name Great Market (*Grote Markt*). The square is in a traditional Frankish form, that of the triangle, and is noteworthy for the stepped facades of the guild houses, some original, others reconstructions. The most exceptional buildings are **l'Ange Blanc** (with an angel at the top), the house of the **Tonneliers** (with a statue of St. Matthew), the **Vieille Arbalète** (with a statue of St. George), that of the young **Arbalètriers** (1500), and the house of the **Merciers**.[1] The Brabo fountain in the center, however, is from 1887.

★★ TOWN HALL (STADHUIS). Grote Markt 1; entrance from Zilversmidsstraat. The monumental renaissance **Rathaus** from Antwerp's Golden Age, was built from 1561 to 1565. It is mentioned in Nannerl's travel notes. During the Spanish fury in 1576, the interior was burned out, and it was decorated in the seventeenth–eighteenth centuries with numerous art works which were plundered or destroyed during the French occupation. Little remains inside from the eighteenth century; the present interior and the numerous paintings are from the nineteenth century. Open weekdays 1–3:30 PM; Saturday 12:30–3:30 PM; Sunday 9 PM–3:30 PM.

Antwerp. Grote Markt (Grand Place).

★★★ CATHEDRAL OF OUR LADY OF ANTWERP (CATHÉDRALE). Handschoenmarkt. Leopold mentioned the "indescribable work of art, 'The Descent from the Cross' by Rubens" in the Church of Our Lady, in his travel notes. And Nannerl, after Mozart's death, wrote that Mozart played the organ here. The massive Brabantine Gothic cathedral, the largest Gothic church in Belgium, was begun in 1352, and provides an architectonic unity that is unparalleled. Inside the cathedral there is a large collection of art, partially recovered through gifts, after the systematic plundering during the French occupation from 1794–1800. The renowned tower, mentioned by Nannerl, was begun in 1420 and finished in 1521. In the transept can still be found the remarkable Rubens triptych (1612) mentioned by Leopold, as well as "The Assumption of the Virgin" and "The Elevation of the Cross" by Rubens. The present organ, however, is from the nineteenth century. Open Monday to Friday 10 AM–5 PM; Saturday 10 AM–3 PM; Sunday 1 PM–4 PM; admission charge.

GENERAL SITE OF THE HOTEL A LA POSTE. Groenplatz. Until 1878, the *Hotel à la Poste*, where the Mozart family stayed 6–7 September 1765, was still found on the Groenplatz, the square on the south side of the Cathedral. Together with the Handschoenplatz, in front of the cathedral, the Groenplatz provides a vital living area of the city, with hotels and numerous cafes.

[★ ★ THE ROYAL MUSEUM OF THE FINE ARTS (KONINKLIJK MUSEUM VOOR SCHONE KUNSTEN)]. Leopold de Waelplaats. Leopold mentioned "The Holy Trinity" of Rubens, which was in the Carmelite church (Church of the Brothers of Our Lady) during their visit in 1765–66. The church has been destroyed, but the Rubens work, which was damaged, is presently in this museum, along with 1,000 other works of ancient masters. Open every day 10 AM–5 PM; closed Mondays and holidays; no admission charge.

★ ★ OLD STOCK EXCHANGE (ALTE BOERSE). 15 Hofstraat; entrance at the door marked "Stad Antwerpen, Dienst van Het." Leopold mentioned the "extremely beautiful *Boerse*" (stock exchange), which most probably referred to this Old Exchange, built in 1515. Inside the fine courtyard from the Spanish period, replete with Gothic arches, is a *pagadder* tower (named after the Spanish paymasters). The building today houses the Municipal Building for Education. Open Monday to Friday 8:30 AM–4:30 PM; closed on national holidays.

★ST. PAUL'S CHURCH (ST.-PAULUSKERK). St. Paulusstraat 29–31; entrance at the corner of Korte Doornik and Zwartzustersstraat. The church, built in Gothic style (1530–71), but furnished in the style of the Counter-Reformation, was mentioned by Nannerl as the Dominican church. The fabulous organ, with woodcarving from 1650, was rebuilt in 1730 by Forceville, and has 52 registers. Outside the church is a Calvary of 36 statues. Open daily 2–5 PM.

★ PAINTERS' ACADEMY (MAHLER ACADEMIE). Mutsaertstraat 29. The painters' academy mentioned in Leopold's travel notes was perhaps the present Royal Academy of Fine Arts, which was an enormous Franciscan monastery in

Antwerp. Old Stock Exchange.

the fifteenth century. Among the future painters who studied here was Vincent van Gogh. The present complex includes several period buildings in classic style, and a picturesque courtyard. Open Monday to Saturday 9 AM–Noon and 2–5 PM; closed Sunday.

[★ ★ ★ CHARACTERISTIC SIGHTS OF ANTWERP]. Among the additional edifices, which the Mozarts may have seen during their stay in Antwerp, from 6–9 September 1765, are the sixteenth–eighteenth century **Maison Plantin** (today the **Musée Plantin-Moretus**), the seventeenth-century house of Rubens (**Rubenshuis**), the original edifice which today houses the **Musé e Mayer van den Bergh,** and the sixteenth-century **Maison des Bouchers (Vleeshuis),** which today houses a splendid art museum and a collection of musical instruments.[2]

N o t e s

1 Michelin, *Belgique*, 37.
2 Michelin, op. cit., 38–9.

Mozart in Brussels

About 5 October 1763 to 15 November 1763 ▪ 8/9 May 1766

The sojourn of the Mozart family in Brussels, during the "Great Western" trip of 1763–66, lasted more than five weeks, as they waited impatiently to perform for Prince Charles of Lorraine. Leopold's patience was severely tested because of the high expense of maintaining his family; he wrote: "It looks like nothing will come from it, as the Prince does nothing but hunt, eat like a pig, and drink, and in the end it turns out that he has no money."

During that period, the Mozart family was able to spend a great deal of time sight-seeing; Leopold noted, in particular, the illumination of the city at night, and the fine paintings in the churches. The children were finally invited to play for the Prince (who was actually an avid musician, with a court chapel including several renowned musicians). For their long wait, they were compensated, both financially, and in terms of artistic recognition.

Music

The Allegro to the Sonata for keyboard, or violin and keyboard, K. 6, has the inscription "by Wolfgango Mozart d. 14. Octob. 1763 in Bruxelles." Probably the Andante and Menuetto I were also composed in Brussels.

Brussels Sites

★ ★ ★ LA GRAND PLACE. Leopold cited "the town hall and the beautiful buildings which stand on the same square" in his travel notes, and wrote enthusiastically about the nearby markets, lighted at night, where one could find "unbelievably beautiful" wares such as silver, gold, mirrors, and other fine things. The Grand Place, the main marketplace of Brussels, dates from as early as the twelfth century; it was reconstructed in four years, after it was bombed by Louis XIV in 1695. The style is largely Italian Baroque, freely reinterpreted by Flemish architects. The facades almost all maintain the gable of the traditional Flemish house, and present a rich originality in their differences, yet with the effect of a uniform style. It has been called "the richest theater in the world."[1]

★ ★ TOWN HALL. Grand Place. The late-Gothic town hall, cited by both Leopold and Nannerl in their travel notes, is a masterpiece of civic architecture, begun in 1402 and completed in 1480. Its remarkable spire, designed in 1449, is topped by Saint Michael the archangel, the patron saint of Brussels. Although the interior was restored in the nineteenth century and is completely changed from the time of the Mozarts' visit, the courtyard has original eighteenth-century statues and fountains, and inside the town hall are found portraits of Prince Charles, Maria Theresia and her father, Charles VI. In addition, there are Brussels tapestries from the sixteenth to eighteenth centuries and original eighteenth-century paintings taken from other houses. Guided visits: Tuesday to Friday 9:30 AM–5 PM; Sunday and holidays 10 AM–4 PM; last visit is a half hour before closing time; closed 1 January, 1 May, 1 November, 11 November, and 25 December; entrance fee.

SITE OF THE HOTEL D'ANGLETERRE. (81), rue de la Madeleine. The Mozarts stayed in the "Hotel of England" during their six-week stay in Brussels, from around 5 October to 15 November 1763. It was a severe trial of patience for Leopold, waiting to perform for Prince Charles of Lorraine, as the bill of the "finest hotel in Brabant" was alarmingly high. However, during the period of their stay in this hotel, Mozart composed the Allegro for the Sonata for Clavier and Violin, K. 6. The hotel was situated on the rue de la Madeleine, at the corner of rue Saint Jean, and was near the Theatre Royal. Later distinguished guests included Napoleon, Wellington, and the painter, Louis David. In 1769 it was remodeled with a large hall for dancing and concerts; in 1904, to enlarge the rue de l'Empereur, the building was expropriated by the city of Brussels, and demolished in 1937. The address no longer exists; instead, the site is in the rue de l'Empereur at the present place de l'Albertine.

★ ★ ST. MICHAEL'S CATHEDRAL (ST. MICHAEL AND ST. GUDULA). Place St. Gudule. Leopold frequently mentioned "the large church" in his letters and notes, and was impressed by the life-sized figures of the Rubens painting "Christ Handing the Keys to Peter." The church, which since 1961 has been the cathedral of St. Michael, was constructed from the thirteenth to fifteenth centuries in Gothic "Brabançon" style. Inside the cathedral, presently undergoing a massive restoration, there are stained-glass windows from the sixteenth century, and a pulpit from the seventeenth century; Charles of Lorraine, the patron for whom the Mozarts had to wait four weeks to perform, is buried in the crypt. Organ concerts are given, including Tuesday concerts at 8 PM in August, and the

Sunday service at 10 AM provides a wide selction of sacred music. Open Monday–Saturday 7 AM–6 PM; Sunday 2 PM–6 PM.

★ PARC DE BRUXELLES. Leopold cited the walks in the woods, where small fallow deer could be seen (the "*Waldpromenaden, wo die Dändle sind*"). Originally the park, the present Parc de Bruxelles, belonged to the Dukes of Brabant and was an enormous "*Warande*," renowned for its natural beauty, ponds, fountains, and rock grottoes.[2] In 1835, the architect Zinner changed the park extensively from its appearance at the time of the Mozarts' visit, creating a symmetrical French garden. Open daily 6 AM–9 PM.

[★ ★ PALACE OF PRINCE CHARLES OF LORRAINE]. 1, Place de Musée. Prince Charles, who promised to hear the Mozarts and kept them waiting, lived in the **Nouveau Chateau** (Hôtel de Nassau) during the Mozarts' stay in 1763.[3] This fifteenth-century Hôtel, renowned for its splendor, no longer exists.[4] In 1756, it was bought by Prince Charles who retained the Gothic chapel (see below), and built the present splendid palace. The palace is attributed to Dewez (about 1766), and is in a refined Louis XVI style with fine statues and bas-reliefs; it forms the right wing of the present complex. The central wing was built by Roget in 1825 in the style of the old palais, while the left wing was built in the last quarter of the nineteenth century.[5] The statue of Charles de Lorraine in the square (1848) is by Jehotte. Inside the former palace is a permanent exhibition of the restored apartments of "Charles of Lorraine and His Time." Of note is the monumental staircase, sculpture by Laurent Delvaux, and the marble rotunda. *To view the apartments, a prior appointment through the Royal Library is required.*

★ ★ ★ NASSAU CHAPEL. Place du Musée, 2. The only part that remains of the residence of Prince Charles of Lorraine during the stay of the Mozarts is the Brabant Gothic-style Saint George's Chapel, constructed in 1760, under the Austrian regime as an annex to the palace, by the architect Jean Faulte. The plan is very similar to that of the chapel of Versailles, with galleries on each side, and Ionic and Corinthian orders, treated with a freedom characteristic of Louis XV. The chapel is decorated completely with a delicate stucco, and there is a beautiful wrought-iron balustrade. *The chapel can be seen only by request*; closed Sundays, public holidays and the last week of August; no admission charge.

★ ★ OUR LADY OF SABLON/ZAVEL (NOTRE DAME DU SABLON). 6, rue Bodenbroeck. Leopold cited "the church on the large Sablon [square]" in his travel notes and cited the chapel of black-and-white marble, containing the tombs of the Thurn und Taxis family. Our Lady of Sablon is one of the most beautiful flamboyant Gothic churches in Belgium, built in 1304 by the guild of crossbow marksmen, the defenders of the city. The choir dates from the fifteenth century and the splendid pulpit was carved in 1697 by Marc De Vos. The two Baroque marble chapels, which impressed Leopold Mozart, were built in the second half of the seventeenth century by the Thurn-und-Taxis family.[6] The "**Ommegang**," a historical procession in Brussels, centers around the legend of a statue of the Madonna which gave the church its name. Nearby, in the Place du Grand Sablon, there are several facades of old master craftsmen's houses. In the center of the square, there is a fountain of Minerva, erected in 1751,[7] expressing the gratitude of Lord Bruce for the hospitality he received in Brussels. Open daily 7:30 AM–6:30 PM; Saturday, Sunday and public holidays 9 AM–7 PM; *no visits during services.*

★ ★ PALACE OF THE DUC D'ARENBERG AND GARDENS (PRESENT EG-MONT PALACE). Petit Sablon 8. Leopold, who had several weeks to visit the sights in Brussels and to accept private invitations for music making, cited the Duke of Arenberg and his family, as well as the Duke's palace in his travel notes. This suggests that the Mozarts were invited here and performed privately. The present edifice, first constructed in the sixteenth century, was profoundly altered in the eighteenth century by the Dukes of Arenberg. The classical facade is decorated with Ionic pilasters and columns, with wrought-iron balustrades.[8] Since the time of the Mozarts' visit, numerous personalities have stayed here, including Queen Christina of Sweden, Louis XV, Rousseau, and Voltaire. Presently the palace, with its opulently furnished salons, is the property of the Ministry of Foreign Affairs and is used for official receptions and large conferences. The interior of the left wing remains almost as it was under the Arenbergs; that of the right was completely renovated after it burned down in 1892.[9] *The palace is never open to the public.* The gardens before the entrance are accessible to the public.

★ MISCELLANEOUS SIGHTS OF BRUSSELS. Many of the sights mentioned by Leopold, such as the large and small Carmelite churches and the Jesuit church, as well as the walks along the ramparts of the city, no longer exist. The present Boulvard-Ring runs over the former ramparts, though remnants can be found at the Porte de Hal, Tour de Villers, and Tour d'Angle. In addition, Leopold mentioned the walks outside the city near the canal, where many ships could be seen. Today the canal still exists (although modernized), connecting Brussels and Antwerp.

N o t e s

1 Jean Cocteau, quoted in Leroy, *Brussels*, 36.
2 Leroy, op. cit., 51.
3 According to the Deutsch/Bauer/Eibl annotations, Prince Charles lived in the Hôtel de Nassau during the Mozarts' visit. However, this building is not the location of the Archives Royaux, as cited in the Bauer/Deutsch/Eibl notes; they are presently located in the nearby palace, 2 rue de la Regence, at the Cour des Comptes.
4 An extensive garden, presently occupied by the square of the Musée and all the site of the Bibliothèque Royale, preceded the Hôtel. A painting (by Van Schoor about 1650), owned by the Musées Royaux des Beaux-Arts, shows the Hôtel as it was. Marez, *Guide illustré de Bruxelles*, 260–264.

5 Ibid., 260–264.
6 Leopold incorrectly called the chapel the St. Barbara chapel. The two chapels are St. Maclou and St. Ursula.
7 Leopold cites the fountain in the Grand Sablon, "upon which the Emperor's and Empress's portraits are found." This "Fontaine de la Minerva" by Bergé still exists; the effigies of Francis I and Maria Theresa can be seen on the medallion held by Minerva.
8 Marez, op. cit., 203.
9 Communicated by Annette Onyn and Jean Leroy, Office de Tourisme et d'Information de Bruxelles.

$\mathcal{M}$ozart in Ghent

4 and 5 September 1765

$\mathcal{M}$ozart and his family, during their "Great Western" trip of 1763–66, stopped briefly in Ghent, returning from Paris and London. During their stay, they managed to see the sights and climb the municipal tower with the carillon, and Mozart played the "large new organ" at the Baudelo chapel.

Ghent Sites

★ BAUDELO CHAPEL. Bibliotheekstraat.[1] Mozart played the Van Peteghem organ here in what Leopold called the "P. P. Bernardinern," or the Baudelo abbey of the order of Cîteaux.[2] The monks called "the Bernardines" belonged to the severe order of Cîteaux and bear the name of the great reformer of medieval monasticism, Saint Bernard of Clairvaux.[3] The buildings of this monastery were confiscated during the occupation of Belgium by the French revolutionaries and the monastery was converted into a public library, which was housed in the chapel, and a school, the "Atheneum," which still exists.[4] The organ, which was built in 1765, was sold in 1819 and transported to the **Nederlands Hervormde Kerk** of Vlaardingen, near Rotterdam; in 1975 it was carefully restored to its authentic state and is a splendid example of classic organ building.[5]

★ ★ TOWN HALL (STADHUIS). Botermarkt. Both Leopold and Nannerl mentioned seeing the Town Hall in their travel notes. The oldest wing, with the Town Council Hall and the Armory Room, dates back to 1482 and is in late Bruges style. The late Gothic part (on Hoogpoort and Botermarkt), is from 1518 to 1539 and includes the Pacification Hall (1535) and the Wedding Chapel (1535). Other rooms of interest include the Parsifal room, where concerts are held, and the Throne room (1635). *It is open to the public only when accompanied by a guide*; visits in several languages from beginning of May to end of October every Monday, Tuesday, Wednesday and Thursday afternoon; 4 PM in English.

★ ★ BELFRY AND CHIMES (CARILLON). Sint-Baafsplein. In Leopold's travel notes, he wrote, "From the tower we saw the city. We saw the Carillon."[6] This municipal tower, a typical city feature for important cities in Flanders, was built about 1300, and the city's privileges were preserved here in the Gothic vault (called the "Secret"). The famous Roeland bell, cast in 1315, was made into 37 bells by Peter Hemony, the Stradivarius of bell makers, in the seventeenth century. On the various floors, the dragon and the bell museum are interesting. Open daily 10 AM–6 PM; admission charge. The Carillon, with 52 bells (almost all from 1660), sounds every 15 minutes; performance on the chimes Friday 11 AM–12:30 PM and Sunday 11:30 AM–12:30 PM.

★ ★ ★ ST. BAVO CHURCH. Sint-Baafsplein. Leopold mentioned visiting several churches, but did not specify which churches. However, because of the importance of this church, and its proximity to the Belfry and Carillon, there is no doubt that this was one of the churches they visited. Inside, there is a theatrical Rococo pulpit of dark oak and marble with life-sized sculptures (1741–45 by Laurent Delvaux), and a splendid dark wood baroque organ case (1653) with life-sized angel trumpeters. Rubens's "St. Bavo's Entry into the Monastery," and the incomparable masterpiece, the polyptych, "The Adoration of the Mystic Lamb" (1432) by Jan van Eyck are found inside.[7] Crypt open 10 AM–Noon and 2–5 PM Monday to Saturday; 1–5 PM Sunday (Summer: 9:30 AM–Noon; Monday–Saturday 2–6 PM; Sunday 1–6 PM).

SITE OF THE SINT-SEBASTIAANSHOF HOTEL. Kouter. The inn where the Mozarts stayed from 4 to 5 September 1765 no longer exists; the *St. Sebastian Hotel*, which originally was the guild house of the archers of Saint Sebastian, was sold to become an inn about 1750, as a result of a financial debacle of the guild; it was located on the site of the present city library and the nineteenth-century opera house on the Kouter.[8] Two remarkable buildings surviving from Mozart's time are the so-called **Corps de Garde**, the headquarters of the city's eighteenth-century police force, and the prestigious **Hotel Faligan**, the residence of a wealthy family of traders.[9]

[★ ★ CHURCH OF OUR LADY OF ST. PETER (SINT-PIETERSKERK)]. Sint-Pietersplein.[10] The monumental dome was built by Huyssens after the model of St. Peter's Basilica in Rome. In this abbey, which is today the Center for Art and Culture, there is a courtyard with Gothic arches, and a room containing capitals, pillars and carved stone artworks. It can be visited, but only during exhibitions. Open 9 AM–12 Noon; 2–5 PM; permission may be requested from the administration to see many rooms restored in original style, with many beautiful details of the monastery, such as the present conference room with huge fireplaces.

★ ★ CHURCHES OF GHENT. Leopold mentioned visiting several churches, but did not cite their names. Important churches in the town center include the thirteenth-century **St. Nicholas's Church** on Korenmarkt, Belgium's finest example of Scheldt Gothic (*presently closed to public*) and **St. James (Sint-Jacobs)**, with a Romanesque tower at the intersection of the nave and transepts.

[★ ★ ★ CHARACTERISTIC SIGHTS OF GHENT]. Important sights which still can be seen from the time of the Mozarts' visit include the Great Meat House (**Groentenmarkt**), a medieval indoor market with a guild hall and a butchers' chapel, built between 1406 and 1410; the Castle of the Counts (**Gravensteen**), the 800-year-old castle of Philip of Alsace, located in the town center; the **Korenlei** with its elegant facades; the old Fish Market (**Oude Vismarkt**) of 1689 with a monumental baroque entrance gate with sculptures, including Neptune; the Castle of Gerard the Devil (**Geraard de Duivelsteen**), a fortified mansion from 1245; and the Cloth Hall (**Lakenhalle**) of 1425.

N o t e s

1 The Bauer/Deutsch/Eibl notes to the *Mozart Briefe* created such a confusion in Ghent that it was necessary to traverse the city repeatedly; numerous letters resulted in the following information, which is published here for the first time in the Mozart literature. In the Bauer/Deutsch/Eibl notes (V, zu 102/72), the "P: P: Bernardinern" is indicated as the "present St. Peterskirche (1629 bis 1714) auf dem Sint-Pietersplein," which has nothing to do with Mozart's stay in Ghent. In fact, Mozart played on the organ in the Baudelo Chapel.

2 Communicated by Joris de Zutter, Stadsarchief, Gent, in response to my queries.

3 Communicated by Joris de Zutter, Stadsarchief, Gent.

4 Communicated by Joris de Zutter, Stadsarchief, Gent.

5 Communicated by Joris de Zutter, Stadsarchief, Gent.

6 This can be no other tower than the Belfry, where the chimes are located, and which come reasonably close to Nannerl's description of the number of steps (326). In the Bauer/Deutsch/Eibl notes, the St. Bavo Tower is also suggested, which is extremely unlikely as it has 446 steps, and they had to climb the Belfry to see the chimes; it is unlikely that they would have immediately climbed another tower several minutes away. There is also a popular tradition in Ghent that Mozart played the carillon; as Leopold indicated with greatest precision that they "looked at the carillon" ("Wir haben die Carillion betrachet"), it is extremely unlikely that Mozart played the carillon, since both Leopold and Nannerl would have documented the event, instead of writing that we "looked at the chimes."

7 It should be noted that, as a result of a theft, this breathtaking masterpiece contains a panel which is a copy (1941), namely that of the Judges. The present chapel in which the masterpiece is displayed is a "bunker," created to discourage future thefts.

8 Communicated by Joris de Zutter, Stadsarchief, Gent.

9 Communicated by Joris de Zutter, Stadsarchief, Gent.

10 This phenomenal eighteenth-century church has, unfortunately, no Mozart connection; it was mistakenly linked to Mozart's visit to Ghent by the Bauer/Deutsch/Eibl notes to the *Mozart Briefe*. However, it is worthy of visit; it represents the finest eighteenth-century Jesuit architecture, which Leopold (and Mozart) praised.

 Mozart in Leuven (Louvain)

Dates

4 October 1763

During the "Great Western" trip of the Mozart family, 1763–66, they stopped in Leuven; they had traveled from Cologne and Aachen, and later continued on to Brussels before arriving in Paris, the goal of their great tour.

Leopold had praise for this "well-populated and well-nourished" city; the fine City Hall, the splendid marble altars, the Dutch paintings, and the quantity of brass were all noted by Leopold during the brief stay of the Mozart family in Leuven.

Leuven Sites

★ ★ ★ ST. PETER'S CHURCH (SINT-PIETERSKERK). Grote Markt. After arriving on 4 October 1763 (on the way to Brussels from Germany during the "Great Western" trip), the Mozarts spent the afternoon seeing Leuven. They "went first to the main church [St. Peter's Church], and attended Mass." Leopold was "transfixed" in front of the famous "Last Supper" by Dirk Bouts, and wrote enthusiastically about the "precious paintings of the Netherlanders," the fine brass pieces throughout the church, and the black-and-white marble altars. Today the side chapels of this fifteenth-century Gothic church have been converted into the Museum of Religious Art, renowned particularly for "The Last Supper" (1467) by Dirk Bouts. The middle panel has always been in the church; two of the four wings later went to Berlin, and two to Vienna; in 1918, they were returned as war reparations. Open Tuesday–Saturday 10 AM–Noon and 2–5 PM; also Sundays and holidays from 25 March to 30 September; closed Mondays; admission charge.

★ ★ TOWN HALL (RATHAUS). Grote Markt. Leopold Mozart admired the "beautiful City Hall," where he brought his family. The edifice, begun in 1448 and finished in 1463, is a masterpiece of late Brabant Gothic, with an ornate, feather-light marble lace facade; the 200 statues were not added until the nineteenth century. Most of the interior was redone in the nineteenth century; numerous Dutch paintings are found in the various rooms. The Gothic Hall has an oak ceiling, and small sculptures depicting the life of Jesus. Guided tours Monday–Friday for individuals (no groups) at 11 AM and 3 PM; Sunday 3 PM; from 25 March to 30 September; also Saturday 11 AM and 3 PM.

SITE OF THE "WILD MAN" INN ("ZUM WILDEN MANN"). Smolder-splein 1. As was usual for the Mozarts, they stayed in the finest inns during their "Great Western" trip, and this inn was the largest, most renowned in the city. Leopold wrote that they were "well-lodged." In 1849, the edifice was bought by Mr. Moerman, the post collector, and turned into a post office; today the central post office is there.[1]

★ ★ UNIVERSITY (CATHOLIC UNIVERSITY LEUVEN). Naamsestraat 22. Leopold was impressed by the "university of world priests" in Leuven, founded 1425 by Pope Martin V at the request of Duke John IV of Brabant. Most of the old university buildings have been preserved. In 1432, the university was housed in the fourteenth-century Gothic Clothmakers' Hall, where it is still located; the upper floor is seventeenth-century Baroque, while the "REGA" wing is eighteenth-century classical style. There are numerous buildings from the period including the fourteenth-seventeenth-century Drapers' Halls (**Hallen**) at Naamsestraat 22, the sixteenth-century Renaissance Van Dale College at Naamsestraat 80, and Premonstrant College at Naamsestraat 61 (Louis XV style).

[★ ★ CHARACTERISTIC SIGHTS OF LEUVEN]. Numerous sites remain from the time of the Mozarts' visit in 1767 and before. The seventeenth-century Baroque St. Michael's Church is of interest, as is the extensive sixteenth-eighteenth-century Beguine Convent, built of sandstone and brick.

N o t e s

1 Communicated by C. Devlies, Mayor/Alderman of Leuven.

Czechoslovakia

Olomouc (Olmütz), Prague

Other Sites of Interest:

Brno (Brünn)

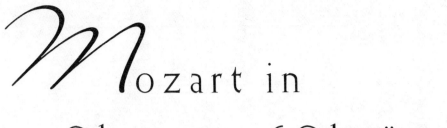

Mozart in Olomouc (Olmütz)

26 October–about 23 December 1767

Leopold left Vienna with his family, after the outbreak of a smallpox epidemic in 1767; Brünn and Olmütz were chosen because of the Mozarts' Salzburg connections with various residents there. After several days in Brünn, they left for Olmütz, where Mozart began to show symptoms of smallpox. After Mass, Leopold informed the cleric, Count Podstatsky, who had Mozart brought immediately to the Deanery of the Cathedral, where Podstatsky's physician, Dr. Joseph Wolff, treated him. During the weeks that Mozart's eyesight had to be protected, Chaplain Johann Hay visited him daily, teaching him card tricks; Mozart also learned fencing during his convalescence. After Mozart recovered, his sister also succumbed to the illness. Mozart wrote a song, to thank Dr. Wolff, and the family left again for Brünn, arriving on Christmas Eve 1767.

Music

Symphony No. 6 in F, K. 43; the inscription "Sinfonia di Wolgango Mozart à Vienne 1767" on the autograph has a change, probably in the hand of Leopold, citing Olmütz, 1767, which was then crossed out. It may have been begun in Vienna and finished in Olomouc.

Einstein contended that "An die Freude" ("To Joy"), K. 53/43b/47e was the song written before 23 December 1767 in Olmütz, to thank Dr. Wolff who had treated Mozart's case of smallpox; this has been somewhat disputed, in the most recent Köchel catalogue (K[6]), for example.

Olomouc Sites

★ ★ "BLACK EAGLE" INN ("ZUM SCHWARZEN ADLER"). Down Square and Lafayette St.[1] The Mozart family, arriving on 26 October 1767, first lodged in the "Black Eagle" Inn, in a "miserable, damp" room, which they had to heat with an unpleasant, smoking stove. Here Mozart's smallpox symptoms appeared, namely a fever, painful eyes, and an irregular pulse; after two days he was taken to the Deanery. The sixteenth-century Renaissance edifice by G. Gialdi, where the inn was located, is today called the Haunschild Palace; it preserves the features of the period, including a fine stone sculpture portal and bay window.[2] The square, Down Square, has numerous old houses and aristocratic palaces in Gothic, Renaissance, and Baroque styles; the Baroque sculpture monuments, St. Mary's Column (1716–27), and the fountains of Neptune (1695) and Jupiter (1735) are also noteworthy.[3] The fine eighteenth-century palace with a double staircase, the King's Town National Theater, was the first stone theater in Olomouc; however, it was built in 1770,[4] after the visit of the Mozarts.

SITE OF THE THEATRICAL ARENA. Courtyard of the "Black Eagle" Inn.[5] Leopold wrote, "The comedians (actors) are here, as they were performing in Salzburg, in the ox stalls." Leopold attended the performance, which took place in the wooded construction in the yard of the inn where the Mozarts stayed two days; in 1770, three years after the destruction of the structure, a new theater was built, the fine Town National Theater.[6]

Olomouc. Bishop's Palace. Unsigned engraving.

★ ★ CATHEDRAL DEANERY (DOMDECHANTEI). On 28 October 1767, Mozart, who was delirious with smallpox, was packed up in furs and driven to the Deanery. Count Leopold Podstatsky took in the whole family, and the chaplain, Johann Hay, came to see Mozart every day. As Mozart was unable to read for several weeks, Hay taught him numerous card tricks, and an instructor taught him fencing. The house, with an adjacent Baroque chapel, St. Barbara (originally a Romanesque fortress rotunda), remains today in the same form as in the eighteenth century; it is in a fine state of preservation, including the restrained facade and the gate composed of slender pillars and wrought iron. A commemorative plaque with a bas-relief portrait recalls Mozart's visit to the Deanery.[7]

★ ★ ★ ST. WENCESLAS'S CATHEDRAL. The cathedral was founded in 1109, and rebuilt in Gothic style from 1265 to 1375. (Later Ludwig van Beethoven wrote his *Missa solemnis* for this cathedral.) Leopold was not impressed by the music here in 1767; he wrote, "The music in the Cathedral is weak, yes, very weak." The cathedral was reconstructed in neo-Gothic style from 1883 to 1890.[8] Adjacent to the cathedral is the small, elegant Renaissance St. Anne's Chapel.

★ HRADISCH WAY (HRADISCHER WEG). Leopold, during Wolfgang's convalescence, often took walks on the *Hradischer Weg* to see the fortifications (which were demolished in 1886). The Hradisch Way leads to the Hradisch Monastery, north of Olmütz.

N o t e s

1 Communicated by Dr. Jiří Musil, Olomouc.
2 Communicated by Dr. Jiří Musil, Olomouc.
3 Communicated by Dr. Jiří Musil, Olomouc.
4 Communicated by Dr. Jiří Musil, Olomouc.
5 Communicated by Dr. Jiří Musil, Olomouc, in response to my queries, and published here for the first time in the Mozart literature.
6 Communicated by Dr. Jiří Musil, Olomouc.
7 Communicated by Dr. Jiří Musil, Olomouc, in response to my queries; this site was overlooked in the Bauer/Deutsch/Eibl notes to the Mozart letters.
8 Communicated by Dr. Jiří Musil, Olomouc.

Mozart in Prague

Dates

11 January–8 February 1787 ▪ 4 October–about 13 November 1787 ▪ 10 April 1789 ▪ 31 May–about 2 June 1789 ▪ 28 August–Middle September 1791

The city of Prague played an important role in Mozart's life, during his last few years; several of Mozart's most renowned and adventurous works were written here. Mozart was first invited here in 1787; his opera, *The Marriage of Figaro*, was highly successful, and he directed the "Prague" Symphony, K. 504, for the first time. During this trip, Mozart received the contract to write *Don Giovanni*.

During Mozart's second stay in Prague, *Don Giovanni* was performed with great success. In addition, he made two brief visits (without Constanze) in 1789, passing through Prague on the way to Berlin with Prince Karl Lichnowsky, and then again when returning to Vienna.

Mozart's last opera, *La clemenza di Tito*, was written for Prague, for the coronation of Leopold II as King of Bohemia in 1791.

Music

German sacred songs, "O Gottes Lamm"; "Als aus Ägypten," K. 343/336c, written in Prague, or Vienna, perhaps in early 1787.

Don Giovanni, K. 527, performed for the first time in Prague on 29 October 1787.

La clemenza di Tito, K. 621, performed for the first time in Prague on 6 September 1791

"Prague" Symphony, K. 504; Vienna, 6 December 1786.

Scene for soprano and orchestra, "La mia bella fiamma . . . Resta, o cara," K. 528, for Josepha Duschek, Prague, 3 November 1787.

Aria for bass, "Io ti lascio," K. Anh. 245/621a, written probably in Prague, September 1791.

Songs, "Des kleinen Friedrichs Geburtstag," K. 529, and "Das Traumbild," K. 530, Prague, 6 November 1787.

Six German Danses for orchestra, K. 509, Prague, 6 February 1787; the Contredanses K. 510/Anh. 293b/C13.02 are probably not authentic.

Theme by Mozart, K. Anh. C 26.11, supposedly written for harpist Joseph Haisler during Mozart's first stay in Prague.

Organ fantasy by Mozart, K. Anh. 27.03; supposedly Norbert Lehmann wrote down this piece after hearing Mozart's improvisation (in 1787).
String quartet, K. 575 and part of K. 589 were written on manuscript paper from the area near Dresden and Prague (see Alan Tyson's work on the autograph scores, 1975).

Prague Sites

★ ★ ★ VILLA BERTRAMKA. Mozartova 169, 540 012 Praha 5. This villa, in the Prague quarter Smíchov outside of the city, belonged to the singer Josepha Duschek, and her husband Franz. Mozart was a frequent guest during his trips to Prague; it was here that Mozart finished *Don Giovanni* in Fall 1787. On 4 October 1787, during Mozart's second trip to Prague (to rehearse and direct *Don Giovanni*), he and Constanze lodged in the "Three Lions" Inn, also staying for a time in this villa; the two rooms in the villa in which they stayed, and the stone garden table where Mozart is said to have composed, can still be seen. During this visit, on 3 November 1787, Mozart presented Madame Duschek with the concert *scena*, "Bella mia fiamma," K. 528, supposedly written down after she had locked him up with writing supplies in her garden pavilion. Again, during Mozart's third trip to Prague, with Constanze, Franz Süssmayr, and Anton Stadler (to direct *Don Giovanni* and *La clemenza di Tito*), Mozart probably stayed here. The villa, furnished with period pieces, is today part of the National Museum of Music; in addition, there is an attractive park, with numerous sculptures, and a bust of Mozart. Villa open daily except Tuesday 10 AM–5 PM; admission charge.

Prague. Engraving, published by Carel Allard, ca. 1700.

★ ★ KONVICTSAAL. Staré Mesto #291 (also #24). Mozart wrote to his friend Gottfried von Jacquin, on 15 January 1787,

At six o'clock [on the eleventh] I drove with Count Canal to the so-called Bretfeld ball, which is known for gathering the cream of Prague's beauties. That would have been exactly for you, my friend! I mean, I see you running after all the lovely girls and women. Do you think I was running after them? No . . . limping after them. I didn't dance and I didn't flirt. The former because I was too tired; the latter because of my inborn, tired nature. I looked on, however, with great pleasure as these people sprang around, enraptured, to the music of my *Figaro* arranged as contredanses and waltzes. For people here talk about nothing but Figaro.

The beautiful complex of the **Konvictsaal** is presently undergoing an extensive reconstruction; inside, there is a characteristic courtyard.

★ ★ "THREE LIONS" INN ("ZU DEN DREI GOLDENEN LÖWEN"). Kohlenmarkt (Uhelný trh #420). During Mozart's first trip to Prague, he stayed in this hotel on 11 January 1787, before moving into the Palais of Count Johann Thun-Hohenstein. Again, on 4 October 1787, during his second trip to Prague, Mozart and Constanze stayed here, as well as at Villa Bertramka for a while. Lorenzo da Ponte, Mozart's librettist for *Don Giovanni*, stayed in the inn "Zum Platteis," directly across from Mozart's lodging. According to the Mozart biographer Niemetschek, the overture to *Don Giovanni* was unwritten two days before the première. Nissen (Constanze's second husband) wrote that Constanze stayed up with Mozart, giving him punch, and telling him stories, letting him doze off for two hours; however, the copyist arrived at 7 AM, and Mozart finished the overture. Today there is an attractive stucco relief of Mozart, commemorating his stay here.

★ INN "ZUM PLATTEIS." Kohlenmarkt (Uhelný trh #11). Here, across from the inn in which Mozart and Constanze lodged, Lorenzo da Ponte stayed from 8 October to about 15 October 1787. Da Ponte later wrote that he spent eight days in Prague rehearsing the actors; he and Mozart were said to have been able to call to one another from their hotels. Although the facade remains essentially intact, the courtyard of the hotel has been converted into a modern marketplace and is not interesting. Although the building is in need of restoration, the classical balcony and windows, as well as the literal "headstones" of the facade, are of interest.

★ ★ ★ NOSTITZ THEATER. Ovocný trh 6, 110 00 Praha 1. In 1783, this new "National Theater" was established by Count Nostitz; it was the site of the first performances of two of Mozart's operas. During Mozart's first trip to Prague, on 13 January 1787, he attended a performance of Paisiello's opera *Le gare generose*, and chatted during the entire performance (from boredom). During this visit to Prague, *Figaro* was performed on 13 January 1787, in the presence of Mozart. Then, on 19 January 1787, Mozart gave a concert here, with his so-called "Prague" Symphony, K. 504, and three improvisations on the piano, the last based on "Non piú andrai" from *Figaro*. Finally, on 22 (perhaps 20) January 1787, Mozart himself conducted *Figaro* from the keyboard. During his second trip to Prague, (to present *Don Giovanni*), Mozart's *Figaro* was presented on 14 October 1787 on the occasion of the visit of Prince Anton Clemens von Sachsen and his future bride, despite the intrigues of a high-ranking woman to have *Figaro* presented as a play without music. *Don Giovanni* was first presented on 29 October 1787, probably with Casanova in the audience. Finally, during Mozart's last trip to Prague, he conducted *Don Giovanni* on 2 September 1791, for the coronation of Emperor Leopold II as King of Bohemia. Mozart then conducted *La clemenza di Tito* on 6 September 1791, in the presence of Emperor Leopold II; the emperor's wife is supposed to have described it as a "*porcheria tedesca.*" ("a German mess"). This remarkable theater, in eighteenth-century scale, was closed for years, and has just received a spectacular renovation.

★ THE NEW INN (NOVÁ HOSPODA), LATER "THE GOLDEN EAGLE." Corner of Zeltner and Fischmarktgasse (Celetná/Rybná). While dining in the restaurant that was located here, Mozart is said to have heard the harpist Joseph Haisler perform variations to *Figaro*; Mozart is then said to have played a theme for him (K. Anh. C 26.11), which he then gave to the harpist, and Haisler then improvised variations on it, which he continued to do for years. Despite the "ring of truth" of the anecdote, and contemporary confirmation, the authenticity of the theme has been called into question. When standing on Celetná, facing the tower, the New Inn was on the left (on the western side of the intersection of Celetná and Fischmarktgasse (Fish Market Street). After the inn was renamed, a golden sign was added. The street is one of the most characteristic parts of Prague; the nearby tower (Prašná brána/Pulverturm) dates back to 1475, and underwent extensive restoration in the 1960s.

★ ★ CLEMENTINUM. Klementinum St. knilovna. On 13 January 1787, Mozart made a visit to the remarkable Clementinum, including the library (with a collection of 130,000 volumes) and the theological seminary. He wrote to Gottfried von Jacquin on 14 January 1787 that he paid "a call on Father [Dr. Karl Raphael] Unger at 11 AM and inspected the Imperial and Royal Library and the General Theological Seminary. After we had stared our eyes out of our heads we thought we heard a little stomach *aria* [air] inside us. We thus concluded that it would be wise to drive to Count Canal's for lunch." Again, in November 1787, Mozart visited the Theological Seminary. The Clementinum was formerly a Jesuit College; today it is the seat of the State Library of Czechoslovakia. Unfortunately, the visitor today does not have the opportunity to "stare the eyes out of the head," since *the spectacular so-called "Baroque Hall" of the Clementinum is closed to the public*; the remarkable architectural design, antique astrolobes, frescoed ceilings, and pavement cannot be seen. In the complex, however, various libraries and facilities, as well the impressive facade, can be seen today.

★ SITE OF THE PALAIS OF COUNT PACHTA. Annaplatz/Annagasse (Anenské nám.). In February 1787, during his first visit to Prague, Mozart wrote the German Dances, K. 509, for one of the large balls given by the Prague nobility. Most likely they were written for Count Johann Pachta von Rájow, who was a Major, as well as a "good musician and composer," and who had his own wind band (*Harmonie*). Count Pachta supposedly invited Mozart to dine at his home before a ball, an hour before the usual time; Mozart found supplies for writing music awaiting him, and wrote some German dances for the Count within a half hour. Later, on 10 April 1789, while stopping in Prague on the way to Berlin with Prince Karl Lichnowsky, Mozart came here to visit Count Pachta, who was not at home. The present edifice, with three arches on the street level, surmounted by a balustrade, is not the Pachta Palais from the time of Mozart; the original was destroyed.[1]

★ ★ "UNICORN" INN ("EICHHORN"). Lazenská. During Mozart's trip to Berlin and Dresden with Prince Karl Lichnowsky, they stopped in Prague on 10 April 1789 at 1:30 PM, where they lodged at the "Unicorn" Inn, departing on the same day at 9 PM. After arriving, Mozart was "shaved, [had his] hair done, and dressed," and went to visit Josepha Duschek, Count Canal and Count Pachta, all without success; however, he did manage to see the impresario Guardasoni, arranging a contract for a future opera at Prague. The fine facade, with green stucco, is impressive, despite the need for restoration; the interior is not interesting. However, the square and the surrounding edifices are extremely characteristic. There is a commemorative plaque on the facade citing the stay of Beethoven (but not of Mozart).

★ ★ ★ NICOLAUS CHURCH. Malostranské námêstí, 110 00 Praha 1. In this splendid Baroque church, on 6 December 1787 (during Mozart's second trip to Prague), one of his Masses (probably in C minor, K. 427) was performed. The work of the architect C. Dienzenhofen and his son Kilian Ignaz, the church has magnificent ceiling paintings, and pink and green decoration, with a gilded pulpit. The organ is original, by Master Schwarz, with 2,500 pipes. Concerts are given here, including those which are part of the **Grosse Musik Festival**, 12 May–3 June. Open daily 9 AM–5 PM (Winter) and 9 AM–6 PM (Summer); admission charge.

★ ★ PALAIS OF COUNT THUN-HOHENSTEIN. Thunstrasse (Thunovská) #14. This palace of Mozart's patron, "old Count Thun" (Count Johann Joseph Thun-Hohenstein), is rich in associations with Mozart's Prague sojourns. Mozart, on his first trip to Prague, traveling with Constanze, the violinist Franz de Paula Hofer (his future brother-in-law), and his servant Joseph, stayed a single night in the "Three Lions" Inn, after which they moved into this palace, from 12 January 1787. The conditions were so pleasant that Mozart remained *sine linea* (without writing a line); instead he slept late, heard the Count's own musicians perform, and played on the "excellent pianoforte" which the Count had sent to his room. On 12 January 1787, in Mozart's room, he performed the Bandel Trio for tenor, soprano, and bass (with violins, viola and bass), K. 441, and a Piano Quartet (probably K. 493). Today the edifice houses the British Embassy; it has been redone into offices and residences, and *cannot be visited inside*. The remarkable fortress-like facade, however, is of interest, with its massive gate.

★ ★ ★ STRAHOV MONASTERY (STRAHOVSKY KLASTER). Strahovské nádvoří 132, 110 00 Praha 1. In this remarkable monastery, founded in the twelfth century, Mozart played the organ during his second visit to Prague. Many years later, the Canon, Norbert Lehmann, wrote to the Mozart biographer, Niemetschek, that Mozart arrived at 3 PM, with Josepha Duschek, and wished to play the organ, which had been restored in 1744 by Ölschlägel. Although Lehmann was not happy to play for such a master, he demonstrated the full strength of the organ and improvised on a theme. Mozart then "for about five minutes struck masterful chords *pleno choro*," and then played the manual

. . . without chest register and choir organ. All four reed stops seemed too loud to him. In addition to the usual pedal without mixtures, he chose the eight-foot trumpet bass. He then began a four-part fugal theme that was even more difficult to perform because it and its imitation consisted of nothing but mordents, extremely difficult to execute with expression on this organ, which required great pressure from the fingers. But his fourth and fifth fingers in both the right and left hands were equal in strength to the first, second, and third; this astonished everyone.

Lehmann described Mozart's modulations from G minor, through B minor to D-sharp major, ending in B major over B flat in the pedal. Lehmann then partly wrote down the improvisation, K. Anh. C 27.03. The large complex of the former Strahov Monastery, which was rebuilt at various times, is today the seat of the Museum of Czech Literature. The most important rooms are the Theological and Philosophical Halls; the library is more than 800 years old. The splendid altars of black marble have remarkable paintings, as well.

[★ ★ ★ CHARACTERISTIC SIGHTS OF PRAGUE]. The Old Town Square is one of the most historic places in Prague, with the old Town Hall, surmounted by a renowned astronomical clock; the Gothic Church of Our Lady, the Rococo Kinsky Palace, and the Monument of Master John Huss are also noteworthy. In addition, the Charles Bridge is of interest; this bridge, the oldest in Prague (begun in 1357), was built by P. Parler, and has thirty Baroque statues and sculptural groups. The Mala Strana (the small town) has gardens, picturesque corners, and numerous fascinating edifices. The Vyšehrad Castle complex on the rock above the Vltava is important in Czech folklore, as the supposed seat of the first Czech princes; the St. Martin's Rotunda, and the Church of St. Peter and Paul, surrounded by a Baroque fortress, are preserved there today. The Prague Loreto, built in the seventeenth–eighteenth centuries, has a carillon which sounds every hour, and a remarkable treasury inside. The Jewish Cemetery, dating from the fifteenth century, is fascinating for its characteristic grave markers and tombs. Finally, the Prague Castle, which dates back to the nineteenth century, is the residence of the Czech presidents. The Gothic Cathedral of St. Vitus is there, with a mausoleum of Czech sovereigns, and with the coronation jewels.

Other Sites of Interest:
Brno (Brünn)

PALACE OF COUNT FRANZ SCHRATTENBACH. Kobližná-Gasse. The members of the Mozart family were guests here, in the palace of the brother of Archbishop Sigismund of Salzburg, from 24 December 1767 to 9 January 1768. Today the facade of the palace is remarkably intact. The architecture is austere, with ornament over the windows on the two floors above the ground floor, and a coat-of-arms over the central entrance. Presently there are shops located on the ground floor. A commemorative plaque, with a bas-relief portrait of Mozart in profile, states, "W. A. Mozart lived here in December 1767 and January 1768."

GENERAL SITE OF THE TAVERN ON THE CABBAGE MARKET (KRAUT-MARKT). Here, on 30 December 1767, Count Schrattenbach gave a concert at which the Mozart children played "to the admiration of all," with the participation of musicians from Brünn. Later, one of the members of the audience wrote an account describing how the young Mozart could not tolerate wind instruments because of their impure intonation.[2]

Prague. Leopold II, Coronation Procession, 1791. Engraving by Karl Pluth after Ph. and F. Heger.

N o t e s

1 Communicated by Ph. Dr. Jitřenka Pešková, library.
2 Schenk, *Mozart and His Times*, 102.

England

Canterbury, London

(and Chelsea)

Other Sites of Interest:

Dover

Mozart in Canterbury

Dates

24–31 July 1765

After their extended sojourn in London, as part of the "Great Western" trip of 1763–66, the Mozart family stopped in Canterbury. During their stay, they were invited to visit for several days by Sir Horace Mann, the nephew of the British Minister in Florence, who lived in a country house outside of Canterbury.

Canterbury Sites

★ ★ ★ **CANTERBURY CATHEDRAL.** Sun Street. Nannerl, in her travel notes, mentioned this breathtaking edifice. Its history goes back to 597 AD, when St. Augustine arrived in Kent and founded the first cathedral. In the structure which was built in 1070–77 by Archbishop Lanfranco, Thomas Becket was assassinated in 1170. This church structure was demolished, and the actual present nave was begun in 1377; the cathedral was completed in 1498. The **Baptismal Font** (1639), the chapels in the crypt, and the cloister are noteworthy.

POSSIBLE HOTEL OF THE MOZARTS. In the eighteenth century, the most important hotels in Canterbury were the "Fountain" in St. Margaret's Street, the "Rose" in the Parade, and the "Red Lion" on High Street. The "Red Lion" was demolished in the early nineteenth century, and the "Rose" and "Fountain" were bombed in WW II.[1]

[★ ★ ★ **CHARACTERISTIC SIGHTS OF CANTERBURY**].[2] Despite wartime bombing, much of the city from the time of the Mozarts' visit still remains. Within a short walk from the cathedral are the **Christ Church Gate**, the main entrance to the cathedral precincts, built in the early sixteenth century; the **West**

Gate, which is the only remaining city gate, built about 1380; the **City Walls,** part of which can be seen behind the cathedral near Broad Street; the eleventh–twelfth century **Castle,** the keep of which can be seen near Rheims Way; the **Dane John,** an ancient burial mound, probably dating from the first century; **St. Martin's Church,** which is the oldest parish church in England still in use, where Christians worshipped even before St. Augustine came to Canterbury in 597 AD; **St. Augustine's Abbey Ruins,** which are the remains of a great monastery destroyed in the reign of Henry VIII (partly in the care of "English Heritage" and open to the public); and numerous old churches, including **St. Paul, St. Peter,** and **St. Mildred,** all of which are still in use today.

★ EXCURSION TO BOURNE PLACE. Seven miles southeast of Canterbury,[3] in the country. From 26 to 29 July 1765, the Mozarts were the guests of Sir Horace Mann, the nephew of the British Minister in Florence; Sir Horace resided several years in this country house of the manor of Bishopsbourne.[4] At some point during their stay in Canterbury, the Mozarts enjoyed seeing horse races,[5] which was noted in Leopold's letters, and in Nannerl's travel notes. The eighteenth-century red-brick Bourne Place has a two-story front and an unusually wide pediment covering five windows, a cornice and hipped roofs; it is apparently unoccupied at the present.[6] *It is not open to the public.*

N o t e s

1 Communicated by David S. Cousins, Reference and Information Librarian, Canterbury Library, in response to my queries; possibilities for the hotel in which the Mozarts lodged had previously been overlooked in the Mozart literature.

2 Contributed by David S. Cousins, Reference and Information Librarian, Canterbury Library.

3 Anderson, *Letters of Mozart,* I, 84.

4 Anderson, op. cit., I, 84–85.

5 It is not completely clear from Leopold's letter which day the Mozarts attended the horse races; Eibl (in contrast to Deutsch) believes that 25 July 1765 was the day they saw the races in Canterbury (which requires the text of Leopold's letter to be somewhat reordered); see Bauer/Deutsch/Eibl, *Mozart Briefe,* VII, zu 102/18–20 (NR). However, horse racing also took place on Barham Downs near the village of Bridge; the modern Bridge bypass road covers part of the land where the racecourse once lay; communicated by David S. Cousins, Reference and Information Librarian, Canterbury Library.

6 Communicated by David S. Cousins, Reference and Information Librarian, Canterbury Library.

Mozart in London (and Chelsea)

Dates

In London from 23 April to 6 August 1764 · In Chelsea from 6 August to about 25 September 1764 · In London from about 25 September 1764 to 24 July 1765

London and Paris were the most important destinations of the extensive tour ("Great Western" trip) on which Leopold took his family from 1763 to 1766, stopping and performing whenever possible in each musical center along the way. The fifteen months in England were a significant period in Mozart's life. Mozart's family was received with particular warmth at the court of George III and Queen Sophie Charlotte; the children performed three times at Buckingham House. In addition to performing at four other concerts, as well as private "exhibitions" in London, Mozart met Johann Christian Bach (one of the most significant influences on Mozart's musical style) and studied voice with the castrato Giovanni Manzuoli. In addition, Daines Barrington, the lawyer and nature scholar, examined the prodigy and later described the encounter; Mozart improvised arias of love and rage for him, singing and accompanying himself on the keyboard.

After an evening at Lord Thanet's on 8 July 1764, Leopold fell seriously ill and required seven weeks in the suburbs of Chelsea (presently part of London) to recuperate. Because of the gravity of Leopold's illness, Mozart and Nannerl were not permitted to touch the keyboard. Instead, during this period, Mozart wrote his first symphony, and notated by himself numerous keyboard pieces/sketches (contained in the "London Sketchbook").

Music

Symphonies K. 16 in E-flat major, K. 19 in D; in addition, the rediscovered K. Anh. 223/19a in F probably also dates from London. Only the Incipit, contained in the Breitkopf catalog, of a lost symphony, K. Anh. 222/19b in C is known.
6 Sonatas for keyboard and violin (or flute) with violoncello *ad libitum*, K. 10 through K. 15 (op. 3)

Motet (sacred madrigal), "God is our refuge," in four voices, K. 20.
Tenor aria with orchestral accompaniment, "Va dal furor portata," K. 21/19c, to a text from Metastasio's *Ezio.*
Keyboard duet in C, K. 19d.
The "London Sketchbook," K. Anh. 109b/15a–ss, consists of short pieces, written on two staves for keyboard (or orchestral sketches).
A third sketchbook, called "Capricci" by Nannerl, has been lost. In addition, the solo keyboard variations, K. Anh. 206/21a, cited in the Breitkopf catalog, have been lost.

Chelsea Sites (London)

★ ★ HOME OF DR. RANDAL. Today 180 Ebury Street. During Leopold's serious illness, from 6 August 1764 to around 25 September 1764, the Mozart family lived in the calm suburb of Chelsea, where they stayed with the Randal family. As the food they had sent in was so poor, Mozart's mother began to cook here, to the enthusiasm of Leopold. The house had to be kept very still, and Mozart was left to composing, during which time he notated a number of piano pieces in the "London Sketchbook" (K. Anh. 109b/15a–15ss), some of which include awkward passages. Mozart also wrote his first two symphonies here, K. 16 in E flat and K. 19 in D, and Nannerl later wrote that Wolfgang had asked her

Chelsea. Unsigned engraving, 18th century. Mozarteum, Salzburg.

to remind him to write a good part for the horn. Presently there is a commemorative plaque on the simple brick facade. The house, which was damaged in the back, has been restored, and today has private apartments.

★ ★ CHELSEA ROYAL HOSPITAL. Nannerl mentioned this *infalitenhaus* or "Invalid Home" which today is still a home for veterans. Wren designed the imposing classic complex, which features spacious courtyards. The **chapel**, with a frescoed apse by Ricci, and the **Great Hall** with an eighteenth-century mural of Charles II are noteworthy.[1] Chapel open daily 2–4 PM; Great Hall open daily 10 AM–Noon, 2–4 PM; no admission charge.

★ RANELAGH GARDENS. Royal Hospital Road. Presently **Botanical Gardens**, on the grounds of the **Chelsea Royal Hospital**. The **Rotunda**, which has been demolished, was the site of a concert on 29 June 1764 by Mozart and his sister, at which time Mozart performed a selection of his own musical works on the harpischord, and a concerto for organ. The concert was for the benefit of the **Lying-in Hospital**, whose foundation stone was laid the next year (1765) in order to "win the affections of this highly unusual nation." Each year, in February, the park hosts the renowned **Chelsea Flower Show.**

★ ★ CHARACTERISTIC STREETS OF CHELSEA. On 9 August 1764, Leopold wrote, "I am now in a spot outside the town, where I have been carried in a sedan-chair, in order to get more appetite and [to get] fresh strength from the good air. It has one of the most beautiful views in the world. Wherever I turn my eyes, I see only gardens and, in the distance, the finest castles; and the house where I am living has a lovely garden." Much of the area between the **Physic Garden** and the **Royal Hospital**, as well as the **Cheyne Walk**, has maintained its appearance from the eighteenth century.

London Sites

★ ★ ★ WESTMINSTER ABBEY. Westminster; London SW1P 3 PA. Both Leopold and Nannerl mentioned visiting this extraordinary architectural masterpiece, begun in the time of Edward the Confessor, and rebuilt in Gothic style in the thirteenth century, with a splendid chapel and numerous later additions. Open 8 AM–6 PM (–8 PM on Wednesday); admission charge for the Royal Chapels.

★ ★ ★ WESTMINSTER HALL. Located in the **Palace of Westminster** is another famous London site visited by the Mozarts, as cited in Nannerl's travel notes. It was built in 1097, and rebuilt in the fifteenth century. The hammerbeam, which weighs almost 700 tons, is considered to be the finest timber roof ever built.[2] *It can be visited only by applying to a member of Parliament.*

★ ★ ★ BUCKINGHAM PALACE. St. James's Park; London SW1; *the entrance to the Queen's Gallery is on Buckingham Palace Road.* Mozart performed for King George III and his wife Sophie Charlotte three times during the sojourn of the Mozarts in London. On the evening of 27 April 1764, from 6 to 9 PM Mozart and his sister performed for the music-loving monarchs. Again on 19 May 1764, they were at court, where Mozart played works by Wagenseil, J. C. Bach, Abel, and Handel at first sight, improvised "the most beautiful melody" on a bass of a Handel aria, played the King's organ, and accompanied the queen who sang an aria.[3] Finally, on 25 October 1764, they were again invited to perform, from 6 to 10 PM. Leopold had six sonatas by Mozart (K. 10 through K. 15) for clavier, violin or flute, and *ad libitum* cello engraved, which were dedicated to Queen Sophie Charlotte. Despite the small honorarium of 24 guineas which they received each time, Leopold wrote about the extraordinary graciousness of the welcome, and of the "easy manner and friendly ways" of the sovereigns. The brick core of the present palace, where Mozart performed, was bought by George III in 1762 for his wife, and was known as **Buckingham House,** or the "Queen's House." It is located at the rear of the present structure, and is difficult to see. The present palace which surrounds it was completed in 1837 to plans of John Nash. *Although the palace is not open to the public, the Queen's Gallery, with exhibitions of paintings and furniture, can be visited.* Open Tuesday–Saturday and holiday Mondays 11 AM–5 PM; Sunday 2–5 PM; closed holidays[4]; admission charge. In addition, the Royal Mews contain a Riding House from 1764, and the Gold State Coach of 1762. They are open Wednesday and Thursday 2–4 PM; closed holidays; admission charge.

★ ★ ★ ST. JAMES'S PARK. Here, in London's oldest park, Leopold wrote that, a week after their appearance in court, they were walking and the King came driving with the Queen. He recognized and saluted them, especially "Master" Mozart. The park was landscaped in the seventeenth century in the style of Le Nôtre, which was the form in which the Mozarts saw it. However, in the nineteenth century, Nash landscaped it, creating islands (with wild fowl) in the long water, as it is today.

★ SITE OF THE HOME OF LORD THANET. 19 Grosvenor Square (formerly 18).[5] **Grosvenor Square** is one of London's largest squares, and here Mozart performed for Lord Thanet (Sackville Tufton, 8th Earl of Thanet)[6] from 6 to 11 PM on 8 July 1764. On the way, Leopold followed the family on foot, as the weather was beautiful and he could not get a second coach. The severe "cold" which he contracted that evening required over seven weeks recuperation in Chelsea. John Adams, the first Minister to Britain and later President of the United States, lived in the building which was formerly at #9. No original buildings of the eighteenth century survive; Lord Thanet's house was much

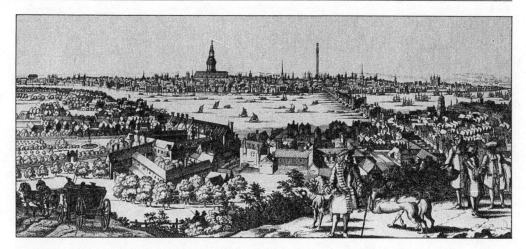

London. Engraving, published by Carel Allard, ca. 1700.

rebuilt and finally demolished in 1933.[7] Neo-Georgian buildings are found on three sides, with Saarinen's modern **American Embassy** on the west.[8]

SITE OF THE SPRING GARDENS. Court adjacent to the Admiralty Arch, on the northern side. Nothing remains of the large exhibition hall of the **Academy of Painters**, located in **Spring Gardens** (the fashionable seventeenth-century gardens with entertainment and refreshments in arbors) where Mozart and his sister played a concert at noon on 5 June 1764. The concert had been postponed twice, probably because of an illness from which Wolfgang was suffering. However, the "grand vocal and instrumental concert," with the participation of the violinist Barthélémon and the cellist Cirri, was so successful that Leopold took in 100 guineas in three hours, and most of the participants refused to accept an honorarium. Mozart and his sister performed a concerto for two claviers, and Wolfgang also performed on the organ.

★ SITE OF THE LITTLE HAYMARKET THEATER. 9–10 Haymarket. The Mozart children, "wonders of Nature," gave a concert in the **Little Haymarket Theater** at 6 PM on 21 February 1765, during which symphonies of Mozart were performed, most likely K. 16, K. 19 and K. Anh. 223/19a. Here, in the **Theatre Royal**, the principal composer of the time was J. C. Bach, a strong influence on Mozart's earliest symphonies. This public "vocal-and-instrumental" concert had been postponed from the 15th because Arne's oratorio *Judith* was being performed; it was then postponed again. The present Theatre Royal at Haymarket was built by Nash in 1821 with a large pedimented portico.[9] The theater no longer exists; it was located adjacent to, and immediately to the north (to the left of the portico of the facade) of, the present theater.[10] The site formerly occupied by the **Little Theatre** is now 9–10 Haymarket, being offices; there are no eighteenth-century buildings in the area.[11]

★ SITE OF THE HOME OF JOHN COUSINS. Today 19 Cecil Court in the St. Martin Lane district near Trafalgar Square and Leicester Square. After a single night in "**The White Bear**" **Inn**, the Mozarts lived here with the haircutter John Cousins, in three small rooms, until Leopold's illness necessitated their move to Chelsea. The present shop complex, with its multicolored shiny brick facade, is from the nineteenth century.

SITE OF "THE WHITE BEAR" INN. 221 Piccadilly. After arriving in London on 23 April 1764, the Mozarts stayed for a single night in this inn before moving nearby to the home of John Cousins. "**The White Bear**" **Inn**, which dated back as far as 1685, was demolished in 1870 and replaced by the **Criterion Restaurant**.[12] There is nothing in the area from the eighteenth century.[13]

★ GOLDEN SQUARE. In the area of this remarkably preserved square, Leopold cited Mr. Kirckman, claviermaker (Broad Street, Golden Square), and other merchants. In addition, Tschudi, the renowned maker of keyboard instruments, was located at 32 Great Pultney Street, Golden Square, after October 1742.[14]

SITE OF HICKFORD'S ROOMS. 63–65 Brewer Street in Soho. **Hickford's Great Room** was the location of a public concert of the Mozart children on 13 May 1765, at which time they performed four-handed music (C Major Sonata for piano, four hands, K. 19d). The concert, for which Leopold had to reduce the price to 5 shillings, again had the participation of the instrumentalists Barthélémon and Cirri, and the singer Cremonini. The concert room, where Gluck had performed on the glass harmonica in 1746,[15] was not used very much for music after 1779; it remained substantially preserved in its original form, and was demolished in 1934, despite its unique historical interest.[16] Presently the site is occupied by the **Regent Palace Hotel** annex of 1937.[17] The neighborhood is partly a red-light district, partly Chinatown. However, the area, including Great Pultney Street and the Golden Square, has interesting historical buildings.

★ SITE OF THE HOME OF THOMAS WILLIAMSON. 20 Frith Street, near Soho Square. After the family returned from Leopold's convalescence in Chelsea, they moved on 25 September 1764 to the home of the corset maker Williamson. In this apartment, and in "the great room in the '**Swan and Harp Tavern**' in Cornhill," Leopold advertised private concerts, where ticketholders could hear Mozart perform any piece of music at sight, including music without a bass line, which he would compose without use of the clavier. Works Mozart probably composed here include the keyboard duet, K. 19d; "God is Our Refuge," K. 20; "Va dal furor portata" for tenor, K. 21/ 19c; the lost solo keyboard variations, K. Anh. 206/ 21a; the lost symphony, K. Anh. 222/19b[18]; and the symphony rediscovered in 1981, K. Anh 223/ 19a. The house (demolished), with a simple brick facade with a moulded brick cornice, may have been built or rebuilt about 1725–26.[19]

★ SOHO SQUARE. Leopold wrote, on 8 June 1764, that the Mozarts attended Mass in the chapel of the French Ambassador, Claude-Francois Regnier, Count of Guerchy. The embassy, with a Catholic chapel, was in **Monmouth House** on Soho Square, of which only the street name remains.[20] *Monmouth House*, which had been the residence of the Duke of Monmouth until his execution in 1685, extended with its ancillary buildings from Soho Square to Queen Street, and occupied the site of 27–28 Soho Square (today a modern commercial building, about 1988) and 29–30 Soho Square (today the **Hospital for Women**; mainly nineteenth century).[21] Also on Soho Square was the renowned concert series of the Venetian opera singer, Theresa Cornelys (Imer-Pompeati), who was mentioned in Leopold's travel notes. She presented the extremely successful concerts directed by J.C. Bach and Karl Abel here from 1765, in **Carlisle House.** Today, at 21a Soho Square, on the site of the former concert room in **Carlisle House, St. Patrick's Roman Catholic Chapel** is located.[22]

[★ ★ SITE OF THE THEATRE ROYAL, COVENT GARDEN]. English national opera, as opposed to Italian opera, had its origins in the work of Arne and Arnold, in the **Theatre Royal**, Covent Garden.[23] During the period of the Mozarts' visit, Gay's *The Beggar's Opera* was still being performed. The present building by Smirke, which opened in 1809, replaced the theater of 1732, which burned down.[24] The present Covent Garden area has been splendidly restored and is a vital area of London.

★ ★ BRITISH MUSEUM. The former museum in **Montagu House**, which was seen by the Mozarts, contained a collection of antique statues, stuffed giraffes, fossils, manuscripts, all without labels, surrounded by heroic frescoes.[25] Nannerl noted the library and the antiquities which she saw, as well as "all kinds of birds, fishes, vermin, and fruit." The present edifice by Smirke was designed in 1824, and took 20 years to complete. Mozart wrote a four-voice *a capella* motet, "God is Our Refuge," K. 20, for the **British Museum**, for which Leopold received a note of gratitude. The museum today has the anthem in its collection, as well as the famous Carmontelle pastel of the Mozarts performing. Open Monday–Saturday 10 AM–5 PM; Sunday 2:30–6 PM; closed holidays. Print department open 10 AM–1 PM and 2:15–4 PM (passport required to view the Carmontelle pastel).

★ ★ LINCOLN'S INN FIELDS. London WC2A 3TL. Both Nannerl's travel notes, which mention **Lincoln's Inn Fields Garden**, and Leopold's addresses cite this historic area of London. The site belonged to the Dominicans until 1276, and was ultimately in the possession of the Earl of Lincoln, who willed his mansion as a college (or resident inn) for lawyers.[26] Most of the brick buildings with stone ornament date from the fifteenth century, while the brick gatehouse with towers on Chancery Lane is from 1518. The gabled brick buildings, called the "**Old Buildings**," are Tudor, refurbished in 1609. The **chapel** (1620–23), where John Donne laid the foundation and preached, has windows commemorating famous benchers and treasurers such as St. Thomas More, Pitt, Disraeli, and Gladstone. The **Old Hall** (1490) contains Hogarth's "St. Paul before Felix."[276] It is possible to walk around the complex; ask at Porter's lodge, except Saturday. The chapel is open Monday–Friday, Noon–2:30 PM; closed bank holidays.

★ ★ SITE OF THE TEMPLEBAR. Near Inner Temple Lane, London EC4. Nannerl cited the major sites visited by the Mozarts (in this case, not cited by Leopold), which included **Templebar**, the city gate. The bar (formerly the city's medieval western "barrier") in 1765 was an arch (1672) designed by Wren, which was used to display heads and quarters of the executed. It was disassembled in 1870, and the present **Queen Victoria memorial pillar** was erected in 1880. However, plans are underway to reassemble it in the churchyard of St. Paul's. The Mozarts undoubtedly also saw the nearby complex of the Temple, including the remarkable **Temple Church** (1160–85). The circular Romanesque structure inside has blind arcades with grotesque heads, six marble pillars, and tenth–thirteenth-century effigies of Templars and their patrons.[28] The church is open 10 AM–4 PM.

★ SITE OF SOMERSET HOUSE. Strand, London WC2. Nannerl also cited "*Soumerset hauss*" in her travel notes. While the present structure is a splendid example of eighteenth-century architecture (1776), it is not the edifice seen by the Mozarts. The remarkably original palace, begun by Somerset in 1547, was destroyed in 1776. The present structure with a Palladian facade on the Strand, and an extensive courtyard, is the location of the Probate Registry.[29]

★ ★ ★ ST. PAUL'S CATHEDRAL. London EC4M 8AD. This spectacular seventeenth-century church by Wren was mentioned by both Leopold and Nannerl. The massive dome has a viewing gallery, while the interior is remarkable for its gold leaf and mosaics. Open 9 AM–6 PM (–5 PM October to March); admission charge for dome, galleries, crypt, treasury, choir and ambulatory. The **Templebar** by Wren, seen by the Mozarts, will be reerected in the churchyard.

★ ★ MONUMENT. Monument Street, London EC3R 8AH. Nannerl mentioned visiting the **Monument**, this Doric column of Portland stone, erected 1671–77, with a relief of Charles II, topped by a gilded urn. It is remarkably preserved in an area which has been substantially developed. The once-spectacular view has been obstructed by the numerous high-rise buildings which surround it. Open April to September 9 AM–6 PM (2–6 PM Saturday and Sunday); October to March 9 AM–2 PM and 3–4 PM Monday to Saturday; admission charge.

★ SITE OF THE ROYAL EXCHANGE. Cornhill and Threadneedle Streets. The Mozarts visited numerous sites in London by mid-March 1765, including the **Royal Exchange**, probably on afternoons and Sunday. The first edifice, modeled after the exchange of Antwerp, was built in 1566, and after the Fire of 1666, it was rebuilt of Portland stone. This structure, seen by the Mozarts, was called "the most beautiful, strong and stately . . . in Europe." In 1838 it burned down, and the present *Exchange* was erected, with a massive Corinthian pediment and allegorical sculpture.[30]

GENERAL SITE OF THE "SWAN AND HARP" TAVERN. Cornhill Street.[31] Leopold advertised several times in July 1765 that the Mozart children were performing from 12–3 PM in the Great Room in this tavern. For these performances, Mozart wrote his first clavier sonatas for four hands, and the children played four-hands on the same keyboard with the keys covered.

★ ★ ★ TOWER OF LONDON. Nannerl mentioned the **Tower** in her travel notes, and Leopold wrote, "I will describe verbally to you the Tower, namely the West Castle, and will tell you how the roar of the lions there frightened our Mr. Wolfgang." From the thirteenth to eighteenth century there was a royal menagerie in the **Lion Tower**, which has since been demolished. The **Crown Jewels**, and the **White Tower** of Kentish and Caen stone, are of particular interest. Open March–October 9:30 AM–5 PM (2–5 PM Sunday); November–February 9:30 AM–4 PM (closed Sunday); admission charge.

Excursions

★ ★ ★ KEW GARDENS. Richmond upon Thames. The spectacular **Kew Gardens** were visited by the Mozarts. Princess Augusta began the botanical aspect of the gardens, and enlarged them from seven to more than a hundred acres.[32] Prince Frederick, who died in 1751, had the garden landscaped, and later, the Princess of Wales appointed Aiton, who had worked at the **Chelsea Physic Garden** (walking distance from the Mozart residence in Chelsea) as gardener (1759–93). The Mozarts would have seen the **Kew Palace** (Dutch House built 1631), which has a remarkable variety of brickwork and Dutch gables.[33] The interior of this small country house is from the period of George III, for whom the Mozart children performed. The **King's Dining Room** and the seventeenth-century **Breakfast Room**, as well as the furniture and restored decoration, are of interest. Behind it is the formal **Queen's Garden**, with *parterres*, a gazebo, and characteristic plants of the seventeenth century. The **orangerie** and the 10-story **pagoda** each date from the period of the Mozarts' visit (1761). Kew Palace open April–September daily 11 AM–5:30 PM); admission charge.

★ ★ GREENWICH. After the Mozarts visited the impressive sights at Greenwich, Nannerl wrote, "I saw the Invalid House, the Queen's ship, [and] the park in which there was a very beautiful view." The **Royal Hospital for Seamen** by

Wren (1694–1704) was a similar concept to the Royal Military Hospital in Chelsea, near which the Mozarts lived during Leopold's illness. The hospital with twin cupolas (Painted Hall and the chapel) became the **Royal Naval College** in 1873, while the extended **Queen's House** (England's first Palladian villa) became the **National Maritime Museum** in 1937.[34] In addition, the **Old Royal Observatory** by Wren (begun 1675) is of interest. The extensive park is open daily from sunrise to sunset. The Royal Naval College is open daily except Thursday 2:30–5 PM. The National Maritime Museum and the Old Royal Observatory are open Monday–Saturday 10 AM–6 PM (–5 PM in Winter); Sunday 2–6 PM (–5 PM in Winter); admission charge.

★ ★ RICHMOND. Thanks to Nannerl's travel notes, we also know that the Mozarts visited Richmond, where there was "a very beautiful view." Richmond is known as one of the most beautiful urban greens in England, and was the royal seat from the twelfth to seventeenth centuries. The **Old Palace**, looking over the Green where Tudor jousting took place, was stripped of its paintings and furnishings after the execution of Charles I, and little remained in the eighteenth century, except for private houses which were erected from the ruins.[35]

Other Sites of Interest: Dover

D a t e s

About 22 April 1764 • 1 August 1765

*T*he eighteenth-century port of Dover, mentioned by Nannerl in her travel diary, was very different from the present port, which was altered considerably in the nineteenth century. The Mozarts, on their way to London, took Easter confession in Calais, and left their coach behind there. Leopold rented a boat (about 22 April 1764), and shared the cost with four strangers; however, with the four Mozart family members, two servants (including Porta, whom Mozart and his father later met in Rome in 1770, and in Vienna in 1773), and the crew, "it was uncomfortable to stay with so many people, who occasionally get seasick in an astonishing way." As a result most of the passengers were extremely seasick. ("We saved money on buying medical emetics," as Leopold described it.) However, the port, and the descending and surfacing "sea-swine" (dolphins) impressed Leopold; both Nannerl and Leopold were impressed by seeing "how the sea ebbed and waned." Unfortunately, when they arrived, 30–

40 insistent porters were waiting for them to take their baggage to the hotel "by force."

On their return from London to the continent, on 1 August 1765, the weather was excellent, and during the trip of 3½ hours, they were not bothered by the previous problems of seasickness.

During their two passages through Dover, the Mozarts probably did not have a great deal of time for sight-seeing; however, places of interest in the eighteenth century which they could have seen still exist, including **Dover Castle**, the **Church of St. Mary the Virgin, Maison Dieu Hall**, (built in 1203 as a hospice for pilgrims; now the Town Hall, although at that time it was a storehouse for the Navy); the ruins of **St. James's Church**, and the **Dover Priory** (now Dover College).[36]

The Mozarts stayed in an inn (probably the night of 22 August 1765), perhaps the same miserable inn where John Bing stayed; he described the state of inns in Dover (about 1790):

. . . in the York Hotel, . . . amidst Noise, and Racket, we procured a mean dirty Parlour for ourselves, and a kind of ship-hold for our Horses. Bad specimen this, To the French, of English comforts!—Bread, and Wine, not to be endured; with a nasty brown fricasse, and old tough Partridges! A Room fill'd with Wind; and ship Stinks!! Up till eleven o'clock.[37]

Later, he wrote:

Never did I Enter a more dirty, noisy, or more imposing Inn, than this York House; for we were charged most exorbitantly, for wine not drinkable, for musty Fowls, and stinking Partridges; never did I leave an Inn with greater Pleasure.[38]

Perhaps, for this reason, Leopold did not mention the inn where the Mozart family stayed overnight in Dover.

N o t e s

1 Michelin, *London*, 44.
2 Michelin, *London*, 168.
3 Buckingham Palace has communicated to me that the location of the organ which Mozart played is no longer known; it is definitely no longer located in the palace. It is not known in which room Mozart played for the monarchs; since the eighteenth century, the interior of the palace has been considerably reconstructed.
4 The 40 acres of gardens of the palace are not open to the public; communicated by Buckingham Palace.
5 *Survey of London* xl (1980), 133.
6 Before he succeeded to the earldom in 1753, he was known as Lord Tufton, the barony of Tufton being the junior title and therefore held as a courtesy title by the eldest son and heir of the Earl. Communicated by Philip McEvansoneya, London Division of English Heritage.

7 Communicated by Philip McEvansoneya, London Division of English Heritage; *Survey of London* xl (1980), 137.

8 Michelin, op. cit., 117.

9 Michelin, op. cit., 134.

10 Communicated by Philip McEvansoneya, London Division of English Heritage.

11 Communicated by Philip McEvansoneya, London Division of English Heritage.

12 Communicated by Philip McEvansoneya, London Division of English Heritage; from *Survey of London* xxix (1960), 253.

13 Communicated by Philip McEvansoneya, London Division of English Heritage.

14 Bauer/Deutsch/Eibl, *Mozart Briefe*, V, zu 99/125–26.

15 Hildesheimer, *Mozart*, 31.

16 Communicated by Philip McEvansoneya, London Division of English Heritage; from Elkin, *The Old Concert Rooms of London* (1955), 44.

17 Communicated by Philip McEvansoneya, London Division of English Heritage; *Survey of London* xxxi (1963), 121.

18 *Survey of London* xxxiii (1966), 160.

19 *Survey of London* xxxiii (1966), 160–61.

20 Bauer/Deutsch/Eibl, op. cit., V, zu 89/33.

21 Communicated by Philip McEvansoneya, London Division of English Heritage.

22 Pohl, *Mozart und Haydn in London*, 4.

23 Schenk, *Mozart and His Times*, 70.

24 Michelin, op. cit., 74.

25 Michelin, op. cit., 36.

26 Michelin, op. cit., 95.

27 Ibid.

28 Michelin, op. cit., 64.

29 Michelin, op. cit., 145–46.

30 Michelin, op. cit., 62.

31 It has not been possible to locate the address of this former tavern; communicated by Philip McEvansoneya, London Division of English Heritage.

32 Michelin, op. cit., 109–11.

33 Ibid.

34 Michelin, op. cit., 79–83.

35 Michelin, op. cit., 128–29.

36 Communicated by C. Waterman, Curator, Dover Museum.

37 Bing, *The Torrington Diaries* (1781–94), 161; sent to me by C. Waterman, Curator, Dover Museum.

38 Bing, op. cit., 163; sent to me by C. Waterman, Curator, Dover Museum.

France

Dijon, Lille, Lyons, Nancy,
Paris, Strasbourg,
Versailles

Mozart in Dijon

About 12 July to about 25 July 1766

A t the end of their "Great Western" trip of 1763–66, the Mozart family stopped in Dijon, *en route* to Salzburg via Switzerland. They were invited by the Prince de Condé to perform at the Assembly of the Estates of Burgundy, and there met the renowned President Charles de Brosses, whose memoirs provide an important document of the eighteenth century. The concert of the children took place at the Town Hall of Dijon, in which they also played four-handed. Leopold had very strong words of contempt for the French musicians whom they met (and who perhaps participated in their concert), calling them "mediocre," "asses," and "miserable." Unfortunately, Leopold's careful travel notes ended with Dijon, and we know very little about what took place after their sojourn here.

Dijon Sites

★ HOME OF CHARLES DE BROSSES. Place Bossuet, 8.[1] In his travel notes, Leopold cited the President of the Court in Parliament, Charles de Brosses, known for his historical and archeological works, and a great music lover; his *Lettres d'Italie* was a notable success. It is very likely that the Mozarts were invited here, to the **Hôtel Fevret de Saint Mesmin,** for private music making during their approximately 15 days in Dijon. The splendid facade, with stone balustrades, mansard roof, and elegant ornament can be seen; the apartments are privately owned.

★ ★ PALACE OF THE DUKES AND OF THE GENERAL STATES OF BURGUNDY (PALAIS DES DUCS ET DES ETATS DE BOURGOGNE). Place de la Liberation. For the sumptuous festivities of the gathering of the States of Burgundy, which began on 14 July 1766, the Mozarts were engaged to perform by the Prince de Condé. In addition to the Mozart concert, which undoubtedly took place in the large room (**la grande salle des Etats**),[2] the **Théâtre italien** performed as well, also probably in this palace. The palace, built on the site of third-century

Roman city walls, had successive additions in the fifteenth–eighteenth centuries. While the present facade dates from 1786, many parts remain from the time of the Mozarts' visit and before, such as the ceremonial Gabriel Stairway, (open only during exhibitions), the **cour de Flores,** the **Chapelle des Elus** (1736–39), the Philip the Good Tower (with its fine panorama), the Bar Tower, and the wing of the Fine Arts Museum (one of the most important in France, installed in 1787). Open 10 AM–6 PM every day except Tuesday; admission charge.

★ HOME OF PHILIPPE-ANTOINE CHARLES DE LA TOUR LE PIN. 41, rue Vannerie.[3] Leopold, in his travel notes, cited the Marquis Tour le Pin, his wife, his daughter and son. Charles de la Tour le Pin was a general and commander of the province; although little is known about the stay of the Mozarts in Dijon, this home was a likely site for a private concert by Mozart. The edifice exists today in essentially the same form as in the time of Mozart.

★ ★ CONCERT ROOM IN THE OLD CITY HALL (SALLE DE LECTEUR OF THE ARCHIVES DE LA COTE D'OR). 8, rue Jeannin. On 18 July 1766, the Mozart children played a concert in the sumptuous **salle d'honneur** (1670; designed by Rancurelle), which is presently the reading room of the archives (**salle de lecture**). The program included compositions by Mozart, and the two children also performed four-hand piano music; the Prince de Condé, instead of sitting on the throne prepared for him, sat among the ladies, who offered him refreshments.[4] The entrance to the former residence of Chancellor Rolin (which became the **Hôtel de Ville**) has a dramatic pillared courtyard with a wrought-iron staircase, decorated with busts and paintings. Inside the carved wood concert room is a fireplace with two marble giants by Rollin and Dodin, as well as four splendid portrait panels, and a commemorative plaque in marble citing the Mozart concert[5]; during the **Premier Empire** some additions were made to the decoration. The small room indicates how select the concert was, and the grandeur of the decoration remains completely intact despite the unfortunate presence of reading tables and lamps. The original program which Mozart played is preserved here. Open to the public Monday–Friday, 9 AM–12:30 PM and 1:30–5 PM.

[★ ★ CHARACTERISTIC SIGHTS OF DIJON]. Here, in the birthplace of Jean-Philippe Rameau, there are numerous edifices dating from before the time of the Mozarts' visit in 1766. The **Hôtel Lantin** (1652–81) at #4, rue des Bons-Enfants is today the **Musée Magnin,** and offers a splendid collection of period furniture and paintings; the Justice Palace (**Palais de Justice**) at #8, rue du Palais, was constructed in 1572, and has numerous fine rooms which may be visited, as well as the original facade with Renaissance niches and windows; the vast **Hôpital Général** (from 1206; largely redone in the seventeenth century) has a precious chapel; the **Certosa di Champmol** was destroyed in 1793, but has many impressive ruins.[6] As practicing Catholics, the Mozarts undoubtably visited, and participated in services in, the fine churches in Dijon, possibly including the

Burgundian-Gothic **Nôtre-Dame,** the late Gothic **St. Michael,** the Cathedral (**St-Bénigne**), and the Baroque chapel of Saint Anne (1699–1709), which today hosts a museum of sacred art.

[★ ★ EXCURSION TO THE ''ROUTE DES GRAND CRUS'']. Leopold enjoyed sampling the fine wines in Dijon, which suggests that he and the family, like many travelers, visited the local vineyards. A characteristic trip through the famous Burgundian vineyards begins at Beaune. Contact the Tourist Office at Place Darcy.

N o t e s

1 This edifice is a site, remarkably intact, which has previously been overlooked in the Mozart literature. In response to my queries, Françoise Vignier, Director of the Dijon Archives, communicated that Charles de Brosses (from 1743 to 1772) rented to his cousin Charles-Marie Fevret de Fontette half of the family *Hôtel des Fevret*; this indicates that de Brosses in fact lived here when the Mozarts visited Dijon in 1766.
2 Fyot, "Mozart à Dijon," 25.
3 Communicated by Françoise Vignier, in response to my queries. This edifice is another example of a well-preserved site which has been overlooked in the Mozart literature.
4 Fyot, op. cit., 26.
5 The plaque of various colors of marble was added by Charles Poisot in 1872; however, the date is wrong. Confirmed by Françoise Vignier, Director of the Dijon Archives.
6 Touring Club Italiano, *Francia*, 191–92.

$\mathcal{M}$ozart in Lille

About 5 August–4 September 1765

$\mathcal{O}$n the way to The Hague for the first time, during the "Great Western" trip of 1763–66, Mozart's family stopped in Lille, where Mozart became very sick for several weeks with a "strong catarrh" (probably angina). After he had recovered, Mozart's father fell ill, with fits of vomiting and dizziness. However, Leopold was impressed by the city, which he described as "beautiful [and] well-built . . . very populated, with a great deal of commerce." On 26 August 1765, the Mozarts heard about the death of Emperor Franz I who died in Innsbruck. Since the Duc de Choiseul was traveling through the city with the Fifth Regiment, they were able to see "the most beautiful war exercises," and Leopold called the daily parade "the most beautiful that I have ever seen."

Lille Sites

★ **GENERAL SITE OF THE APOTHECARY JACQUEMAND.** Place du Théâtre.[1] Leopold mentioned Jacquemand in his travel notes, probably in the context of the illness of Mozart, who became very sick for several weeks with a "strong catarrh" (probably angina); this was followed by the illness of Leopold himself, who had fits of vomiting and dizziness. The pharmacist Jacquemand lived "on the little square," about 100 meters from the Mozarts' lodging. Today the **Place du Théâtre** is dominated by the flamboyant opera house (built 1910–24); across the street from the opera house is the **Rang du Beauregard**, an interesting example of Franco-Lilloise architecture from the late seventeenth century.

★ **SITE OF THE "HOTEL DE BOURBON."** Grande Place 17 (entrance to **Hôtel Bellevue** is on Place du General de Gaulle at 5, rue Jean Roisin. During the stay of the Mozarts in Lille, from around 5 August 1765 to 4 September 1765, they lodged in the **Hôtel de Bourbon** with Mr. Cousin, probably Charles Cousin, who was very involved in theater and theater direction in Lille.[2] Here, Wolfgang became very sick (probably angina), and after he recovered, Leopold fell ill. Doctor Merlin, who was later called in by Leopold, lived nearby. Nothing remains of the edifice where the Mozarts stayed; the hotel was replaced, after 1831, by the **Belle-Vue**.[3] Today, the three-star hotel, **Grand Hôtel Bellevue**, has a commemorative plaque concerning Mozart in the lobby; the present building is from 1912.

★ GRAND GUARD (HAUPTWACHE). Place du General de Gaulle. Leopold cited this imposing building in classic style, which was built by Gombert in 1717 to accommodate the police of the King of France, and to keep a watchful eye on the population of Lille. The facade is completely intact from the time of the Mozarts' visit, while the interior has been completely redone as a theater. The facade features a clock topped with a "sun," and the coat-of-arms of Lille on the right wing, those of France and Navarre on the left.[4]

★ GRAND PLACE. Presently Place du General de Gaulle. The "beautiful, large square" cited by Leopold, although it has lost a great deal of charm since the eighteenth century, is still of interest for the **Grand Guard**, for small seventeenth-eighteenth-century middle-class houses, and for the seventeenth-century Old Exchange (**Vieille Bourse**). The ensemble of twenty-four identical houses of the Old Exchange, circling a courtyard, was built by Julien Destrée in 1652–53, and has an ornate facade decorated with *cariatides*, garlands, and grotesque masks.[5]

[★ GENERAL SITE OF THE OPERA HOUSE]. Rue de la Comédie, almost at the corner of Place Rihour.[6] Leopold mentioned several musicians who performed for the **Comédie**, or opera house, in his travel notes. In their month in Lille, it is quite likely that the Mozarts attended one of the performances here, of which there were 186 in the 1765–66 season.[7]

[★ ★ PLACE RIHOUR]. The Mozart family undoubtedly passed through this characteristic square, in close proximity to their lodging and to the Opera House. The **Place Rihour**, which is dominated by the fortress-like **Palais Rihour** (1453–73) was built for Philippe Le Bon and was the residence of the Dukes of Burgundy in the fifteenth century. On the ground floor, where the **Office du Tourisme** is located, is the Gothic-style "Room of the Guard"; on the floor above, the former chapel has an unusual nave of star vaulting.[8]

GENERAL SITE OF THE HOME OF DR. MERLIN. Rue de l'Hôpital Militaire, across from the rue St.-Etienne. Leopold cited the name of this physician, who lived on the former Rue des Jésuits, undoubtedly in the context of the successive illnesses of Wolfgang and himself. The nearby stone facade of the eighteenth-century Church of St. Etienne is of interest.

★ ★ CITADEL AND "EXERCISE SQUARE" (CITADELLE AND CHAMPS DE MARS). Both Leopold and Nannerl cite the "parade," and the "exercise," which were undoubtedly among their most impressive experiences in Lille.

These refer, most likely, to the daily parade, and the war exercises of the Fifth Regiment of the Duc de Choiseul; they would have taken place on the "Esplanade." The Citadel, in the shape of a five-pointed star, is a splendid example of seventeenth-century military architecture, built by Vauban from 1667 to 1670 after Louis XIV conquered the city.[9] Today the complex of historic buildings houses an army post, which can be visited during the day; the ornate marble gate is noteworthy. Numerous parks and gardens surround the fortress; however, the actual **"Exercise Square"** is a parking lot today,[10] and of little interest. The Citadel is open all year for groups and April–October for individuals; contact Vera Dupuis, Tourist Office of Lille, Place Rihour.

SITE OF THE COLLEGE ST.-PIERRE. Avenue du peuple Belge. The Abbé Grare, cited in Leopold's notes, was a regent at this institution. During the French Revolution, the building burned, although the rich library formed much of the basis of the present collection of the **Bibliothèque communale** in Lille. Of the building, only the crypt remains, where the present **Palais de Justice** is located.[11]

★ HOSPICE GENERAL (HOPITAL GENERAL). Avenue du Peuple-Belge. Leopold cited "Cuvelier, Receveur de l'Hopital general" in the travel notes. Due to Leopold's illness, and that of Mozart, Arthur Schurig was led to suppose that Wolfgang lay in this hospital during his illness.[12] However, it was a home for beggars, orphans and invalids, and not a hospital where Mozart could have stayed. The fine building by Vigné de Vrigny, an example of classic eighteenth-century style, was erected in 1738. Other historic "hospitals" in Lille include the fifteenth-century **Hospice Gantois** on the Rue de Paris near the Paris Gate, the splendid fifteenth-eighteenth-century **Hospice Comtesse** at 32, rue de la Monnaie, and the **Pavillon Saint-Sauveur,** with its alternation of brick and stone, on Rue Saint-Sauveur, the last remaining building of the former charitable organization, founded in the thirteenth century.

★ ABBEYS OF LILLE. Leopold mentioned the "noble convent outside the city," in his travel notes, which could refer to one of the two Cistercian abbeys (**de Loos** or **de Marquette**), each located outside of the city ramparts.[13] Most such religious refuges were destroyed and plundered during the French Revolution. However, the Loos Abbey (**Abbaye de Loos**) on rue Jean-Jacques-Rousseau, the refuge of the Marciennes Abbey (**l'Abbaye de Marchiennes**) off Rue Gustave-Delory, and the Court of the Brigittines (**Cour des Brigittines**), on Rue Gustave-Delory between Rue Saint Sauveur and Rue de Paris, still present an architectural view of the convents of the period.

GENERAL SITE OF "LA NOUVELLE AVENTURE." Today Place de la Nouvelle Aventure. This busy site of entertainment, eating, and drinking was cited by both Leopold and Nannerl in their travel notes. It was built in 1754, and demolished in 1858; today only the name of the square recalls the building.

[★ ★ CHARACTERISTIC SIGHTS OF LILLE]. Despite the poor state of preservation, Lille is rich in buildings of architectural interest which remain from 1765, and before. These include seventeenth-eighteenth-century houses on the **rue de la Grande-Chausée**, the **Place des Patiniers**, with two small seventeenth-century houses with arches in "diamond point," and the aristocratic seventeenth-century houses of Rue Royale. Characteristic churches include the fifteenth-century Gothic Saint Catherine Church (**Eglise Sainte-Catherine**), the domed Saint Mary Magdalen Church (**Sainte-Marie-Madeleine**), begun in 1675 and finished by the architect Gombert in 1713, and the Saint Maurice Church (**Eglise Saint-Maurice**), which was constructed over five centuries. Numerous gates include the fifteenth century **Noble-Tour**, the only vestige of the medieval fortifications of the city, at Rue des Déportés, the Ghent Gate (**Porte de Gand**), built by Pierre Raoul in 1621, the Paris Gate (**Porte de Paris**), built from 1685 to 1692 to commemorate the conquest of Lille by Louis XIV, and the **Roubaix Gate** (**Porte de Roubaix**), constructed in 1621 by Michel Wattrelos.[14]

N o t e s

1 Kampé de Fèriet, "Mozart à Lille," 6.

2 In 1761, Charles Cousin (probably the Mr. Cousin mentioned by Leopold in his travel notes), opened a café called "La Redoute" (mentioned by both Leopold and Nannerl), which was located at the beginning of the esplanade along the *Canal de la Deule*. Communicated by M. Decrois; quoted by Kampé de Fèriet, op. cit., 11.

3 Kampé de Fèriet noted, in 1957, as an amusing detail, that #17 was occupied by the *Cinéma* (with the same name) "*Le Bellevue.*" Kampé de Fèriet, op. cit., 5.

4 *Lille vous accueille*, 44. The Bauer/Deutsch/Eibl notes to the Mozart letters overlook this imposing edifice, the facade of which is intact, and splendidly preserved.

5 *Lille vous accueille*, 46.

6 Kampé de Fèriet, op. cit., 9.

7 Lefebvre, *Histoire du Théâtre à Lille*, 257; quoted by Kampé de Fèriet, op. cit., 9.

8 *Lille vous accueille*, 45.

9 *Lille vous accueille*, 43.

10 Communicated by Vera Dupuis, Office du Tourisme de Lille.

11 Communicated by Vera Dupuis, Office du Tourisme de Lille.

12 Kampé de Fèriet, op. cit., 6.

13 Kampé de Fèriet, op. cit., 12.

14 *Lille vous accueille*, 39–46.

Mozart in Lyons

About 6 July 1766 to about 20 August 1766

Leopold had wanted to take his family to Italy (over the Alps from Lyons), but instead, proceeded on to Salzburg via Switzerland. During his month in Lyons, he wrote to his landlord, Lorenz Hagenauer, about the fine silk wares, and about how he had his family's new wardrobe made. The Mozart family also gave a concert in Lyons, which was an enormous success financially. Staehelin published a letter describing it:

A few days ago, they gave a concert here, where they played the most difficult pieces, and all the symphonies played were compositions of the young virtuoso. He improvised for a quarter-hour with the most capable musicians from here, and did not stand behind them. In short, one must see him to believe it, as stated on the poster, and I was really, like everyone else, enchanted.

We know very little about their stay in Lyons, as Leopold's careful travel notes ended in Dijon, and, strangely enough, neither he nor Nannerl mentioned the concert later.

Lyons Sites

SITE OF THE CONCERT ROOM ON THE PLACE DES CORDELIERS. Place des Cordeliers. On 13 August 1766, Wolfgang and Nannerl participated here in a concert that normally took place each Wednesday; the wife of the renowned composer of *clavecin* and organ pieces, Jean-Jacques Charpentier, sang first, and the program concluded with dances from a Rameau opera.[1] A letter by Forcarts describes the concert: "They played the most difficult pieces, and all the symphonies . . . were compositions of the young virtuoso. He improvised for a quarter hour with the most capable masters from here . . . In short, one must see him, to believe it." The demolition of **la Maison des Concerts** took place in 1856 (during the transformation of the *place des Cordeliers*), to make access to the Lafayette Bridge more easy[2]; it was a charming, small eighteenth-century French theater with elongated windows on the third floor and a classic bas-relief in the tympanum. When facing the church **Saint-Bonaventure**, the theater was located to the left, almost perpendicular to the church; an unattractive modern street has replaced it, and the *place des Cordeliers* as well.

[★ BONAVENTURE CHURCH]. Place des cordeliers. This church, begun in the early fourteenth century and finished at the end of the fifteenth century, is located in close proximity to the site of the concert hall where Mozart performed. It was severely damaged several times, such as in 1562 and 1783, and the exterior has undergone considerable changes throughout the centuries. The major facade was reconstructed in 1859, but is, however, very similar to that which the Mozarts saw in 1766. Four Aubusson tapestries based on the life of St. Bonaventure, donated to the church about 1744, are of interest; in addition, there are numerous carved altars which were reinterpreted and constructed in the nineteenth century, and stained glass windows which were redone in the nineteenth-twentieth centuries.

[★ ★ CHARACTERISTIC SIGHTS OF LYONS]. The Mozarts, who inevitably saw the sights of each city they visited, were in Lyons four weeks, from about 26 July to about 20 August 1766. The sights they most likely saw at this time were the City Hall (**Hôtel de Ville**), **Palais St-Pierre** (an old Benedictine abbey, presently the location of the Museum of Fine Arts), the Roman Theater (dating from the first century AD), the **Place du Gouvernement**, and St. Paul's Church. In addition, they could have visited the **Fourvière Basilica** (where there was only a chapel at the time), the Square Bellecour and **les Terreaux**, the **Abbaye d'Ainay** (Romanesque abbey), **Mercière Street**, the intersection of the Saone and the Rhône rivers (which was located south of the Place Bellecour), **St. Nizier**, the **Hotel Dieu**, and the Charité Hospital; the Old City, with the exception of the nineteenth-century **Palais de Justice**, presents an exceptional historical look into the Lyons which the Mozarts saw in 1766.[3]

N o t e s

1 Beaumont, "Mozart et la musique lyonnaise en 1766."
2 Ibid.
3 Communicated by Valérie Mesle, Office du Tourisme, Lyons.

$\mathcal{M}$ozart in Nancy

About 3 October to about 13 October 1778

$\mathcal{M}$ozart's stay in Nancy lasted about one week; he claimed (perhaps with mock presumption) that he was "never happy in a city where he was not well known." However, Mozart had been deeply offended by the shoddy treatment he received from Baron Melchior Grimm, who sent him on a slow coach from Paris (perhaps to save money). However, Mozart was thoroughly impressed by the unified, "progressive" architecture of Nancy; the splendid vision of King Stanislas and his architect Héré is still in evidence today.

Nancy Sites

[★ ★ ★ CHARACTERISTIC SIGHTS OF NANCY]. On his trip from Paris back to Salzburg, about 3 October 1778, Mozart wrote to his father from Nancy, "Please forgive me that I cannot write much, because when I am in a town where I am not well-known, I am never in a good mood; nevertheless I believe that, if I were well-known here, I would gladly stay, because the city is, in fact, charming—beautiful houses, beautiful broad streets, and superb squares." Few places in the world present a more untouched view of the sights which Mozart saw than Nancy.[1]

"beautiful houses." Mozart's allusion to the "beautiful houses" undoubtedly would have included the splendid facades of the palaces which surround Stanislas Square, Alliance Square, and the **Place de la Carrière.** This unique complex consists of classical, symmetrical buildings, connected by elegant wrought-iron gates. The private houses on the streets near the Ducal Palace include the **Hôtel des Loups** (1, rue du Haut-Bourgeois), **Hôtel Ferrari** (29, rue de Haut-Bourgeois), **Hôtel de Fontenoy** (4, rue du Haut-Bourgeois), the **Hôtel du Marquis-de-Villé** (10, rue de la Source), the **Hôtel d'Haussonville** (9, rue Trouillet), and the Ducal Palace (64, Grand Rue; presently the Historical Museum of Lorraine).[2]

"**beautiful broad streets.**" The **Grande Rue**, leading from the fourteenth-century **Porte de la Craffe** (infamous for its prisons and torture chambers) to Stanislas Square, and the linden tree-lined avenues of the **Place de la Carrière** (opened in the sixteenth century), are some of the numerous broad streets of Nancy, which can be seen today in a state of remarkable preservation.

"**superb squares.**" Stanislas Square is one of the most outstanding squares in France, a masterpiece of the eighteenth century, carried out from 1752 and 1760 for King Stanislas by the architect Héré. On the southern side, the spectacular City Hall (**Hôtel de ville**) of 1775 is found, surmounted by the coat-of-arms of King Stanislas. On the north side is a triumphal arch (1752) by Héré, dedicated to King Stanislas and Louis XV. Stanislas Square, Alliance Square, and the **Place de la Carrière** together form a unique eighteenth-century complex. In addition, **Place de Grève** (now **Place Carnot**) and **Cours Léopold** are noteworthy.[3]

[★ ★ CHURCHES OF NANCY]. Among the various churches that Mozart could have seen during his visit in 1778 are the imposing cathedral, begun in 1703 on the plans of Betto, and finished in 1742 by Boffrand; the flamboyant Gothic Church and Monastery of the Cordeliers, erected in 1482–86 by Duke Renato II; Saint Sebastian Church (1720–31); the Church of Our Lady (**Nôtre Dame de Bonsecours**), the work of Héré (1738–41), containing the tomb of King Stanislas; and the octagonal Ducal Chapel, which was inspired by the Medici Chapel in Florence.

N o t e s

1 The historical complex created by Héré for Stanislas, the former King of Poland, has been included by U.N.E.S.C.O. among the monuments which form the world's heritage. These include the *Place Stanislas* (originally *Place Royale*), with splendid wrought iron gates, decorated with gold-leaf ornament, by Jean Lamour; the *Place d'Alliance*, with a unique Rococo fountain representing the three major rivers of Lorraine; and the spacious esplanade of *Place de la Carrière*, with four rows of linden trees.
2 Communicated by Christiane Drouin, Manager, Office de Tourisme de Nancy.
3 Communicated by Christiane Drouin, Manager, Office de Tourisme de Nancy.

Mozart in Paris

18 November 1763–10 April 1764 · 10 May–9 July 1766 · 23 March–26 September 1778

Paris was the goal of the 3½-year "Great Western" trip of Leopold Mozart and his family, 1763–66. They stayed in Paris twice during the extensive trip; during the first sojourn, they were invited to Versailles for two weeks, and the children performed for the Court of Louis XV.

After an extended stay in London, and travel to various cities including The Hague and Brussels, the Mozart family again returned to Paris.

Years later, Leopold wanted Mozart to return to Paris, to develop as a musician, and to find a permanent position; Mozart traveled with his mother, who later died in Paris. Despite many setbacks in Paris, including financial difficulties, and a host, Baron Grimm, who offered little encouragement, some of Mozart's most renowned works were written in this musical center.

Music

SACRED WORKS Kyrie, K. 33, Paris, 12 June 1766.
Stabat mater, K. 33c, written in Paris and Salzburg, 1766; lost.
Miserere, K. Anh. 1/297a, in eight movements, Paris, March–April 1778; lost.

ORCHESTRAL WORKS Ballet, "Les petit riens," K. Anh. 10/299b, Paris, May–June 1778; in addition, there is a movement (in Gavotte rhythm), K. 300, which was perhaps discarded from this ballet; also sketches for a ballet, K. 299c, composed supposedly in Paris in early 1778, or summer 1778.
"Paris" Symphony, K. 297/300a, Paris, June 1778.
Symphonie concertante, K. Anh. 9/297B, for flute, oboe, bassoon, and horn, probably written in Paris, April 1778; R. Levin's convincing examination, *Who Wrote the Mozart Four-Wind Concertante?* concludes that the parts are by Mozart (although adapted), while the orchestral ritornelli are later additions.
Concerto for flute and harp, K. 299/297c, Paris, April 1778.

VOCAL WORKS Scene for soprano and orchestra, "Popoli di Tessaglia ... Io non chiedo," K. 316/300b, composed in Paris, July 1778, with the manuscript date of 8 January 1779, in Munich.

Scene for soprano and orchestra, K. Anh. 3/315b, written for Tenducci, in St. Germain, August 1778, has been lost.

CHAMBER MUSIC Sonatas for keyboard and violin, K. 6 (written in Salzburg, Brussels, and Paris, 1762–64) and K. 7 (Paris, end of 1763–beginning of 1764).

Sonatas for keyboard and violin, K. 8 and K. 9, Paris, 1763–614.

Sonatas for keyboard and violin, K. 304/300c and K. 306/300l, Paris, summer of 1778

Flute Quartet, K. 298; the Köchel catalog places the work in early 1778, or summer 1778, Paris; Wyzewa-St. Foix place it in Vienna, 1787.

"La Chasse," K. Anh. 103/299d is a fragment.

KEYBOARD MUSIC Solo keyboard sonata, K. 310/300d, written in Paris, in the summer of 1778.

Solo keyboard variations, "Je suis Lindor," K. 354/299a, written in Paris, in early 1778 (or summer 1778); "Lison dormait," K. 264/315d, written in Paris, summer 1778.

Paris Sites

★ ★ ★ **PALACE OF THE DUCHESSE DE CHABOT.** Former "Place Royale,"[1] (#15,[2] Place des Vosges); Metro 1, 5, or 8: Bastille. One of Mozart's most unpleasant Paris experiences took place here, about which he wrote to his father in detail.[3] While paying a visit here at the end of April 1778, Mozart "had to wait a half-hour in an ice-cold, unheated room without even a fireplace," at

Paris. Engraving, published by Carel Allard, ca. 1700.

which time he was asked to play for Elisabeth-Louise de La Rochefoucault, Duchesse de Chabot, the wife of Louis-Antoine-Auguste de Rohan, Duc de Chabot. Unable to play because of numb fingers, Mozart asked to be taken to a room with a fire, and instead "had the honor of waiting for a full hour" in a room with the windows and doors open, while the Duchess and her circle of gentlemen drew. When the Duc de Chabot arrived, however, Mozart, despite his headache and the cold, eventually played as when he was "in the best mood." The symmetrical square, one of the finest in Paris, was built in 1605–12 under Henri IV, influenced by the Florentine Renaissance conception of Catherine de Medici. It was built like a stage set for tournaments and marriages with a unified design of arcades on the ground floor, surmounted by high "French windows" (which appeared here for the first time) and smaller windows topped by a high roof. In the middle of the south side is the **Pavillon du Roi**, with the **Pavillon de la Reine** opposite. In the middle of the square is a copy of the equestrian statue of Louis XII, destroyed during the Revolution.[4]

★ ★ PALACE OF COUNT VAN EYCK. Today 68, rue de Francois-Miron; Metro 1 or 11: Hôtel-de-Ville. From 18 November 1763 to 10 April 1764, during the first Paris sojourn, the Mozarts stayed in a room of the palace of the Bavarian Minister, Count van Eyck. Leopold wrote, "We have the Countess's harpsichord in our room . . . it is good, and like ours has two manuals." The Countess van Eyck, despite a severe illness, "chatted . . . with unbelievable amiability with Wolfgang," and was a remarkable hostess during five months the Mozarts stayed in Paris. The palace received its present form largely in the seventeenth century. Count van Eyck lived here from 1755 (as owner from 1769) and had a private casino, where Leopold Mozart perhaps played.[5] The imposing facade is presently intact, although in bad condition, with the interior abandoned. It is austere, with a mansard roof above the cornice, and long unornamented windows with simple wrought-iron balconies. Nearby, there is the City Hall mentioned by Leopold (see Place de Grève, below), as well as St. Gervais Church, where the Mozarts would have attended Mass, which has a commemorative plaque about Couperin on the left exterior wall. On the street there are several half-timbered buildings from the fourteenth century.

★ ★ PLACE DE GRÈVE. Today Place de l'Hôtel-de-Ville; Metro 1 or 11: Hôtel-de-Ville. Leopold wrote on 22 February 1764 about the Place de Grève (near the Hotel-de-Beauvais, where the family was staying), ". . . the Seine has been so full here for 14 days that one must travel on the Place de Grève with boats, and many areas of the city . . . cannot be crossed." It was also the place "where misdoers are sent to the next world. Whoever loves these executions has something to see every day." The City Hall, built in 1533 in early French Renaissance style, was enlarged to the present size from 1837 to 1849, in the original style, with the addition of sculpture in the niches.[6] After destruction by fire in 1871, the whole complex was completely restored.

[★ ★ SITE OF THE ACADEMY OF THE AMATEURS: HOTEL DE SOUBISE]. 60, rue des francs-bourgeois; Metro 11: Rambuteau. On 3 December 1777, Mozart wrote, "[Wendling] has been to Paris twice, and has only just returned. He maintains that it is still the only place where one can make money and a great reputation . . . Once a man has written a couple of operas in Paris, he is sure of a settled yearly income. Then there is the Concert Spirituel and the Academie des Amateurs, which pay five louis d'or for a symphony." The Academy of the Amateurs was founded in 1769 as competition to the Concert Spirituel. The twelve yearly concerts of the Academy were held from December to March/ April[7] in the Hôtel de Soubise, where the National Archives are presently located. Mozart arrived in Paris at the end of the concert season of the Academy, too late to compose anything for the concerts. It is not known if he attended any concerts here.[8] The interior decoration of the Hotel (1735–38), in the oval salon by Boffrand, for example, is one of the most representative examples of French Rococo. Open 2–5 PM daily except Tuesday.

SITE OF THE TEMPLE. Rue Dupetit-Thouars and Rue Gabriel Vicaire; Metro 3: Temple. Louis François de Bourbon, Prince de Conti, who had his own music chapel, lived in the "Temple," a fortress-like palace, which was the original settlement of the Order of the Temple (dissolved in 1307). A remarkable painting of the young Mozart at the harpsichord, about to accompany the singer Pierre Jelyotte, comes from June 1766. It depicts a tea in the "salon de quatre glace" in the Temple. Schobert, whose sonatas Mozart used in his early *pastiche* piano concertos, was a clavecinist here for the Prince de Conti. Nothing remains of the palace, the tower of which served as a prison to Louis XVI and Marie Antoinette during the French Revolution. However, a commemorative plaque and a map about the Temple can be found today at the site.

GENERAL SITE OF THE HOME OF MAYER. Rue Bourg l'Abbé; Metro 4: Etienne Marcel. Here, near the former "Silver Lion" Inn, Mozart and his mother lived after they arrived in Paris on 14 March 1778. Mayer was the Parisian Agent Mayer of the Augsburg merchant Arbauer, whom Leopold knew. On 9 April 1778, Grimm visited Mozart's mother here. The building was completely destroyed in the nineteenth century, although the street name remains the same.[9]

★ ★ ST. EUSTACHE. Quartier "les Halles"; Metro 4, Les Halles. The body of Mozart's mother, Anna Maria, was blessed here on 4 July 1778, and then buried in one of the three graveyards of the church (probably either that of the Church of the Innocents, or St. Jean-Porte-Latine).[10] The church was begun under Francois I in 1532, in Renaissance style, and was completed in 1640. The present facade dates from 1754 to 1788. Inside the chapel of St. Cecilia, there is a red-marble memorial marker to Anna Maria Mozart, as well as a memorial to Rameau. The Berlioz *Te Deum* was first performed here. Concerts on the organ (1854) are given here frequently.

★ GENERAL SITE OF THE PALACE OF THE COMTE DE GUINES. Quai de Conti[11]; between Pont des Arts and Pont Neuf; Metro 1: Louvre. Beginning in April 1778, Mozart gave composition lessons here to Marie-Louise-Philippine,[12] daughter of Adrien-Louis de Bonnières, Louis Comte de Guines, Governor of the Artois. For the Count and his daughter, Mozart wrote the Concerto for flute and harp (K. 299/297c). The resistance of the Count to pay him the fee he had earned left Mozart, who was in difficult financial straits, embittered. Since there are today two complexes on Quai de Conti from the time of Mozart (the present **Institut de France**, and the **Hôtel de la Monnaie**), the Count must have lived in one of the four houses (eighteenth-nineteenth century) which are found, beginning at #13, between the two complexes. The first (#13) was the Hôtel Brulart de Genlis (from the period of Louis XV), and is presently an art gallery/exhibition room; however, the Rococo carved wood interior is preserved in the Musée Carnavalet.

GENERAL SITE OF THE PALACE OF COUNTESS LILLEBONNE. Rue de l'université. On 8 December 1763, Leopold wrote, "Tomorrow we must go to the Marquise Villeroy and to the Countess de Lillebonne" (Françoise-Catherine-Scholastique), where Mozart and his sister would have performed, as a matter of course.

GENERAL SITE OF THE HEINA MUSIC BUSINESS. Rue de Seine in Faubourg St. Germain. Here, in the Hôtel-de-Lille, Franz Joseph Heina (or Haina), who was born near Prague, had a music instrument business and a music publishing firm. Heina and his wife, (born Gertrude Brockmuller) were Mozart's truest friends during his stay in Paris. In 1776, he lived "chez le Sr Bordet," which published for the first time Mozart's K. 179/189a, K. 180/173e, K. 254, K. 311/284c, and K. 354/299a, as well as the masterpiece, the Piano Sonata in A minor, K. 310/300d.

★ ★ LUXEMBOURG PALACE AND GARDENS. 15, Rue de Vaugirard; Metro 4 or 10: Odéon. The horn player Heina and his wife had visited Anna Maria (Mozart's mother) often during her illness. She dined with them on 10 June 1778, while Mozart was at Grimm's house, and they took her to the gardens and gallery of the Luxembourg Palace. A few weeks thereafter Anna Maria died. The palace, built for Maria de Medici in 1615 by de Brosses to resemble the Florentine Palazzo Pitti, has changed little, although the gardens were considerably changed at the beginning of the nineteenth century by Chalgrin. The two large galleries, open to the public from 1750, were designed for a famous series of paintings by Rubens, today found in the Louvre. The present seat of the Senate is located here; *it is closed to the public*.

★ ★ SITE OF THE PARIS OPERA AT THE PALAIS ROYAL. 202, Rue St. Honoré. The Paris opera (called the Royal Academy of Music) was located to the right of the cul-de-sac (202, Rue St. Honoré) from 1770 to 1781 in a hall constructed by Moreau from 1763 to 1770.[13] Here, Mozart heard the operas of the major warring factions, Gluck's *Armide* and Piccinni's *Roland*. On 11 June 1778, Mozart's ballet, "Les Petits Riens," choreographed by Noverre, was first performed here after Piccinni's opera *Le finte gemelle*. Only "about 12 pieces" of the 21 numbers of the ballet were actually by Mozart. After the performance of his "Paris" Symphony at the **Concert Spirituel**, Mozart came to the Palais-Royal for an ice (see eighteenth-century Cafés of Paris). The original palace, built 1634–39 by Le Mercier for Cardinal Richelieu, was enlarged by Mansart, with a garden surrounded by a colonnade, and numerous cafés and businesses. The theater where Molière performed his last *Malade Imaginaire*, had been located in the wing of the palace at the south-east angle, from 1673 to 1763 (to the left of the cul-de-sac at 202 Rue St. Honoré[14]). At present, in the splendid courtyard of the Palais-Royal, with unified facades, there are controversial striped modern pillars/seats emerging from the pavement, and a modern fountain. The present building by d'Ivry is essentially from 1752 to 1770.[15]

★ ★ CAFES OF PARIS: [CAFE CHARTRES], FORMER CAFE DE FOY, [CAFE PROCOPE]. After the performance of the "Paris" Symphony, Mozart went to the Palais-Royal "out of pure joy," enjoyed an ice, and afterwards "said the rosary." Although Mozart did not cite which café in the Palais-Royal, the Café de Foy (founded 1749), which no longer exists, served an excellent ice. In addition, at the Café Procope (founded 1686), which still can be found at 13, rue de l'Ancienne Comédie, numerous personalities were regulars—Voltaire, Rousseau, and Beaumarchais, as well as Diderot, d'Alembert, Benjamin Franklin and, perhaps, Mozart. At the former Café du Caveau, the present 89, Galerie Beaujolais, members of the warring factions of Gluck and Piccinni met. Finally, at the west angle of the Rue St. Honoré and the Place du Palais-Royal, the Café de la Régence was located (relocated since 1854 to 161, Rue St. Honoré); it was frequented by Grimm, Diderot, Voltaire, Robespierre, and Philidor. Today a remarkable example of authentic eighteenth-century decoration can be seen at the Café Chartres at 17, rue de Beaujolais, which was, however, opened in 1784.

SITE OF THE LODGING OF MOZART AND HIS MOTHER. Rue du Sentier across from the Rue du Croissant. Around 11 April 1778, Mozart and his mother moved into a new apartment with two rooms facing the street, in the Hôtel des 4 fils Haimon, which Madame d'Epinay found for them. Although the rooms were "cold, even with a fire," the apartment was "closer to the nobility and near the theater." On 24 June 1778, a doctor was called for Anna Maria, who had been complaining about headache, chills and fever, and lost her hearing suddenly on 23 June. On 3 July, after being unconscious for several hours, Mozart's mother died in the presence of Mozart, a servant, and their friend Heina. The building no longer exists; on the site, there are modern apartments and offices.

★ SITE OF THE PALACE OF LOUISE D'EPINAY AND BARON GRIMM. 5, Rue de la Chaussée d'Antin. On 25 March 1778, Mozart visited Baron Grimm and his mistress, Louise d'Epinay. He was invited here often, and shortly after the death of his mother on 3 July 1778, Mozart moved in with them, in the unfurnished room that had been used as a "sick-room." The heavy conflicts with Grimm prompted Mozart in September to write to his father about Grimm, who had loaned him 15 louis d'or, that "he is on the Italian side—is false—and tries to suppress me." Although Mozart was treated well by Madame d'Epinay, Grimm was overbearing, and put pressure on Wolfgang to leave Paris, which he did on 26 September 1778, with bad feelings. Nothing remains of the building, where Chopin also occupied a room from 1833 to 1836.

SITE OF THE HOME OF BADEMEISTER BRIE. Rue Traversière (today 8 rue Molière); Metro 7: Pyramides. On 10 May 1766, after returning to Paris from England, Holland and Belgium, the Mozart family moved into a "closed apartment" here, owned by Bademeister Brie. It was very close to the Palais Royal and was obviously very expensive as Leopold wrote, "what it costs, I will save to tell you in person." The building no longer exists; today #8 is the address of the post office Palais Royal, near the present Comédie Française.

★ SITE OF THE CONCERT SPIRITUEL. Tuileries; Metro 1: Tuileries. The **Concert Spirituel**, the first regular concert undertaking in Paris, with choir and orchestra, was founded by Philidor in 1725. The performance of Mozart's "Paris" Symphony, written for these concerts, took place on 18 June 1778, in the "Room of the 100 Swiss" in the Palace of the Tuileries, with "all applause." It was repeated on 15 August 1778 with a new Andante movement. Earlier, at the beginning of April 1778, Mozart had worked on an arrangement of a "Miserere" by Holzbauer (K. Anh. 1/297a) on commission of the director of the **Concert spirituel**, Joseph Le Gros, that was performed only in part during Holy Week. Supposedly, Mozart's lost second "Paris" symphony was also performed here on 8 September 1778. The palace has been demolished; however, the site is near the Arc du Carrousel, at the extension of the axis of the Pont Royal.

GENERAL SITE OF THE CONCERT ROOM OF MR. FELIX. Rue et Porte St. Honoré. Here, on one of the most illustrious streets in Paris, Mozart and his sister gave their first concert in Paris on 10 March 1764, in the home of "a distinguished lady where there is a small theater often used by the nobles for their private theatricals." Leopold later wrote that Grimm "arranged our first concert," including distributing 320 tickets and paying for the candles. Their second concert, where Gavinies the violinist and Picinelli the singer participated, was given here. The concert, which took place on 9 April 1764, was probably the concert to which Leopold referred in 1778 when he cited the music-loving dilettante Baron Karl Bagge, "who contributed his musicians." Bagge, a composer of quartets and violin concertos, invited numerous artists to participate in his household concerts. The two Paris concerts were extremely successful financially.

★ GENERAL SITES ON RUE ST. HONORÉ. The Mozarts had many connections to this historic street. On the section near the Place Vendôme lived the bachelor, Monsieur Bourgade; at his home the Mozart children performed, and he was very kind to the children, later giving Leopold "many louis d'or." Leopold cited Madame Marie-Thèrése Geoffrin, "La reine de salon," whose salon on Rue St. Honoré (and Rue Royale[16]) was a center of artistic and literary life for 60 years, and whose frequent guests included Baron Grimm. The apartment in the home of Notary le Noir that Leopold had first paid 100 livres to reserve (forfeited when the family was invited to live with Count van Eyck) was on this street, across from Rue d'Echelle. Eckard, whose piano sonatas Mozart used as movements in his early Salzburg *pastiche* piano concertos (K. 37, K. 39, K. 40, K. 41) lived with le Noir, as did Christian von Mechel, who engraved the Carmontelle portrait of the Mozarts. Later, in 1778, Mozart was in close contact with the music publisher, Jean-Georges Sieber, who paid Mozart 15 louis d'or for the sonatas for the Electress Elisabeth Auguste that he published in November 1778 as *Oeuvre premier*. Sieber lived at that time in the Hôtel d'Aligre (although the building was demolished in 1852, the site is today #121–25 Rue St. Honoré[17]).

★ ★ PALACE OF MADAME POMPADOUR. 55, Rue du Faubourg-St-Honoré. Today the Palais d'Elysee, the residence of the President of the Republic. Leopold wrote on 1 February 1764, "[Madame Pompadour] is extremely dignified and uncommonly intelligent … In Paris she has a most splendid Hotel, entirely rebuilt, in the Faubourg St. Honoré. In the room where the clavecin is found (which is all gold-leaf and most artistically lacquered) hangs a life-sized portrait of herself and beside it a portrait of the King." This description indicates that the Mozarts visited here, at which time they would have performed on the clavecin mentioned. The palace, built in 1718, was remodeled in 1754 for Madame Pompadour in the light, elegant Rococo taste which was a reaction to the pomp of Louis XIV style. In 1764, under Louis XV, the palace became a foreign embassy, and after the Revolution, Napoleon lived here. Since 1873, it has been the seat of the French president. *The palace cannot be visited.*

N o t e s

1 The Bauer/Deutsch/Eibl notes to the Mozart letters (V, zu 448/18) lists her as living on "Place Royale." However, the eighteenth-century name of "Place Royale" has been changed, and is presently "Place des Vosges"; it is one of the most remarkable and well-preserved areas of Paris.
2 Communicated by Madame Felkay, Archives de Paris.
3 Although it is quite possible that the Duc du Chabot lived here, Leopold Mozart transcribed many of the Paris names and addresses, which he sent to Mozart in Mannheim in 1778, from his travel notes dating back to 1763–66, and which could have changed within the period of over a decade. P. de

Bruyn, Paris, has communicated to me that several Rohan-Chabots had palaces on the rue de Varenne (as well as on the present Place des Vosges); in the Almanach Royal 1765, a Duc de Chabot is listed on rue de Varenne (they owned 1750–91 the Hôtel Mazarin, and perhaps the Hôtel d'Estampes-d-'Orsay, as well). In addition, he notes, the "Almanach Royale" of 1778 gives an address of a Duc de Chabot on rue de Seine (where the Rohan-Rochefoucauld-Chabots had a vast set of buildings).

4 Wachmeier, *Paris*, 96–98.

5 Bauer/Deutsch/Eibl, *Mozart Briefe*, V, zu 74/39, 60.

6 Wachmeier, op. cit., 83.

7 Angermueller, *Musikalische Umwelt*, LXXI.

8 Angermueller notes that the documents and programs concerning the Concerts des Amateurs are missing. Angermueller, op. cit., LXXI.

9 Communicated by Paul de Bruyn, Archives de France.

10 According to Valentin, Cemetery St. Jean-Porte-Latine; according to Deutsch in the Cemetery of the Church of the Innocents.

11 Communicated by P. de Bruyn, Archives de Paris.

12 P. de Bruyn has communicated to me that this was the address of the Duc in 1778; his daughter, Marie-Louise-Philippine married Armand de Castries on 29 July 1778, moving to the Hôtel de Castries on rue de Varenne. Her father moved in 1781 to the petit hotel de Castries at 76, rue de Varenne; *Chartier de Castries*, ed. Archives Nationales, 1975, 306 AP 601. Papiers personnels, 7–8.

13 Hillairel, *Dictionnaire historique des rues de Paris*, 431–32.

14 Ibid.

15 Wachmeier, op. cit., 80.

16 Communicated by Madame Felkay, Archives de Paris.

17 Hillairel, op cit., 424.

Mozart in Strasbourg

Dates

About 14 October–3 November 1778

After Mozart's sojourn in Paris, marred by the death of his mother, and his strained relationship with Baron F. Melchior Grimm, Mozart returned to Salzburg, via Mannheim and Munich. Apparently to save money, Baron Grimm put Mozart on the slow coach through Nancy and Strasbourg, which distressed Mozart, who had to get up each morning at 3 AM (and who twice had "the honor of getting up at 1 AM"). Mozart wrote to his father, "You know that I cannot sleep in a coach." In Mozart's three weeks here, he played "in public on the two best organs by Silbermann," and was well received by the musicians of the city; his concerts, however, were financially disastrous to the artist, whose financial situation was severely strained.

Music

The three concert programs given by Mozart in Strasbourg are not known. However, Mozart wrote on 23 October 1777 that he played [in Augsburg] "the Strasbourg Concerto; it flowed like oil." J. Liebeskind, in 1908, wrote of the similarity of the *musette* theme in the third movement of K. 218 to the "Ballo Strasburghese" musette in Dittersdorf's Carnival Symphony (IMF P 153/2), strongly suggesting that Mozart was referring to his violin concerto, K. 218, as the "Strasbourg Concerto."

Strasbourg Sites

★ ★ ST. THOMAS CHURCH (L'EGLISE SAINT-THOMAS). Mozart wrote, "I have played here in public on the two best organs built by Silbermann, which are in the Lutheran churches: the New Church, and the Thomas Church." The small, fascinating Silbermann organ (1737–40) in this church, built in eighteenth-century scale, is remarkably intact; it was restored in 1970. The exterior of the church, which is Gothic from the thirteenth-fourteenth centuries, is severe; it was later converted into a Protestant church. Inside is found a magnificent tomb of Marshal de Saxe, which was executed 1756–77 by order of Louis XV.

★ HOME OF PHILIPP JAKOB FRANCK.[1] 7, du quai Saint-Nicolas.[2] Franck, who was elected mayor of Strasbourg three times, and his brother, a violinist, are among the few known people with whom Mozart had contact during his stay in the city. Leopold wrote that Baron Grimm had arranged for Mozart's mail to be sent to Franck, *banquier* of the firm Sigmund Haffner. The edifice where Franck lived was constructed in 1587, and bought by Franck in 1765; today it is owned by the **Hospices Civils de Strasbourg.**[3]

[★ ★ MEETING HALL (SALLE DU MIROIR)].[4] 3, rue du Miroir. While it is not known where Mozart's first concert in Strasbourg, on 17 October 1778, took place, it has been suggested that it was here in the present **Salle Mozart,** which was the meeting hall of the merchants, the **Corporation des Marchands.**[5] The concert, without orchestra, was not successful financially, although Mozart was encouraged by the presence of Prince Max von Zweibrücken. The room has been reconstructed in eighteenth-century style with gold stucco ornament, pilasters in painted rippled marble and a painted harpsichord. Concerts are now held here regularly.

SITE OF THE RESTAURANT OF J. B. JOSEPH MARCHAND. 5 de la rue des Orfèvres.[6] Mozart, who frequently made contact with people involved in theater in a city, would very likely have frequented this restaurant, owned by the brother of the director of the German theater troupe in Mannheim and Munich.[7] The building was destroyed in WW II, and was reconstructed in 1953; today the fashionable clothing store **Céline** is located on the ground floor.[8]

[★ ★ ★ PALAIS ROHAN]. 2, place du Chateau. When Mozart arrived in Strasbourg, the relay station of the post was in the **Cour du Corbeau** on the **quai d'Ill**, opposite this grand edifice.[9] Mozart wrote, "If the Cardinal (who was very ill when I arrived) had died, I might have gotten a good appointment. . . ." He undoubtedly saw, and most likely paid a visit to, this vast complex where the Cardinal lived, which is presently the Museum of Fine Arts. Built 1731–42 from plans by architect Robert de Cotte, it is one of the most splendid examples of elegant eighteenth-century French architecture, and today houses an excellent painting collection from the fourteenth to nineteenth centuries.

★ ★ ★ CATHEDRAL OF NOTRE-DAME. Mozart heard a new Mass by F.X. Richter here at Nôtre-Dame, on Sunday (probably 25 October 1778). The interior presents remarkable sense of height and weightlessness. In addition to a spectacular astronomical clock, carved altarpieces, and an impressive Baroque chapel, the cathedral has a magnificent fifteenth-century Krebs organ, modified in the beginning of the eighteenth century by Andreas Silbermann. Open 7–11:40 AM and 12:45–7 PM.

★ NEW TEMPLE (TEMPLE-NEUF). Place du Temple-Neuf. Mozart played the organ (built 1747–49) in the **Temple Neuf,** which he called the "new church"; the church, as well as the organ, were destroyed by fire during 24–25 August 1870. The present Protestant Church was rebuilt in imitation of Romanesque-style architecture.

SITE OF THE STRASBOURG THEATER. Place Broglie; near the present Municipal Theater. Despite the lack of financial success of his first concert, Mozart later played two concerts in the Strasbourg Theater, on 24 and 31 October 1778. The concert on 24 October was with a very poor orchestra; the receipts for both concerts were surprisingly poor, although Mozart reported that "my ears hurt from the applause . . . , as if the whole theater were full." The theater in which Mozart played no longer exists; it burned on 30 May 1800, and was reconstructed 1804–05 near the present theater. The previous site was actually closer to the **Palais du Gouverneur Militaire.** The present facade has sculptures of the Muses, added in 1821, by Ohmacht, which ornament the peristyle; this facade survived the fire of 1870.[10]

N o t e s

1 Philipp Jakob Franck was not a musician, as Massin writes in *Wolfgang Amadeus Mozart,* but a banker. Communicated by François Fuchs, Illkirch.
2 Communicated by François Fuchs, Illkirch.
3 Communicated by François Fuchs, Illkirch.
4 The Strasbourg Archives confirmed for me that there are no documents which indicate that Mozart performed in this hall; it is only affirmed by a popular tradition.
5 François Fuchs, who has done a study of Mozart's stay in Strasbourg, and who presented a paper, "Mozart et l'Alsace," on 27 January 1989, has communicated to me that Mozart's first Strasbourg concert may have been given in this hall. The arguments, in addition to the popular tradition, are that J. G. Schertz, from whom Mozart borrowed 8 louis d'or, lived on the rue de l'Epine, only a short distance from the *Salle du Miroir;* in addition, Philipp Jakob Franck, who was an important contact for Mozart in Strasbourg, was a member of the *Corporation des Marchands,* which met in this hall.
6 Communicated by François Fuchs, Illkirch.
7 Communicated by François Fuchs, Illkirch.
8 Communicated by François Fuchs, Illkirch.
9 Massin, op. cit., 275.
10 Fritsch, Jocelyne. *Le Théâtre Français à Strasbourg de 1830 à 1870.* (Master's Thesis, Université des Sciences Humaines, Strasbourg, 1989), p. 9.

Mozart in Versailles

Dates

24 December 1763–8 January 1764 ▪ 28–30 May 1766

The Mozart family made two visits to the court during the "Great Western" trip of 1763–66. A vivid account of the first trip is found in Leopold's letter of 1 February 1764. Mozart was accompanied frequently to the court chapel by his father to hear the choir sing motets during Mass so that he would become familiar with the French choral style. At court, the children were received with great enthusiasm; the King's daughters, for example, "approached them ... kissed them and let themselves be kissed by them countless times." During the great dinner on the evening of New Year's Day, Wolfgang was requested to stand beside the Queen, Marie Leczinska, and to entertain her, while she interpreted everything for the King, Louis XV.

Years later Nannerl recollected that Mozart performed on the organ in the chapel, to the applause of the court; in addition, when Madame de Pompadour refused to allow Mozart to kiss her, he responded, "Who does she think that she is? . . . the Empress herself kissed me!" Two additional academies were played at Versailles; the precious gifts received indicate that they were for Adrienne-Catherine, Comtesse de Tessé, and Victoire-Marie-Anne de Savoie, Princesse de Carignan.

During Mozart's ill-fated Paris trip in 1778, he wrote his father that Jean-Joseph Rudolphe, a member of the King's private orchestra, had offered him the position of organist at Versailles. Despite Leopold's encouragement, Mozart wrote that, on Grimm's advice, he did not pursue it, as he was interested only in a position as Kapellmeister.

Music

Sonatas for clavier and violin, K. 6 (written in Salzburg, Brussels, and Paris) and K. 7 (written in Paris) were dedicated to Victoire-Marie-Anne de Savoie, Princesse de Cari-

gnan, while K. 8 and K. 9 (written in Paris) were dedicated to Adrienne-Catherine, Comtesse de Tessé.

Kyrie for four-voice choir with string accompaniment, K. 33, using the melody of a French song, was written in Paris after the second Versailles trip.

Versailles Sites

★ ★ ★ **PALACE OF VERSAILLES.** 78000 Versailles. Here, on 1 January 1764, the Mozarts were invited to the grand dinner of the King, Louis XV, and his Queen, Maria Leczinska, during which Mozart was invited to stand by the Queen, conversing with her the whole time in German. The "grand dinner" which Mozart attended was in the Queen's Antechamber (**Antichambre ou salon du Grand Couvert**), which can be visited today as part of the **Grands Appartements royaux**, specifically part of the **Appartement de la Reine**.[1] In addition, gifts received by the Mozarts indicate that Mozart played for the daughter of Louis XV, Madame Victoire (Louise-Marie-Thérèse de Bourbon), and for Adrienne-Catherine, Comtesse de Tessé, to whom Mozart dedicated his Piano/Violin Sonatas, K. 8 and K. 9. There is also a tradition in Versailles that Mozart played for another of the four daughters of Louis XV, Madame Adélaïde; the spectacular Golden Chamber, or **Cabinet Doré** (1753) of Madame Adélaïde can be seen today[2] (although in a form somewhat altered by Louis XV and Louis XVI). Construction of the palace was begun in 1668 by Le Vau, while

Versailles. Unsigned engraving. Bibliothèque des Beaux Arts, Paris.

maintaining the Marble Court of the Hunting Palace of Louis XIII. The style of Louis XV, the King who received the Mozarts, can best be seen in the ceiling painting of the Hercules Salon (1736), and in the wall decoration of the Louis XV rooms (around 1750), which are considered among the finest examples of Rococo ornament. In addition, it can be seen in the **Petit Trianon** and the Opera theater, examples of the transition to classicism.[3] Also of interest for the time of Mozart's visit are the small apartments from the time of Louis XV (1738), and the apartments of Madame de Pompadour. Apartments, Hall of Mirrors, and Museum of History are open 9:45 AM–5 PM.

★ ★ ★ ROYAL CHAPEL AT VERSAILLES. The Mozarts heard Christmas Mass here in 1763, and later, Wolfgang played the organ before the entire court. Mozart's Kyrie for four-voice choir with string accompaniment (K. 33) was most likely destined for the Court Chapel. Years later, in 1778, Mozart wrote to his father that he had not pursued the post of organist, which would have brought him to Versailles six months a year. The chapel (1699–1710, by Jules Hardouin-Mansard) features a lofty colonnade of Corinthian pillars over a low "Roman" arcade, and a splendid apse ceiling fresco, "The Ascension of Christ" by Charles de la Fosse. The organ, by Robert Cliquot and Tribuot, is from 1708[4]; the organ case was carved from drawings by architect Robert de Cotte by several sculptors.[5] Open 9:45 AM–5 PM.

★ ★ ★ PARK OF THE PALACE OF VERSAILLES. Nannerl, in her travel notes, mentioned the beautiful marble and alabaster vases, the spectacular Latona fountain, the Neptune pool, "Diana at Her Bath," and "The Rape of Proserpina" (a masterpiece by François Girardon which is in the part of the park known as the Colonnade). The present "English landscape garden" was not yet created during the Mozarts' visit. Park open 8 AM–5 PM; the Petit Trianon only Tuesday to Friday 2–5 PM.

GENERAL SITE OF THE HOTEL AU CORMIER. Rue du Peintre Lebrun. This hotel, where the Mozarts lived from 24 December 1763 to 8 January 1764, and from 28 May to 1 June 1766, was in close proximity to the Palace of Versailles.

N o t e s

1 Communicated by Guy Kuraszewski, Direction des Musées de France, Versailles.
2 Ibid.
3 Wachmeier, *Paris*, 142.
4 Wachmeier, op. cit., 150.
5 Communicated by Guy Kuraszewski, Direction des Musées de France, Versailles.

Germany

Aachen, Augsburg, Berlin, Bonn (and Brühl), Coblenz, Cologne, Dillingen, Donaueschingen, Dresden, Frankfurt, Heidelberg, Leipzig, Mainz, Mannheim, Munich, Passau, Potsdam, Schwetzingen, Ulm, Wasserburg am Inn, Worms

Other Sites of Interest:

Hohenaltheim, Kirchheimbolanden, Markt Biberbach

Mozart in Aachen

Dates

30 September–2 October 1763

During their "Great Western" trip of 1763–66, Mozart and his family stopped in Aachen on the way from Cologne, traveling in the direction of Paris by way of the Austrian Netherlands. It was "the most expensive place" they had seen during the trip, and the abundance of kisses that Princess Amalia gave them, and particularly Mozart, did not help to offset those expenses, as "neither the innkeeper nor the postmaster can be paid in kisses."

In Aachen, the Mozart family met members of the aristocracy, the middle class and the army. Princess Amalia, who was the sister of Frederick II of Prussia, tried to convince them to travel to Berlin, instead of Paris, making promises that Leopold did not believe; he hesitated even to write them down in a letter.

Aachen Sites

[★ ★ ★ CATHEDRAL (MÜNSTER)]. Münsterplatz. Leopold mentioned Anton Joseph Lacand, the director of music in the cathedral. Because of its importance, Leopold and the Mozart family would undoubtedly have visited the cathedral. Charlemagne, who settled in Aachen, ordered the construction of this domed basilica before 800 AD; the coronations of thirty princes as King of Germania took place here.[1] The Gothic chancel was consecrated in 1414, the 600th anniversary of Charlemagne's death. The spectacular altar (the "Pala d'Oro") and Charlemagne's relics are noteworthy. Open every day 7 AM–7 PM; guided tours are possible except Saturday; admission charge.

SITE OF THE "GOLDEN DRAGON" INN ("ZUM GOLDENEN DRACHEN"). Komphausbadstrasse 9.[2] Here, in the inn where the Mozarts lodged during their stay in Aachen from 30 September 1763 to 2 October 1763, the children performed a concert that was only mentioned by Nannerl in 1792.[3] The hotel no longer exists; on the site there is a wide street.[4]

SITE OF THE HOTEL OF PRINCESS AMALIE OF PRUSSIA. Nr. 13 Komphausbadstrasse. The Mozarts met with Princess Amalie, the sister of King Frederick II, at the beginning of October 1763. The concert of the Mozart children took place either here or in the ballroom which belonged to it, at Nr. 11.[5] The expensive city, coupled with the fact that the Princess paid them only with kisses, prompted Leopold to write, ". . . neither the landlord nor the postmaster can be paid with kisses." The building no longer exists; on the site today there is a wide street.[6]

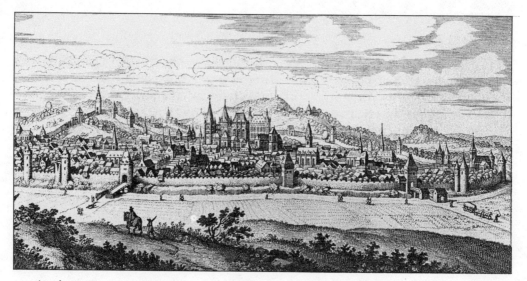

Aachen. Engraving by Matthaeus Merian, 17th century.

[GENERAL SITE OF THE HOME OF RUDOLPH GEYR VON SCHWEPPENBURG]. Former Felsgasse; it was the first parallel alley south of the present Blondelstrasse.[7] While it is not known if the Mozarts were invited here, Leopold cited Geyr, the **Geheimrat** (privy council) of Cologne, in the travel notes. Geyr, the administrator of the poor for St. Adalbert Church, had a home which was an important gathering point in Aachen. Neither the building nor the street exist today.[8]

[★ ★ ST. ADALBERT CHURCH]. Kaiserplatz. Rudolph Geyr von Schweppenburg, cited by Leopold, was linked with this church. The abbey and church were dedicated 1005; today the original church (which was renovated 1873–76) represents one of the oldest basilicas (with pillar construction) found in the area of the Rhein.[9] The Mozarts did not see the tower, which is a nineteenth-century addition.

[★ ★ CHARACTERISTIC SIGHTS OF AACHEN]. Typically the Mozarts visited the most important sights of each city they visited. Today these include the fourteenth-century Town Hall (**Rathaus**), built on the site of Charlemagne's palace, of which the Granus Tower remains; the marketplace (**Marktplatz**) with the Charles Fountain (**Karlsbrunner**) and the **Lousberg** before the gates of the city can also still be seen today.[10] The superb Treasury (**Domschatzkammer**) collection includes an arms chest from the thirteenth century, and a gold cross with precious stones from 990. In addition, the Postwagen Inn of 1657, and the restored Gothic Löwenstein House are of interest, as is the present Couven Museum, a reconstructed eighteenth-century pharmacy with a collection of seventeenth-eighteenth century furnishings.[11] Although it was not yet constructed during the Mozarts' visit, the carefully restored old Bath House (**Altes Kurhaus**), designed by Jakob Couven in 1782, is a fine example of eighteenth-century architecture.

N o t e s

1 Michelin, *Germany*, 33–34.
2 Poll, "Mozart in Aachen," 361.
3 Ibid., 365; Bauer/Deutsch/Eibl, *Mozart Briefe*, V, zu 65/131.
4 Communicated by A. Pauels, Archivoberinspektorin, Stadtarchiv Aachen.
5 Poll, op. cit., 365; Bauer/Deutsch/Eibl, Ibid.
6 Communicated by A. Pauels, Archivoberinspektorin, Stadtarchiv Aachen.
7 Located, in response to my queries, on maps of the period sent by A. Pauels, Archivoberinspektorin, Stadtarchiv Aachen; previously, the site had been ignored in the Mozart literature.
8 Communicated by A. Pauels, Archivoberinspektorin, Stadtarchiv Aachen.
9 *Aachener Reisefuehrer*, 113.
10 Communicated by A. Pauels, Archivoberinspektorin, Stadtarchiv Aachen.
11 Michelin, op. cit., 34.

Mozart in Augsburg

22 June–6 July 1763 ▪ 7 November 1766 ▪ 11–26 October 1777 ▪ 7–10 March 1781 ▪ about 28/29 October 1790

At the beginning of their "Great Western" trip of 1763–66, the Mozart family stopped in Augsburg, the city of Leopold's birth; here the children gave three public concerts, and Leopold bought a travel clavier by the renowned maker Johann Andreas Stein. Returning from this trip in 1766, they again stopped here. During Mozart's trip to Paris with his mother, 1777–78, he stopped in Augsburg, where his relationship to his cousin, Anna Maria Thekla (to whom he wrote numerous scabrous letters) became more animated. This visit was marred by the bad manners of Jakob Alois Karl Langenmantel, who made fun of Mozart's Order of the Golden Spur when Mozart was a guest at the Langenmantel home. Mozart's academy here featured, among other works, his concerto for three pianos, K. 242. In 1781, Mozart and his sister made a brief excursion from Munich, where his *Idomeneo* was being performed. Finally, after Mozart's ill-ventured trip to Leopold II's coronation in Frankfurt, he stopped again in Augsburg.

M u s i c

Concerto for three pianos, K. 242 (composed for Countess Antonia Lodron and her two daughters) was performed here on 22 October 1777 with Mozart playing the second piano, the cathedral organist J. Michael Demmler the first, and the piano maker Johann Andreas Stein the third. The same evening, Mozart played his piano concerto, K. 238. Mozart wrote on 17 October 1777 that he played here, and in Munich, all six of his piano sonatas from memory. The piano sonatas which were Mozart's repertoire during his visit to Augsburg in 1777 were the six sonatas, K. 279/189d; K. 280/189e; K. 281/189f; K. 282/189g; K. 283/189h; and K. 284/205b. He mentioned, in particular, the last two in the set.

On 19 October 1777, during a little evening music in the *Stift Heilig-Kreuz*, Mozart

played his "Strasbourg" violin concerto, K. 218, and the piano variations on a theme by Fischer, K. 179/189a.

The opera *Idomeneo* was written for Munich, 1781, during which time Mozart and Nannerl made an excursion to Augsburg.

Augsburg Sites

★ HOLY CROSS CHURCH AND MONASTERY (HEILIG-KREUZ-KIRCHE). Heilig-Kreuz-Strasse 3. Here in the Augustine Monastery, accompanied by his uncle, Mozart met the music-loving prelate Bartholomaeus Christa, and played the Stein organ for him on 13 October 1777; he had "never heard anyone play the organ so effectively and earnestly." Mozart played evening music, including a symphony, a violin concerto by Vanhal, and his "Strassburg" concerto (K. 218) on 19 October 1777. After dinner, he performed the Fischer Variations (K. 179/189a), and then improvised on fugue themes until 11 PM, including creating a double fugue, to the astonishment of the monks. During other visits 23–25 October 1777, Mozart left manuscripts of his sacred music to be copied, in gratitude for the hospitality, including *Misericordias Domini* (K. 222/205a), and two short Masses (K. 192/186f and K. 220/196b). The former Augustine Monastery, founded in 1195, had a Gothic church (fifteenth-sixteenth century), reconstructed in Baroque style in 1719. The Stein organ no longer exists; it was dismantled in 1890. After destruction in 1949, the church was rebuilt in a simple late Gothic style. The painting "The Ascension of the Virgin" from Ruben's studio (1627) and the wrought-iron work are of interest.[1] Open 10 AM–6 PM.

[★ ★ PROTESTANT CHURCH OF THE HOLY CROSS]. Ottmarsgässchen 6. Adjacent to the former Augustine church and monastery is this well-preserved Protestant church, by the same name, with a fine wood caissoned ceiling, and numerous paintings from the seventeenth to eighteenth centuries, including a Tintoretto. Usually closed; open by request.

★ SITE OF THE "WHITE LAMB" INN ("ZUM WEISSEN LAMM"). Ludwigstrasse 36. When Mozart and his mother arrived on 11 October 1777, they lodged here, and when they departed on the morning of 26 October 1777, there was a tearful farewell given to them by Bäsle, with Stein and Mozart's relatives gathered in front of the hotel. Again, returning from the coronation of the Emperor in 1790, Mozart stayed here, on 28 or 29 October 1790. The old inn was destroyed in 1944, but has been rebuilt in an old style; it now houses the **Bezirksfinanzdirektion** (District Administration of Finances). An attractive commemorative profile of Mozart in bronze, over pink marble, cites the sojourns of Mozart and Goethe.

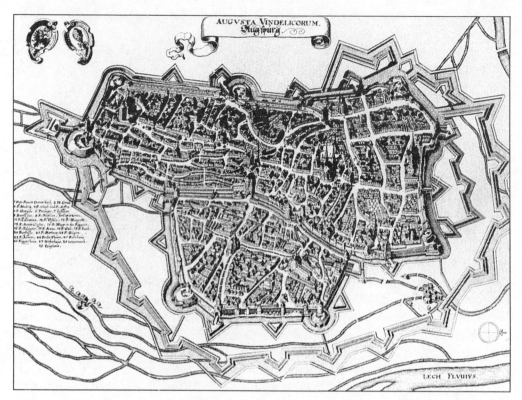

Augsburg. Engraving by Matthaeus Merian, 17th century.

[★ ★ HOME OF HANS GEORG MOZART (1647–1719)]. Today Äusseres Pfaffengässchen 24. This edifice from the sixteenth century in the Cathedral quarter is one of the few Mozart-related sites preserved in Augsburg. It was acquired on 23 December 1681 by Leopold's uncle Hans Georg, the master builder.[2]

★ ★ ST. MARY'S CATHEDRAL. Kornhausgasse 8. Although Leopold did not specifically cite the **Dom** in his travel notes (for sights in Augsburg he wrote "the city hall, etc., etc."), it is likely that he brought his family here at the beginning of July 1763. The church, reconstructed in Gothic style in the fourteenth century, has a remarkable Gothic south portal, "The Doorway to the Virgin," and 32 Romanesque bronze bas-relief panels.[3] In the nave there are four altars with paintings by Holbein the Elder; the twelfth-century windows with alabaster panes of the Prophets are also noteworthy. Sacred choral music concerts are given here. The peaceful gardens outside with eighteenth-century statues, and the surrounding facades, are also of interest. Open 10 AM–6 PM.

★ ★ SITE OF THE ST. SALVATOR MONASTERY (INCLUDING THE "LIT-TLE GOLDEN SALON"). Jesuitengasse 12. Mozart's uncle Alois (Leopold's brother) lived in the complex of this monastery with his wife and his daughter Anna Maria (Bäsle), and Leopold had studied here for two years after high school.[4] Mozart and his mother first called here after arriving in Augsburg on 11 October 1777. Wolfgang amused himself a great deal with his cousin, Anna Maria, whom he called "[like me], a little wicked," and to whom he later wrote numerous scatological letters. The monastery was destroyed in 1803 (including the organ), and the house where Bäsle lived, at #26 Jesuitengasse, was destroyed in 1944 and not rebuilt. The splendid Rococo "little golden salon" (1765) at #12 Jesuitengasse was the former congregation room of the Jesuits, and has a large painting by Guenther, a student of Asam; it would very possibly have been seen by Mozart. The small golden salon is *closed to the public*; it is open only for concerts and lectures (contact tourist office). St. Salvator Church is open by request only.

★ ★ ★ BIRTHPLACE OF LEOPOLD MOZART. Frauentorstrasse 30. During their first visit to Augsburg, Leopold probably showed his wife and children the various homes of his family, including this house where he was born. In 1937, 150 years after the death of Leopold, a monument was made of his house. The edifice (sixteenth-seventeenth century) with a gable roof, has been restored in period style inside and out with great attention to detail, and, with the numerous scores, etchings, paintings and instruments, presents a valuable view into the period. There is a fine *Hammerklavier* (1785) by Augsburg's master builder, Johann Andreas Stein, who was both hospitable and influential during Mozart's 1777 visit. It is used for concerts here. Museum open 10 AM–12 Noon, 2–5 PM; Fridays 10 AM–12 Noon, 2–4 PM; Saturdays 10 AM–12 Noon; Sundays 10 AM–12 Noon; closed Tuesdays.

Augsburg. Jesuitengasse. Engraving by Jeremias Wolff, before 1724.

★ ST. GEORGE ABBEY AND CHURCH. Georgenstrasse 12. Leopold Mozart's parents were married here, and Leopold was baptized here, in the Catholic church whose abbey was built by Hans Georg Mozart, the great-granduncle of Mozart.[5] The late Gothic building was erected 1490–1505. While the onion-domed tower was added in 1681, it was severely damaged in 1944. Inside, the large marble statue of St. Salvator (probably by Loy Hering) and the remainder of an altar (1512) are of interest.[6] Open 10 AM–6 PM.

SITE OF THE LANGENMANTEL HOME. Hinter dem Schwalbeneck 1/Am Schwalbeneck 1.[7] On the day after his arrival, 12 October 1777, Mozart made one of his first visits to the Langenmantels, who ultimately offered him insults and excuses of empty coffers instead of the hospitality of the city of his father. The influential Catholic town patrician, Jakob Wilhelm Benedikt Langenmantel, spoke to Mozart in a grammatically condescending way, and then gave him "the honor of playing for his lumpy son, his long-legged daughter-in-law and his vapid wife" for 45 minutes. The day after next, Langenmantel's son, Jakob Alois Karl, and his younger brother-in-law made a steady stream of jokes in bad taste about buying an order like Golden Spur which Mozart was wearing, prompting Mozart's decision to leave Augsburg immediately. Only the intercession of Stein persuaded Mozart to stay and perform. The house was destroyed in 1944.

★ ★ CITY HALL (RATHAUS). Maximilianstrasse 1. At the beginning of July 1763, Leopold Mozart took his family to visit the Late Renaissance town hall (1618) by Elias Holl, with its two onion-domed towers, and its impressive golden salon (**Goldener Saal**). At the end of WWII, the town hall was destroyed, and has since been splendidly rebuilt. In the golden salon, the gold ceiling, wood parquet, wall frescoes, and carved wood portals and doors (with gold leaf) create a magnificent impression. The "Prince's Chamber" has also been restored; three other rooms have not yet been. Open daily 10 AM–6 PM.

SITE OF THE GENEOLOGICAL ROOM OF THE MERCHANTS (GESCHLECHTERSTUBE). Formerly Maximilianstrasse 2. On 16 October 1777, stopping *en route* to Paris with his mother, Mozart performed here for an academy of the patricians of Augsburg, with a local orchestra so bad that it was "enough to give you St. Vitus's Dance." After his initial ignoble treatment by the patrician family Langenmantel, his concert, in which he played a concerto and a sonata (K. 283/189h), was a success; Mozart's two concerts did not, however, cover his expenses in Augsburg. The **Geschlechterstube** was located, when facing the edifice (with the Perlach Tower on the left), behind, to the right. The present Maximilianstrasse is lined by many beautifully restored Renaissance homes of Augsburg's wealthy burghers.

★ ★ BAREFOOT CHURCH (BARFÜSSERKIRCHE). Mittlerer Lech 3. On 17 October 1777 Mozart was introduced to the famous organ by its builder, Stein, who had been organist here for decades. The organ unfortunately no longer exists. Today the church of the former Franciscan Monastery, which was severely damaged in WW II, is a Protestant church. Of the Gothic edifice of 1398, only much of the choir remains. Inside there are Baroque paintings, carved wood sculptures by Petel (about 1630), and a fine forged choir grating (1760); the cloister still has the star net vaulting of the late-Gothic period.[8] Open 10 AM–6 PM.

Augsburg. Geschlechterstube. Engraving by Matthias Seutter and J. C. Weyermann, 1741.

★ SITE OF THE THEATER (KOMÖDIENSTADEL). Address was Bei der Jakobskirche 3.[9] It was after Mozart's visit to the theater with his cousin and young Langenmantel, to see Reuling's *Singspiel* "Der Teufel is los" coupled with the ballet "The Drunken Farmer," that Mozart was made the object of ridicule by young Langenmantel and his brother-in-law. The nearby Protestant Jacob's Church, the Jacob Gate, and the Jacob Wall are interesting examples of fourteenth-eighteenth-century architecture.

[★ ★ FUGGER QUARTER (FUGGEREI)]. Fuggerei 56 (Administration building). This quarter, founded in 1519 by Fugger the Rich to house the town poor, is the first social settlement of its kind in the world, and still charges only a token rent (with the obligation to pray each day for the souls of the founders). The complex, with 66 gabled houses, has eight streets which have been closed every evening for centuries, and its own church.[10] The house at #14 Mittleren Gasse, which today has a commemorative plaque, was the second apartment of Franz Mozart, the great-grandfather of Mozart, who lived here from 1681, and died here, impoverished, in 1694.[11] At #13 Mittleren Gasse, there is a Fugger Museum, open 9 AM–5 PM (April to October).

SITE OF THE "THREE KINGS" INN ("ZU DEN DREI KÖNIGEN"). Jakoberstrasse 28. The three public concerts of the Mozart children, on 28 June, 30 June, and 4 July 1763, were probably given in this inn. Years before, on 14 January 1756, two of Leopold's most renowned works, the program symphonies "Peasant Wedding" and "Musical Sleigh Ride," had first been performed here.[12] The audience for the Mozart children was predominantly Lutheran, with few Catholic countrymen, and the financial results were less than satisfying. The inn no longer exists; it was destroyed in 1944.

SITE OF THE HOME AND PUBLISHING BUSINESS OF THE LOTTER FAMILY. Oberer Graben 53, near the Vogeltor. Leopold's violin treatise was published here by Johann Jakob Lotter in 1756, the year Mozart was born, and when the Mozart family visited Augsburg in 1763, they were often invited to the Lotter home.[13] The nearby Bird Gate (**Vogeltor**) was erected in 1445.

★ ★ ST. ULRICH AND AFRA. Ulrichsplatz. At the beginning of July 1763 Leopold took his family to see the church treasure here, where he used to sing as a child during church.[14] The former Benedictine abbey, founded by Maximilian I in the fifteenth century, and redone in the seventeenth-eighteenth centuries, is adjoined by a Protestant church of the same name (a tradition characteristic of Augsburg). Mozart wrote in October 1777 that he had played on the old organ by Stein, but he could not get a positive impression of the instrument. The three altars and pulpit by Hans Degler and the remarkable Baroque wrought iron grille in *trompe l'oeil*, are among the fine works of art in the church.[15] Open 10 AM–6 PM; *the treasury cannot be visited.*

★ ★ HOME OF ANDREAS STEIN. Ulrichsplatz 10. One of the most important sites for Mozart's 1777 visit was the home of the master organ/clavier builder Johann Andrea Stein, to whom Mozart facetiously introduced himself as "Trazom" (backward spelling) on 12 October 1777. Stein soon recognized him from his playing, and a great mutual respect followed. Stein persuaded Mozart to stay after his bad experiences with the Langenmantels, and arranged for a concert. Here, Mozart rehearsed the poor orchestra of the Protestant Musical Society on 19 October 1777 for his academy in the Fugger concert rooms. He was invited to lunch here, along with his cousin Bäsle and his uncle, and also heard Stein's young daughter play clavier, who squirmed and grimaced awkwardly. The charming facade, with a commemorative plaque, remains; the building behind it is modern. At the first address of Stein (not known), Leopold took Mozart in 1763, bought a portable Stein clavichord, and heard the extraordinary violin virtuoso Nardini play.

[★ ★ ★ SCHÄTZLERPALAIS]. Entrance Maximilianstrasse 46. Although this palace (1765–70) has no connection to Mozart's visits to Augsburg, it is a splendid example of eighteenth-century decoration; there is a breathtaking Rococo theater with lavishly carved wall decoration, stucco, and ceiling painting. Several fine art galleries are located in the palace. Open daily except Mondays, 10 AM–4 PM October to April; 10 AM–5 PM during other months; admission charge.

★ SITE OF THE "THREE MOORS" INN ("DREI MOHREN"). Maximilianstrasse 40. Leopold and his family, arriving on 22 June 1763 from Munich, stayed in this splendid hotel. All that remains of the 1723 hotel, which was demolished in 1951 following severe war damage, are the three busts of the Moors which are incorporated into the restrained, modern facade of the present luxury hotel. In addition to the Mozarts, Frederick the Great, Goethe, Emperor Francis II, and Napoleon stayed in the former hotel. On 16 March 1821, Mozart's son Franz Xavier stayed here.[16] In the square is a fine Hercules fountain (1602) by Adriaen de Vries.

★ ★ SITE OF THE FUGGER PALACE WITH CONCERT HALL. Maximilianstrasse 36–38. Mozart gave an academy here on 22 October 1777, playing his concerto for three claviers with the cathedral organist Johann Michael Demmler, and with Stein. In addition, Mozart conducted the orchestra of "connoisseurs and amateurs" in two symphonies, performed a piano concerto and a sonata (K. 284), and improvised fugues. Mozart's mother and a local newspaper notice noted that it was a magnificent success, although the two concerts in Augsburg did not cover their expenses there. A member of the

Augsburg. Gasthof zu den Drey Mohren (The Three Moors Inn). Engraving by F. P. Edelwirth and A. Klauber, early 19th century.

audience, who did not introduce himself, was Baron Melchior von Grimm, who was to play such an important role (largely negative) in Mozart's Paris sojourn in 1778. The broad complex (**Fuggerhäuser**), centering around many courts, was rebuilt in 1951 over the ruins of the town palace of Jacob "the rich," built in 1515. The facade, with long rows of windows, has been restored to its appearance in 1632. The attractive arcaded **Damenhof**, entered at #36, is noteworthy.[17] Open 8 AM–6 PM.

N o t e s

1 Baedeker, *Augsburg*, 28.
2 Mançal, "Augsburger Mozartstätten," 15.
3 Michelin, *West Germany*, 48.
4 Mançal, op. cit., 18.
5 Mançal, op. cit., 16.
6 Baedeker, op. cit., 29.
7 Mançal, op. cit., 23.
8 Baedeker, op. cit., 19.
9 Mançal, op. cit., 24.
10 Michelin, op. cit., 47.
11 Mançal, op. cit., 12.
12 Mançal, op. cit., 20.
13 Ibid.
14 Mançal, op. cit., 18.
15 Michelin, op. cit., 47.
16 Mançal, op. cit., 26.
17 Baedeker, op. cit., 14.

$\mathcal{M}$ozart in Berlin

19 May–28 May 1789

$\mathcal{I}$n 1789, Mozart was asked by Prince Karl Lichnowsky to accompany him to Berlin. Upon arriving, Mozart presented the landlord Moser with a copy of his six "Haydn" String Quartets, (K. 387, K. 421/417b, K. 428/421b, K. 458, K. 464, and K. 465). When it was known that Mozart was arriving in Berlin, the National Theater presented his *Abduction from the Seraglio*, which Mozart attended; during Pedrillo's aria, "Frisch zum Kampfe, frisch zum Streite," the second violin had a D# in the parts (instead of D), and Mozart supposedly finally called out, "Damn it, play D!" According to the anecdote, soon the whole audience and orchestra realized that Mozart was present.

Mozart wrote to his wife from the Tiergarten that he would soon play for Queen Frederick, but did not expect much to come of it. However, instead, Mozart received a commission from King Frederick William II to compose six string quartets, and six easy piano sonatas for young Princess Frederick Charlotte. Mozart is also believed to have attended the concert of his pupil, the ten-year-old Johann Nepomuk Hummel, while visiting Berlin.

M u s i c

Mozart later finished the string quartets, K. 575, K. 589, and K. 590 for King Frederick William II, and the piano sonata, K. 576, for Princess Frederick.

Berlin Sites

GENERAL SITE OF THE INN IN THE TIERPARK. Southern border of the park, near the present Tiergartenstrasse. Here Mozart wrote his letter to Constanze of 23 May 1789, "in an inn in the Tiergarten (in a summer house with a lovely view) where I lunched today *all by myself* in order to devote myself wholly to you." It is one of Mozart's most openly loving (and erotic) letters. In the 1780s, on the south end of the park, numerous inns were located, including the

"Court Hunter" and "Richard's Coffee Garden," which provided the meeting point of Berlin society; visitors to Berlin did not fail to visit them. None of these inns still exist today.[1]

★ TIERPARK. Although the present park is an attractive area of Berlin, the park as Mozart saw it no longer exists; from 1833 to 1840, this **Tiergarten** was redone in a landscape from English models by Lenné, although the Baroque groundplan of the crossing paths was maintained. The eighteenth-century sandstone statues have not survived.

Berlin. Engraving by Matthaeus Merian, 17th century.

[★ ★ ★ KNOBELSDORFF WING OF THE CHARLOTTENBURG PALACE]. Luisenplatz. On the night of 25 May 1789, Queen Frederick gave a reception at **Schloss Monbijou**; Mozart performed for her the next day. While this strongly suggests that the performance also took place in *Schloss Monbijou*, it does not eliminate the possibility that she received Mozart the next day at Charlottenburg, which was only a few miles away.[2] This summer palace of Frederick William II has, therefore, no documented Mozart connection; however, the wing designed by Knobelsdorff, and built 1740–49, provides a unique view of Berlin during the time of Mozart's visit. Frederick William II's apartments include two rooms decorated in the Chinese style and one room in the Etruscan style. The painting collection of Frederick the Great, the concert hall, the Rococo Golden Gallery, and the Banquet Hall should be seen. The park was landscaped in English taste by Frederick William II; the Belvedere today houses an exhibition of eighteenth-century Berlin porcelain.[3]

★ ★ ★ GENDARMENMARKT (TODAY PLATZ DER AKADEMIE). Mozart probably stayed on the Square, in the home of the trumpeter Moser, who lived at Charlottenstrasse 53; today the headquarters of the Christian-Democratic Union is located on the site.[4] Located on this magnificent square are the German Cathedral (consecrated 1708) and the French church. Since the two churches on the square were not imposing enough, Frederick II ordered that two cupolas be built. Destroyed during WW II, the square has undergone a splendid restoration, which is still in progress.

★ SITE OF THE NATIONAL THEATER. Platz der Akademie. Mozart is supposed to have attended his opera, *The Abduction from the Seraglio*, here on the day of his arrival in Berlin, 19 May 1790. The original theater that Mozart visited in 1789 was far different: a slender structure from 1776. The present building near the site is the **Schauspielhaus**, built by Schinkel from 1818 to 1821, after the **Nationaltheater** of Langhans burned in 1817. The theater was located in front of the Schauspielhaus, at the left side.[5] It was destroyed in WWII and reopened in 1984 after a splendid reconstruction.

[★ ★ FRENCH CHURCH]. Platz der Akademie. The church, built 1701–05, is the oldest building on the square. Between 1780–85, a cupola was added, making the two churches on the square like twins. Destroyed in WW II, it was reopened in 1983. Open Tuesday to Saturday Noon–5 PM; Sundays 1–5 PM.

[★ ★ DOME OF THE FRENCH CHURCH]. The dome was built between 1780–85 after the plans of von Gontard. Today the beautifully restored tower houses a museum and a wine restaurant with a view.

[★ ★ ★ UNTER DEN LINDEN]. Although very little is known about Mozart's week in Berlin, he undoubtedly visited the center of Berlin life, the broad avenue, Unter den Linden, where the Court Opera House was located. Nearby, Bebel Square (originally named Opera Square) can be found, with St. Hedwige Cathedral. The splendid facade of the former Royal Library, built from 1774 to 1780, can also be seen.

[★ ★ DEUTSCHE STAATSOPER]. *Opera seria* was held in the large Court Opera House, designed by Knobelsdorff in 1743. Today, numerous opera performances are held here.

[★ ST. HEDWIG]. Bebelplatz. Although the facade has been beautifully restored, the interior is modern and unsatisfying. The cathedral was built between 1747–1773, to plans by Knobelsdorff with the Pantheon in Rome as a model. It burned in 1943, and was rebuilt between 1952 and 1963.

Berlin. Schloss (Monbijou Palace). Engraving by J. G. Rosenberg.

GENERAL SITE OF MONBIJOU PALACE (SCHLOSS MONBIJOU). On the Oranienburger Strasse, south of the Sophienkirche; on the northern bank of the river Spree, east of the present Monbijou-Strasse.[6] A surprising oversight in the Mozart literature is the question of where Mozart performed for Queen Frederick on 26 May 1789; it was most likely in Monbijou Palace which stood on this site.[7] During this court appearance, Mozart most likely received the commission from King Frederick William II to write six string quartets (of which he wrote three, K. 575, K. 589, and K. 590), and six easy piano sonatas for Princess Frederick Charlotte (of which only that in D, K. 576, is known to have been completed). The former palace, built by Nehring in 1708, and enlarged by Knobelsdorff in 1788 for Queen Frederick, was completely destroyed in WW II, and the ruins were torn down in 1945; today the site of the palace has been laid out with a public park area.[8]

N o t e s

1 Communicated by Manfred Pahlmann, Berlin.
2 Communicated by Director Bliss, Geheimes Staatsarchiv Preussischer Kulturbesitz, Berlin.
3 Michelin, *Germany*, 65.
4 Communicated by Dr. Schmidt, Office of City History Documentation, Stadtarchiv, East Berlin.
5 Communicated by Dr. Schmidt, Office of City History Documentation, Stadtarchiv, East Berlin. Concerning the site of the Corsican Room (*Corsikaschen Konzertsaale*), where Hummel, a pupil of Mozart for about two years, gave a concert on 23 May 1789, and is said to have left the platform to embrace his teacher at the end of the program, Director Bliss communicated to me:

> In the "Berlinischen Nachrichten" in the advertisement about the concert in question, it was only communicated that "Tickets can be had from Mr. Corsica and Mr. Toussaint in the Poststrasse in the Inn "Zum Goldener Adler." Ten years later, in the "Anschaulichen Tabellen von der gesamten Residenzstadt Berlin," two inns of a Mr. Corsica are named, with the address "An der Ger-

traudenbruecke 4 and Oranienburger Strasse 8" (across from the Monbijou Castle). Since in the Berlin Address Calender of that time only a selection of inns are mentioned, it cannot be determined whether these inns existed in 1789.

6 Communicated by Director Bliss, Geheimes Staatsarchiv Preussischer Kulturbesitz, Berlin, and Manfred Pahlmann, Berlin.
7 The Prussian Archives located the Queen for me, by way of the "Berlinischen Nachrichten": on 25 May 1789 (the night before Mozart performed for her), Queen Friederick gave a reception at *Schloss Monbijou*. This does not eliminate the possibility that she received Mozart at Charlottenburg, only a few miles away. Communicated by Director Bliss, Geheimes Staatsarchiv Preussischer Kulturbesitz, Berlin.
8 Communicated by Director Bliss, Geheimes Staatsarchiv Preussischer Kulturbesitz, Berlin.

Mozart in Bonn (and Brühl)

Dates

27/28 September 1763 ▪ **(excursion to Brühl)**

In the first leg of their "Great Western" trip of 1763–66, *en route* to Paris, Mozart and his family stopped briefly in Bonn, arriving by boat from Coblenz (where Mozart had a cold). As they were not received by the elector, they visited the castle, and made a brief pilgrimage to the "Holy Steps." They traveled on to visit the castle at Brühl, and then continued their journey to Cologne.

Bonn Sites

★ ★ TOWN HALL AND SQUARE (RATHAUS UND MARKTPLATZ). Am Markt. Leopold cited the market square, with the Town Hall (1737–38), an ornate pink-and-grey Rococo structure designed by Leveilly, which has a colorful coat-of-arms and an emblem of the four seasons. The free staircase with the wrought-iron and gold railing was added in 1765, after the Mozarts' visit. The building, with the Elector's Room, and the Gobelin Room inside, is *closed to the public*. The foundation stone of the obelisk fountain in the square was laid by Elector Max-Friedrich in 1777.

[★ MINORITENKIRCHE (TODAY ST. REMIGIUS)]. Brüdergasse 8. Leopold cited the **"Kapuziner"** church, which was torn down in the nineteenth century. However, this former Minorite church off the Market Square existed in the time of the Mozarts' visit, and was in close proximity to the Market Square which they visited.[1] The high Gothic church with three naves, rebuilt 1738–48 under Elector Clemens August, has been redone in a simple but elegant modern style with several features in the old style, such as the carved pulpit. The church, where Beethoven played the Baroque organ (destroyed 1944), has been called St. Remigius since 1806.

Bonn. Marktplatz. Engraving by Balthasar Friedrich Leizel, 1780. Stadtarchiv Bonn.

★ ★ ELECTORS' RESIDENCE (KURFÜRSTLICHE RESIDENZ). Am Hof/ Regina-Pacis-Weg. The Mozarts visited the residence of the Archbishops of Cologne on 28 September 1763, and Leopold noted the numerous features which they saw: costly beds, paintings, porcelain, clocks, and a machine with a hand which wrote *vivat clemens*. The interior was destroyed by fire in 1777; only the exterior remains intact from the time of the Mozarts' visit, with an imposing sculpture group. In 1926–30, extensions based on the original plans were added to the building of 1697 on the city side. The gallery over the street in the form of a triumphal arch with the coat-of-arms of Elector Clemens August (today called the Coblenz Gate) originally held the archives for the Order of St. Michael. Leopold also cited the gardens, which are today simple lawns, and the menagerie, which no longer exists.

[★ ★ OLD CUSTOMS (ALTEN ZOLL)]. A few minutes from the Residence by foot, this former "Three King" Bastion from 1642 was a likely brief visit of the Mozarts for the view of the Rhein which it affords. The site, where the customs for the Rhein were formerly located, is one of the few remaining fortifications of the city from the seventeenth century.

★ ★ KREUZBERG CHURCH. Stationsweg 21. On 28 September 1763, in addition to seeing the Residence, the Mozarts made a visit to the church at the **Kreuzberg** with the "Holy Steps," where they had "the most beautiful view in the direction of Cologne." The church was built 1627–28. The extensive staircase by Balthasar Neumann, the middle part of which could only be ascended on the knees, was added by Elector Clemens August in 1746–51. Open daily 9 AM–6:30 PM (Summer); 9 AM–5 PM (Winter); the "Holy Stairs" are open daily 9 AM–5 PM.

SITE OF THE "GOLDEN CARP" INN ("ZUM GOLDENEN KARPFEN"). Rheinstrasse 24. After arriving in Bonn by boat on the evening of 27 September 1763, the Mozarts stayed in this inn overnight. It was torn down in the nineteenth century; because of the numerous changes in the street pattern, it is difficult to determine the exact location, but probably it was at #24, next to the present Hotel Beethoven.[2]

Bonn. Engraving by Matthaeus Merian, 17th century.

★ ★ POPPELSDORF CASTLE (POPPELSDORFER SCHLOSS) AND POPPELS-DORFER ALLEE. Leopold wrote that "we saw the Residence, Poppelsdorf, and everything there is to see." The castle, called "Clemensruhe," was built for Elector Clement Augustus in 1715 by Robert de Cotte, and is linked to the residence by a splendid avenue of chestnut trees. The French-influenced facade has three gables, while the Italianate inner courtyard has a semicircular colonnade. The building today houses the Mineral-Petroleum Museum of the University of Bonn. In the back, where there was once a moat, are found the botanical gardens of the University. Museum open Wednesdays 3–7 PM; Sundays 10 AM–5 PM; closed holidays; no admission charge. Part of the castle is open Monday–Friday 9 AM–6 PM (April to September); Monday–Friday 9 AM–4 PM (October to March); 9 AM–1 PM Sundays and holidays; closed on Saturdays.

Bruhl Sites

★ ★ BRÜHL CASTLE (AUGUSTUSBURG) AND FALKENSLUST HUNTING PAVILION. After visiting Bonn, the Mozarts traveled with the post to Brühl on 28 September 1763, where they visited Brühl Castle and Falkenslust. Elector

Clemens August von Bayern had the castle built largely from 1725 to 1748, after plans by Cuvilliés, as his summer residence. Leopold cited the splendid Rococo staircase with caryatids (attributed to Balthasar Neumann), which was built 1743–48. At Falkenslust, Leopold was impressed by the mirror room, the Chinese Room, the Indian house, and the "Snail's Shell."[3] In addition, he praised the inlaid black stone tables, created to appear as if copper etchings were lying on them, as well as the jewels, paintings, statues, and clocks. He also cited the garden, which today offers splendid formal flower gardens and extensive woodlands. The **Falkenslust** hunting pavilion (1729), as well as the Shell Chapel (**Muschelkapelle**) are still intact today and can be visited. Schloss Augustusburg is open 9 AM–Noon and 1:30–4 PM; closed Monday; closed December–January and holidays; admission charge. Schloss Falkenlust open 9 AM–Noon and 2–4 PM; closed Mondays; closed December–January and holidays; admission charge.

GENERAL SITE OF THE "ENGLISH GREETING" INN ("ZUM ENGLISCHEN GRÜSS"). On 28 September 1763, on their way to Cologne, the Mozarts stopped to see the Brühl Castle, and stayed overnight in this inn. The inn no longer exists; today on the former site, there is a large apartment building with stores.[4]

Bruehl. Augustusburg Castle of the Elector of Cologne. Engraving by Mettely after J. M. Metz. Stadtarchiv, Bonn.

N o t e s

1 This corrects the information in the Bauer/Deutsch/Eibl notes in which the Minorite church is suggested as the "Kapuziner" church referred to by Leopold. Bauer/Deutsch/Eibl, *Mozart Briefe*, V, zu 65/79.

2 Communicated by Frau Schulze, Stadtarchiv Bonn.

3 The *Fasanery* and the Indian House were demolished in 1822; the so-called *Schneckenhaus* (Snail's House) was demolished at an even earlier time; jewels, clocks and *objets d'art* mentioned by Leopold are unfortunately no longer in the possession of the Schloss Brühl. The original wall tapestries have also, in the course of the years, been lost. Communicated by Herr Mahlert, Verwaltung Schloss Brühl.

4 Communicated by Herr Mahlert, Verwaltung Schloss Brühl.

Mozart in Coblenz

Dates

17–27 September 1763

During their "Great Western" trip of 1763–66, Leopold and his family traveled down the Rhein from Mainz on a boatride interrupted by heavy winds and storms, arriving in Coblenz on 17 September 1763; from here they traveled to Bonn, then on to Brühl and Cologne. In Coblenz, during the approximately ten days they spent here, Mozart and his sister played for the Elector in the Philippsburg and visited the many sights of the city.

Coblenz Sites

SITE OF THE PHILIPPSBURG CASTLE (SCHLOSS PHILIPPSBURG). The Philippsburg Castle was the residence of the Elector of Trier since 1690. On the afternoon of 18 September 1763, Mozart and his sister played for the Elector Johann Philipp von Walderdorff in the **Rittersaal** of the Philippsburg; the castle was destroyed by the French army in 1801,[1] and was not rebuilt afterwards. The palace was located below Ehrenbreitstein fortress at the shore of the Rhein. The German Railroads (**Reichsbahn**) built the present railroad station on the site in 1936.[2]

★ ★ EHRENBREITSTEIN CITADEL (FESTUNG EHRENBREITSTEIN). The Ehrenbreitstein fortress seen by the Mozarts was destroyed in 1799 by the French, and the present neoclassical fortifications were built by the Prussians (1816–32). However, at the foot of the hill, the royal stables (1762), which belonged to the elector's residence and the **Dikasterial** building, built by Elector Schönborn to plans of Balthasar Neumann (1739) can be seen today. Leopold mentioned a well which descended "all the way to the Rhein," which was later cited by Jules Verne; there is now a cistern which no longer reaches the Rhein.[3]

In addition, Leopold had heard that a tunic of Christ was in the fortress; is now preserved in the Trier Cathedral. There is a Regional Museum and a Rhein Museum, as well as an extensive panorama of the Rhein from the end of the fortress at the left. The Rheinmuseum in the Ehrenbreitstein Fortress is open during the day.

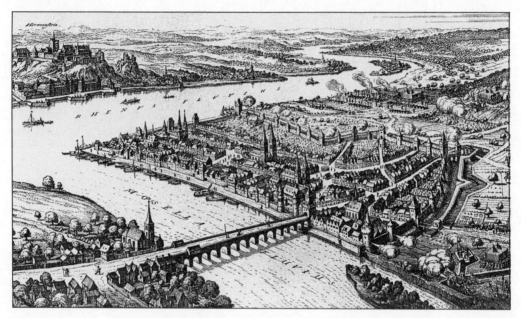

Coblenz. Engraving by Matthaeus Merian, 17th century.

★ ★ MOSEL BRIDGE (BALDUINBRÜCKE). One half of this fine stone bridge over the Mosel, mentioned by Leopold, is original. It was built from 1337 by Elector/Archbishop Balduin, who is commemorated by a modern stone statue. Formerly the bridge had fourteen arches; today eleven remain.

SITE OF THE "THREE CROWNS OF THE KINGDOM" INN ("ZU DEN DREI REICHSKRONEN"). Entenpfuhl. After a sail down the Rhein from Mainz which had to be interrupted due to heavy winds and storms, the Mozarts arrived in Coblenz on 17 September 1763, and stayed at this inn, which was destroyed in WW II[4]; they departed on 27 September 1763. It was later known for the casino and the "day and night" banqueting during the stay of the French emigrants in Coblenz.[5]

★ CHURCH OF OUR LADY (LIEBFRAUENKIRCHE). Florinspfaffengasse 14. Leopold cited the organist Harras at the **Liebfrauenkirche** in his travel notes. The Romanesque basilica was begun about 1180, and was finished in the thirteenth century, with the addition of a Gothic chancel in the fifteenth century, and domed Baroque towers in the seventeenth century.[6] Open Monday–Friday 8:30 AM–5:30 PM.

★ ST. CASTOR'S CHURCH (STIFTSKIRCHE ST. KASTOR). Kastorhof 8. Leopold mentioned Johann Kopp, canon in this historic Romanesque church, as well as the singer Johann Mehlen, who was also *Canonicus capitularis* here. This suggests that the Mozarts had close connections to this church during their stay in Coblenz. The art treasures are of interest, including 16 painted panels, with a portrait of St. Castor. Nearby the church, the attractive former administrative building of the **Deutschherrenhaus** and the flower court are noteworthy.

[★ CHARACTERISTIC SIGHTS OF COBLENZ]. While much of Coblenz has been destroyed, numerous buildings, both original and rebuilt, from the time of the Mozarts' visit can be seen today.[7] The German Corner, (**Deutsches Eck**), which received its name in 1216 from the Teutonic Order of Knights, is a scenic area of Coblenz. The **Deutscher Kaiser** is a sixteenth-century "residential tower" with battlements which survived the war. On Kornpfortstrasse (the name of which recalls the "Corn Gate" cited by Leopold), the "Three Kings" (**Drei Könighaus,** 1701; after reconstruction, it has been the home of the City Library since 1977[8]) has a fine bay window; it is directly in the area of the "Three Crowns of the Kingdom" Inn, where the Mozarts stayed. The Franconian Royal Palace, with rear towers from the fourth-century Roman wall, is an early eighteenth-century Baroque building on the site of a Merovingian palace which stood here from the fifth century. St. Florin's Church, with three naves, is a Romanesque basilica from the twelfth century with a Gothic chancel (1350). One of the finest groups in the Old Town, the **Altes Kaufhaus and Schoeffenhaus,** were built in 1419 and 1530; presently the Middle Rhein Museum (**Mittelrhein-Museum**) is located in the **Altes Kaufhaus.** The Old Castle, built in the thirteenth century, with extensions in Renaissance and Baroque style, is also of interest. The Mint Master's House of 1763 also remains, as do the "Four Towers" at Loehrstrasse (1689–91), buildings with ornamental oriel turrets. Finally, the seventeenth-century Town Hall (former Jesuit College), undoubtedly seen by the Mozarts, has a splendid portal and Rose window which remain, as well as a stone crucifix from the sixteenth century. An example of eighteenth-century architecture, which was built after the Mozarts' visit, is the pure neoclassical Electors' Palace (**Kurfürstliches Schloss**), built 1777–86 by the last elector, Clemens Wenzeslaus.

N o t e s

1 Bauer/Deutsch/Eibl, *Mozart Briefe,* V, zu 65/40–41 (N).
2 Communicated by Rolf E. Scheid, Verkehrsamt Koblenz.
3 Communicated by Rolf E. Scheid, Verkehrsamt Koblenz.
4 Communicated by Herr Schmidt, Stadtbibliothek, Koblenz.
5 Bauer/Deutsch/Eibl, op. cit., zu 65/38 (N).
6 Michelin, *West Germany,* 162.
7 For more detailed information, refer to "Koblenz an Rhein und Mosel," published by the Tourist Information Agency Coblenz.
8 Communicated by Herr Schmidt, Stadtbibliothek Koblenz. Schmidt also communicated that it was not possible to locate the home of Geheimrats (Secret Counselor) Lothar Franz von Kerpen, or the residence of the French or Imperial Envoys.

Mozart in Cologne

29/30 September 1763

During their "Great Western" trip of 1763–66, the Mozart family stopped briefly in Cologne, after visiting Bonn and Brühl. In Cologne, they visited the cathedral and the Treasury in the cathedral. Little is known about their visit to Cologne; perhaps (as Schenk speculated), Mozart played in the Jesuit Church and the Ursuline Church. After their visit, the family went to Aachen, before traveling on in the direction of Paris.

Cologne Sites

★ ★ ★ CATHEDRAL (DOM OR MÜNSTER). On 29 September 1763, the Mozarts visited what Leopold, with his distaste for medieval architecture, called the "dirty Cathedral." Although it is still blackened, the cathedral is an overwhelming experience, both for its size and its ornate decoration. It was the first Gothic church in the Rhineland, begun in 1248, with work suspended in 1550. The Mozarts saw it in an unfinished state, as it was not until 1880, after a feverish period of Neo-Gothic revival in Germany, that the cathedral was finished. The five splendid glass windows from about 1500 are noteworthy, as are the large Flemish polyptych (1520) called the "Altarpiece of the Five Moors," the tenth-century Othonian "Cross of Gero," the breathtaking twelfth-century "Magi's Shrine," and the Lochner altarpiece, "The Adoration of the Magi."[1] Leopold and Nannerl both mentioned the fascinating treasury (**Domschatzkammer**), and Leopold cited "the beautiful monstrance," stolen in 1976, and since recovered. The treasury is open 9 AM–5 PM (–4 PM from 1 November to 30 April); Sundays and holidays Noon–4 PM.

★ ★ JESUIT CHURCH (ST. MARIA HIMMELFAHRT). Mazellenstrasse 32–
40. In this splendid church visited by the Mozarts on 29 September 1763, *en
route* to Paris and London during their "Great Western" trip, it has been
suggested that Mozart played the organ.[2] The theatrical black-and-gold leaf
Baroque altar and the carved pulpit and canopy are of interest.

[★ ★ CHURCH OF ST. URSULA (KIRCHE ST. URSULA)]. Ursulaplatz 24.
Although Leopold cited the "Ursulinerkirche" in his travel notes, there is a
possibility that he was referring to this remarkable church, which is more
famous than the nearby Ursuline Church, and which is dedicated to the patron
saint of Cologne, St. Ursula.[3] This thirteenth-century Romanesque edifice has a
macabre aspect; hundreds of bones have been arranged in an ornamental fashion. The renowned treasury (**Goldene Kammer**) has numerous reliquary busts
(fourteenth-seventeenth century), and, in addition, there is the fine Aetherius
shrine (1170), embossed in copper, with enamel and gold.[4] The organ is original
from the time of the Mozarts' visit. The treasury is open Monday 11 AM–12
Noon, Wednesday 3–4 PM, Thursday 11 AM–Noon, Friday 3–4 PM, Saturday
4–5 PM; admission charge.

★ URSULINE CHURCH. Machabärstrasse. Leopold cited the "Ursulinerkirche" in his travel notes, and it has been taken for granted that he was referring
to this small Baroque church; in addition, it has been speculated that Mozart
would have played the organ here.[5] Leopold's taste in architecture leaned
heavily toward that of the eighteenth century, and this church, built 1709–
1712, would have been more in keeping with those tastes than the above-
mentioned Romanesque St. Ursula's Church.

★ ★ LARGE ST. MARTIN'S CHURCH (GROSS ST. MARTIN). Brigitten-
gasse. Leopold mentioned "Cologne St. Mergen" in his travel notes, in the
section on Coblenz. This is believed to indicate St. Martin's,[6] an impressive
twelfth-century Romanesque church, with a large square tower and four smaller
towers, in the traditional Rheinland style with three apses.

[★ OLD CITY HALL (RATHAUS)]. Alter Markt. Although not mentioned by
Leopold, this ediface, today largely reconstructed, lies between the cathedral
and the Heumarkt; the Mozarts would most likely have seen the original
structure from that period. It is partly Gothic from the fourteenth century, and
has a porch in Italian Renaissance style.

HEUMARKT. Leopold cited this small square near the Rhein in his travel notes.
Today, the small, nearby St. Martin's Church (**Klein St. Martin**) is of interest.

GENERAL SITE OF THE "HOLY GHOST" INN ("ZUM HEILIGEN
GEIST"). Rheinstrasse. For their overnight lodging in Cologne on 29 Septem-

ber 1763, the Mozarts stayed in this inn. Although Cologne has changed radically since the eighteenth century, today, on the Rheingasse, the thirteenth-century **Overstolzenhaus** presents an aspect of the city from the time of the Mozarts' visit.

NEUMARKT. This square, dominated by the impressive Romanesque church of the Holy Apostles (**St. Aposteln**), was also cited by Leopold in his travel notes. The eleventh-century church, with a fine apse from the thirteenth century and two octagonal lantern turrets, is a example of classic Rheinland Romanesque style.

N o t e s

1 Michelin, *Germany*, 93–95.
2 Schenk, *Mozart eine Biographie*, 88.
3 Cologne has two churches, one dedicated to St. Ursula, and the other called the Ursuline Church, in close proximity to one another. This unusual situation could easily have led to confusion on the part of Leopold. The original communication from the Cologne Historical Archives, in the Bauer/Deutsch/Eibl notes to the Mozart letters, cited the Ursuline church on Machabäerstrasse, without acknowledging the possibility for confusion which is inherent in the situation.
4 Michelin, op. cit., 97.
5 Schenk, op. cit., 88.
6 Bauer/Deutsch/Eibl, *Mozart Briefe*, V, zu 65/61.

Mozart in Dillingen

Dates

About 3–6 November 1766

The Mozart family stayed in Dillingen from 3 (or 4) to 6 November 1766, on their way back to Salzburg during the last leg of their "Great Western" trip, which lasted about three and a half years. At this time Mozart (who was ten years old at the time) and his sister performed for the Prince-Bishop Joseph I von Augsburg (Landgraf Joseph Ignaz Philipp von Hessen-Darmstadt), with a fine orchestra maintained by the Prince-Bishop.

Dillingen an der Donau Sites

★ ★ **RESIDENCE OF THE PRINCE-BISHOP (SCHLOSS).** Schlossstrasse 3. The Mozart family stayed in Dillingen from 3 (or 4) to 6 November 1766, on their way back to Salzburg during the last leg of their "Great Western" trip, which lasted about three and a half years. At this time Nannerl and Wolfgang (who was ten years old at the time) performed for the Prince-Bishop Joseph I von Augsburg (Landgraf Joseph Ignaz Philipp von Hessen-Darmstadt), who had just returned from a cure in Belgium. For their performance, including playing with the fine orchestra maintained by the Prince-Bishop, the children were given two rings; one, a beautiful ring representing a miniature of a vase of flowers made of turquoise, ruby, emerald, and a half-diamond, is today found in the Mozart birthhouse on Getreidegasse in Salzburg. The residence in Dillingen still exists; the oldest part of the castle dates from the thirteenth century, and was rebuilt in the fifteenth-sixteenth centuries, and it served for centuries as a residence for the

Prince-Bishops of Augsburg. It is no longer in the same form as in the eighteenth century; today the Bureau of Revenue and the local courts have their offices there. While there is no documentation about the room in which Mozart and his sister played, it is generally assumed that it was the festival hall of the castle; the hall with its remarkable stucco ceiling is still found in the castle, revealing the opulence of the decoration, although the room was subdivided into offices in the nineteenth century.[1] There are no set times to view these rooms; permission to view the rooms will be given by the administration. The Gothic Madonna (about 1517) at the west entrance, and the fourteenth-century Chapel of St. Ulrich, located in the garden (which has been restored to its form of 1740) are noteworthy.

[★ ★ "GOLDEN STAR" INN ("GOLDENER STERN")]. Corner of Königstrasse and Schlossstrasse. It can be assumed that the Mozarts lodged at this inn, which was the finest hotel in Dillingen at the time; it was also the post hotel, and only 50 meters away from the castle, the goal of the Mozarts during their stay in Dillingen.[2] The "Golden Star," an inn since 1652, has been the seat of a local savings bank (**Kreis- und Stadtparkasse Dillingen**) since 1955; however, it maintains the architectural structure and its exterior appearance from the time of the Mozarts' visit.[3]

[★ ★ CHARACTERISTIC SIGHTS OF DILLINGEN]. Dillingen offers many sights which the Mozarts may have seen in 1766. Spectacular Rococo interiors are represented in the University Church (today **Studienkirche**); the former Library Room of the Jesuit University (**Bibliotheksaal in der Akademie für Lehrerfortbildung**) at Kardinal-v.-Waldburg-Strasse 6; and the sumptuous Rococo Golden Room (**Goldener Saal**) of this same former University, with a large ceiling painting by Anwander from 1761–64. The Parish Church (**Basilika St. Peter**) at Klosterstrasse 5 was built 1619–28 by Alberthals, and has stucco decoration and a ceiling fresco from 1734/35; the eight-sided tower was built by David Motzhardt, the great-grandfather of Mozart, a hundred years before the Mozarts' visit. In addition, not far from Dillingen, David Motzhardt built the Pilgrimage Church in Kicklingen, which the Mozarts perhaps included in their itinerary. The convent of the Franciscans (**Franziskanerinnenkloster**), at Klosterstrasse 6, has a church which was built by Fischer in 1736–40; the ceiling fresco and altar paintings by Scheffler are noteworthy, as is the large crucifix (about 1520). Buildings from before 1766 are found at Heinrich-Roth-Platz 1 (1610), Weberstrasse 14 (seventeenth century), Kasernplatz 6 (1722–23), and Hafenmarkt 11 (inner structure from fifteenth-sixteenth century). The only remaining city gate (**Mitteltorturm**), at Königstrasse 25, has a structure from the thirteenth century; its present appearance dates from 1753. Other churches include that dedicated to Mozart's patron saint, St. Wolfgang (**St. Wolfgangskapelle**), at Kapuzinerstrasse 8 (1591), which has a large sculpture group by Luidi from 1728/29; **St. Leonhardskapelle**, at Donauwörther Strasse 20 (the oldest remaining sacred edifice in Dillingen); and the church of the **Kapuzinerkloster** at Kapuzinerplatz 1 (which dates from 1695 to 1697).

N o t e s

1 Communicated by Karl Baumann, Dillingen.
2 Layer, "Mozart und Dillingen," 20.
3 Communicated by Karl Baumann, Dillingen.

Mozart in Donaueschingen

19 October–about 1 November 1766

*M*ozart and his family did not have to announce their arrival in Don-aueschingen, as their arrival was awaited by the Prince von Fürsten-berg, a great lover of music. Their former servant who had accompanied them to Paris, Sebastian Winter, was in the service of the Prince at the time. During their stay in Donaueschingen, they performed "something special all the time" from 5–9 PM for nine evenings. Upon leaving, the generous Prince gave the Mozarts 24 Louis d'or and a diamond ring each for Nannerl and Mozart.

Music

Mozart performed many things during his nine evenings of music-making in the palace of Prince Joseph Wenzel von Fürstenberg. These included a set of solos for cello with bass, for the Prince of Fürstenberg; Leopold Mozart mentions them in his catalog of 1768, next to K. 33a and other violin and viola di gamba solos which have been lost. In addition, Mozart must have performed his previous works, such as the "Gallimathias Musicum," K. 32, the early manuscript of which is found today in the Donaueschingen Archives.

Later, in 1784, when Mozart was living in Vienna, Leopold sent Prince Joseph Maria Benedict von Fürstenberg, upon request, six of Mozart's piano sonatas, (probably K. 310/300d, K. 311/284c, K. 330/300h, K. 331/300i, K. 332/300k, and K. 333/315c), in addition to three piano concertos (K. 413/387a, K. 414/385p, and K. 415/387b, which were advertised in the "Viennese Newspaper" of 15 January 1783). Again, in 1786 Mozart sent three symphonies, K. 425, K. 319, and K. 338, to Prince Joseph Maria von Fürstenberg, as well as three piano concertos, K. 451, K. 459, and K. 488. As usual for his piano concertos, Mozart was very concerned and insistent that no one copy them.

Donaueschingen Sites

★ ★ PALACE (SCHLOSS DONAUESCHINGEN). Fürstenbergstrasse 2. Upon their arrival on 19 October 1766, the Mozarts were keenly awaited by Prince Joseph Wenzel von Fürstenberg, who invited them immediately to his palace where, for nine days, from 5 to 9 PM, they performed "something special all the time." The palace, built in 1723, however, is not in the same state as that seen by the Mozarts; it underwent extensive reconstruction and expansion from 1893–96.[1] Today it is the private residence of Prince von Fürstenberg and is in an excellent state of preservation. The reception room features a carved wood Florentine throne and sixteenth-century Flemish tapestries, and the large salon is noteworthy for its wall decoration, mirrors, portraits, and antique furniture (not necessarily from the time of the Mozarts' visit). The music room (**Festsaal**), where the princes assembled with their guests on important occasions throughout history, features wood parquet, a huge oval painted ceiling, and French

Donaueschingen. Schloss (Palace).

tapestries from the eighteenth century. It is the site of the Donaueschinger Contemporary Music Concerts, an important forum for contemporary music.[2] Open Easter to September 9–11:30 AM and 1:45–4:30 PM; closed Tuesdays; admission charge.

★ ★ GARDENS OF THE PALACE. Fürstenbergstrasse 2. Guests of the Prince enjoyed the opportunity of exploring the enormous gardens and parks of the palace, which are so extensive that a walk easily takes an hour-and-a-half. Open 24 hours a day; no admission charge.

[★ ★ ST. JOHN'S PARISH CHURCH (STADTPFARRKIRCHE ST. JOHANN)]. Karlstrasse 71. During their stay in Donaueschingen, the Mozarts, who were practicing Catholics, undoubtedly visited this splendid church, built 1724–43, next door to the palace. The multicolored veined marble and gold-leaf altar and pulpit, characteristic of Bohemian Baroque, are highly theatrical. The organ (1581), by Chrysosotomus von Breisach, was installed in the church in 1733. Open 8 AM–7 PM.

[★ ★ PAINTING GALLERY (FÜRSTENBERG COLLECTION)]. Karlsplatz 7. The gallery of paintings collected by the Fürstenberg family features works by Holbein the Elder, Grünewald, and Cranach. It was built in 1868, yet many paintings that the Mozarts saw in 1766 can be seen here.[3] Open 9 AM–Noon and 1:30–5 PM; closed Monday, and the month of November.

[FÜRSTENBERG LIBRARY (FÜRSTLICHE FÜRSTENBERGISCHE HOFBIB- LIOTHEK)]. Haldenstrasse 5. The library contains two original letters from Mozart to Sebastian Winter, as well the Mozart autographs "Geh'n wir in den Prater," K. 558, and "Ave Maria," K. 554.

N o t e s

1 "The palace was built in 1723; however, from 1893 to 1896 it underwent an extensive reconstruction and expansion." Communicated by Georg Goerlipp, Archivar, Fürstlich Fürstenbergisches Archiv.
2 Graf zu Lynar, *Schloss Donaueschingen*, 14.
3 "The painting gallery of the Fürstenberg house did not exist in the present form during the visit of the Mozarts; the present building was built in 1868. Certainly, however, a large number of paintings that were in the castle, and in other Fürstenberg buildings, are [in the present gallery]. Mozart certainly would have been able to see them." Communicated by Georg Goerlipp, Archivar, Fürstlich Fürstenbergisches Archiv. In response to my queries about Franz Anton Martelli, Herr Goerlipp responded, "[He] was the music director in the court from 1762, and left the service of the Fürstenberg court in 1770. Where Herr Martelli lived is unknown."

Mozart in Dresden

Dates

12–18 April 1789

During Mozart's trip to Berlin with Prince Karl Lichnowsky in 1789, they traveled from Vienna, stopped in Prague, and continued on to Dresden. Here, in addition to a private concert in their hotel, **Hotel de Pologne**, Mozart, with the singer, Josepha Duschek, and the nine-year-old cellist Nikolaus Kraft (for whose father Haydn wrote the Cello Concerto in D), performed at court for Elector Frederick August III von Sachsen and his wife Amalie, performing the Piano Concerto in D, K. 537. In addition, Mozart played a competition with the organist, Johann Hässler on the organ of the Hofkirche, after which they continued on fortepiano at the home of the Russian Ambassador. A quiet event of great interest took place during Mozart's stay in Dresden; Doris Stock made a silverpoint drawing of Mozart, which is one of the most touching (and representative) of all known portraits.

Music

At his private concert in the Hotel de Pologne, Mozart performed the String Trio, K. 563; Frau Duschek sang arias from *The Marriage of Figaro* and *Don Giovanni*.
During his concert for Elector Frederick August III von Sachsen, Mozart performed the Piano Concerto in D ("Coronation"), K. 537.
Also, according to Alan Tyson's studies of paper types and stave rulings, Mozart began work on the String Quartets, K. 575 and part of K. 589, using paper that came from a mill between Dresden and Prague.

Dresden Sites

[★ ★ ★ ZWINGER PALACE]. Despite the fact that he did not mention it, Mozart did not fail to see this monumental edifice because of the proximity of the opera house to the Zwinger. The palace was built in 1711/12, during the great era of Dresden Baroque, which began under Frederick August I; the architect Pöppelmann created a truly theatrical edifice, which presented a fabulous stage set to the court activities which now took place here.[1] Although destroyed in WWII, the Zwinger has been sumptuously rebuilt.

GENERAL SITE OF THE OPERA HOUSE. Connected to the Zwinger Palace.[2] On the evening of 15 April 1789, Mozart heard Cimarosa's opera, *Le trame deluse*, which he termed "truly wretched." However, he was surprised to meet the singer Rosa Manservisi here, who had sung in his opera *La finta giardiniera* in Munich in 1775. Frederick August I commissioned Pöppelmann to build the opera house, which was linked to the Zwinger Palace; it was constructed 1717–19.[3] Despite numerous renovations, the opera house could no longer meet the demands placed upon it, and in 1834 the architect Gottfried Semper built the renowned opera house.[4] This Semper Opera House was destroyed in 1944, and has recently reopened after a spectacular restoration.

Dresden. Engraving by Matthaeus Merian, 17th century.

★ ★ **CATHOLIC COURT CHAPEL (KATHOLISCHE HOFKIRCHE OR HOF-KAPELLE).** On 13 April 1789, Mozart heard a Mass by the chief *Kapellmeister* Johann Gottlieb Naumann (which Mozart termed "very mediocre") in this splendid church, built 1738–55 by Gaetano Chiaveri. In addition, here Mozart and Johann Hässler each played the famous Gottfried-Silbermann instrument for Prince Lichnowsky and Naumann. Mozart cited Hässler's skill with the pedals, but noted that he "is incapable of executing a fugue properly." In addition, Mozart's letter of 16 April 1789 indicates that Mozart performed *in quattro* with the organist Anton Teiber here in the chapel. The **Hofkirche** was destroyed in the night from 13 to 14 February 1945; the pipes of this last organ by Silbermann were saved, as they had been removed from the church, while the Rococo organ case was destroyed.[5] The instrument, as a result of a reconstruction project, sounded again for the first time in 1971.[6]

★ ★ **RESIDENCE PALACE (RESIDENZSCHLOSS).** Schlossstrasse. Here in the Residence of the Elector Frederick August III and his wife Amalie, Mozart played a court concert on 14 April 1789 at 5:30 PM in the room of the Electress. Included on the program was Mozart's Piano Concerto, K. 537 ("Coronation"); also participating were Josepha Duschek, the flutist Prinz, and the nine-year-old son of the cellist Kraft. Mozart noted, "This is something altogether extraordinary for this city; usually it is very hard to get a hearing in Dresden." Mozart wrote to Constanze that he received "a very fine snuffbox," but failed to mention the 100 ducats which were enclosed. The palace was the seat of the Sachsens (the House of Wettin) for centuries. In the eighteenth century, the rooms of the Electress were located in the west wing of the palace over the Green Vault (**Grünes Gewölbe**); the palace, almost completely destroyed in February 1945, is presently being rebuilt and will be used primarily as a museum.[7] Today the treasury of August the Strong is found in the Albertinum.

SITE OF THE HOTEL DE LA POLOGNE. Corner Schlossstrasse and Grosse Brüderstrasse. Both Mozart and Prince Lichnowsky stayed in this hotel from their arrival in Dresden on 12 April 1789 until their departure on the 18th. Later Lichnowsky was to stay here when visiting with Beethoven. A private concert, with Mozart on viola, Anton Kraft on cello, and supposedly Anton Teyber on violin, was performed here on 13 April 1789. The string trio, K. 563, was performed, and Josepha Duschek also sang "a great deal from *Figaro* and *Don Giovanni*. The inn stood until 1869, after which time the **Sächsische Bank** stood on the site; these buildings and all others on Schlossstrasse were destroyed in 1945, and the street was not rebuilt in its original form.[8]

Dresden. View of the Frauenkirche. Engraving by Canaletto, 1750.

SITE OF THE HOME OF JOHANN NEUMANN. Schlossstrasse 36, near the former *Hotel de Pologne*. On 12 August 1789, in the home of the secretary of the Privy War Council (who had written librettos for operas by Naumann), Mozart visited Josepha Duschek, who was staying here at the time. The next day, Mozart was invited here for breakfast with Prince Lichnowsky. The home, like the **Hotel de Pologne**, and all other houses on Schlossstrasse, were destroyed in 1945.[9]

GENERAL SITE OF THE HOME OF CHRISTIAN KÖRNER. Neustadt.[10] Mozart was invited here on 16 or 17 April 1789, at which time Doris Stock, the sister-in-law of Körner, sketched his last portrait, the famous silverpoint drawing. In addition, Mozart is said to have improvised at the piano, instead of sitting down for dinner, thereby providing his hosts with the "most refined dinner music." The house belongs to those buildings which were destroyed in the air bombing attack in February 1945.[11]

[★ ★ ★ **CHARACTERISTIC SIGHTS OF DRESDEN**]. Although all buildings connected with Mozart's visit to Dresden were destroyed in February 1945, there are numerous edifices (many reconstructed) in Dresden from 1789 and before. These include the **Kreuzkirche**, the **Torhäuser des Coselpalais** (1762–63), the monumental staircase before the **Johanneum** (1728–29), the **Stallhof** (1586–91), the equestrian statue of August II, which is called the Golden Rider, or **Goldene Reiter** (1736), the **Neustädter Wache** (1749–55), and the **Japanese Palace** (1727–37).

N o t e s

1 Communicated by Herr Zenker, Direktor des Stadtarchivs, Dresden.
2 Ibid.
3 Ibid.
4 Ibid.
5 Ibid.
6 Ibid.
7 Ibid. The Bauer/Deutsch/Eibl notes to the Mozart letters, and the Mozart literature surveyed by them, does not indicate where Mozart played for the Electress Amalie. Zenker's communication indicated that it was not the Zwinger but the Residenzschloss.
8 Communicated by Herr Zenker, Direktor des Stadtarchivs, Dresden.
9 Ibid.
10 The Körners also owned a summer house, in the Dresden suburb of Loschwitz; however, because of the early time of year of Mozart's visit, it is not to be assumed that Mozart visited there. The house in Dresden-Loschwitz still exists. Friedrich von Schiller stayed there repeatedly. Communicated by Herr Zenker, Direktor des Stadtarchivs, Dresden.
11 Communicated by Herr Zenker, Direktor des Stadtarchivs, Dresden. It was not possible to locate the home of the Russian Ambassador Belovselski-Beloserky, who had published a book on Italian music, and where Mozart was invited for lunch. In addition, after Mozart and Hässler played the organ in the Court Chapel, Mozart performed in the ambassador's home on the pianoforte for Hässler.

Mozart in Frankfurt

About 10–31 August 1763 ▪ 28 September–16 October 1790

ozart and his family first traveled to Frankfurt from Mainz, during their "Great Western" trip of 1763–66. Here, the children gave the first concert of five, one of which was attended by Goethe. They then returned to Mainz, continuing in the direction of Paris.

The visit of Mozart at the end of his life was for the coronation of Leopold II. It was, however, marked by bitterness; he wrote to Constanze, "If people could see into my heart, I would have to be ashamed; everything is cold, ice-cold." Despite dining with the "richest merchant in all Frankfurt," Franz Maria Schweitzer, Mozart and his fortunes were not improved in Frankfurt; the performance of *Don Giovanni*, planned in Mozart's honor by the Mainz Theater Company, was canceled in favor of an opera of Dittersdorf. In addition, the concert given by Mozart, at which he performed the "Coronation" Concerto, K. 537, was a success artistically, but not financially.

M   u   s   i   c

Mozart worked each day on the Adagio [of the Adagio and Allegro "for the clock-maker"], K. 594, "a work that is so disagreeable to me." On 12 October 1790, there was a performance of Mozart's *The Abduction from the Seraglio* by the director of the troupe of the Elector of Trier, Johann Böhm.

At his academy on 15 October 1790, at which Margareta Schick and Francesco Ceccarelli performed, Mozart played the Piano Concertos in F, K. 459, and in D, K. 537 (which is known as the "Coronation" Concerto, because of Mozart's performance in Frankfurt, during the coronation festivities of 1790).

Frankfurt Sites

★ ★ ★ ST. BARTHOLOMEW CATHEDRAL (DOM ST. BARTHOLOMÄUS). Domplatz 14. The festivities surrounding the crowning of Leopold II were the impetus for Mozart to travel to Frankfurt in 1790. The cathedral has been the site of imperial coronations since 1562, and it was here that Leopold II was crowned 9 October 1790. Inside the Gothic building dating from the thirteenth century, there are splendid altars of carved, painted wood, and impressive frescoes are found in the choir. The fifteenth-century tower, surmounted by a dome, is impressive. The **Wahlkapelle** (chapel where the seven Electors of the Holy Roman Empire made their choice) has an extraordinary altarpiece and two fine paintings.[1] Open 9 AM–6 PM.

Frankfurt. Engraving by Matthaeus Merian, 17th century.

SITE OF THE MOZART LODGING. Bendergasse 3. On 12 August 1763, the Mozarts may have lived here, as a window pane from the attic room, etched by Leopold, remains from this house. Today the area is entirely modern, comprising the **Kunsthalle** between the Römerberg and the cathedral. The glass is preserved in the Frankfurt Historical Museum.[2]

★ ★ ★ RÖMERBERG PLATZ. Leopold cited this square before the **Rathaus** (City Hall) in his travel notes of 1763; the Mozarts, in their traditional habit of seeing the particular sights of a city, did not fail to see this square (today reconstructed) of fifteenth-century houses. It received its name from the center house "Zum Römer," which, along with three adjacent buildings, became the City Hall. The small inner courtyard has a remarkable Renaissance stairway.[3]

SITE OF THE CONCERT ROOM OF HERR SCHARFF. Schärfengässchen 6/Holzgraben 15. The Mozart children gave public exhibitions here, on 18 August, 22 August, 25 (or 26) August and 30 August 1763, in the room furnished with two large crystal chandeliers, and 18 silverplated candleholders. For one performance, young Goethe attended with his family, and Goethe later remembered clearly "the little man in his wig and sword." In 1765, the building was replaced by a new structure. Today, parts of the ground floor are older, while the upper floors are modern and unobtrusive.

Frankfurt. Römerburgplatz. Engraving by Delkeskamp.

SITE OF THE HOME OF BANKER FRANZ SCHWEITZER. North side of Kaufhausstrasse "Zeil" between Brönnerstrasse and Schäfergasse.[4] Here, on 2 October 1790, Mozart dined with the Frankfurt Banker Franz Maria Schweitzer, whom he described as "the richest merchant in all Frankfurt"; Mozart would most likely have performed here as well. The early classical building was demolished at the beginning of this century.[5]

★ **LIEBFRAUKIRCHE.** Schärfengässchen 3. This church near the Scharff concert room was rebuilt in Gothic style in 1954, after damage in WW II. Open 9 AM–6 PM.

★ **ST. KATHERINE CHURCH.** Katharinenplatz. Supposedly Mozart played the organ here after Mass in 1790 and was rudely shoved by the church organist, who cited Mozart's daring modulations as being against "pure style."[6] The fourteenth-century church was burned in 1944, and has been redone in a simple modern style. The modern stained glass, vaulted wood ceiling, and modern altar are interesting. The present organs are also modern.

[★ ★ HAUPTWACHE]. This low watch building, an attractive edifice from the eighteenth century, is in close proximity to the St. Katherine Church.

SITE OF THE INN "THE WHITE SWAN" ("WEISSEN SCHWANEN"). Am Steinweg 12, on the corner of Theaterplatz. On the night of 29 September 1790, Mozart stayed in the hotel formerly on this site. There is a commemorative plaque with a relief in bronze showing the former hotel (no mention of Mozart) and citing the signing of the Frankfurt Peace by Bismarck. Today a cinema is located on the site.

SITE OF THE LARGE COMEDY THEATER (KOMÖDIENHAUS/ SCHAUSPIELHAUS/FRANKFURTER THEATER). Rathenauplatz.[7] Here, on 15 October 1790, at 11 AM, during the period of festivities for the coronation of Leopold II, Mozart played a private concert. A "new symphony" by Mozart (perhaps either the "Paris," K. 297/300a, K. 319, or K. 385) was performed, probably in two parts at the beginning and the end of the concert.[8] However, of greatest interest are the two Piano Concertos performed, probably K. 459 and K. 537, each of which has received the designation "Coronation." In addition, the singers Schick and Ceccarelli performed. The concert was satisfying "in regards to honors," but financially unsuccessful. Mozart attended the opera the same day, probably *Oberon, King of the Elves* by Paul Wranitzky. The earlier production of *Don Giovanni* scheduled for 5 October 1790 to honor Mozart was replaced by Dittersdorf's *Die Liebe in Narrenhause*. After the opening of the new Opera House (1880), the structure was demolished (1902), and was replaced by a commercial building, which survived the destruction of the war.[9]

★ ★ HOUSE OF BÖHM. Kalbächer Gasse 10 (Fressgasse). On 30 September 1790, Mozart moved in here with the theater director Johann Heinrich Böhm, whom he had met in Salzburg. Mozart wrote on 3 October 1790 that here, in his "hole of a room," he was working daily for Joseph Deym on the "Adagio and Allegro" in F minor and F, K. 594, for a mechanical organ. Although it was severely damaged in the war, the house has been attractively restored in style; presently it houses the pastry shop Lochner.

★ DOMINICAN CHURCH. Battonnstrasse (Kurtschumacherstrasse 23). Of the church cited in Leopold's travel notes from 1763, only the choir (1470–72) remains. Both the church and the monastery have been rebuilt after WW II, in a simple, elegant modern style; the modern stained glass in the choir is noteworthy.

SITE OF THE ''GOLDEN LION'' INN (''GOLDENEN LÖWEN''). (Fahrgasse 41.)[10] For part of the time from 10 to 13 August 1763, the Mozarts stayed in this inn. The street number no longer exists; it is intersected by the present Bahnhofstrasse.

★ DEUTSCHORDENSHAUS. Brückenstrasse 7, near the **Alte Brücke**. This massive Baroque structure with three wings was cited by Leopold in his travel notes of 1763. It was remodeled in 1709–15 by Kayser, and was the location of the former German Order. In 1943 it was damaged, and rebuilt, with alterations in 1963–65.

[★ ST. MARIA CHURCH]. Brückenstrasse 3–7. This Baroque church, attached to the German Order complex, is from 1741 to 1751 with a facade by Kirchmeyer. It was damaged in 1943, and was restored in Baroque style.

SITE OF ''THE THREE OXEN'' INN (GASTHOF ''ZU DEN DREI RINDERN''). (Brückenstrasse 26.)[11] On the night of 28 September 1790, Mozart stayed in this inn, near the House of the German Order. The address no longer exists; the site is presently in the modern intersection.

N o t e s

1 Michelin, *Germany*, 121–22.
2 As the message is etched in glass, it is impossible to make a handwriting analysis to determine if this is, in fact, by Leopold Mozart. I am very skeptical that Leopold Mozart wrote this message, as he would have risked censure for damaging the property of the inn.
3 Michelin, op. cit., 120.
4 Prior to the publication of this book, the location of this site has been overlooked in the Mozart literature. Communicated by Dr. W. Klötzer, Stadtarchiv, Frankfurt.
5 Communicated by Dr. W. Klötzer, Stadtarchiv, Frankfurt.
6 Schenk, *Mozart and His Times*, 427–28.
7 Published for the first time in the Mozart literature. Communicated by Dr. W. Klötzer, Stadtarchiv, Frankfurt.
8 Bauer/Deutsch/Eibl, *Mozart Briefe*, VI, zu 1140/3.
9 Communicated by Dr. W. Klötzer, Stadtarchiv, Frankfurt.
10 One of the many addresses repeatedly cited in the Mozart literature that no longer exists.
11 One of the addresses cited in the Mozart literature that no longer exists.

Mozart in Heidelberg

D a t e s

About 25 August 1763 • **9 December 1778**

During the beginning of the "Great Western" trip of 1763–66, Mozart and his family took an excursion from Schwetzingen to Heidelberg, where they spent a great deal of time walking through this beautiful city. Mozart played the organ in the Church of the Holy Ghost, "arousing such admiration that . . . his name and the circumstances were inscribed on the organ for a perpetual remembrance."

On his way back to Salzburg from the ill-fated Paris sojourn of 1778, Mozart again passed through Heidelberg.

Heidelburg Sites

★ ★ CHURCH OF THE HOLY SPIRIT (HEILIG-GEIST-KIRCHE). Heiliggeist-strasse. On about 25 July 1763, Mozart played on the organ in this Protestant church, which has a history reaching back to the fifth century. Leopold wrote, on 3 August 1763, ". . . our Wolfgang played the organ to such astonishment that, as a perpetual reminder his name was inscribed there by the order of the Dean." The Gothic church has a chancel which formerly was the sepulcher of the palatine electors; since 1693 only the tomb of Ruprecht III remains.[1] The organ from the time of Mozart no longer exists.[2] The International Heidelberger Organ Summer (**Orgelsommer**) offers concerts in July and August: Fridays and Saturdays 9–10 PM, Sundays 11:30 AM–12:30 PM; regular concerts take place during the year 11:30 AM–12:30 PM on Sundays and holidays.

★ ★ ★ HEIDELBERG CASTLE (SCHLOSS). The castle, which the Mozarts came to Heidelberg to see, is a ruin of the fortress of 1689–93, and showed the "sad fruit of the former French wars" of Louis XIV. The great vat cited by

Leopold, built for Elector Karl Theodor in 1751, holds 49,000 gallons; it is in the cellar of the Friedrich's Wing.[3] The wallpaper and silk workshops cited in the travel notes of Leopold and Nannerl were destroyed by lightning in 1764.[4] The well cited by Nannerl is the Upper Prince's Well (**Obere Fürstenbrunnen**) which has the date 1738 hidden in a text, on the right staircase walls.[5] Leopold cited "the most beautiful view," perhaps from the **Rondell** or the gardens (**Schlossgarten**), landscaped by Friedrich V between 1616 and 1619. Also of note are the Fat Tower (**Dicker Turm**), the elegant Elizabeth Gate (**Elisabethen-tor**), built in a single night in 1615 as a surprise for the wife of Friedrich V, the defensive Sprung Tower (**Gesprengter Turm**), the Gothic **Library** building and loggia, **Friedrich's Wing**, the **Great Terrace**, and the **Otto-Heinrich Wing**.[6] Open daily 9 AM–5 PM (1 April–31 October); 9 AM–4 PM (1 November–31 March); admission charge.

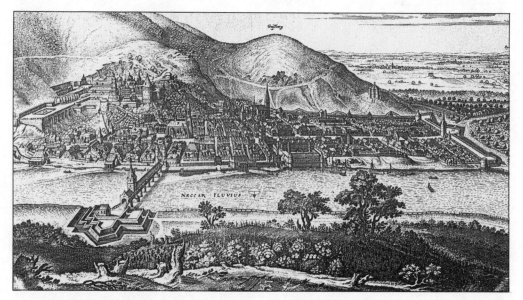

Heidelberg. Engraving by Matthaeus Merian, 17th century.

SITE OF THE "THREE KINGS" INN ("ZU DEN DREI KÖNIGEN"). Hauptstrasse Nr. 160. The inn where the Mozarts stayed no longer exists. However, since 1832, the Three Kings Street recalls the name former **Gasthof**.[7] The edifice has been rebuilt numerous times, and nothing remains of its original appearance, except perhaps the sandstone window casings and the cornice frieze.[8] Presently it has an unassuming, functional facade with a commemorative plaque citing Robert Schumann's stay in Heidelberg.[9]

★ ★ ★ CHARACTERISTIC SIGHTS OF HEIDELBERG. The marketplace (**Marktplatz**) lies between the church in which Mozart performed and the City Hall (**Rathaus**); the Knight's Mansion (**Haus zum Ritter**) built in 1592 is a masterpiece of the late Renaissance; the Baroque palace, presently the Electoral Palatinate Museum (**Kurpfälzisches Museum**) has an outstanding altarpiece by Riemenschneider (1509) of the twelve Apostles.[10]

N o t e s

1 Michelin, *Germany*, 149.
2 Despite the belief for many years that single parts of the organ still existed, rebuilt into the present organ, this has been conclusively disproved. It is not known if the inscription cited by Leopold has survived. Mauthe, "Heidelberger 'Mozart-Orgel,' " 262.
3 Michelin, op. cit., 148.
4 Bauer/Deutsch/Eibl, *Mozart Briefe*, V, zu 57/18.
5 Mauthe, "Heidelberger 'Mozart-Orgel,' " 255–6.
6 Michelin, op. cit., 147–48.
7 Bauer/Deutsch/Eibl, op. cit., 57/15.
8 Mauthe, op. cit., 254.
9 Mauthe, op. cit., 253–55.
10 Michelin, op. cit., 149.

Mozart in Leipzig

Dates

20–about 23 April 1789 ▪ 8–17 May 1789

During Mozart's trip to Berlin with Prince Karl Lichnowsky in 1789, they traveled from Dresden to Leipzig. Here Mozart improvised "without compensation" for a delighted large audience in the church of J. S. Bach, St. Thomas, on themes including the choral "Jesu, meine Zuversicht." In addition, Mozart copied Bach's music enthusiastically from parts placed all around him.

After leaving for Potsdam, Mozart again returned to Leipzig, where he found his friend, Josepha Duschek, the singer. Together, they gave a concert in the Gewandhaus; at the rehearsal with many elderly musicians in the orchestra, Mozart took the Allegro of one of his symphonies very rapidly, to their annoyance, in order to avoid a concert with faltering tempos. Supposedly, Mozart refused to rehearse the piano concertos, saying, "The parts are correctly written; they play correctly, and so do I." During the concert, consisting entirely of his own compositions, Mozart performed the C Major Piano Concerto in C, K. 503, from a type of musical shorthand, perhaps to prevent pirated copies from being made; as usual, Mozart ended the concert with generous encores.

Music

"Little Gigue for Clavier," K. 574, inscribed in the album of Karl Immanuel Engel, Leipzig organist of the Saxon Court.
A six-voice double canon, K. Anh. 4/572a, supposedly written at the home of Doles, is lost.
At Mozart's Gewandhaus concert, he performed the Piano Concertos, K. 456 and K. 503. Josepha Duschek sang the Scene with Rondo, K. 505, and probably also the Scene, "Bella mia fiamma," K. 528, which Mozart wrote for her in Prague. As an encore, Mozart improvised in C minor (probably the C minor Fantasy, K. 475), and closed with his piano variations in E flat, "Je suis Lindor," K. 354/299a.

Leipzig Sites

★ ★ ST. THOMAS CHURCH (THOMASKIRCHE). Thomaskirchhof. In the presence of the choirmaster Friedrich Doles and the organist Karl Goerner, Mozart improvised here for about an hour on 11 April 1789, "without previous announcement and without compensation." The organ that Mozart played no longer exists, although the exterior of the church remains substantially in the form which Mozart saw. However, the Baroque interior was completely changed from 1884–89 to neo-Gothic style. The crucifix by Loebel, the splendid baptismal font from 1614/15 (where Richard Wagner, and 12 of Bach's children were baptized), and the magnificent bas-relief (the epitaph of Leicher from 1612) depicting Daniel in the Lion's Den are exceptional works of art to be found in the church. Numerous vocal and organ concerts are given in the church today. Open daily 8 AM–6 PM (March–October); 8 AM–5 PM (November–February); 8 AM–4 PM (December–January).

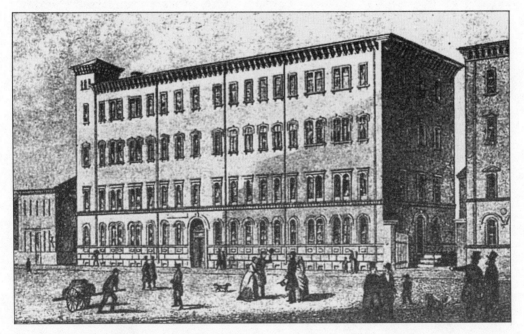

Leipzig. Gewandhaus. Unsigned engraving, early 19th century.

SITE OF THE THOMAS SCHOOL (THOMASSCHULE). Thomaskirchhof 18. During Mozart's visits to Leipzig in 1789, he heard the choir of the school perform Bach's motet, "Singet dem Herrn ein neues Lied," which delighted him, according to the eyewitness, Rochlitz. In addition, Mozart is said to have looked enthusiastically at a great deal of Bach's music from separate parts, and to have asked for copies. Here, where the present Superintendent's building is located, was the **Thomasschule**, which was demolished in 1902. A commemorative plaque notes the site of the old school, as does a small relief on the back of the Bach monument of 1909.[1]

Leipzig. St. Thomas Church and St. Thomas School. Engraving by Georg Balthasar Probst. Stadtgeschichtliches Museum.

SITE OF THE HOME OF THOMAS SCHOOL CANTOR DOLES. Thomaskirchhof 18. In addition to performing for Johann Friedrich Doles at the Thomas Church on 22 April, Mozart is believed to have visited him several times, and to have written the lost canon in 6 voices (K. Anh. 4/572a) for him. Doles, like his teacher and predecessor, J. S. Bach, lived in the sixteenth-century **Thomasschule** building,[2] which was demolished in 1902.

SITE OF THE HOME OF UNIVERSITY RECTOR PLATNER. Katharinenstrasse 12.[3] During his visits to Leipzig, Mozart was invited by the rector of the university, the medical doctor Ernst Platner, and performed for him on the fortepiano. This Baroque edifice was destroyed in 1943 during a bombing attack.

SITE OF THE FORMER GEWANDHAUS. Universitätsstrasse.[4] Mozart's only Leipzig concert, in which Josepha Duschek also participated, was held here on 12 May 1789 at 6 PM. Mozart performed the Piano Concertos K. 456 and K. 503, and probably the Fantasie in C minor, K. 475, and variations. It is said that he refused to rehearse the piano concertos prior to the concert, noting, "The parts are correctly written; they play correctly, and so do I," and that he performed from a special notation consisting of only the figured bass part and the principal ideas, to prevent the concertos from being pirated.[5] The **Gewandhaus** in which Mozart performed was demolished in 1895; the **Neue Gewandhaus**, built in 1884 in the area of the city center, was destroyed in 1944. The present modern **Neue Gewandhaus** is on Karl-Marx-Platz, across from the new Opera House.[6]

Leipzig. Promenade. Engraving by J. A. Rosmaesler, 1777. Stadtgeschichtliches Museum, Leipzig.

[★ ★ MISCELLANEOUS SITES OF LEIPZIG]. Although the center of Leipzig was over 80 percent destroyed in WW II, several original or reconstructed sites are representative of the time of Mozart's visit in 1789. Among the few buildings or monuments which remain from the time, and have been preserved, are the old City Hall, rebuilt in Renaissance style in 1556 and today Museum of the City of Leipzig; the **Nikolaikirche**; several Baroque houses on Katharinenstrasse; the 1770 monument to Gellert by Öser; the King's House (**Königshaus**); and **Barthels Hof** on the Market Square.[7] Other original or reconstructed buildings include the **Bosehaus**, the present Johann-Sebastian-Bach Museum, with occasional Mozart exhibitions; the Old Exchange (**Alte Boerse**) built in 1678–87 in Baroque style; the old Weighing Station (**Alte Waage**) built in 1555 and rebuilt in 1964 after destruction in WW II; the Coffee Tree (**Kaffeebaum**), founded in 1694, where numerous personalities gathered; the vaulted **Auerbachs Keller**; the

Romanushaus, the most beautiful Baroque building in Leipzig, built 1701–04; and the Rococo **Gohliser Schlösschen** (Little Palace) built in 1756.

N o t e s

1 Communicated by Dr. Klaus Sohl, Museumsdirektor, Museum für Geschichte der Stadt Leipzig.
2 Ibid.
3 From the Leipzig Address Book (1789); communicated by Dr. Klaus Sohl.
4 Communicated by Dr. Klaus Sohl.
5 Schenk, *Mozart and His Times*, 414.
6 Communicated by Dr. Klaus Sohl.
7 Ibid.

Mozart in Mainz

**About 3 August to about 10 August 1763 · 31 August–middle September 1763 ·
16–21 October 1790**

During the extensive "Great Western" trip of 1763–66, Leopold took his two musical prodigies to Mainz. Unfortunately, the Elector Josef von Breidbach-Bürresheim was very ill; instead, for the first time, Leopold gave a public concert. In addition, they met Anna de Amicis, a Neapolitan singer who later sang in Mozart's Milanese opera, *Lucio Silla*.

While in Mainz, Mozart's family made an excursion to Frankfurt am Main on the market boat. Mozart and his sister gave another concert in Mainz when they returned to Mainz, before traveling to Coblenz; they also visited Wiesbaden and Kostheim.

Toward the end of his life, Mozart stopped in Mainz during his financially unsuccessful trip to Frankfurt for the coronation of Leopold II in 1790. Mozart's letter to Constanze from Mainz, despite "many tears" on the last page, is full of "a great number of kisses flying around." Before continuing on to Mannheim, Mozart played a concert at the Elector's Palace.

Mainz Sites

★ ★ ST. AUGUSTINE CHURCH. Augustinerstrasse 34. Mozart probably played the organ here during his visit to Mainz in 1790.[1] The splendid church, built in 1768 as a monastery church, has been a seminary church since 1805. It reopened in 1990 after a restoration, and features a facade of pink sandstone with a sculpture group. The organ is original; it was built by Stumm in 1773.[2]

★ ★ "ROMAN KING" INN ("ZUM RÖMISCHEN KÖNIG"). Grebenstrasse 26. On 13 August 1763, Leopold wrote, "We lodged at the 'King of England' and, in the meantime, gave a concert at the 'Roman King.'" In a later letter, from 4 December 1777, Leopold wrote that they had given three concerts in Mainz, taking in 200 gulden, although they "did not play before the Elector who happened to be ill." The 'Roman King' was not destroyed in the war, and is today beautifully restored.[3] The Rococo figure of the Roman King is from 1774.[4]

★ ★ CATHEDRAL ST. MARTIN AND STEPHAN. Am Markt. Inside this mammoth, reconstructed Romanesque structure, mentioned in Leopold's travel notes, there are attractive mosaics and altars of carved stone. Open (May to September) Monday–Friday 9 AM–6:30 PM, Saturdays 9 AM–4 PM, Sundays 12:30–2:45 PM and 4–6:30 PM; (October to April) Monday–Friday 9 AM–5 PM, Saturdays 9 AM–Noon and 2–4 PM, Sundays 2–2:45 PM and 4–4:30 PM.

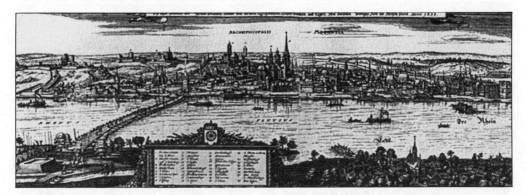

Mainz. Engraving by Matthaeus Merian, 17th century.

SITE OF THE "KING OF ENGLAND" INN ("KÖNIG VON ENGLAND"). Liebfrauplatz.[5] The Mozart family stayed here, in one of the most elegant inns of Mainz, during their visits to the city in 1763. About 80 percent of the city center of Mainz was destroyed in WW II, including this edifice; the inn was in the immediate vicinity of the "Roman Emperor" Inn, approximately where the present building of the Gutenberg Museums, with exhibition rooms, stands.[6]

★ ★ ★ "ROMAN EMPEROR" INN ("ZÜR RÖMISCHEN KAISER"). Liebfrauenplatz 5. In 1763, the seven-year-old Mozart and his sister gave a concert here. As the Elector was ill, they were unable to appear at court, and Leopold decided for the first time to present them in a public concert. Today the splendid edifice, with an ornate vaulted entrance of white stucco, houses the administrative offices for the Gutenberg Library. The structure, built as a private castle, became the "Roman Emperor" in 1742. It burned in the last war and has been beautifully rebuilt, maintaining the late Renaissance and Baroque features. The courtyard between the building and the modern Gutenberg Library are noteworthy.

★ ★ OSTEINER HOF. Schillerplatz 1. Leopold met and visited Count Ostein here during his trip to Mainz in 1763, which suggests that Mozart also played here. The facade has a splendid pink-and-white bow front (traditional colors for Mainz), and wrought-iron balconies. The facade, from 1749, has been restored to perfection with a massive coat-of-arms, while the interior has been reconstructed partly in eighteenth-century style. As it is the seat of the West German Armed Forces, *it can only be viewed from outside.*

★ BASSENHEIMER HOF. Schillerplatz 2. Leopold, and perhaps his family, visited Count Johann Bassenheim here. Today the building is the seat of the Minister of the Interior. Since the inside has been modernized, only the restrained facade (1750–56), which has been beautifully restored, is of interest.

★ ★ SCHÖNBORNER HOF. Schillerplatz 11. Leopold met and visited Count Hugo Schönborn here in 1763. Of the three buildings cited on Schillerplatz, this one has many original architectural features inside, and has been maintained in eighteenth-century style. Today it houses the **Institut Français**. The marble staircase with wrought iron and gold leaf can be seen, as well as a large salon on the *piano nobile* which has undergone numerous changes in style.

SITE OF THE "ARNSBERGER HOF." Schusterstrasse 45.[7] When he arrived in Mainz on 16 October 1790, Mozart stayed in the modest inn previously on this site, across the street from the "Casino." Today this part of Schusterstrasse is dominated by modern structures; the inn was demolished in 1906 to make way for the department store **Tietz**.[8] The building across the street, at the corner of Schusterstrasse and Christofstrasse, belonged to the society "Kasino Hof zum Gutenberg," and burned at the end of the nineteenth century; it was replaced with a new building and today a pharmacy is located on the site.[9] At # 42, there is a charming edifice with the date 1737 inscribed in the facade.

★ ★ DALBERGERHOF. Klarastrasse 4; formerly named the "pig's head" ("*Bey dem Saukopf*"). Leopold called here on the director of court music, Baron Friedrich Dalberg, in hopes of performing at court. The splendid monumental structure, with a sculpture group on the facade, has been remodeled inside in a modern style, although the staircase is in the original style. Today it is no longer the Police Headquarters, but instead houses the Peter Cornelius Conservatory, and the **Landesmusikrat**.

★ ★ ★ ST. PETER'S CHURCH. Petersstrasse 3. Mozart is believed to have played on the organ in this church, one of the most splendid Rococo churches (1752–56) in the Rheinland before its destruction in 1945.[10] The restoration, however, is breathtaking: the rococo pulpit, entirely frescoed ceiling, and altars of gold, black, and pink marble are noteworthy.

★ ★ ELECTOR'S PALACE (KÜRFÜRSTLICHES SCHLOSS). Ernst-Ludwig-Platz 2. On 30 October 1790, Mozart played a concert in the Academy Room (**Akademie-saal**) for the Elector Friedrich von Erthal. While the splendid, ornate

Renaissance facade remains, inside there is nothing of its previous splendor, as it was destroyed by American troops in WW II; the original **Akademie-saal** no longer exists.[11] Today the palace houses the Roman-German Museum.

★ MISCELLANEOUS SITES OF MAINZ.[12] Nannerl mentioned the Elector's palace "**An der Favorite**" in her travel notes. While the palace no longer exists, today there is a restaurant of the same name, with a view of the city. Only the outline remains of the Fish Tower noted by Leopold in his travel notes, although the medieval structures, the Wood Tower and the Iron Tower, have been beautifully restored, and can be seen. Leopold and his family traveled with the **Marktschiff** from Mainz to Frankfurt, and it is still possible to go by boat from April until the end of October.

N o t e s

1 Schenk, *Mozart, Eine Biographie*, 553.
2 Communicated by Jürgen Schmidt, Mainz Tourist Information Office.
3 Communicated by Herr Schütz, Archivdirektor, Mainz.
4 H. Schrohe, *Bilder aus der Mainzer Geschichte (Hessische Volksbücher*, Band 48, 1922), 66ff.
5 The Bauer/Deutsch/Eibl annotations to the Mozart letters cite the address Am Markt 37. This address, like many cited repeatedly in the Mozart literature, no longer exists.
6 Communicated by Herr Schütz, Archivdirektor, Mainz.
7 Communicated by Herr Schütz, Archivdirektor, Mainz, in response to my queries, and published here for the first time in the Mozart literature.
8 Communicated by Herr Schütz, Archivdirektor, Mainz.
9 Ibid.
10 Bauer/Deutsch/Eibl, *Mozart Briefe*, V, zu 60/14; compare A.B. Gottron, *Mozart und Mainz*, 27.
11 Communicated by Jürgen Schmidt, Mainz Tourist Information Office.
12 Leopold cited the Lord High Chamberlain Baron von Eltz in his travel notes, which suggests that he also visited him, and that Mozart played for him (Schenk writes, "Leopold called upon the Lord High Chamberlain, Baron Eltz"; *Mozart and His Times*, 55). Herr Schütz, Director of the Mainz Archives, located the home of Count Anselm Casimir Franz zu Eltz in response to my questions. He owned a city *palais*, the Eltzer Hof at Bauhofstrasse 3–5 and the corner of Grosse Bleiche, in which he lived when he was in Mainz.

Mozart in Mannheim

Dates

About 30 July to about 1 August 1763 ▪ 30 October 1777–14 March 1778 ▪ 6 November–9 December 1778 ▪ About 23–25 October 1790

*I*n addition to the stay of the Mozart family during the "Great Western" trip of 1763–66, Mozart had two important sojourns in Mannheim in 1777–78, on the way to Paris, and *en route* to Salzburg from Paris. The amount and quality of music written by Mozart here indicate the significance of his visits to Mannheim.

The splendid Mannheim orchestra, which later transferred to Munich along with the Elector Karl Theodor, was an important influence in the eighteenth century, both for musical taste and style. Despite good relations with Mannheim musicians (composers Christian Cannabich and Ignaz Holzbauer, and the flutist G. B. Wendling), Mozart was unsuccessful in finding an appointment in the city, and fell deeply in love with Aloisia Weber, who was not interested; Mozart later married her sister. In reaction to Mozart's increasingly apparent independence, Mozart's mother suggested to Leopold that she continue on to Paris with him, instead of returning to Salzburg as planned; she ultimately died in Paris.

Finally, on the return from his trip to Frankfurt, where Mozart performed during the coronation ceremonies of Leopold II (for which he pawned the family silverplate), Mozart stopped in Mannheim, and heard his opera, *The Marriage of Figaro*.

Music

Piano sonatas K. 309/284b and K. 311/284c.
Concerto for flute, K. 313/285c, and Concerto for flute (also in a version for oboe), K. 314/285c, were both written in early 1778; also an Andante for flute, K. 315/285e.
Flute quartets K. 285 and K. 285a.
Sonatas for keyboard and violin, K. 301/293a; K. 302/293b; K. 303/293c; K. 305/293d; and K. 296.

Songs, "Oiseaux, si tous les ans," K. 307/284d, and "Dans un bois solitaire," K. 308/295b, both written in the winter of 1777–78.

Arias for soprano, "Alcandro lo confesso … Non só d'onde viene," K. 294 (in two versions) and "Basta vincesti … Ah, non lasciarmi," K. 486a/295a, both written in February 1778; in addition, aria for tenor, "Se al labbro mio non credi," K. 295 (in two versions), written in February 1778

Two Kyrie fragments, K. 322/296a, and K. Anh 12/296b

Nineteen vocal cadenzas to three opera arias of Johann Christian Bach, K. 293e

Duodrama, *Semiramis*, which was cited in the Gotha theater calendar of 1779, has never been discovered; perhaps Mozart never began it.

Rondo K. 284f, written in November 1777, has been lost.

Fragment of a Concerto for piano and violin, K. Anh. 56/315f

Mannheim Sites

SITE OF THE "PRINCE FREDERICK" INN (GASTHOF "PRINZ FRIED-RICH"). B–2, 8.[2] During the first visit of the Mozart family to Mannheim, from about 30 July to 1 August 1763, they stayed three days in this elegant inn, which was located at Josefsgasse, on the corner of Wormsergasse. It proved to be too expensive for Mozart and his mother when they returned at the end of October 1777. Nothing remains of the inn.

★ ★ PALACE OF THE ELECTOR (KURFÜRSTLICHES SCHLOSS). Bismarckstrasse. During their first visit to Mannheim, in 1763, the Mozart family visited this enormous Baroque palace complex, built 1720–1760 under the Electors Carl Philipp and Karl Theodor of the Palatinate. Leopold, in his travel notes from 1763, mentioned the painting gallery and the library.[3] During his second stay in Mannheim, Mozart played a concerto, a sonata, and an improvised fantasia in the Knight's Hall (**Rittersaal**) at an academy on 6 November 1777. Today the massive complex houses the University; at the main entrance there is a commemorative plaque. The monumental staircase has splendid original stucco by Paul Egell, as well as stucco by others which has been recreated; the *Rittersaal* has been restored to its former grandeur, with a recently frescoed ceiling, as well as original paintings, and original sculptures of Karl Theodor and his wife.[4] Of all the rooms in the palace, only the Library of the Electoress (**Bibliothekskabinett**) is completely original. Daily tours 1 April–31 October (except Monday) 10–12 AM and 3–5 PM; November–March (only Saturdays and Sundays) 10–12 AM and 3–5 PM. For special tours call ahead; admission charge.

SITE OF THE COURT OPERA (GROSSE HOFOPERNHAUS). Located in the Elector's Palace. This fine theater was visited by the Mozart family in 1763, during their first visit to Mannheim. On 5 November 1777, during his second stay in Mannheim, Mozart sat in this theater, with the flutist Johann Baptist Wendling in the orchestra for the performance of **Günther von Schwarzburg** by Holzbauer, with ballet music by Christian Cannabich. The opera house was destroyed in 1795.[5]

★ COURT CHAPEL (HOFKAPELLE; TODAY CALLED SCHLOSSKIRCHE). In the west wing of the Palace of the Elector. On 9 Nov 1777, Mozart played organ at the religious service here; he wrote to his father a description of the effect which his playing had on the receptive congregation, and on Cannabich. The splendid bas-relief of the Trinity from 1731 by Egell has been preserved, although the interior of the chapel was destroyed, including the organ.[6] It has been restored in a simple style revealing little of the former splendor. Private church; open daily 9 AM–5 PM.

★ ★ PALAIS HEYDECK (TODAY BRETZENHEIM-PALAIS). A-2; across the street from the Elector's Palace. In this palace, built 1781–88 as a present of the Elector Karl Theodor for the children of his twenty-year-old mistress, Josefa Seiffert (Countess Heydeck), Mozart played for the Countess and her children on 7 and 8 November 1777, with the Elector present for a time.[7] Mozart also offered his services to the Elector as a teacher for the countess. In WW II, particularly on 1 March 1945, the building was destroyed, except for the walls. It was carefully reconstructed by the bank, **Rheinische Hypotheken**, which it has housed since 1901[8]; the elegant exterior features wrought-iron balconies in black and gold.

★ ★ COURT CHURCH/JESUIT CHURCH (GROSSE HOFKIRCHE/ JESUITENKIRCHE). A-4. Leopold mentioned this church, built between 1733 and 1760 by Bibiena and Rabaliatti, in his travel notes from the Mozarts' visit in 1763. Later, Mozart attended religious services of all kinds here. It is the largest church of the city, and one of the important Baroque churches in southwestern Germany. The massive portal, the fine wrought-iron of the entrance, and the unique holy water fonts are original, as are the side altars and relative appearance of the organ.[9] The splendid altar by Egell seen by Mozart, which was destroyed in 1943/44, is being reconstructed. The spacious interior has bright green and red *faux-marbre* wall panels. Open daily 7 AM–Noon and 2–6 PM; continuously on Sundays and holidays.

★ "COLD ALLEY" ("KALTE GASSE"). Between A-4 and B-4, behind the Jesuit Church.[10] Some of the few original Mannheim edifices from the time of Mozart can be seen here: for example, B-4, 13 (**Götzelmann**), and the slender tower of the Observatory (**Sternwarte**) built 1776–78, and renowned as a result of the first long-term weather prediction. Mozart visited the Observatory on 16 November 1778 where he signed the guest book. House B-5, 20 has an original ground floor; around the corner at B-5, 17/18 is a carefully preserved edifice with a characteristic courtyard inside.[11]

[SITE OF THE NATIONAL THEATER (NATIONALTHEATER)]. Today the empty square B-3. During Mozart's third visit to Mannheim, from 6 November to 9 December 1778, Heribert von Dalberg, the Director of the National Theater, offered his *Cora* to Mozart to set to music, which Mozart declined. Mozart wrote him a letter saying that he had called on him twice unsuccessfully, which was most likely here, or at his home at N-3, 4 (**Dalberghaus**).[12] During his fourth and last stay in Mannheim, Mozart attended the major rehearsal of *Figaro* here, and on the next day, 24 October 1790, he conducted its first performance in Mannheim, in German. This historic theater, which stood here until 1943, faced a large square which is today called Schillerplatz; commemorative plaque about the theater. The adjacent building at B-2, 12 is an old eighteenth-century Mannheim house, with an inn called "Between Acts" ("**Zum Zwischenakt**"), which recalls the theater history of the square. Some other buildings that are essentially from 1780 or earlier are the Baroque house **Cunzmannsche Haus** at C-4, 9 (today **Volksbank**), and C-3, 18.[13]

[★ ★ ARSENAL (ZEUGHAUS)]. Today Reiss Municipal Museum C-5. This massive late-Baroque edifice designed by Verschaffelt was being built during Mozart's second and third visits to Mannheim in 1777–78, and is significant as one of the few buildings remaining in Mannheim that Mozart would have seen.[14] The museum offers municipal history and a decorative arts collection which includes fine local Frankenthal porcelain.[15] Open weekdays 10 AM–1 PM and 2–5 PM (–8 PM Wednesdays); Sundays and holidays 10 AM–5 PM; closed Monday.

SITE OF THE "PALATINE COURT" INN ("ZUM PFÄLZISCHEN HOF"). D-1, 5 on Paradeplatz. Leopold had recommended against Mozart and his mother staying in the "Prince Frederick" Inn, where they had lodged in 1763; for that reason, they stayed in this inn, which had been recommended to them by travelers, when they arrived on 30 October 1777. However, even their simple attic room proved to be too costly, as expensive wood for heating was required during the cold and wet fall of 1777.[16] Today there is a clothing department store, C & A, on the site; commemorative plaque. Some other nearby buildings that are essentially from 1780 or earlier are D-4, 4 (Catholic Sister House), and E-2, 8 (Bakery Herrdegen).[17]

SITE OF THE HOUSE OF SERRARIUS. F 3–5. An irreplaceable landmark destroyed during WW II was the house where Mozart and his mother stayed from 12 December 1777 to 14 March 1778 during their second stay in Mannheim. A majority of Mozart's Mannheim works originated here; works from the winter 1777–78 include "Oiseaux, si tous les ans" and "Dans un bois solitaire"; the Concerto for flute, K. 313/285c and the Concerto for oboe (or flute), K.

314/285d; the Flute quartets, K. 285 and K. 285a; the Sonatas for keyboard and violin, K. 301/293a, K. 302/293b, K. 303/293c, K. 305/293d, K. 296; the Piano sonatas, K. 309/284b and K. 311/284c, and the Rondo, K. 284f. The house stood here from 1740–1943; no commemorative plaque. There is a 1941 drawing of the house, and the artist had also been commissioned to draw the interior; however, he was called to serve in the war.[18] In Schwetzingen, the preserved "Red House" Inn has somewhat the same architectural style and features.[19]

★ ★ CITY PARISH CHURCH OF ST. SEBASTIAN (STADTPFARRKIRCHE ST. SEBASTIAN). F-1 Marktplatz. From the letters of Mozart's mother, we know they mostly attended this church during their second visit to Mannheim, 30 October 1777–14 March 1778. The church stands intact from the time of Mozart's visits, with the exception of the famous altar by Egell, which is no longer in the church; it was sold to Berlin. The three-member gable inscription is dedicated to justice and piety.[20] Open daily 8 AM–7:30 PM.

[★ ★ CITY HALL (RATHAUS)]. F-1. Although there is no known connection of this building to Mozart's travels, the splendid facade remains from the time of his visits and is the oldest edifice (1700–23) remaining from the period of the Electors. The City Hall and the church are built symmetrically around a tower, a characteristic Mannheim construction. The Glockenspiel plays at 7:45 AM, 11:45 AM, and 5:45 PM.

SITE OF THE LUTHERAN CHURCH (TRINITATIS KIRCHE). G-4. On 18 December 1777, Mozart played and was delighted by the new organ by the renowned organ builder Stumm from Sulzbach, installed in December 1777.[21] In addition, Abbé Georg Joseph Vogler also performed, with the renowned Mannheim composers Ignaz Holzbauer, Christian Cannabich and Carlo Giuseppe Toëschi present. Renowned visitors to the church included the Prussian King Friedrich Wilhelm I and his famous son, later Frederick the Great, about 1730. Both the church and the organ were destroyed in WW II.

SITE OF THE HOME OF THE WEBERS. M-1, 10; across from the present Chamber of Commerce and Industry, which is at L-1, 2.[22] The Weber family, which was to play such an important role in Mozart's life, lived here in 1778, in the Oberstadt, across from the Lottery House. Before leaving on his trip to Kirchheimbolanden (which lasted from 23 to 29 January 1778) with Aloisia Weber, with whom Mozart fell in love, and her father, Fridolin, Mozart came here to have compositions for the trip copied.

★ ★ HOUSE OF BARON VON SICKINGEN (DALBERGHAUS). N-3, 4. This beautiful edifice, of which the facade is original, belonged to Baron von Sickingen until 1778. Sickingen, who lived in Paris as the Palatine Ambassador, and who met Mozart there in 1778, was an enthusiastic supporter of Mozart, and a loyal friend to him. Later, when Mozart called on Dalberg, the Director of the National Theater, at the end of 1778 during his third stay in Mannheim, from 6 November to 9 December 1778, it was very likely here at the **Dalberghaus**. The facade of the building, where the **Stadtbücherei** (City Bookstore and Music Bookstore) is located, has been beautifully restored by the city.[23]

SITE OF THE "MAINZ ELECTOR COURT" INN ("CHURMAINZISCHER HOF"). 0-3, 4. Here, in what was later the "*Mainzischer Hof*," Mozart visited his pupil F. G. Duval de la Pottrie. The building no longer exists; today on the site is a pharmacy, **Mohrenapotheke**. Other nearby buildings from 1780 or earlier are 0-4, 4 (**Badische Bank** since 1870), P-5, 9 (**Eichbaum**), Q-3, 15, and T-2, 5.[24]

★ ★ CONCORDANCE CHURCH (KONKORDIENKIRCHE). R-2. In December 1777, Mozart came here, and played the organ, with his Swiss student of "gallanterie" and "general bass," Guillaume Duval de la Pottrie, who was serving as a Dutch officer. First erected in 1665 in wood, the church served the French Reformed congregation, and later, the German Reformed congregation. After it was destroyed in 1689, the church became known as the Twofold National Church. In 1795 it was destroyed, and again in 1952; the organ was also lost. Today a wing houses a school named after Mozart. The church can be visited during services, or by calling.

N o t e s

1 The exhaustive research of Hans Budian ("Mannheimer Mozartgedenkstätten" in *Das Mannheimer Mozart-Buch*), provides the basis of my discussion of Mannheim sites. Few cities other than Salzburg and Augsburg have received this type of detailed study regarding Mozart sites. Budian located the sites of the inns where Mozart stayed, where the Webers lived, and the buildings remaining in Mannheim from the period. The important site of the home of Christian Cannabich has not yet been located. As I have done for each Mozart city, Budian organized his article into a systematic itinerary.

2 Budian, "Mannheimer Mozartgedenkstätten," 22.

3 Leopold mentioned the painting gallery, the library, and the treasure chamber in his travel notes. Today the painting gallery, which was taken to Munich when the elector relocated his court there, is in the Alte Pinakothek in Munich. Eibl, in the notes to the Mozart letters, states that the library to which Leopold was referring was probably the still-existing library; however, an extensive library containing hundreds of leather volumes, which has been destroyed, is more likely the library to which Leopold was referring. Bauer/Deutsch/Eibl, *Mozart Briefe*, V, zu 68.

4 Budian, op. cit., 26–27.

5 Budian, op. cit., 27.

6 Budian, "Mannheimer Mozartgedenkstätten," 27.

7 Haas, "Mozart im Bretzenheimschen Haus zu Mannheim," 46.

8 Budian, op. cit., 29.

9 Ibid.

10 Ibid., 30–31.

11 Ibid.

12 Ibid., 35.

13 Ibid., 31.

14 Ibid.

15 Michelin, *West Germany*, 176.

16 Budian, op. cit., 22.
17 Ibid.
18 Ibid., 32.
19 Stief, "Mozart in Schwetzingen," 269.
20 Budian, op. cit., 32.
21 Ibid., 33.
22 Vögele, Wolfgang, "Wo stand das Mannheimer Weber-Haus?" *Acta Mozartiana* 30 (1983), 25–30.
23 Budian, op. cit., 35.
24 Ibid., 34.

$\mathcal{M}$ozart in Munich

$D\ a\ t\ e\ s$

About 14 January to the middle of February 1762 ▪ 12–22 June 1763 ▪ 8–about 27 November 1766 ▪ 7 December 1774–6 March 1775 ▪ 24 September–11 October 1777 ▪ 25 December 1778–about 13 January 1779 ▪ 6 November 1780–12 March 1781 ▪ 29 October–about 6 November 1790

$\mathcal{M}$ozart had frequent and important contacts with Munich during his lifetime, and the city was the site of several of his most renowned works. His first trip, at the very beginning of his travels as a child prodigy, was to perform, with his sister, for the Elector Maximilian Joseph III.

At the beginning of the "Great Western" trip to Paris and London of 1763–66, Mozart and his family stopped in Munich, and they did again at the very end of the extensive journey.

During the "second Munich trip," in 1774–75, Mozart's opera *La finta giardiniera* was performed in the Salvator Theater.

On the way to Paris with his mother in 1777, Mozart again stopped here for about two weeks; his attempts to find a permanent position were met with a polite, but negative, response. In 1778, when Mozart was returning to Salzburg from Paris (where his mother had died), he stayed in Munich with the Webers; his serious affection for Aloisia Weber was met with a rebuff.

The splendid Munich Residence Theater (by F. Cuvilliés) was the site of the first performance of Mozart's *Idomeneo*, which his father and sister attended. Mozart's altercation with Archbishop Hieronymus Colloredo took place shortly thereafter in Vienna.

Finally, in 1790, toward the end of his life, Mozart traveled to the coronation ceremonies of Leopold II in Frankfurt am Main. He again stopped in Munich, this time performing for the King of Naples.

$M\ u\ s\ i\ c$

La finta giardiniera, opera buffa, performed in Munich, 13 January 1775
Idomeneo, opera seria, performed in Munich, 29 January 1781

Ballet music for *Idomeneo* in five movements, K. 367; composed before 18 January 1781 in Munich

Scenes for soprano, "Popoli di Tessaglia ... Io non chiedo," K. 316/300b, (dated Munich, 8 January 1779; probably begun in Paris in June 1778) and "Warum, o Liebe ... Zittre, töricht Herz," K. Anh 11a/365a (Munich, November 1780), and "Misera, dove son ... Ah! non son' io che parlo," K. 369 (Munich, 8 March 1781)

Songs, "Die Zufriedenheit," K. 349/367a, "Komm, liebe Zither," K. 351/367b (both Munich, winter 1780/81)

Duo for bassoon and cello, K. 292/196c, Munich, early 1775

Oboe Quartet, K. 370/368b, Munich, 1781

"Great" Serenade for 13 instruments, K. 361/370a; composed during the first half year 1781 in Munich and Vienna

Piano Sonatas, K. 279 to K. 283/189d-h, Munich, early 1775; Piano Sonata K. 284/205b, Munich, February-March 1775; Piano Sonatas, K. 330/300h, K. 331/300i, K. 332/300k, written in Munich or Vienna, 1781–83

Capriccio for solo keyboard, K. 395/300g, Munich, October 1777

Offertory "Scande coeli limina," K. 34, written for the Monastery at Seeon, in Bavaria, in early 1767

Offertory "Misericordias Domini," K. 222/205a, Munich, early 1775

Kyrie, K. 341/368a, composed supposedly between November 1780 and March 1781, in Munich, although recent research (Tyson, 1987) suggests Vienna, 1788

Missa Brevis, K. 220/196b, composed supposedly in January 1775 in Munich

Fragment of a Kyrie, K. Anh. 16/196a, composed supposedly in January 1775 in Munich

Six Sonatas for clavier and violin, K. 301 to K. 306/293a-e, written in Mannheim and Paris, dedicated to the Electress of the Palatinate, and presented to her when Mozart was in Munich

Munich Sites

★ ★ ★ NYMPHENBURG CASTLE. On 13 June 1763, during their second trip to Munich, the Mozarts visited Nymphenburg. Here they received an order to appear in the palace, where from 8–11:15 PM Wolfgang and his sister performed before Elector Maximilian Joseph III and the Bavarian nobility. Nannerl was the principal performer on 20 June 1763,[1] and received "the greatest applause." Years later, on 21 November 1766, the Mozart children performed for the Bavarian Elector, with Mozart displaying his new talent for improvised composition, using a theme by the Elector. During his visit in 1777, Mozart spoke to the Elector privately about a position in Munich, at table in Nymphenburg, where he was told, "It is too early now." The oldest part of the castle dates to 1664, with later additions by Max Emmanuel, Karl Albrecht and Maximilian Joseph III. The banqueting hall was decorated by the Zimmermanns with

Rococo stucco and frescoes. Open 1 April to 30 September 9 AM–12:30 PM and 1:30–5 PM; the rest of the year 10 AM–Noon and 1:30–4 PM; closed Mondays; admission charge.

★ ★ ★ NYMPHENBURG PARK. In 1763, Nannerl noted, "I saw the Nymphenburg..., the garden and the four castles..." Before Wolfgang's performance for Elector Maximilian Joseph III, the Mozarts spent four hours in the park, later running for shelter from rain and thunder. The park features a large flower bed, white marble sculptures, and a large canal which ends in a waterfall. The "castles" mentioned by Nannerl include: **Amalienburg**, a hunting lodge built 1734–39 by Cuvilliés for the Electress Amalie (open the same times as the castle), featuring a world-renowned circular Hall of Mirrors in blue and silver; **Badenburg**, built 1718–21 by Effner for Elector Max Emanuel (open 1 April to 30 September; 10 AM–12:30 PM and 1:30–5 PM; closed Monday; admission charge), featuring a pool with frescoed ceiling and an ante-chamber with hand-painted eighteenth-century Chinese paper; **Pagodenburg**, an octagonal tea-pavilion, built in east Asian style by Effner in 1716 (open the same times as Badenburg); and the **Ermitage**, a retreat for the aged Elector Max Emanuel, built 1725–28 by Effner (open the same times as Badenburg).[2]

Munich. Engraving by Matthaeus Merian, 17th century.

★ ★ ★ THE PALACE (RESIDENZ). Max-Joseph-Platz 3. The fourteenth-century *Residence* was extended by the Dukes of Wittelsbach to its present seven inner courts. It was seriously damaged 1943–45, including many rooms relevant to Mozart, and the original plans were destroyed. However, it has now been magnificently reconstructed. The Emperors Room (named after the pictures of the Roman-German Kings and Emperors from Rudolph von Habsburg to Charles VI and replaced in 1799 by the Hofgarten Room[3]) figured prominently in Mozart's life; on 22 January 1775 at the academy held here in honor of Archbishop Colloredo, it is possible that Mozart performed. Then, in 1778, Leopold wrote to Mozart that an academy held in the Emperors Room had featured music almost exclusively by Mozart; and on 4 (or 5) November 1790, when Mozart played for the Elector Karl Theodor and Ferdinand IV, King of Naples, this academy was held in the Emperors Room. In addition, when Mozart presented his six Sonatas for clavier and violin, K. 301/293a to K. 306/300e, to the Electress Elisabeth Auguste on 7 January 1779, it is likely that it was in the Residence. Open Monday–Saturday 10 AM–4:30 PM; Sundays and holidays 10 AM–1 PM; closed Mondays and certain holidays; admission charge; to visit the entire collection it is necessary to make separate morning and afternoon tours.

★ ★ ★ TREASURY ROOM IN THE RESIDENCE (SCHATZKAMMER). On 21 January 1775, Leopold wrote, "Nannerl is coming with me to the court to see the rooms, the jewels and so forth." The old Treasury Room seen by the Mozarts has become the porcelain museum today. The splendid treasure that they saw, including crowns, diadems, and relics, is found in the present **Schatzkammer**. Open Monday–Saturday 10 AM–4:30 PM; Sundays 10 AM–1 PM; closed Mondays; admission charge.

★ ★ ★ CUVILLIÉS THEATER (ALTES RESIDENZTHEATER). Residenzstrasse 1 (today located in the Residence). This unique Rococo court theater, of splendidly carved wood in red, white and gold, was built by Cuvilliés (1751–53) with four individually decorated tiers. Here, on 29 January 1781, Mozart's opera *Idomeneo, King of Crete* was first performed, with Leopold and Nannerl in the audience to witness the resounding success. The theater was originally on the site of the present New Residence Theater; it was disassembled and stored in 1943/44, which prevented its destruction in 1944, and has been reassembled in the Residence. Open Monday–Saturday 2–5 PM; Sundays and holidays 10 AM–5 PM; admission charge.

★ ★ COURT CHAPEL IN THE RESIDENCE. Several Masses by Wolfgang, conducted by Leopold, were performed in the court chapel on 12 and 19 February 1775 (probably *Missa brevis* in F, K. 192/186f, and *Missa brevis* in D, K. 194/186h). The restrained seventeenth-century chapel has an interesting *caisson* ceiling.

SITE OF THE "GOLDEN STAG" INN (GASTHOF "ZUM GOLDENER HIRSCHEN"). Formerly Theatinerstrasse 18.[4] *En route* to Paris, the Mozart

Munich. Elector's Residence.

family stayed in the inn of Johann Stürzer from 12 to 22 June 1763. After Mozart's performance for the Elector ended at 11:15 PM on 18 June 1763, they returned here, tired, for supper and sleep. On the return leg of the trip, from 8 to about 27 November 1766, they again stayed in this inn. The building no longer exists; during WW II, the Theatinerstrasse was severely damaged, and new numbers were allocated, with the result that there is no longer a number 18 on Theatinerstrasse. When standing on Theatinerstrasse, facing the beginning of Salvatorstrasse (with the Theatiner Church to the right), the site is on the left (a modern building constructed after WW II),[5] near the present corner of Salvatorstrasse and Theatinerstrasse.[6]

SITE OF THE OLD COURT THEATER ON SALVATOR PLATZ (ALTEN HOFTHEATER AM SALVATOR PLATZ). Salvatorstrasse, near Salvator Platz. The premiere of *La finta giardiniera* on 13 January 1775 was not, as previously believed, in the **Redoutenhaus** on Prannergasse, but here,[7] directed by Vice Concertmaster von Croener. Mozart described the premiere: "My opera was . . . such a success that it is impossible for me to describe the applause . . . the whole theater was so packed that a great many people were turned away. Then after each aria there was a terrific noise, clapping of hands and cries of 'Viva Maestro.'" The Old Court Theater was located on the present Salvatorstrasse, adjacent, and to the north of, the church on Salvatorplatz (in the direction of the Theatinerstrasse).[8] The theater was built 1651–58 by Santurini, and opened in 1662. In 1778 Elector Karl Theodor declared it the Court and National Theater; it was demolished in 1802.[9]

SITE OF THE REDOUTENSAAL. Prannergasse 8. Leopold wrote in 1774, "In the **Salle de Redoute** only operettas, or rather *intermezzi* [that is, comic operas] are given, during which . . . hundreds of masks stroll around, chatter, jest and gamble." Mozart wrote on 11 January 1775 that he went to the masked academies, which were held here each Tuesday and Thursday in the **Redoutensaal** which, with the gambling tables, belonged to Count Joseph Anton Seeau.[10] In addition, on each of the first two days after his arrival in Munich on 24 September 1777, Mozart went to the home of Count von Seeau, the theater director, seeking a permanent position. The count was described as "a gambler," who fought several duels, and remained "a libertine, a gluttonous eater and a heavy drinker" into old age.[11] The **Redoutensaal**, which had been built by Gärtner in 1718, was rebuilt in 1818 by Leo von Klenze, and became the seat of the Bavarian Parliament. The building was destroyed during WW II, and remained in ruins until 1961. Since 1980, Tela Insurance is located at Prannergasse 8.[12] Several fascinating facades from the period include the **Palais Gise** (about 1760) at Prannerstrasse 9 and **Palais Neuhaus-Preysing** (about 1735–40) at Prannerstrasse 2; the facade of **Palais Seinsheim** (1764) at #7 was redone in neo-Baroque around 1900.[13]

SITE OF THE HOME OF COUNT SALERN. Maffeistrasse 7. After his unsuccessful attempt to secure a position at court in 1777, Mozart called upon Count Joseph Salern, the director of music and opera. He was invited to dine at Salern's for two days, and played many things from memory, including the two cassations, K. 247 and K. 287/271H, and the serenade rondo, K. 250/248b. Mozart wrote, "You cannot imagine how delighted Count Salern was." The house bought by Count Salern in 1766 was on Maffeistrasse (at #7).[14] When standing on Maffeistrasse facing the beginning of Windenmacherstrasse, it was the building almost directly on the corner to the right. Today the site has been incorporated into the Loden Frey store.[15]

★ **SITE OF THE HOME OF FRAU VON DURST.** Residenzstrasse 7. In 1777, Mozart visited Frau von Durst (who in her previous home had hosted Nannerl), who lived in the "Mayor Schmädel house," across from the present post office. It was very close to the Franciscan monastery, which formerly had a church on the site of the present Max-Josephs-Platz. Today, where Frau von Durst lived, there is a furniture shop "Seitz KG Internationale Einrichtung HR Möbel"[16]; the three former buildings were not reconstructed after the war, and a provisional building (one story high) was built, which now belongs to the Franziskaner Restaurant.[17]

SITE OF THE HOME OF COUNT AND COUNTESS BAUMGARTEN. Theatinerstrasse 8.[18] It was probably through the mediation of Countess Baumgarten that Mozart received the commission for the opera *Idomeneo*.[19] Mozart wrote on 13 November 1780, "Yesterday I dined with [Christian] Cannabich at Countess Baumgarten's . . . this is the best and most useful house here for me. In addition, through this house, everything has succeeded for me, and will—God willing—continue to do so." Mozart then used a string of ribald language in code to explain to Leopold that the Countess Baumgarten was the mistress (favorite) of the Elector, Karl Theodor. It was for the Countess that Mozart wrote the scene, "Misera, dove son!"—"Ah! non son'io che parlo," K. 369, to a text from Metastasio's *Ezio*.[20] Count Johann Joseph von Baumgarten[21] bought the edifice in 1763. The building was replaced by a new structure in 1912[22]; the building is today owned by the bank, **Bayerischen Hypotheken- und Wechselbank**[23]; the renowned restaurant **Böettner's** is located in the building today.

★ SITE OF THE FIAT (FIALA) HOME. Corner of Burgstrasse and Altenhofstrasse. Mozart stayed here from 6 November 1780 to 11 March 1781, when he came to Munich for his opera *Idomeneo*. His two rooms with alcoves were in the home of a Mr. Fiat (perhaps Fiala). The modern, restrained building is distinguished by a commemorative plaque noting Mozart's stay and his completion of *Idomeneo*. Burgstrasse is a characteristic street with painted facades, such as #5, from the sixteenth century; the house in which Cuvilliés (who designed the Old Residence Theater) died is also on this street, marked by a commemorative plaque.

★ ★ CHURCH OF OUR LADY (FRAUENKIRCHE). Frauenplatz 12. During the trip of Leopold and Wolfgang in 1774/75 for Mozart's opera *La finta giardiniera*, Mozart's "Grand Litany," K. 125, was performed, most likely here in the **Frauenkirche**. The church, in late Gothic style, with two massive towers topped by onion domes, was built 1468–88 by Ganghofer. The sober red brick structure was damaged in 1944, and has been reconstructed.

SITE OF THE "BLACK EAGLE" INN (GASTHOF "ZUM SCHWARZEN ADLER"). Kaufingerstrasse 25 to Frauenplatz 4. In this inn, where the Mozarts had apparently stayed during a previous visit, friends from Salzburg who had come for the premiere of Mozart's *La finta giardiniera* took lodging. In the winter 1774/75, a competition between Mozart and Ignaz von Beecke, arranged by the innkeeper Franz Joseph Albert, probably took place here. On 24 September 1777, Mozart and his mother arrived here for a stay of over two weeks. Albert, an enthusiastic music lover and generous friend to Mozart, conceived an ill-fated plan to keep Mozart in Munich by soliciting a ducat a month from ten friends. During this same trip, on 4 October 1777, a small academy was held here with the weak violinist Dupreille, probably in the former dance hall with mirrors; Mozart's cassation, K. 287/271b, was performed at this time.[24] Finally, on 29 October 1790, during his last trip to Munich, Mozart again stayed here. Nothing remains of the original building. In its place is a simple building with a gambrel roof, next to the cathedral, presently the music store Hieber.

★ SITE OF THE HERZOG HOSPITAL AND CHURCH. Today Herzogspital-strasse 9. Here, in October 1777, Mozart visited the renowned composer Mysliveček, disfigured by venereal disease; Mysliveček assured Mozart that he could have him write an opera for Naples, a plan that never materialized. The hospital, built from 1555 to 1601, was demolished in 1944, as was the Herzogspital Church, St. Elisabeth. The tower still exists, however, and the church has been reconstructed with a modern interior. A fine wood figure from 1651, "Mary Suffering," can be seen.

SITE OF THE LITTLE PALACE OF CLEMENS (CLEMENS-SCHLÖSSCHEN). Prielmayerstrasse 7. On their visit to Munich in 1762, the Mozarts "waited on" Clemens Franz de Paula, Duke of Bayern, and cousin of the Elector, who maintained his own music chapel. The little palace, where the Mozarts visited the Duke, stood on the site until 1891. It was located outside the city walls, in the area of the present Palace of Justice (**Justizpalast**), near the present **Karlstor-Stachus**. A commemorative plaque on the north side of the Palace of Justice on Elisenstrasse recalls the former edifice.[25]

★ ★ ★ CHURCHES OF MUNICH. Frau von Durst entertained Nannerl during her visit to Munich in 1775 to attend the premiere of *La finta giardiniera*, by taking her to services at a different church each day. These included, most probably, **St. Peter's**, **St. Michael's**, and the **Theatiner Church**, among others.

N o t e s

1 Münster notes that 20 June 1763 was the first date that Nannerl could have performed, as opposed to Eibl's date of 19 June 1763 in *Chronik*. Münster, "München und Wasserburg," 40.
2 Michelin, *Germany*, 193–94.
3 Biller/Rasp, *München Lexikon*, 142–153.
4 Almost all references to this site in the Mozart literature cite Theatinerstrasse 18; however, this address no longer exists. Even recent specialized publications continue to publish this error, including Münster, "München und Wasserburg," 35, and Münster, "Mozarts Münchener Aufenthalt von 1766," 2.
5 Communicated by Vera Golücke, Fremdenverkehrsamt München.
6 Several agencies in Munich were unable to locate what is presently on the site of what was Theatinerstrasse 18. However, using the *Häuserbücher der Stadt München*, II, I was able to locate the site. Stadtarchiv München, 336–337.
7 Bauer/Deutsch/Eibl, *Mozart Briefe*, VII, zu 301/19 (NR).
8 Presently it is the site to the left of #19 Salvatorstrasse. Stadtarchiv München, op. cit., II, 257.
9 Stadtarchiv München, op. cit., II, 257.
10 The Katasterplan in the *Häuserbuch der Stadt München*, showing the site, with a garden, suggests to me that Count Seeau may have lived here as well.
11 Schenk, *Mozart and His Times*, 37–38.
12 Communicated by Dr. Verena Schäfer and Herbert Winkler, Manager, Tourist Office of Munich.
13 Biller/Rasp, op. cit., 174–75.

14 Stadtarchiv München, op. cit., II, K 127. Another nearby house, bought by his wife, Countess Maria Josepha (born von La Rosee) was at Theatinerstrasse 45. Today, standing on Theatinerstrasse, facing Perusastrasse, the site is the corner immediately on the right, now partly in the intersection. Stadtarchiv, *Häuserbuch* I, G 432. This second site is discussed by R. Münster, "Zwei verlorene Münchener Mozart-Stätten," 11; however, I am not sure if the author of that publication was aware of the house at Maffeistrasse 7, which was acquired several years earlier by Count Salern, or if there is any documentary evidence linking Mozart's performance with this second house.

15 Communicated by Vera Golücke, Fremdenverkehrsamt München.

16 Communicated by Herbert Winkler, Manager, Tourist Office of Munich.

17 Communicated by Vera Golücke, Fremdenverkehrsamt München.

18 Published in the Mozart literature for the first time. Stadtarchiv München, op. cit., I, K 321.

19 Bauer/Deutsch/Eibl, *Mozart Briefe*, VI, zu 535.

20 Bauer/Deutsch/Eibl, op. cit., VI, zu 537/9–10.

21 Bauer/Deutsch/Eibl, op. cit., VII, zu 537/7–8 (NR).

22 Stadtarchiv München, op. cit., I, K 321.

23 Communicated by Vera Golücke, Fremdenverkehrsamt München.

24 Münster, "Zwei verlorene Münchner Mozart-Stätten," 13.

25 Münster, "München und Wasserburg," 37.

Mozart in Passau

Dates

20–26 September 1762

After Leopold's successful trip to Munich with Mozart and his sister, the family traveled to Vienna, by way of Passau and Linz. After waiting several days, the new Bishop, Count Joseph Thun-Hohenstein, decided to hear Mozart only (not his sister); afterward Leopold complained about receiving a single ducat.

Passau Sites

★ ★ ★ ARCHBISHOP'S RESIDENCE. Residenzplatz 8. Mozart, and not his sister Nannerl, was "permitted" to perform for Count Joseph Thun-Hohenstein (1713–63) during the stay of the Mozarts in Passau, from 20 to 26 September 1762; for this performance, the Prince-Bishop gave the disappointed Leopold a "whole" ducat. The **Residenzplatz** is surrounded by buildings of the former bishops, dating from the Renaissance.[1] Today the fine staircase in the residence can be visited without asking permission. The nearby splendid Gothic Cathedral of St. Stephen, which the Mozarts undoubtedly visited, was reconstructed in Baroque style in the seventeenth century; the east end (**Chorabschluss**) of the cathedral is a spectacular piece of flamboyant Gothic architecture.[2]

★ THE "RED CRAB" INN ("ZUM ROTEN KREBS," LATER "GREY HARE" INN, OR "ZUM GRAUEN HASEN"). Oberer Sand 1. The Mozarts probably stayed in the inn which was here, the "Red Crab" Inn, which after 1826 was called the "Grey Hare"; another possibility for an inn was the "Golden Sun" Inn ("Goldene Sonne").[3] The "Grey Hare" Inn was rebuilt and modernized in 1951; an attractive commemorative plaque of dark red Trent marble was placed on the south side of the inn in 1957. However, there is no documentation which indicates definitively in which inn the Mozarts lodged.[4] Today, instead of the "Grey Hare" Inn, the building houses the Café Kowalski.

Passau. Engraving by Jeremias Wölff, 19th century.

★ THE "GOLDEN SUN" INN ("ZUR GOLDENEN SONNE"). Unterer Sand 18. Another possibility where the Mozarts lodged was this inn, which was the more expensive of the two inns, and which had existed since 1323.[5] In the building today, there is no longer an inn but a small restaurant (**Wirtshaus**).

★ ★ MARIA HILF CHURCH. Mariahilfberg. Leopold wrote to his landlord, Lorenz Hagenauer, on 3 October 1762, that Nannerl wanted Mrs. Hagenauer to know that she kept her promise; they all made a trip to the church to pray for Hagenauer's son Johann Lorenz (who died on 18 January 1763). This pilgrimage church, built 1624–27 (probably by Garbanino) has a seventeenth-century copy of the painting of Mary by Lucas Cranach, the original of which is found in Innsbruck.[6]

★ ★ OBERHAUS FORTRESS (VESTE). Ferd-Wagner Strasse. Leopold, in his letter of 29 December 1762 to Lorenz Hagenauer, wrote that he had planned to leave Pressburg, but that he was suffering from an unusual toothache in the entire row of his upper front teeth. During the night his whole face swelled up, and he wrote that he looked like the trumpeting angel, a reference to the Passau "Tölpel" (Oaf), a stone head on the Veste Oberhaus in Passau.[7] The imposing fortress was built by the bishops of Passau on the wooded Georgsberg hill.

N o t e s

1 Michelin, *Germany*, 210.
2 Ibid.
3 Saam, "Mozart in Passau," 13; Bauer/Deutsch/Eibl, *Mozart Briefe*, V, zu 46/10.
4 Ibid.; ibid., 32/16.
5 Saam, "Mozart in Passau," 14.
6 Ibid., 13; Bauer/Deutsch/Eibl, op. cit., V, zu 32/16.
7 Ibid.; ibid., 32/41.

Mozart in Potsdam

About 25 April–about 6 May 1789

Toward the end of his life, Mozart traveled with Prince Karl Lichnowsky (via Prague) to Dresden, Leipzig, Potsdam and Berlin. In "expensive Potsdam," where Mozart was temporarily "abandoned" by Prince Lichnowsky, Mozart had himself announced to King Friedrich Wilhelm II, who, instead of receiving him, referred him to the chamber music director, Jean-Pierre Duport. From this meeting, however, arose a series of solo piano variations on a theme by the cellist, Duport.

Music

Solo keyboard variations, K. 573, on a Minuet from the sonata for violoncello, Op. 4, No. 6, by J. P. Duport; written in Potsdam, 29 April 1789.

Potsdam Sites

[★ ★ ★ PALACE SANS SOUCI]. During his trip in April 1789, Mozart had himself announced in the palace of King Frederick William II,[1] but was referred to the director of chamber music Jean-Pierre Duport. This extraordinary palace, first erected 1745–47 according to sketches by Frederick the Great, and designs by Knobelsdorff, is a remarkable monument; marble sculpture and decoration, frescoes and stucco combine to form a unique example of eighteenth-century architecture. Although the **Neue Anlage** [between the New Palais (1755, 1763–65) and the Belvedere] and the **Fasanerie** are from the nineteenth century, there are many important eighteenth-century monuments; the Obelisk Gate of 1747 (**Obeliskportal**) by Knobelsdorff leads to extensive gardens, representative of eighteenth-nineteenth-century landscape architecture.

★ HOME OF TUERRSCHMIDT. Am Bassin 10. Here in the Blankenhorn House, home of the horn player Tuerrschmidt, Mozart is believed to have lived during his stay in Potsdam in late April/early May 1789. A commemorative plaque is today found on the site.

Potsdam. The Royal Palace. Unsigned engraving.

[★ ★ CHARACTERISTIC SIGHTS OF POTSDAM]. Potsdam has a large number of edifices from the eighteenth century. In the area of the Old Market is the **Marstall** (1746), the **Knobelsdorffhaus**, erected in 1750 by Knobelsdorff (damaged in the war and rebuilt in the original style), the Nicholas Church (**Nikolaikirche**), and the City Hall (**Rathaus**), both destroyed on 14 April 1945 and rebuilt. In the area of Wilhelm-Külz-Strasse is the **Ständehaus** (today Potsdam Museum), the former Military Orphanage (**Militärwaisenhaus**) of 1722, the obelisk by Knobelsdorff (1753), and the "Old Watch" Inn (**Gastätte "Alte Wache"**) of 1772, with several other houses from before 1775 in the area.

N o t e s

1   The Mozart literature does not indicate if Mozart was received in the City Palace (*Stadtschloss*), which was destroyed in 1945, or in Sans Souci. Since I received no response to my letters to the Archives or to the Tourist Office in Potsdam, it was not possible to determine more precise information. In addition, it was not possible to cite where the home of Sophie Nichlas was located. Supposedly, at a gathering there, Mozart improvised individually on three themes offered to him, combining all three at the end.

Mozart in Schwetzingen

D a t e s

About 14 July to about 29 July 1763 ▪ 29 October 1777 ▪ 24 October 1790

On their way to Paris during the "Great Western" trip of 1763–66, the Mozart family and their servant Sebastian Winter traveled through Munich, Augsburg and Ulm, and visited Schwetzingen, the summer residence of the Elector of the Palatinate, Karl Theodor. It was Mozart's first encounter with the splendid Mannheim orchestra, and the visit was a success; as Leopold noted: "My children have set all Schwetzingen talking. The Elector and his consort have shown indescribable pleasure and everyone has been amazed." The children performed in the elector's palace, along with the flutist Wendling, good singers, and "the best orchestra in Germany."

On his way to Paris during the trip of 1777–79, Mozart and his mother left Augsburg, stopped in Hohenaltheim, and traveled through Schwetzingen on the way to Mannheim.

Finally, returning home to Vienna after his visit to Frankfurt for the coronation ceremonies of Leopold II, Mozart again passed through Schwetzingen.

Schwetzingen Sites

★ "RED HOUSE" INN (HOTEL-GASTHOF "DAS ROTE HAUS"). Dreikönigstrasse 6.[1] The Mozarts stayed in the "Red House" Inn from 13 to 18 July 1763, during their visit to Schwetzingen. The inn, whose location on the same site can be documented since 1700, still exists although it was closed as an inn in 1920. It is under monument protection, but is in a bad state of repair; at present, it serves as housing facilities for guest workers from Turkey.[2]

★ ST. PANCRATIUS CHURCH. Leopold noted about Schwetzingen, "It is only a village, [but] has three churches, one Catholic, [one] Lutheran, and [one]

Calvinist: and it is so throughout the entire Palatinate." Two churches are still found today in the center of Schwetzingen: the Catholic church (**St. Pancratius**), which is near the castle, and a Protestant church as well.[3]

★ ★ ELECTOR'S RESIDENCE. The building, originally a hunting palace from the middle of the seventeenth century, was rebuilt as a **Lustschloss**, or pleasure palace, after the devastating Orleans War (1688–97). Wolfgang and Nannerl played here for Elector Karl Theodor on 18 July 1763 from 5–9 PM, along with "an admirable flutist, Wendling," "good singers," and what Leopold termed "without doubt, the best orchestra in Germany." The entire castle, including the rooms and the Rococo Theater are in the original form in which Mozart and his family saw them.[4] Open the entire year; the Schwetzingen Festival in May and June presents concerts and operas.

★ ★ GARDENS OF THE PALACE (SCHLOSSPARK). Both Leopold and Nannerl cited the gardens of the palace, a jewel of landscape gardening. It was completed mostly between 1721 and 1734, and in 1748 redone under the French model. The major perspective begins with a semicircle of elegant buildings and a round garden with fountains. Features from the time of the Mozarts' visit include various sculptures of cherubs, the "bird bath," the "wild boar" group, as well as Agrippina, Arion, and Bacchus," plus "the famous "stag group," the Temple of Apollo, the Temple of Minerva, and the Orangerie."[5] Leopold and Nannerl each noted the Star Alley (**Stern-Allee**). While there is a semicircle in the garden behind the castle that is crossed by numerous small walking paths, in the form of a star,[6] the Star Alley to which Leopold and Nannerl were referring is today overgrown with woods, near the **Jägerhaus** and the sports field east of Hockenheimer Strasse; the circumference and radial outlines can still be recognized.[7] Park open April–September 8 AM–7 PM, March and October –6 PM, the remainder of the year –5 PM; admission charge.

★ ★ ★ THEATER OF THE PALACE (SCHLOSSTHEATER). Leopold wrote on 19 July 1763, "It is time to go to the French theatre, which could not be improved on, especially for its ballets and music." The unique Rococo Theater, built in 1752 and enlarged in 1762, is located in the park; it is still in the original style.[8] In May and June, operas are produced here as part of the Schwetzingen Festival.

N o t e s

1 Mossemann, K. "Ortgeschichtliche Betrachtung über die Gaststätte 'Das rote Haus' in Schwetzingen," n. d.
2 Communicated by Herbert Thürmer, Manager, Tourist Information Schwetzingen.
3 Ibid.
4 Ibid.
5 Stief, "Mozart in Schwetzingen," 264.
6 Communicated by Herbert Thürmer.
7 Stief, op. cit., 265–68.
8 Communicated by Herbert Thürmer.

$\mathcal{M}$ozart in Ulm

Dates

6/7 July 1763 ▪ About 2 November 1766 ▪ End of October 1790

On the first leg of their "Great Western" trip of 1763–66, Mozart and his family left Augsburg, and stopped here overnight. Leopold, who did not like medieval architecture, called the town "a dreadful, old-fashioned . . . place, built in bad taste." In 1766, while returning to Salzburg after this extensive trip, they again stopped in Ulm.

At the end of his life, Mozart traveled to Frankfurt am Main, for the festivities of the coronation of Leopold II; on the return trip to Vienna, Mozart again passed through Ulm.

Ulm Sites

★ ★ CATHEDRAL (MÜNSTER). Münsterplatz. The morning after arriving in Ulm on 6 July 1763, the Mozarts went to the remarkable **Münster**, drawn more by the fine organ than the building itself. The organist, Johann Christoph Walther (son of the first German music lexicographer, and a nephew in the second degree of Bach) demonstrated the forty-five registers, three manuals and pedal of the fine Schmal instrument (1730–35).[1] The cathedral was begun in 1377, but the present spire (528 feet—the tallest in the world), was not seen by the Mozarts, as only a modest spire was completed at that time: The massive spire and the two towers were erected in 1890. The Renaissance doors at the entrance are highlighted by Multscher's statue, *Man in Sorrow* (1429). The splendid wood carving of the choir stalls (1469–74), in which figures from the Bible face writers and philosophers of pagan antiquity, and the pulpit (surmounted by a "second pulpit" of 1510 for the invisible Preacher, the Holy Spirit) are of interest.[2] Open 1 May to 31 August 7 AM–6:45 PM; other months 9 AM–4:45 PM; admission charge.

★ ST. MICHAEL'S ABBEY "ZU DEN WENGEN." 6 Wengengasse. Another visit of the Mozarts, on 7 July 1763, was to Dr. Peter Obladen, Canon at this Augustine abbey. The abbey was erected in 1399, and the Gothic interior was remodeled in the Baroque style in 1629. The exterior burned in 1944, and was rebuilt in a modern style, larger than the original.[3] There is a small chapel to the left, which was the choir and a part of the nave of the previous church, which has been restored with some Rococo elements, including grey-and-salmon marble pilasters and gold stucco. In the main church, the former altarpiece (1766) by Kuen can still be seen. At Ulmer Gasse 15, the fifteenth-century stepped grain tower, formerly belonging to the abbey, can be seen.

SITE OF "GOLDEN WHEEL" INN ("ZUM GOLDENEN RAD"). Neue Strasse 65. When the Mozarts arrived in "dreadful, old-fashioned" Ulm on 6 July 1763, they stayed overnight in the fine inn, the "Golden Wheel." Although the inn was completely destroyed, a modern "Golden Wheel" Inn, constructed in an austere style, and completely renovated recently, is located approximately on the site. The exact site was at the present street crossing in front of the present building; when Neue Strasse was laid down in 1954, an entire house length was demolished to give it the present breadth.[4]

[★ TOWN HALL (RATHAUS)]. Marktplatz 1. The Mozarts could not have failed to see this elegant Gothic/Renaissance structure, located so near their lodging. It was constructed around 1370, and merchandise was sold in the cellar vaults from the sixteenth century. The southeast wing is the oldest, followed by the north wing with an open arcade (1539) and the west wing (1905). Rebuilt in 1951 according to the old forms, the town hall is interesting for its pieced gables, the facades painted in *trompe l'oeil*, and the astronomic clock.[5]

[★ ★ SCHWÖRHAUS SQUARE]. Also near the Mozarts' hotel is this attractive square, which was the location of wine markets from the fourteenth to nineteenth centuries (and which Leopold would not have overlooked). The **Schwörhaus** (present location of the Ulm Archives), with its vigorous Baroque gables (1613), was rebuilt in its old form after the bombing of 1944.[6]

[★ ★ OLD QUARTER OF ULM]. The medieval Gothic town Ulm, with the numerous half-timbered and gabled facades that appeal so much to our present historical aesthetic, seemed ugly, old-fashioned and in bad taste to Leopold Mozart, who had lived in the progressive Baroque/Rococo atmosphere of Salzburg. Much of the old quarter of Ulm, rebuilt and restored, recalls the medieval atmosphere. There is a fine view from the right bank of the Danube of the gabled Butchers' Tower (**Metzgerturm**) from 1345, and of the cathedral.[7] The Shoe House (**Schuhhaus**) of 1537 was once the shoemakers' guildhall. The Mozarts may have visited the Church of the Trinity (**Dreifaltigkeitskirche**) of 1617, today called the "**Haus der Begegnung**." Other buildings which can still be found today include the **Zeughaus** (1522), the **Reichenauer Hof** (1535), the **Salzstadel** (1592), and the **Gänsturm** (1360).[8] In addition, the picturesque Fishermen's Quarter (**Fischerviertel**) including the fifteenth-sixteenth-century, half-timbered **Schiefes Haus** and the town ramparts (1480), capture the characteristic charm. The Ulmer Museum has a fine arts section containing works by the artists of Ulm throughout the centuries.

N o t e s

1 Bauer/Deutsch/Eibl, *Mozart Briefe*, V, zu 51/19–20.
2 Michelin, *West Germany*, 258.
3 Baedeker, *Ulm*, 61–62.
4 Communicated by Dr. Eugen Specker, Stadtarchiv Ulm.
5 Baedeker, op. cit., 45.
6 Ibid., 43.
7 Michelin, op. cit., 259.
8 Communicated by Hildegard Osswald, Verkehrsverein Ulm.

Mozart in Wasserburg am Inn

Dates

10–12 June 1763 · 6/7 December 1774 · 6/7 March 1775 · 23/24 September 1777

On 9 June 1763, Leopold Mozart, his wife, his two children, and their servant Sebastian Winter, set out in their own coach in the direction of Munich, at the beginning of the "Great Western" trip of 1763–66. The unfortunate mishap of a broken wheel on 9 June 1763 turned into a new musical experience for Mozart, however. Leopold, who was forced to wait several days with his family in this Bavarian town while the coach was being repaired, brought Mozart to the parish church to teach him the use of the pedals. After an initial try with the pedals, Mozart "began to improvise preludes . . . as if he had already practiced it for many months. Everyone was amazed."

At the beginning and at the end of the "second Munich trip," (at which time Mozart's *La finta giardiniera* was performed), Mozart and his father stopped here. Again, when Mozart left on his ill-fated trip to Mannheim and Paris, with his mother, they stopped in Wasserburg.

Wasserburg am Inn Sites

★ ★ ST. JAMES PARISH CHURCH (STADTPFARRKIRCH ST. JAKOB). The unfortunate mishap of a broken wheel on 9 June 1763 (on the first leg of the Mozarts' three-and-a-half year "Great Western" trip to Paris and London) turned into a new musical experience for Mozart. Leopold, who was forced to wait with his family until 12 June in this Bavarian town, while the coach was being repaired, brought his son to the parish church to teach him the use of the pedals. After an initial try with the pedals, Mozart "began to improvise preludes . . . as if he had already practiced it for many months." The large square tower of the church stands out above the picturesque outline of the old town in Wasserburg. The Gothic interior boasts an ornate carved wooden pulpit from 1638, with a theatrical canopy.[1] The organ unfortunately no longer exists, and church documents do not reveal any information about it.[2]

★ "GOLDEN STAR" INN (GASTHOF "ZUM GOLDENEN STERN"). Färbergasse 3.[3] Wasserburg, about halfway between Salzburg and Munich, became a frequent stop for Mozart and his family. He stayed in this inn numerous times, first with his family (10–12 July 1763, and probably also 6 December 1774 and 6 March 1775), and most likely again with his mother, on the way to Paris via Munich (23 September 1777).[4] The inn is today called "Gassner-Bräu," and has a marble commemorative plaque on the facade, recalling Mozart's visits[5]; today it is privately owned (by the Gassner family), and *is not open to the public.*[6]

Wasserburg. Unsigned engraving, early 19th century.

[★ ★ CHARACTERISTIC SIGHTS OF WASSERBURG AM INN].[7] This picturesque Bavarian town, with aspects still reminiscent of the Middle Ages, has numerous preserved or reconstructed monuments. These include the Duke's castle (**Schloss**; 1531–37) with its fifteenth-century chapel, the late-Gothic Town Hall (**Rathaus**; 1457–59), St. Michael's chapel (and the former crypt located on the bottom floor), the fourteenth-century Holy Ghost Hospital and Church, the Bridge Gate, the Inn Bridge, the "Kernhaus" at Maria's Square (1738), the Gothic Maria's Church, and the Red Tower.

N o t e s

1 Michelin, *West Germany*, 263.
2 Bauer/Deutsch/Eibl, *Mozart Briefe, V*, zu 49/51.
3 Communicated by Frau Peharlach, Städtisches Verkehrsbüro, Wasserburg am Inn.
4 Bauer/Deutsch/Eibl, op. cit., V, zu 309/24ff (N); zu 535/10 (NR).
5 Ibid., V, 48/2–3.
6 Communicated by Frau Peharlach, Städtisches Verkehrsbüro, Wasserburg am Inn.
7 "Wasserburg am Inn," Städtisches Verkehrsbüro, Wasserburg am Inn.

Mozart in Worms

About 1–2 August 1763 ▪ 29 January–2 February 1778

During the "Great Western" trip of the Mozart family, 1763–66, they stopped in Worms, which Leopold described as "an old-fashioned place, ruined through the old French Wars . . . however, noteworthy because of the old events concerning the cathedral, and particularly the Lutheran Church, where Luther appeared before the Council."

Mozart again stopped in Worms in 1778, with Aloisia Weber, with whom he fell in love, and her father, Fridolin. They had performed for the Princess of Nassau-Weilburg in Kirchheimbolanden, after which they stopped in Worms, before returning to Mannheim.

Worms Sites

★ ★ ST. ANDREAS MONASTERY (ST. ANDREASSTIFT). Weckerlingplatz. Mozart, in the company of Aloisia Weber and her father, Fridolin, "lunched and dined every day" here during their stay in Worms from 29 January to 2 February 1778. The Dean of the Monastery was the brother-in-law of Fridolin, P. Dagobert Stamm, whom Mozart called "an excellent and sensible man." The St. Andreas Monastery, with a church, cloister, and an inner courtyard, today serves as the **Museum der Stadt Worms.** The buildings from the twelfth to thirteenth century present characteristic features of Worms architecture, such as the choir of the church with two towers, which appears straight from the outside, and the decoration of the west wing of the choir walk.[1] Open Tuesday–Sunday 10 AM–Noon and 2–4 PM.

★ ★ ★ BASILICA. Leopold, in his travel notes, cited "the old cathedral church," which, today, is no longer a cathedral with a bishop, but is instead a parish church; it was built in its late Romanesque form 1125–81, and is completely intact.[2] The basilica has two apses divided by four round staircase towers; the exterior west chancel (about 1230) is one of the finest examples of

Romanesque architecture in Germany.[3] In the time of the Mozarts' visit, the splendid Baroque altar of Balthasar Neumann already stood in the basilica, as did the fine organ loft from the middle-eighteenth century, which has fine wood carving depicting musical instruments; the interior of the cathedral has scarcely changed since that time.[4] Open from 1 April to 31 October, 8 AM–6 PM (the rest of the year 9 AM–5 PM).

★ ★ GENERAL SITE OF THE EPISCOPAL PALACE. Stephansgasse; the **Kunsthaus Heylshof** is today located on the site of the former imperial and episcopal palace.[5] Leopold wrote that "we ate in the evening in Worms at Baron von Dalberg's," which referred to Karl Friedrich von Dalberg, the General Vicar of the Cathedral. In 1763, the imperial and episcopal palace, with the court church of St. Stephan, was located, as it had been for almost 1,500 years, in the shadow of the cathedral; the Baroque structure was destroyed by French revolutionary troops, and around 1800 the ruins were removed.[6] Presently the remarkable art gallery, *Kunsthaus Heylshof*, in the midst of a spacious park, contains what is regarded as one of the finest private collections in Rheinland-Pfalz; it consists of fifteenth-to-nineteenth-century paintings, as well as sculptures, porcelain, and furnishings once owned by the Barons of Dalberg.[7] Open Tuesday–Sunday 10 AM–5 PM (May–September); Tuesday–Saturday 2–4 PM; Sundays 10 AM–Noon and 2–4 PM (October–April).

SITE OF THE "SWAN" INN ("ZUM SCHWAN"). 49 Kämmererstrasse.[8] The inn where the Mozarts stayed in the beginning of August 1763 (perhaps 1–2 August 1763, during the first months of the "Great Western" trip) no longer exists; in its place there is a modern apartment house with shops. Nearby, the site of the former "Johanniterhof," where Martin Luther lodged during the 1521 **Reichstage** in Worms, is on Kämmererstrasse 39.[9]

★ ★ LUTHERAN CHURCH. In 1763, Leopold mentioned that Worms was "noteworthy because of the old events concerning the cathedral, and particularly the Lutheran Church, where Luther appeared before the Council." It has been suggested that Leopold was referring to the **Church of St. Martin (Martinskirche)** of 1265, which was the first Protestant church in southwest Germany.[10] The Romanesque west door, with eight columns, and the decorative vines on the tympanum, are noteworthy.[11] Another possibility as the "Lutheran church" includes the **Church of St. Magnus (Magnuskirche)**, which is very near the St. Andreas Monastery, which it served as parish church until the Reformation; it was originally a one-room Carolingian structure that was extended in the twelfth-thirteenth century.[12] Finally, the main Lutheran church in the second half of the eighteenth century was the Baroque **Church of the Holy Trinity (Dreifaltigkeitskirche)** on Marktplatz, which was built 1709–25, and had a large painting by Seekatz, "Luther Before Emperor Charles V"; the church burned in 1945, and has been restored in a modern fashion, while preserving the Baroque exterior walls.[13]

[★ ★ CHARACTERISTIC SIGHTS OF WORMS].[14] Sites which Mozart could have seen include the late-Romanesque **St. Paul's Church (Pauluskirche)**, with two towers, the tops of which are modeled after the **Grabeskirche** in Jerusalem; the **Synagoge**, first mentioned in 1034, that has been restored to its form of 1175–76, after it was destroyed in 1938–42; the remarkable **Jewish Cemetery (Judenfriedhof)**, with tombstones from as early as 1076; and the **Church of Our Lady (Liebfrauenkirche)**, which gave its name to the renowned *Liebfraumilch*, or "Milk of Our Lady" wine, that comes from the surrounding vineyards (Leopold was keenly interested in fine wines).

Other Sites of Interest: Hohenaltheim

Dates

26–28 October 1777

On their way from Augsburg to Mannheim, *en route* to Paris, Mozart and his mother took an excursion from Nördlingen to visit Prince Kraft Ernst von Öttingen-Wallenstein, who had heard Mozart perform several times in Rome in 1770. They arrived in Hohenaltheim at 7 PM on 26 October 1777, after lunching at Donauwörth and driving to Nördlingen. The timing was particularly unfortunate: The prince was "in the deepest depression" because of the death of his wife, and was unable to listen to any music. Mozart visited him in his palace (**Lustschloss Hohenaltheim**), and, according to Marianna's letter of 31 October 1777 to her husband, the prince could not "look at anyone without bursting into tears." Wolfgang visited with him, but the prince was so distracted that he asked Mozart four or five times about the same thing. They would have left immediately, except that Marianna contracted a bad cold, which necessitated their staying another night.

During their stay in Hohenaltheim, Mozart visited the pianist Ignaz von Beecke, and apparently "took a violin, and danced around and played," which resulted in Mozart being depicted as a "jovial, high-spirited and brainless fellow." This account, which gave "Herr Beecke the opportunity to disparage [Mozart's] merits" caused Leopold great consternation, when hearing about it later in Salzburg from Anton Janitsch and Joseph Reicha.

When Mozart and his mother left Hohenaltheim on 28 October 1777, it was after a brief visit which combined an unfortunate set of experiences: "a bad cold," "a miserable inn," and a prince who was unable to listen to any music.

★ ★ HOHENALTHEIM PALACE (LUSTSCHLOSS HOHEN-ALTHEIM). Mozart did not perform during his visit to Prince Kraft Ernst von Öttingen-Wallerstein in late October 1777, as the prince was in a profound depression after his wife's death, and could not listen to any music. The prince had first met Mozart in Rome in the spring of 1770, when the fourteen-year-old Mozart was traveling in Italy with his father, and the prince was on the "grand Tour." He also heard Mozart perform shortly thereafter in Naples. It was at this time that the Mozarts were (probably quite casually) invited to the prince's palace in Wallerstein. Leopold remembered this meeting and made the suggestion that his son and wife plan to include Öttingen-Wallerstein in their itinerary. He noted that at this time of the year (October) the prince probably would be found in his Lustschloss Hohenaltheim, not far from Wallerstein. The Lustschloss Hohenaltheim is still standing today in the tiny village of Hohenaltheim. There is, in fact, a member of the Wallerstein family who still lives there.[15] *The Lustschloss is closed to the public.* The geometric formal gardens, including topiary and sculpture, are well maintained.

"BETTER" INN ("OBERE WIRSTSCHAFT"). Marianna Mozart (Mozart's mother) wrote her husband that she and Mozart spent two nights in a "miserable inn." This was most likely the "Obere Wirtschaft," although the "Stag" Inn ("**Zum Hirschen**") is also possible. The "**Obere Wirstschaft**" is the most likely inn in which Mozart and his mother stayed; it belonged to a Herr Bergdolt, and seems to have been frequented by musicians from the court.[16]

Représentation du Château de Plaisance de Hohenaltheim.

Hohenaltheim. Castle of Prince Oettingen-Wallerstein. Unsigned engraving, later 18th century. Oettingen-Wallerstein Archiv, Wallerstein.

Other Sites of Interest: Kirchheimbolanden

Dates

23–29 January 1778

hile Mozart's brief trip to Kirchheimbolanden and Worms was intended only as a "vacation trip, and nothing more," it contributed to a family crisis resulting in Mozart's mother's decision to accompany her son to Paris, where she ultimately died. The Mozarts had already become acquainted with the Princess of Nassau-Weilburg, the sister of the Prince of Orange, during their visit to The Hague in 1765. When he heard that she wanted to see him, Mozart set off with Aloisia Weber, with whom he fell in love, and her father, Fridolin. Mozart's letter of 4 February 1778 has a compelling postscript from his mother (who had continually deferred to her son):

> **You will have seen from this letter that when Wolfgang makes new acquaintances, he immediately wants to give them his life and property. . . . I never liked his being in the company of Wendling and Ramm, but I never dared to raise any objections, nor would he ever have listened to me. . . . I do not consider his journey to Paris with Wendling to be at all advisable. I would rather accompany him myself later on. . . . I am writing this quite secretly, while he is at dinner, and I shall close, as I do not want to be caught.**

This was a striking change from the original plan for her to return to Salzburg while Wolfgang went on to Paris.

On the other hand, Mozart's letter describes a carefree excursion at a time when his father and sister were supposedly experiencing considerable financial problems. Between 23 and 29 January 1778, Mozart performed twelve times for the Princess, and once in the Lutheran church. However, it was after Mozart wrote to his father that he wanted to take Aloisia and her father to Italy, and to write an opera in Venice, that Leopold began to vent his wrath, culminating in his command, "Off with you to Paris, and soon."

Other Sites of Interest:
Market Biberbach

D a t e s

6 November 1766

★ PILGRIMAGE CHURCH OF MARKT BIBERBACH. Here, in the renowned pilgrimage church of the Fugger family, a competition on the organ took place between Mozart and the 12-year-old Joseph Eugen Bachmann, on 6 November 1766. Young Bachmann had a phenomenal memory, and knew more than 200 pieces at the age of nine; "each did his utmost to show himself to best advantage, and the competition turned out very creditably for both." Bachmann later became a Premonstrant monk at Obermarchthal on the Danube.[17]

N o t e s

1 Reuter, *Worms*, 17.
2 By a papal decree of 1925, the church was raised to "Minor Basilica"; communicated by Fritz Reuter, Stadtarchivdirektor, Worms.
3 Michelin, *Germany*, 271.
4 Communicated by Fritz Reuter, Stadtarchivdirektor, Worms.
5 Reuter, op. cit., 20–21.
6 Ibid., 20.
7 Ibid., 21.
8 Communicated by Fritz Reuter, Stadtarchivdirektor, Worms. This updates and elaborates on the Bauer/Deutsch/Eibl notes to the Mozart letters, V, zu 57/26 (N).
9 Today there is a modern apartment building with shops on the site; the commemorative plaque concerning Martin Luther's stay in 1521 is found, nevertheless, at Hardtgasse 2. This was the site of the garden of the "Johanniterhof," through which Luther was led to the interrogation by Emperor Charles V in the "Bischofshof." Communicated by Fritz Reuter, Stadtarchivdirektor, Worms.
10 Bauer/Deutsch/Eibl, *Mozart Briefe*, V, zu 59/40.
11 Michelin, op. cit., 271.
12 Communicated by Fritz Reuter, Stadtarchivdirektor, Worms.
13 Ibid.
14 Ibid.
15 Contributed by Sterling E. Murray, West Chester University, West Chester, Pennsylvania; source: Elizabeth Jeanette Luin, "Mozarts Beziehungen zum Hause Öttingen," *Zeitschrift des Historischen Vereins für Schwaben—Neues Augsburger Mozart-Buch*, LII-LIII (1962), 469–78.
16 Contributed by Sterling E. Murray, West Chester University, West Chester, Pennsylvania. Queries to Hohenaltheim remained unanswered, and Sterling E. Murray did not know of the location of the two inns. This is also true for the home of Ignaz von Beecke, the keyboard virtuoso. Leopold had chastised Mozart for taking up a violin, and dancing around while playing, at the home of von Beecke. As Sterling E. Murray notes, "Beecke knew Mozart from previous meetings, and the Mozarts (father and son) had very little that was kind to say about him."
17 Schenk, *Mozart and his Times*, 94.

Italy

Bologna, Bolzano, Brescia, Cremona, Florence, Lodi, Mantua, Milan, Naples, Padua, Rome, Rovereto, Turin, Venice, Verona, Vicenza

Other Sites of Interest:

Civitá Castellana, Loreto, Parma

Mozart in Bologna

Dates

24–29 March 1770 • 20 July to about 13 October 1770 • (Outside the city, in Croce del Biacco, from 10 August to 1 October 1770)

During the first trip to Italy, Mozart and his father stopped in Bologna before continuing on to Florence, Rome and Naples. Returning from Rome, they again stopped in Bologna, before returning to Milan.

The day after arriving in Bologna, Mozart and his father visited Field Marshal Count Giovanni Luca Pallavicini-Centurioni and his wife Maria Caterina, in whose home a son of Count Kaunitz-Rietberg was staying. Musicians they later met included the famous castrato, Farinelli, whom they visited on his country estate outside of Bologna,[1] the castrato Giuseppe Manfredi, and "la Spagnoletta." In addition, they visited Padre Martini, the world-renowned contrapuntalist, who presented themes upon which Mozart then composed fugues. After a concert at the home of Pallavicini for 150 guests, Mozart and his father left for Rome, by way of Florence.

During their second visit to Bologna, Leopold suffered from a leg injury received on the trip back from Rome. Mozart received the libretto to *Mitridate*, and began work on the opera. Their patron, Pallavicini, invited them to his country estate outside of Bologna, where Mozart and his father spent many pleasant weeks. Another interesting encounter, after a sacred music concert in Bologna, was with Dr. Charles Burney, the historian. Finally, Mozart received a great honor, after passing an exam (with the help of Padre Martini): He was accepted as a member into the renowned **Accademia Filarmonica**.

Music

A Vienna manuscript of the Symphony in D, K. 84/73q (perhaps not by Mozart) cites Mozart as the composer, and cites Milan and Bologna, 1770.

Mozart solved four trick canons from Padre Martini's *Storia della Musica*, K. 73r (probably in Bologna, July and August 1770).

Sacred music includes Miserere, K. 85/73s (written in Bologna, July–August 1770), "Quaerite primum," K. 86/73v (the exercise Mozart wrote for the Accademia Filarmonica), and "Cibavit eos," K. 44/73u.

Menuett, K. 94/73h, composed either in Bologna in March 1770, or in Rome in April 1770.

Fragment of a fugue for clavier, K. 73w, probably composed in Bologna 1770.

Menuett, K. 122/73t, for violins, bass, oboes and horns, may have been written in Bologna, August 1770.

Many recitatives to *Mitridate* were written in Bologna.

Bologna Sites

★ ★ **VILLA PALLAVICINI.** via San Felice, 24. On 25 March 1770, the day after their arrival in Bologna for the first time, Mozart and his father paid a visit to Field Marshal Giovanni Luca Pallavicini-Centurioni and his wife, with a letter of recommendation from Count Firmian in Milan. Count Pallavicini, praised by Leopold for his "friendliness, generosity, tranquility, and special affection for and understanding of all branches of knowledge," organized a reception the next day, with a concert from 7:30 to 11:30 PM for 150 persons of the highest nobility; Mozart directed an orchestra and the castratos Giuseppe Aprile and Giuseppe Cicognani participated. Among the guests was Padre Giovanni Battista Martini, in retirement, who rarely attended concerts.[2] Mozart received a generous gift of 205 Bologna lire from Pallavicini. Despite the sober street entrance, with a facade redone in 1788, the interior of the villa is remarkably intact today, although converted into office space. Two enormous reclining sculptures flank the staircase, which leads to apartments on each side that are occupied by business firms. Numerous splendid rooms with bas-reliefs, original stucco, and frescoed ceilings are intact; permission may sometimes be granted to see the rooms.

★ ★ **CHURCH OF SAINT FRANCIS (SAN FRANCESCO).** Piazza S. Francesco. Mozart and his father visited Padre Martini several times, on 25 and 26 March 1770.[3] Martini, one of the most important contrapuntalists of the eighteenth century, was regarded as "a kind of international oracle," for music history and theory.[4] He suggested themes to Mozart who then wrote out fugues, and he gave the visitors two volumes of his history of music. The thirteenth-century church, with a monastery, has several fine works of art; the *ancona* of the main altar, a carved filigree of marble (1392), was done by Venetian sculptors. The organ, which was made by Andre and Petronio Giovagnoni with the consultation of Padre Martini, dates from 1759, and can still be played today.[5] Open 6:30 AM–Noon and 3–7 PM.

SITE OF THE "PILGRIM" INN (L'OSTERIA DEL PELLEGRINO). via Ugo Bassi, at the top of Via Calcavinazzi.[6] Upon arriving in Bologna for the first time on 24 March 1770, Mozart and his father lodged here, at "the best hotel." Leopold wrote they had "the honor of paying a ducat each day," as the city was full, as there were "over 1,000 Jesuits alone, who were driven here." In 1924–30, the former Via Vetturini was transformed into Via Ugo Bassi.[7]

Reception of Mozart into Accademia Filarmonica, Bologna. Unsigned portrait in oils. Mozart seated left. Museum of Drottningholm Theater.

SITE OF THE "SAINT MARK" INN (L'OSTERIA DI SAN MARCO). Vicolo della Zecca, at the corner of via Ugo Bassi.[8] Returning to Bologna on 20 July 1770, after their trip to Rome and Naples, Leopold and Wolfgang stayed here, at the official hotel of the post, across from their previous lodging at the "Pilgrim." Leopold suffered from a severe leg wound, which kept him from leaving their room for nine days; he complained that "being sick in an inn is no fun." The composer Joseph Mysliveček paid them a visit, bringing the contract for the Milan opera and for an oratorio in Padua; during this period Mozart also received the libretto to *Mitridate* by Cigna-Santi for Milan. The inn, considered one of the best in Bologna, also hosted the Archduke and Archduchess of Tuscany in 1770; in 1943 the hotel was bombed.[9] The present via Ugo Bassi is the result of an urban renewal during the nineteenth and twentieth centuries, and buildings from the previous epochs are gone.[10]

★ ★ BASILICA OF SAINT PETRONIUS (SAN PETRONIO). Piazza Maggiore. Returning to Bologna after a splendid summer visit at Villa Pallavicini outside the city, Mozart and his father attended the services here on 4 October 1770, the feast day of Saint Petronius. "All of the musicians of Bologna" attended the musical event, which Mozart described as "beautiful but long," with trumpeters from Lucca who "blew terribly." The immense church, begun in 1390, has a breathtaking pink marble facade, begun in 1556, which is unfinished. The main portal (on which Jacopo della Quercia worked from 1425 to 1438) has one of the most beautiful Madonnas of the fifteenth century above in the lunette. The massive interior has fine paintings affixed to many pillars and a ciborium by Vignola over the main altar. Twenty-two chapels by renowned artists feature a marble statue by Sansovino on the ornate marble altar of St. Anthony of Padua, fifteenth-century frescoes by Giovanni da Modena in the first and fourth chapels on the left, a fifteenth-century Ferrarese Saint Sebastian, and a fifteenth-century pavement in Faenza ceramic in the fifth chapel on the left.[11] The organ to the right, also from the fifteenth century, is noteworthy.

[★ ★ ANATOMICAL THEATER (ARCHIGINNASIO)]. Piazza Galvani 1. The theater, built 1638–49 by Levanti, is a wonder of classical architecture, realized completely in wood. Although it was not mentioned by Leopold, it is very possible that he and Mozart saw this remarkable structure, which was the seat of the university in 1770,[12] during their sight-seeing in Bologna. Today the library (**Biblioteca comunale**) is housed in the building. Open 9 AM–1 PM; closed Sundays and holidays.

★ ★ CHURCH OF SAINT DOMINIC (SAN DOMENICO). Piazza San Domenico, 13. During their second visit in Bologna, Mozart and his father visited numerous churches, and, apparently, San Domenico most of all.[13] On 6 October 1770, Mozart played the organ here, either the organ of the Basilica, or that in the Chapel of the Rosary[14] (also called the Chapel of the Holy Sacrament). The Basilica was built 1221–33, and remodeled in the eighteenth century. This frescoed chapel, and the other side chapels, are of interest: The sixth chapel on the right has a superb bas-relief (1267), narrating the life of Saint Dominic, by Nicola Pisano and Fra Guglielmo; it is maintained that the kneeling angel at the right front, as well as Saint Proclus and Saint Petronius, are works of Michelangelo's youth.[15] In addition, the compelling gold-leaf altarpiece, the fourteenth-century tomb of Rolandino dei Passeggeri, and the sixteenth-century inlaid stalls in the choir are of interest. Open 8 AM–Noon and 3:30–7 PM.

★ ★ ★ CHURCH OF SAINT JOHN (SAN GIOVANNI IN MONTE). Piazza San Giovanni in Monte. During their second stay in Bologna, Mozart and his father heard a special *pasticcio* Mass and Vespers here (composed by ten different members of the Accademia Filarmonica) in honor of St. Anthony of Padua on 30 August 1770. It was an annual event, which also drew Dr. Charles Burney, who was collecting material for his history of music, and who had a long discussion with Leopold about Mozart. The original church dates back to 433; the facade (with a highly theatrical location) was begun in 1441, and the Gothic bell tower is from the thirteenth or fourteenth century. Inside, there are 17 chapels with important art treasures, including a breathtaking 'Throned Virgin with Saints' by Lorenzo Costa (fifteenth century) in the sacristy, and a crucifix (1361) by Jacopino da Bologna (1361) in the major chapel. In 1944, the church was seriously damaged; it was restored 1947–50.

★ ★ PHILHARMONIC ACADEMY (ACCADEMIA FILARMONICA).[16] via Guerrazzi, 13. At 4 PM on 9 October 1770, Mozart took an entrance examination to become a member of the **Accademia Filarmonica.** An antiphon was selected, which Mozart was to set in four voices; the result was "Quærite primum regnun Dei," K. 86/73v. Usually it took several hours to complete such an exam, but Mozart "wrote it in a good half-hour." Members then voted with black or white balls, and Mozart was accepted unanimously with all white balls; he was greeted with applause as he entered. The academy building, with an austere facade, is remarkably intact; there are numerous frescoed ceilings, and both the library where Leopold was locked, and the adjacent room with seventeenth-eighteenth-century dark carved wood furniture, where Mozart is said to have written the exam, have been maintained. The large *sala* of the academy, which has been enlarged since 1770, has an original small organ from 1673. Because of the excellent acoustics, concerts are still given here. In the academy, the clean copy of the exam antiphon by Mozart is preserved, as are numerous antique viols and wooden flutes. Open Tuesday and Friday 9:30 AM–Noon and 4–6 PM.

★ CIVIC MUSICAL MUSEUM (CIVICO MUSEO BIBLIOGRAFICO-MUSICALE). Piazza Rossini, 2. Besides all of the extensive library of Padre Martini, Mozart's counterpoint teacher, historical instruments and numerous fragments of musical codices are found here. The original version of Mozart's exam antiphon is preserved here, with corrections by Padre Martini; this suggests either that Mozart's counterpoint would have been too original for the taste of the members, or that corrections were needed. In addition, the unique collection of portraits collected by Padre Martini is found here, including Gainsborough's portrait of Johann Christian Bach, Joshua Reynolds's portrait of Charles Burney, and a famous portrait of Mozart wearing the Order of the Golden Spur; in addition, a recently identified portrait of G. B. Sammartini is also found in the collection. Open 9 AM–1 PM Monday–Saturday; closed Sundays; admission charge.

★ ★ FORMER INSTITUTE (ISTITUTO). via Zamboni 31 (main entrance at 33). Leopold, who was extremely keen on scientific curiosities, brought Mozart to the **Istituto** (or Institute), which is in the present University complex. Leopold wrote, "What I saw here surpassed the British Museum, because here there are not only rarities of nature, but everything that is related to science, like seeing a lexicon of beautiful rooms, clearly and orderly preserved." The sixteenth-century Poggi Palace (Via Zamboni 33) housed the Science Institute from 1714; today it hosts numerous museums, including Zoology, Geology, Paleontology, Mineralogy, and an anatomical museum with splendid works in wax. The many corridors of the university offer frescoed ceilings and a fine courtyard with sculpture. Adjoining this building is the University Library, built in 1744 by Lambertini, who became Pope Benedict XIV; it is still in its original state. Library open 9 AM–1 PM. Most historical museums of the University open Monday–Saturday 9 AM–1 PM; some 9 AM–4:30 PM (Saturday to 1 PM).

★ ★ CITY THEATER (TEATRO COMUNALE). Piazza Verdi; box office at Largo Respighi, 1. Mozart and his father met numerous opera singers during their stay in Bologna, including "la Spagnoletta," (Giuseppa Useda), Farinelli (Carlo Broschi),[17] and Giuseppe Manfredini. During their time in Bologna, two operas were performed there: *La Nitteti* by Joseph Mysliveček, and *Armida* by Vincenzo Manfredini. This unique theater, constructed by Antonio Galli Bibiena in 1756–63, presents a highly theatrical effect, much like a stage set. It is constructed completely in wood, and underwent a fabulous restoration 1980–81.

★ ★ ART COLLECTION OF THE ACCADEMIA CLEMENTINA (ACCADEMIA DI BELLE ARTI). via delle belle arti, 54. Leopold Mozart, accompanied by Wolfgang, saw a statue (which can no longer be located) by their countryman, J.B. Hagenauer, who had won first prize in a competition of the **Accademia Clementina.** Leopold wrote, "We were in the Institute, and saw beautiful statues in the Court Sculpture Gallery." The collection of the **Accademia Clementina,** which in 1770 was housed at via Zamboni 31, is now housed in this Fine Arts Museum, and includes works of the finest painters of Bologna and Ferrara. Open Tuesday–Sunday 9 AM–2 PM; admission charge.

★ ★ VILLA PALLAVICINI DELLA CROCE DEL BIACCO. via Bassa dei Sassi, 7; presently the school **Ospizio Trentina,** outside the city; accessible by public transportation (Bus #14A from Porta S. Vitale to Via Massarenti). Mozart and his father experienced the generous hospitality of Field Marshal Count Giovanni Luca Pallavicini-Centurioni here on his summer estate from 10 August to 1 October 1770. Leopold's right leg and his left foot had been injured on the return from Rome, and this estate in the country was an ideal place to recuperate, while Mozart began on 29 September to compose the recitatives to his opera for Milan. Surrounded by silver and linen finer than a "nobleman's shirt," they enjoyed the fresh figs, melons, and peaches of the season. Wolfgang became a close friend of the count's son, who was his age, and who, like Mozart, was "highly talented," spoke German, French, and Italian, and played the clavier. The villa, renowned for the originality of its construction, is composed of a central part and two wings, set within a vast park. The former grandeur of the villa is still visible in the spacious, luminous salons, the magnificent staircase, and in the stucco and the frescoes on the walls and ceilings, of landscapes and hunting scenes. Although the villa was not severely damaged during WW II, it is presently occupied by a school, and vandalism has taken its toll; it is in need of restoration. Leopold wrote that they placed two stools together in the chapel for him to rest his foot; a small, gracious chapel within the villa exists, but is in a bad state of repair, and is not accessible.

★ CHIESA CROCE DEL BIACCO. 4, via Martelli, Croce del Biacco. Here, a pleasant stroll from the Villa Pallavicini della Croce del Biacco, is an attractive church, renovated in 1691, with two marble side chapels, completely intact, where the Mozarts came before lunch, and took part in services. There is a fine altar painting, and a splendid Bolognese panel from 1600 in the side chapel. Open daily 7 AM–Noon and 2–6:30 PM.

N o t e s

1 Unfortunately Farinelli's *palazzo* no longer exists.
2 Schenk, *Mozart and His Times*, 129.
3 Leonida Busi, in *Il Padre G. B. Martini Musicista-Letterato del secolo XVIII* (Bologna, Zanichelli, 1891), indicates that Padre Martini lived in the Monastery of S. Francesco. Communicated by Dr. Giorgio Marcon, Archivio di Stato, Bologna.
4 Schenk, op. cit., 129.
5 Communicated by Servizi e Informazioni alle Attivitá Turistiche, Bologna.
6 Communicated by Dr. Giorgio Marcon, Archivio di Stato, Bologna.
7 Barblan, *Mozart in Italia*, 78.
8 Dr. Giorgio Marcon, Archivio di Stato, Bologna, located at the site of the *Osteria di S. Marco*, which was at Vicolo della Zecca 85, at the corner of via Vetturini (which is the present via Ugo Bassi).
9 Barblan, op. cit., 78.
10 Communicated by Dr. Giorgio Marcon, Archivio di Stato, Bologna.
11 Michelin, *Italia*, 60.
12 Communicated by Servizi e Informazioni alle Attivitá Turistiche, Bologna.
13 Bauer/Deutsch/Eibl, *Mozart Briefe*, V, zu 172/16–17
14 Ibid., 213/29.
15 Michelin, op. cit., 61.
16 Two of the most important works which deal with Mozart in Italy, Barblan's *Mozart in Italia* and the Bauer/Deutsch/Eibl annotations to the Mozart letters, overlook this historic building, which still exists, in a fine state of preservation.
17 Mozart and his father visited Farinelli outside of Florence at his estate, which has since been demolished; cf. Barblan, op. cit.

Mozart in Bolzano

21–23 December 1769 ▪ 16 August 1771 ▪ 28/29 October 1772

During their first trip to Italy, *en route* to Milan, Mozart and his father stopped in Bolzano for two nights. Their hectic schedule included invitations by the violinist Anton Kurzweil, the Stockhammer family, who entertained them "in a very costly way," and Anton von Gummer, a member of the financial aristocracy of Bolzano.

On the way from Salzburg to Milan, during the second Italian trip, they again stopped in Bolzano. Finally, on the third trip to Italy, Leopold and Wolfgang again stopped here, and visited Father Vincenz Ranftl in the Dominican Monastery.

After experiencing the pouring rain in Bolzano, Mozart wrote a poem to his sister:

"If I should ever come to Bolzano again,
I'd rather kick myself in the cunt."

M u s i c

Leopold wrote on 28 October 1772 that Wolfgang was composing a string quartet, "out of boredom." This refers to the String Quartet, K. 155/134a, written in Bolzano and Verona, October–November 1772.

Bolzano Sites

★ ★ **DOMINICAN MONASTERY.** Piazza Domenicani. On their third trip to Italy, Leopold and Wolfgang stopped in Bolzano (28–29 October 1772) and called on Father Vincenz Ranftl (an instrumentalist whom they had met in

Salzburg) in the Dominican Monastery of "this gloomy town." In the church of the monastery, the chapel of San Giovanni is noteworthy for the splendid fourteenth-century frescoes. Other beautiful frescoes ornament the nave and the late Gothic cloister.[1] The monastery today houses the Monteverdi Conservatory of Music, known for the annual Busoni piano competition.[2]

SITE OF THE "SUN INN" ("ZUR SONNE"). Piazza delle Erbe. This inn, where Leopold and Wolfgang stayed from 21 to 22 December 1769 (and perhaps again in October 1772, when Mozart wrote his string quartet, K. 155/134a), was on the most characteristic square of Bolzano. The inn was located on the south side of the square (also called the **Obstmarkt**) bordering on the beginning of via Museo[3]; it was demolished in 1873.

★ ★ GENERAL SITE OF THE HOME OF ANTON VON GUMMER. via dei portici.[4] On the evening of 22 December 1769, Leopold and Wolfgang were invited to the home of Anton von Gummer, who was part of the financial aristocracy of Bolzano; the famous house of exchange of Giovanni Gummer, in 1761, loaned 200,000 florins to the emperor, and Francesco Gummer, in 1780, founded the masonic lodge of Bolzano.[5] Usually such invitations were accompanied by Mozart performing for his hosts. The house no longer exists[6]; however, the characteristic street is noteworthy for its fifteenth to eighteenth-century houses, with covered arcades (*loggias*) and unusual portals.[7] At #30, the Baroque **palazzo Mercantile** (**Merkantilgebäude**), built 1708–27, is also of interest.[8]

★ HOME OF MR. STOCKHAMMER. Talfergasse 2.[9] On 23 December 1769, Leopold and Wolfgang lunched here at the home of the middle-class Stockhammer family, including Stockhammer's wife and his mother. Leopold wrote that here they were "received with great honor, and were entertained in a very costly way," and that he met his old acquaintance Mr. Stickler. The house is today in the possession of Frau Glauber (born von Walther); a commemorative plaque cites the visit of Mozart.[10]

[★ ★ CHARACTERISTIC SIGHTS OF BOLZANO]. Leopold and Wolfgang undoubtedly saw the picturesque **Piazza delle Erbe**, which opens to the **via dei Portici** (Laubengasse). In addition, they would not have missed the Romanesque-Gothic **Duomo** (Cathedral) with its beautiful bell tower and the Church of the Franciscans (**Chiesa dei Francescani**), built in 1348, with a beautiful small fourteenth-century cloister. The eighteenth-century **Castel Roncolo** (Runkelstein Castle), which lies two miles to the north, is also noteworthy, as is **Castel Mareccio** (Maretsch Castle), which was built in the thirteenth century and rebuilt in 1564.[11]

N o t e s

1 Michelin, *Italia*, 62.
2 Communicated by Dr. Rudolf Ausserer, Terlano (Bolzano).
3 Ausserer, "W. A. Mozarts Reisen durch Südtirol-Trentino," 120.
4 The house could have been on via dei Portici, as the present "Gummergasse" (via Gummer) stretches along the back of via dei Portici, from the *Rathausplatz* to the *Kornplatz*. Communicated by Dr. Rudolf Ausserer, Terlano (Bolzano); it is cited here for the first time in the Mozart literature. In regard to the home of the violinist Kurzweil, with whom the Mozarts lunched on 22 December 1769, Dr. Ausserer communicated that "nothing is known about the house. The Mozarts probably met him during their stay in his native city, Pressburg."
5 Barblan/Lunelli, *Mozart in Italia*, 41.
6 Communicated by Dr. Rudolf Ausserer, Terlano (Bolzano).
7 Michelin, op. cit., 62.
8 Communicated by Dr. Rudolf Ausserer, Terlano (Bolzano).
9 Ausserer, op. cit., 120. This edifice, which is still standing, was overlooked in the Bauer/Deutsch/Eibl notes to the Mozart letters.
10 Communicated by Dr. Rudolf Ausserer, Terlano (Bolzano).
11 Ibid.

Mozart in Brescia

Between 4 and 11 February 1771 ▪ 20/21 August 1771 ▪ 6/7 December 1771 ▪ 3/4 November 1772 ▪ About 5 March 1773

Mozart and his father stopped in Brescia five times during the three Italian trips. During the first visit, *en route* to Venice during the first Italian trip, they saw an *opera buffa* in Brescia. The second and third visits were overnights stops, during the second Italian trip. The fourth and fifth visits, during the third Italian trip, were spent as guests of the great patron of the arts, Count Fausto Lecchi.

Music

The five sonatas for clavier and violin, K. 55-60/Anh. 209c-209h/C 23.01-6, which Wyzewa believed were written in the context of Mozart's stay in Brescia (and perhaps influenced by the music of Tartini), are today listed as doubtful works in the Köchel catalog.

Brescia Sites

★ ★ PALAZZO OF CONTE LECCHI. Corsetto S. Agata, 22. During their stops in Brescia on 3 to 4 November 1772, and around 5 March 1773, Mozart and his father were guests of the distinguished patron of the arts, Count Faustino Lecchi. Lecchi was a "strong violinist, with a great understanding and love of music," according to Leopold's description of him. Count Lecchi had a spectacular collection of paintings (which included Raffael's "The Marriage of the Virgin," presently in the Brera in Milan, and the "*Madonnina*," presently in the Hermitage in Leningrad; in addition, his large collection of musical instruments included several harpsichords (one extremely rare by Domenico da Pesaro) and viols and violins by Amati and Stradivarius.[1] At least the visit of the Mozarts in March 1773[2] was spent in this town palace of Lecchi. In 1799, the edifice was sacked by Austro-Russian forces. Today the palace is surrounded by a small arcade of shops called the **Loggia delle Mercanzie**; in the two courtyards there are antique pillars incorporated into the renovated structure, with a sixteenth-century main portal depicting two imperial profiles, and seventeenth-eighteenth-century stucco decoration, including the window ornament reflecting Austrian Baroque influence.

★ ★ RIDOTTO IN THE THEATER (TEATRO GRANDE). Corso Zanardelli. During their first stay in Brescia, sometime between 4 and 11 February 1771, Mozart and his father attended the *opera buffa* in this theater. The prima donna of the performance was Angelica Maggiore, a former acquaintance of the Mozarts from Frankfurt and The Hague, who was "completely astonished" to see them. While the main hall of the theater (which stands on the same site as the first public theater of Brescia in 1664) was rebuilt 1809–10, several remarkable features remain from the theater which the Mozarts saw: the seventeenth-century facade (with a portico added in 1780), the seventeenth-century portal, and the superb *ridotto*, decorated lavishly with frescoes and stucco. Despite the addition of marble stucco, frescoed statues, and mirrors in 1894, the **ridotto** (which was constructed 1760–69 by A. Marchetti) has essentially retained the form as it was during the time of the Mozarts' visits.[3] It can be seen during a performance, or can be visited by asking permission in the rear entrance to the theater at Via Paganora Monday–Friday 9 AM–12:30 PM, or 3–6 PM.

[★ ★ CHARACTERISTIC SIGHTS OF BRESCIA]. During the five times the Mozarts passed through Brescia, they undoubtedly saw a few of the city's most renowned monuments, as was their habit. The fine square, **Piazza della Loggia**, is dominated by the **Loggia** (the present Municipal Palace), which dates from 1489; in the other noted square (**Piazza del Duomo**), are found the seventeenth-century "new Cathedral" (**Duomo Nuovo**) with a tower of white marble, and the circular Romanesque "old Cathedral" (**Duomo Vecchio**).[4] Behind the Cathedral, the library (**Biblioteca Queriniana**) of 1650, and the adjacent Archbishop's Palace of 1570, are important edifices which Mozart and his father would have seen. In addition, the medieval castle (**Castello**) is surrounded by a fine park. Interesting churches include **San Francesco**, in Lombard Romanesque style with a Gothic cloister, **SS. Nazaro e Celso**, with several art masterpieces, **S. Alessandro**, and the fifteenth-seventeenth-century **San Giovanni**.[5]

Excursion to Montirone

★ VILLA LECCHI AT MONTIRONE. During their visit to Brescia on 3–4 November 1772, Mozart and his father were guests of Count Faustino Lecchi, who owned this summer house in the neighboring town of Montirone; because of the time of year, the Mozarts were very possibly guests here.[6] The villa, which was constructed in 1736–46 by Antonio Turbino, has remained essentially in the original style; the walls in several rooms are frescoed, and there are gardens from the eighteenth century.[7] In the villa, which was once the location of Lecchi's famous painting gallery, Napoleon was the guest of the three Lecchi sons, who were generals in his army. The villa, as a stipulation in the will, can never be divided; it is owned by the present Count Lecchi.[8] *The villa is private property and cannot be visited*; however, the well-preserved facade can be seen.

N o t e s

1 Sartori, "Mozart in Brescia," 141ff.
2 Because their visit was during fall (November), C. Sartori believes that Lecchi "most certainly hosted them in his villa of Montirone." Sartori, "Mozart in Brescia," 141ff. Wyzewa also cites this tradition, in mentioning Lecchi's "chateau in the area of Brescia."
3 Mondini, "Guida al Teatro Grande," 42.
4 Michelin, *Italia*, 66.
5 Michelin, op. cit., 67.
6 See footnote #2.
7 Communicated by Andrea Pola, Municipio Monteroni.
8 Ibid. Although Mr. Pola was under the impression that the villa would be shown to scholars by advance permission, the present Count Lecchi (a descendant of the gracious patron and friend of the Mozarts) was unwilling to show the villa, or to respond to correspondence concerning this historic villa.

Mozart in Cremona

Dates

20 to about 22 January 1770

Little is known about the visit of Mozart and his father in Cremona; they were traveling from Salzburg to Milan, during the first trip to Italy. Leopold, who kept a travel notebook, cited the director of the orchestra in Cremona, as well as the organist of the Cathedral. In Cremona they heard the opera, *La clemenza di Tito*, by Michele Valentini, based on a libretto by Metastasio; Mozart, in the last year of his life, set the libretto to music in Prague.

Cremona Sites

★ ★ ★ THE CATHEDRAL (DUOMO). During their stay in Cremona, Mozart and his father met the cellist and concertmaster Antonio Ferrari here, as well as the cathedral organist Giacomo Arrighi.[1] The cathedral, in Romanesque-Lombard style, was consecrated in 1190, and boasts the highest bell tower in Italy (the thirteenth-century **Torrazzo**). The interior of the church has vaults and sides completely covered with frescoes and stucco. In addition, there are splendid side altars, a unique pulpit of marble bas-reliefs, and an ornate carved organ with a case in gold leaf. Open Monday–Saturday 7 AM–12 Noon and 3–7 PM; Sundays and holidays, 7 AM–1 PM and 4–7 PM.

★ "DOVE" INN ("HOTEL COLOMBINA"). via Sicardo, 11. The Mozarts are believed to have stayed in the "Dove," the historic inn across from the Duomo, where Emperor Joseph II, Napoleon, and Prince Alexander, the son of Czar Nicholas II, later stayed. The exterior of the building has antique pillars and wrought-iron balconies, two of which have carved doves underneath, as suggested by the name. The building today houses private apartments, remodeled since the eighteenth century, and offices on the ground floor.

★ ★ TEATRO NAZARI (TODAY TEATRO PONCHIELLI). Corso Vittorio Emanuele II, 52. This remarkable theater, reconstructed according to eighteenth-century plans, was designed in 1747 by Zaist and Galli Bibiena. It burned in 1806 and 1824, and today it is difficult to imagine how it was in the time of the Mozarts, when they heard the opera *La clemenza di Tito* by Valentini.[2] The **ridotto**, with painted *trompe-l'oeil* designs and Corinthian pillars, is in typical eighteenth-century scale.

Cremona. Inn, "The Dove."

[★ ★ CHARACTERISTIC SIGHTS OF CREMONA]. Mozart and his father usually saw the most characteristic monuments in each city they visited; during their stay in Cremona, from 20 January, to about 22 January 1770, these would have included the thirteenth-century **Palazzo Comunale**, which was remodeled during the Renaissance, including the terra-cotta decoration.[3] In addition, the three palaces, the sixteenth-century Renaissance **Palazzo Fodri** at Corso Matteotti, 17, **Palazzo Stanga** on via Palestro (decorated with sixteenth-century terra-cotta), and the Renaissance **Palazzo Raimondi** on Corso Garibaldi, present a view of the city which is representative of Cremona in the eighteenth century.[4] Important churches which have remained from the time of the Mozarts' visit include the fourteenth-century Lombard Gothic **Chiesa di Sant'Agostino**, and the fifteenth-century **Chiesa di San Sigismondo** (over a mile outside the city), constructed on the site where Francesco Sforza and Bianca Visconti were married in 1463.[5]

N o t e s

1 Schenk, *Mozart, eine Biographie*, 178.
2 Not by Hasse, as cited by Schenk. See Bauer/Deutsch/Eibl, *Mozart Briefe und Aufzeichnungen*, V, zu 158/41 (N).
3 Michelin, *Italia*, 88.
4 Ibid., 89.
5 Ibid.

Mozart in Florence

Dates

30 March–6 April 1770

During his week in Florence, despite a bout with the flu and travel fatigue, Mozart managed to circulate among the highest levels of Florentine society, perform feats at a gala evening with the same effort as "eating a piece of bread," and develop a close friendship with Thomas Linley, in addition to visiting "everything there is to see" in Florence. In his academy at Villa del Poggio Imperiale, Mozart performed, accompanied by the renowned violinist Nardini; Mozart also played the "most difficult fugues," in addition to improvising on the "most difficult themes," presented by Marquis Ligniville, the "strongest contrapuntalist in all of Italy." On 3 April, they were entertained by the castrato Giovanni Manzuoli, who later later sang the title role in Mozart's *Ascanio in Alba*; on 4 April, they were invited by the poetess Corilla, where Wolfgang played alternately with the young English violinist, Thomas Linley. On 6 April, Linley and Mozart were again entertained and played "not as boys, but as men," at the home of Administrator General, Gavard de Pivet. Other people they met included the castrato Nicolini, the Ambassador from England, Horace Mann, and Count Kaunitz. The city of Florence, with its extraordinary artistic heritage, left a dramatic impression.

Music

There is no known music written by Mozart during his week in Florence. Mozart's stay in Florence, however, was dominated by encounters with the two violinists Pietro Nardini, pupil of Tartini, and Thomas Linley; that Mozart's four collections of keyboard-violin music had been published as op. 1, 2, 3, and 4 (K. 6/7, K. 8/9, K. 10/15, K. 26/31, respectively) is also significant. This strongly indicates (despite the fact that it has been overlooked in the Mozart literature) that Mozart performed many of his own keyboard sonatas in Florence, as well as hearing numerous works of Tartini, the teacher of Nardini. In addition, his symphonies were most likely performed; these include (despite problematic dates) Symphony No. 9 in C, K. 73, as well as the earlier symphonies.

In addition, Mozart had just written various arias in Milan which could very possibly have been performed in Florence as well. These include K. Anh. 2/73A (lost), K. 143/73a, K. 78/73b, K. 88/73c, K. 79/73d, and K. 77/73e.

Florence Sites

★ **VILLA OF CORILLA.** via Fernando Zanetti, on the corner of Via de' Cerretani. On 3 April 1770, shortly after their arrival in Florence, Mozart and his father were entertained by Corilla Olimpica (Maddalena Morelli-Fernandez, poetess at the Florentine Court). Leopold wrote to his wife on 21 April 1770, "In Florence we discovered a young Englishman who is a pupil of the famous violinist, Nardini. This boy, who *plays wonderfully*, is about Wolfgang's age and height. He came into the home of the learned poetess Signora Corilla. . . . These two boys performed alternately the whole evening embracing each other continuously." The interior, mostly privately owned apartments, has been remodeled since the visit of the Mozarts, and little remains from the eighteenth century. One floor is occupied by the **Centro Studi e Documentation.** The austere, unimposing facade, with a massive wooden cornice, has been preserved. Commemorative plaque regarding Corilla.

★ **THE "BLACK EAGLE" INN (L'AQUILA NERA).** via Borgognissanti, 4. Mozart and his father arrived in Florence on 30 March 1770, and Leopold, in his travel notes, cited "al Aquila" as their lodging, which is most likely the "Black Eagle" Inn.[1] Here at their lodging, on 4 April 1770, Mozart played together with the young violinist Thomas Linley, with whom he performed the next day for the Finance Administrator Gavard. Today in the building at Via Borgognissanti, 4, there is a 3-star hotel, Hotel Goldoni, on the second floor. Like much of Florence, the facade has been maintained, while the interior of the building has been completely renovated. The only architectural detail in the hotel reminiscent of the past is the antique marble fireplace, with frescoed tiles. Close to the site, however, is a square (**Piazza d'Ognissanti**) which features splendid architecture similar to that which the Mozarts saw, and a view of the **Ponte alla Carraia**; a nearby church (**Chiesa di Ognissanti**), completely redone in the seventeenth century, has a thirteenth-fourteenth-century bell tower and a remarkable "Last Supper" by Ghirlandajo.[2]

[★ **RESIDENCE OF SIR HORACE MANN**]. via Santo Spirito 23.[3] Leopold cited the name of "Cavalier" Horace Mann, who was Ambassador of Great Britain to Florence from 1740 to 1786, in his travel notes. He was the uncle of his namesake, Sir Horace Mann, whom the Mozart family had visited at his country estate outside of Canterbury on 24 July 1765, during their "Great Western" trip. As the salon of Horace Mann in Florence was known for its artistic and intellectual brilliance, it has been speculated that Mozart and his father were invited here to this villa with a garden, on the Fondaccio di Santo Spirito.[4] During the period of the Mozarts' visit, Mann lived in the **Palazzo Manetti,** constructed in the fifteenth century.[5] The nearby Renaissance church (**Chiesa di Santo Spirito**), begun by Brunelleschi in 1444, has a fine Madonna by Filippino Lippi among other art treasures.[6]

★ **RESIDENCE OF GIOVANNI MANZUOLI.** After #20, via de' Bardi, at the Church of Santa Lucia dei Magnoli.[7] On 3 April 1770, Mozart and his father spent the afternoon at the residence of the world-famous soprano castrato, Manzuoli, whom the Mozarts had met in London in the autumn of 1764, and who later sang the title role in Mozart's *Ascanio in Alba* in Milan. The high standards and quality of singing "like Manzuoli" was a repeated phrase in the letters of Mozart and his father. During their afternoon with him, Manzuoli sang for them, including some arias by Mozart. The quarters of Manzuoli, where he invited the Mozarts, were at the church of Santa Lucia dei Magnoli (also called S. Lucia fra le Rovine), which is found on Via de' Bardi, across the Arno River from the city center.

★ ★ ★ **PALAZZO PITTI.** Piazza de' Pitti. On 1 April 1770, after Mass in the Chapel, the Mozarts received an audience with Archduke Peter Leopold, the third son of Maria Theresa, who knew the Mozarts since 1762 in Vienna. Leopold Mozart wanted to secure a post with the Archduke for his son, a desire which was to go unfulfilled. However, on 3 April 1770, Leopold wrote with enthusiasm, "Count Rosenberg sent us immediately to the Court, to the Duke de Salviati with the announcement that he wanted to introduce us to the Archduke. There in the Chapel we heard a sermon and Mass, and after the Mass we had an audience [in the Pitti Palace]. The Archduke was unbelievably kind and immediately asked how Nannerl was. He said that his wife was very eager to hear Wolfgang, and spoke a good quarter hour with us." The spectacular palace, as in the time of Mozart, is distinguished by a rough, imposing facade, constructed from plans by Brunelleschi, and features the splendid Palatine gallery and the Boboli Gardens. The chapel, although in the same place today as in 1770, no longer has the appearance it had in 1770, as it was refurnished with neoclassical decoration and frescoes in 1791 by the Ademollo brothers.[8] While it is difficult to say where the Archduke received his visitors in 1770, the state rooms of the Medici are a possibility; except for some stucco ceilings, however, little remains of the decoration from 1770, as they were changed in the 1850s.[9] Open 9 AM–2 PM (–1 PM on Sundays and holidays); closed Monday.

★ ★ **VILLA DEL POGGIO IMPERIALE.** Viale del Poggio Imperiale; 1 km southwest of the Piazzale di Porta Romana. Mozart played an academy here in the summer residence on 2 April 1770, accompanied by the virtuoso violinist Nardini. Leopold wrote, on 3 April 1770, "Things went as usual, and the astonishment was even greater, as the Marquis Ligniville [Eugene Marquis von Ligniville], the music director, is the strongest contrapuntalist in all of Italy, and

Florence. Palazzo Pitti. Engraving by Johann Sebastian Müller after Giuseppe Zocchi.

consequently gave Wolfgang the most difficult fugues and the most difficult themes, that [he] played off as one would eat a piece of bread." It has been suggested that for the ensemble performance of Mozart and Nardini, Ligniville chose the "Six Sonatas" for clavier and violin, op. 5 (1768) of Luigi Boccherini.[10] Today the villa houses an exclusive girls' school (**Collegio Statale della SS Annunziata**). In addition to lavishly renovated frescoed walls and ceilings

Florence. Villa del Poggio Imperiale. Engraving by Giuseppe Zocchi.

(often in nineteenth-century style), the villa features a *parterre* garden of box-woods overlooking an untouched area of Florence, as well as a hidden tunnel to Porta Romana. Although *it is generally closed to public*, permission to see the villa may be requested from the Direction during the morning.

★ ★ ★ CHARACTERISTIC SIGHTS OF FLORENCE. On 3 April 1770, Leopold wrote, "In these few days, I will see everything that there is to see." Wolfgang and Leopold undoubtedly visited the important architectural and artistic sites of Florence, including the **Palazzo Vecchio**, the **Cathedral Santa Maria del Fiore** (with the famous dome of Brunelleschi), the "Doors of Paradise" by Ghiberti, and the bell tower of Giotto), and Michelangelo's **Medici Chapel**; the spectacular walk to the eleventh-thirteenth-century Romanesque church, **Chiesa di San Miniato al Monte**, presented a fine panorama of Florence, as it does today.

N o t e s

1 Barblan/Damerini, *Mozart in Italia*, 88. See p. 80 for an eighteenth-century map of the area.
2 Michelin, *Italia*, 112.
3 Communicated by Dr. Angelo de Scisciolo, Archivio di Stato, Florence. In response to my questions, Dr. Scisciolo was able to locate this residence precisely, and that of Giovanni Manzuoli, in archival sources; they are presented here in the Mozart literature for the first time. It was not possible to locate the residence of Giuseppe Maria Gavard.
4 Barblan/Damerini, op. cit., 90.
5 Communicated by Dr. Angelo de Scisciolo, Archivio di Stato, Florence.
6 Michelin, op. cit., 112.
7 Communicated by Dr. Angelo de Scisciolo, Archivio di Stato, Florence.
8 Communicated by Dr. Cristina Piacenti, Direttore, Soprintendenza per i Beni artistici e storici di Firenze e Pistoia.
9 Ibid.
10 Fausto Torrefranca, cited in Barblan/Damerini, op. cit., 94.

$\mathcal{M}$ozart in Lodi

About 16 March 1770

$\mathcal{I}$n 1770, when Leopold and Wolfgang stayed the night in an inn in Lodi, the town was one of the changing posts for the coach horses for the route from Milan to Piacenza (which for Mozart then led to Parma and Bologna). The primary interest in Lodi lies in the fact that it was here that Mozart wrote his first string quartet, in an inn at 7 PM. Perhaps it was after hearing the chamber music of Sammartini that Mozart decided to write this three-movement string quartet; four years later, in Salzburg, he added a rondeau as the fourth movement, and he liked the work well enough to take it to Paris eight years later.

M u s i c

Three-movement string quartet, K. 80/73f.

Lodi Sites

★ **GENERAL SITE OF THE INN (LOCANDA)**. Piazzale 3 agosto. On 15 March 1770, on the first leg of their extensive trip to Bologna, Florence, Rome, and Naples, Mozart and his father stopped in Lodi overnight. In the inn, "at seven in the evening," Mozart wrote his first string quartet, the three-movement K. 80/73f, to which he later added a rondeau movement. The location of the **Locanda**, which would have been in close proximity to the post stop, has been a source of dispute; however, it was most likely here, where a post station stood near the former convent of the nuns of San Giovanni in 1770.[1] Nearby, at Via Colle Eghezzone 5, some remaining walls of the monastery can be seen. At #100 Corso Archinti, there is a building, in poor repair, which suggests the characteristic appearance of an eighteenth-century inn.

[★ **POST STOP**]. via Archinti, 16. Another post stop in Lodi, built by the Mola brothers to replace the post stop near the convent of San Giovanni was located here; however, it probably was constructed after the time of the Mozarts' visit.[2] The restrained Austrian Baroque facade, and the courtyard with stucco ornament present a characteristic glimpse into the eighteenth century.

[POST STOP]. Corso Mazzini, 88. The Mola brothers also built this post stop to succeed that near the convent of San Giovanni, perhaps around the same time as the post stop at Via Archinti.[3] For many years it was believed that this was the location of the inn where Mozart wrote his first string quartet, and a commemorative plaque with the erroneous date of 10 March 1770 was erected in 1956. It can still found on the building. However, in 1770, there was no post stop here, and the edifice, with the adjacent inn annex, did not exist at that time.[4]

★ COACH ITINERARY OF THE MOZARTS.[5] The route of the post coach from the old gates through Lodi in the time of the visit of Mozart and his father provides an interesting itinerary of the city in the eighteenth century. The partial remains of the old gate where visitors entered the city can be seen, covered by vines, in Piazzale Fiume; today there is a small pedestrian street. The route led through the present streets, Via dell ' Acquedotto, Viale Dante, and Corso Vittorio Emmanuele, crossing Piazza Maggiore *en route* to the inn.

[★ ★ CHARACTERISTIC SIGHTS OF LODI]. With Leopold's keen interest in the important architectural monuments of each city he visited, it is likely that he and Mozart strolled to the fine **Piazza Maggiore**, located a few minutes from the post stop near the convent of San Giovanni. The austere twelfth-century Lombard Romanesque Cathedral (**Duomo**) and the fourteenth-century **Palazzo Vistarini**, which is opposite the cathedral, are noteworthy. The fifteenth-century cloister of the Holy Spirit in the Old Hospital (**Chiostro dell' Ospedale Vecchio**) is also of interest, as is the nearby fifteenth-century **Palazzo Mozzanica-Vignati**, with a facade in terra cotta. Important churches include the frescoed fourteenth-century **S. Agnese**, the twelfth-century **S. Francesco**, the sixteenth-century **S. Christoforo**, and the imposing Baroque church **S. Filippo**, with the adjacent monastery which today contains the civic museum and library (**Museo Civico e Biblioteca Comunale**). However, the most spectacular sight of Lodi is the **Tempio dell' Incoronata**, begun in 1488. With the polyptych by the Piazza brothers, it presents a masterpiece of architecture and fresco; the treasury, located under the church, contains numerous miniatures and liturgical vessels.

N o t e s

1 Agnelli, ". . . lapide mozartiana alla Gatta." This site was overlooked in the Bauer/Deutsch/Eibl notes to the Mozart letters.
2 Agnelli, ". . . lapide mozartiana alla Gatta."
3 Ibid.
4 Ibid.
5 This itinerary, presented here for the first time, was communicated by Dott. Alessandro Caretta, Liceo "P. Verri."

Mozart in Mantua

Dates

10–19 January 1770

After arriving in the afternoon from Verona during their first Italian trip, *en route* to Milan, Mozart and his father went immediately to the opera. On 11–12 January 1770, they tried, unsuccessfully, to visit Prince Thurn-and-Taxis and his wife Theresia. However, their subsequent reception by Count Francesco Eugenio Arco was more pleasant. On 16 January 1770, Mozart gave his concert for the Royal Academy of Science; a newspaper article later described him as a "marvel of music."

Music

Neal Zaslaw, author of *Mozart's Symphonies*, notes, "Symphonies played at Verona, Mantua, Bologna, Milan, Florence, and Naples apparently were brought from Salzburg, following Leopold's policy to have ready while on tour 'four or six symphonies with the parts doubled for concert use.' Likely candidates include K. 62a, the three Viennese symphonies (K. 43, 45, and 48), the revised version of K. 45a, and (if it is genuine and has been correctly placed chronologically) K. Anh. 216/73g/C. 11.03)" Einstein speculated that the three symphonies likely performed at Mantua were K. Anh. 215/66c, Anh. 217/66d, and Anh. 218/66e. However, they have been lost; only their *incipits* are known from the Breitkopf catalog.

In any case, the program played in Mantua is astonishing. Mozart first directed one of his symphonies, after which he played a keyboard concerto at sight. This was followed by an aria of a local composer, then a keyboard sonata, with variations performed by Mozart, and then transposed. There was then an aria composed and sung by Mozart on a theme presented to him on the violin. In addition, there was an aria by a local composer, followed by an oboe concerto by a local composer, a fugue played by Mozart on the keyboard on a theme presented to him, a symphony played by Mozart based on a single violin part, a duet by a local composer, a trio in which Mozart played a violin part at sight, and finally a symphony by Mozart.

Mantua Sites

★ ★ ★ THEATER OF THE PHILHARMONIC ACADEMY (TEATRO AC-
CADEMICO DEL BIBIENA). via Accademia, 47. Leopold wrote about the new
theater by Galli Bibiena which had opened only six weeks earlier: "I wish that
you had seen the place where the academy was held. . . . I have never seen
anything more beautiful of this kind. . . . It is not a theater, but like the hall of an
opera house with boxes." The academy Mozart performed here on 16 January
1770 included three of his symphonies. The theater is a miniature jewel, in a
severe classical style; it was renovated 1962–63 and has a small seating room,
surrounded by small tiers of boxes in grey and pink wood *faux-marbre* with gold
leaf. The stucco sculptures and bas-reliefs of the ridotto, and the portraits in the
Maria Theresa Room are of interest; they can be seen upon request. Open daily
9 AM–Noon and 3–5:30 PM; closed Sundays and holidays; admission charge.

SITE OF THE HOME OF SIGNORA SARTORETTI. Contrada Due Catene;
today via Dario Tassoni. Very little is known about the kind woman who gave
Mozart a salve for his hands, which were cracked from the frost. On 17 January
1770, she invited the Mozarts to her home, and later sent Wolfgang a present of
four ducats, with a poem and a bouquet. She was perhaps Margherita Sartoretti,
the wife of Tomaso Sartoretti who lived on Contrada Due Catene near the
Palazzo d' Arco.[1] The home of Sartoretti has been encompassed within two
edifices from the nineteenth century.[2]

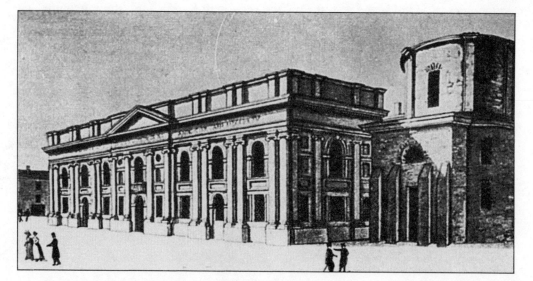

*Mantua. Accademia Virgiliana (Filarmonica). Engraving by Lanfranco-
Puzzi after F. L. Montini.*

★ ★ PALACE OF COUNT ARCO. Piazza d' Arco, 4; entrance at Piazza d' Arco, 1. On 12 January 1770, Mozart and his father were invited here by Count Francesco d' Arco, cousin of the Salzburg Count Georg Arco; Leopold wrote that they received "every grace and courtesy" in this home. The present palace, completely renovated inside in 1784 with a new Palladian facade by Colonna, is on the same site of the palace which the Mozarts visited in 1770. Since that time a garden has been added, and the Renaissance buildings (with the spectacular sixteenth-century frescoed "Zodiac Room") behind it have been annexed. Numerous paintings, antiques, and household utensils remain from the time of Mozart's visit, as well as features from some rooms such as original ceilings and tiles, and parts of the facade on Via Portazzolo. Open 9 AM–1 PM daily except Monday; 2:30–5 PM (1 March–30 September); 2:30–3:30 PM (1 October–28 February); admission charge.

★ HOME OF GAETANO BETTINELLI. via Fratelli Bandiera, at the corner of Via Certosini.[3] Leopold wrote on 26 January 1770, "In Mantua . . . especially a certain Mr. Bettinelli, together with his brother and his brother's wife made themselves completely at our service." This gracious host of the Mozarts was Gaetano Bettinelli, the mathematician, who almost certainly invited Mozart and his father here to his home.

SITE OF THE "GREEN CROSS" INN (ALBERGO "CROCE VERDI"). Behind the present Teatro Sociale (built in 1822), towards the present Corso Umberto Iº (which was previously contrada Croce Verde, then contrada Monticelli Bianchi).[4] When Mozart and his father arrived in Mantua at 5 PM on 10 January 1770, they lodged here in the "Green Cross," an inn which no longer exists. Within an hour of their arrival at the inn, they were at the opera to hear Hasse's *Demetrio*.[5]

★ ★ PALACE OF PRINCE MICHAEL II VON THURN UND TAXIS. via Pietro Frattini, (old street number 2062).[6] The treatment of Leopold Mozart and Wolfgang by Prince Thurn und Taxis and his wife was a remarkably bad experience from their first Italian journey. On 12 January 1770, the prince was too busy to see them, as his wife had been the day before. In two letters, Leopold described in detail his unpleasant experience attempting to visit Prince von Thurn and Taxis, even after following the Prince's carriage after church; this prompted him to write, "Heaven help me, if I wanted to disturb a person's work." The *palazzo*, which belonged to the noble family de Soardi of Mantua, has been recently restored by the local government, and is presently the seat of the government offices. Inside, a fresco, including the coat-of-arms, dating back to the second half of the sixteenth century, has been restored.[7]

[★ ★ CHURCHES OF MANTUA]. Leopold and Wolfgang regularly visited the important churches in each city, which included in 1770 **St. Andrea**, the monumental basilica built in 1472 from plans by Alberti, with a cupola added many years later by Juvaro; the theatrical Chapel of the Immaculate and the frescoed dome are of interest, as are the beautiful organ case and the altar of green marble. In addition, Luigi Gatti, mentioned in Leopold's notes, was vice Kapellmeister of the Court Church (**Cappella Santa Barbara**) in the Ducal Palace. The Renaissance basilica was commissioned by the Gonzagas and built 1562–65, and shows surprising originality. Finally, Mozart and his father undoubtedly visited the cathedral (**Duomo**), dedicated to St. Peter. The facade is by Baschiera and dates from the eighteenth century; the right flank is Gothic, and the bell tower is Romanesque. Giulio Romano reconstructed the interior after a fire in 1545; paintings by the school of Giulio Romano and the fine stucco decoration are noteworthy.

[★ ★ CHARACTERISTIC SIGHTS OF MANTUA]. Important sights remaining from the time of Mozart's visit include the Ducal Palace (**Palazzo Ducale**), the seat of the Gonzagas, a complex of buildings including 500 rooms, gardens, colonnades, squares and courtyards; it was built between the thirteenth and eighteenth centuries incorporating the fourteenth-century **Castello San Giorgio**. The *palazzo* contains Mantegna's masterpiece, the *"Camera degli Sposi"* of 1471. Also of interest is the Gonzaga country villa **Palazzo Té**, constructed between 1525 and 1535 by Raphael's pupil, Giulio Romano.[8]

N o t e s

1 Bauer/Deutsch/Eibl, *Mozart Briefe*, V, zu 156/13.
2 Communicated by Prof.essa Giuseppina Pastore, Mantua.
3 Barblan/Schenk, *Mozart in Italia*, 59
4 Communicated by Prof.essa Giuseppina Pastore, Mantua.
5 In the "Guida numerica alle casee agli stabilimenti di Mantova" (Mantova, 1858), among the old edifices, an inn is mentioned called "Croce Verde," which at that time was part of the adjacent inn called the "Phoenix" (La Fenice). It is probably the same inn as the one where the Mozarts stayed; presently the inn no longer exists. The edifice, much remodeled, is still used today as residences. Communicated by Prof.essa Giuseppina Pastore, Mantua.
6 Bauer/Deutsch/Eibl, op. cit., 155/10.
7 Communicated by Prof.essa Giuseppina Pastore, Mantua.
8 Michelin, *Italia*, 135.

Mozart in Milan

23 January–15 March 1770 ▪ 18 October 1770–about 4 February 1771 (with two weeks in Turin in January 1771) ▪ 21 August–5 December 1771 ▪ 4 November 1772–about 4 March 1773

ozart and his father traveled to Milan from Salzburg three times, during which time three of Mozart's theatrical works were performed in the Theater "Regio Ducale." During their first trip, they met Sammartini at the house of their major patron, Count Firmian, and it was arranged for Mozart to write as the first opera of Carnival season 1770–71; *Mitridate* was later chosen as the opera. They left for an extensive tour of Italy, traveling as far as Bologna, Naples and Rome. Returning to Milan on 18 October 1770, Mozart began seriously to compose *Mitridate*, which, despite several intrigues, was a success. Mozart and his father left Milan for two weeks in Turin (about which very little is known), then returned soon after to Salzburg.

Mozart's second visit was tied to the marriage of Archduke Ferdinand, for whom Mozart wrote the *festa teatrale, Ascanio in Alba*, which apparently overshadowed Hasse's opera *Il Ruggiero*, written for the same occasion. Despite Ferdinand's interest in engaging Mozart, his mother, Maria Theresa, wrote to him, discouraging him to engage "useless people."

Mozart's third visit to Milan was related to his commission to write the opera, *Lucio Silla*; Leopold's quest to obtain a position for Mozart in Florence was, like that in Milan, unsuccessful (most likely due to the negative intervention of Maria Theresa).

M u s i c

ARIAS K. A. nh. 2/73A, K. 88/73c, K. 79/73d, K. 77/73e; several perhaps written to prove Mozart's ability to write an opera in Milan.
K. 74b written for Milan or Pavia, early 1771; suggests that Mozart and his father traveled to Pavia, without doubt visiting the renowned Certosa di Pavia along the way.

THEATRICAL WORKS *Mitridate*, K. 87/74a.
Ascanio in Alba, K. 111.

Ballet music for *Ascanio in Alba*, K. A. nh. 207/A. nh. C27.06, probably in Milan, late 1771; nine numbers have survived, arranged for keyboard
Lucio Silla, K. 135.
Ballet music for *Lucio Silla*: "Le gelosie del serraglio," K. A. nh. 109/135a, probably written in Milan, late 1772, although this has been contested.

WIND ENSEMBLE Divertimento, K. 113.
Divertimento K. 186/159d; Milan, March 1773, and its companion piece, K. 166/159d.

MOTET "Exsultate jubilate," K. 165/158a; written for the castrato Venanzio Rauzzini; performed 17 January 1773.

SYMPHONIES K. 84/73q; either Milan or Bologna, 1770; attributed to others.
K. 74, Milan 1770; questionable if Mozart is the author.
K. A. nh. 216/74g/A. nh C11.03; Milan or Salzburg, 1770–71.
K. 120/111a; Milan, October–November 1771; a finale was written to form symphony with the overture to *Ascanio in Alba*.
K. 96/111b; Milan, October–November 1771.
K. 112; Milan, 2 November 1771.
In addition, the symphonies written for Rome in 1770, K. 81/73l, K. 97/73m, and K. 95/73n, should be regarded as part of the extended cultural milieu of Milan.

STRING QUARTETS K. 80/73f; written in Lodi (presently less than 40 minutes from Milan) on 15 March 1770 (first 3 movements only).
K. 156/134b; Milan, end 1772.
K. 157; Milan, end 1772–early 1773.
K. 158, Milan, end 1772–early 1773.
K. 159, Milan, early 1773.
K. 160/159a; Milan, early 1773.

DANCE MUSIC Contredanses, K. 123/73g; written in Rome, 13–14 April 1770, should perhaps also be regarded within the Milan cultural milieu; also the dance music, K. 122/73t, written perhaps in Bologna, August 1770, should be seen within this context.

Milan Sites

★ ★ CHURCH AND MONASTERY OF SAINT MARK (CHIESA E CONVENTO DI SAN MARCO). 2, Piazza S. Marco. During Mozart's first trip to Milan, from 23 January 1770 to 15 March 1770, he and his father stayed in the monastery lodgings for foreigners (*forestieria*). Leopold described the quarters in a letter dated 26 January 1770:

We have three large guest rooms. In the first room we have a fire burning; there we eat and entertain visitors. . . . We each sleep on four good mattresses, and each night the bed is warmed, so that Wolfgang is always happy to go to bed. We have our own Brother, Father Alphonso to serve us, and we are very comfortable here.

Although it was previously believed that the *forestieria* where the Mozarts stayed was in the area surrounding the existing courtyard, it was recently discovered that it was, in fact, in a wing within a second major courtyard, which has been demolished; on the site of the wing today stands a school, **Liceo Parini**, at Via Goito, 4.[1] The church of Saint Mark was founded in 1254, and has a facade finished in 1871 with an ancient portal, a pointed arch in stone. The interior, in Baroque style, is in the form of a Latin cross; the series of chapels along Via Fatebenefratelli preserve their original form from the thirteenth century.[2] In a second courtyard there is a commemorative plaque citing Mozart's soujourn. The existing courtyard, with several architectural features of the monastery that are intact from the time of the Mozarts' visit, can be seen by asking permission at #2, to the left of the church; there is a small museum as well containing numerous frescoes and other art works, and a fine chapel in carved wood paneling. The church is open Monday–Saturday 7:30 AM–Noon and 4–7 PM; Sundays 7:30 AM–1 PM and 4–7 PM.

SITE OF PALAZZO MELZI. via Fatebenefratelli, 21. During their three trips to Italy, the palace of Count Firmian in Milan was a focal point for Mozart and his father. The palace, which was owned by Princess Melzi, was the home of the important patron of the arts, Count Karl Firmian, the Governor General of Lombardy; in addition, later, Princess Maria Beatrice Ricciardi d'Este resided here and also in the **Palazzo Regio Ducale.** It was in this palace that Mozart met the important composer of symphonies, string quartets, and opera, G. B. Sammartini, on 7 February 1770, at which time Mozart performed. On 18 February 1770, the Duke of Modena and his daughter, the future wife of Archduke Ferdinand, came here to hear Mozart, an occasion which probably resulted in Mozart receiving the commission to write *Ascanio in Alba*. Again, on 12 March 1770, Mozart performed in a concert here, to which more than 150 people of the "highest nobility" were invited; a recitative and three soprano arias by Mozart to texts by Metastasio (K. Anh. 2/73a, K. 88/73c, and K. 77/73e, most likely performed by a castrato) were performed at this time.[3] On 4 January 1771, Mozart again performed for Count Firmian, playing a "new, beautiful, and difficult concerto" at sight. It was also here that Mozart was invited with the famous composer J. A. Hasse on 8 November 1771, and presented with a watch set with diamonds. Other concerts here by Mozart took place on 21, 22, and 23 December 1772 as well. The palace was bombed in 1943; on the site today is the Hotel Cavour. Nearby, the twelfth-century city gate, with a fourteenth-century "Virgin with Child" in stone, **Porta Nuova**, still remains from the time of Mozart's sojourns.

★ ★ ★ CATHEDRAL (DUOMO). 18, Piazza Duomo. This famous cathedral was the site of the wedding of Archduke Ferdinand and Maria Beatrice Ricciardi d'Este on 15 October 1771, for which occasion Mozart was commissioned to write the theatrical work, *Ascanio in Alba*. Leopold reported seeing "20,000 pounds of wax candles, that have been laid out, in order to light the Cathedral, the Court, and other places on the 15th." The square of the cathedral was also the site of another event in Mozart's life: On 30 November 1771, Mozart wrote to his sister that he witnessed the hanging of "four guys" here. The **Duomo** was begun in 1386, and reflects late-Gothic style, with neoclassic features; at the time of Mozart's visits, it was without a facade, which was not finished until 1805–13, as a result of Napoleon's orders. The edifice, recently restored, boasts more than 3,400 statues, of which about 2,300 are on the outside. It is the third largest Catholic structure in the world, and has a spectacular interior supported by 52 pillars; there is magnificent stained glass which dates from the fifteenth century, as well.[4] The view from the terrace (*terrazzi*) is extraordinary.

Milan. Reggio Ducale Theater. Engraving by Marco Antonio Dal Rè.

★ ROYAL PALACE (PALAZZO REALE) AND SITE OF THE "REGIO DUCALE" THEATER (TEATRO REGIO DUCALE). via Palazzo Reale, adjacent to the cathedral. This imposing neo-classic palace, built upon an ancient Roman foundation and a Spanish structure, was designed by Piermarini, the most important eighteenth-century architect of Milan (who designed the La

Scala opera house); however, the reconstruction based on Piermarini's designs took place 1773–78, and Mozart therefore did not see it in its present form. Mozart and his father heard numerous operas and attended balls frequently in the former theater located in the right wing of the palace, on the site of which the **Salone delle Cariatidi** is found today. Three of Mozart's stage works were first performed here. *Mitridate*, directed from the keyboard by the fourteen-year-old Mozart, premiered on 26 December 1770. Including the three ballets, it lasted six hours. For the spectacular wedding of Archduke Ferdinand, Mozart was commissioned to write *Ascanio in Alba*, which premiered 17 October 1771, and was significantly more successful than Hasse's *Il Ruggiero*, written for the same occasion. Finally, on 26 December 1772, the first performance of *Lucio Silla* took place. Despite Mozart's success, however, he was not permanently engaged in Milan. The theater, which was the predecessor of the renowned La Scala opera house, was built in 1717, and completely destroyed by fire in 1776. The interior of the palace is completely modernized; one section is open for art exhibitions daily except Monday 9:30 AM–7:30 PM (–10:30 PM on Thursday); hours subject to change; admission charge. Another wing houses the Cathedral Museum.

GENERAL SITE OF THE "THREE KINGS" HOTEL ("ALBERGO TRE RÉ"). via Giardino, near Piazza Diaz.[5] On 21 September 1771, Leopold wrote:

A few days ago Miss Davies arrived here; she drove past our lodging in the mail coach. I recognized her and she recognized us, as we had just been standing on the balcony. I went a few hours later to the "Three Kings" to visit her; I guessed that she would be staying there as it is the most distinguished hotel. It is not far from us.

Marianne Davies was a virtuoso on the glass harmonica, an instrument which had been significantly improved by Benjamin Franklin. The site of her hotel is of interest, as it is not known where the Mozarts stayed during their second Milanese soujourn, from 21 August to 5 December 1771.

★ CHURCH OF THE TEATI BROTHERS (CHIESA DI S. ANTONIO ABATE DEI FRATI TEATI). via di S. Antonio. On 17 January 1773, Mozart's "Exsultate, jubilate," K. 165/158a, was performed here.[6] Mozart, on 16 January 1773, wrote that his motet for the *primo uomo* (castrato) Rauzzini, would be performed the next day at the "Theatinern." The church was not a "theater" church, but a church of the Teati brothers, part of a former monastery (at #5), which has a twelfth-century courtyard from which the fourteenth-fifteenth-century bell tower can be seen.[7] The church was erected in 1367, and reconstructed in 1582; the somber classic facade (not from the time of Mozart; unfinished, from 1832), with a Greek pediment, and statues of four saints in niches, can be seen. The interior, with seventeenth-century Milanese stucco and frescoes, can only be seen when the church is open for special services, such as Confirmation, which takes place on the second and fourth Sunday of each month, at 9 AM. Nearby, at #6, via Festa del Perdono, is the picturesque **Ospedale Maggiore**, dating back to the fifteenth–seventeenth centuries, which today houses the humanities department of the university. A large part of the *Ospedale* was destroyed in 1943 and reconstructed.

[★ ★ SFORZESCO CASTLE (CASTELLO SFORZESCO)]. Piazza Castello. Milan in the eighteenth century was a leading center of instrumental music, and several times a week, open-air concerts were given with a large orchestra on the ramparts of **Castello Sforzesco**.[8] The massive structure, which has its origins in the fourteenth century, was reconstructed by Francesco Sforza; it has been altered numerous times in the past centuries.[9] Mozart's "Divertimento," K. 186/159b, with a progressive orchestration of two each of oboes, clarinets, English horns, horns, and bassoons, written in Milan in March 1773, and its companion piece, K. 166/159d with the same orchestration, may have had a connection with this open-air tradition.

★ ★ PALAZZO LITTA. 24, Corso Magenta. On 10 February 1770, Leopold wrote:

Meanwhile we have had the opportunity of hearing various kinds of church music and yesterday we listened to the High Mass or Requiem for old Marchese Litta, who died during Carnival, much to the annoyance of his large family, as they would have gladly granted him the possibility of living until Lent. The "Dies Irae" of the Requiem lasted about three quarters of an hour . . . we didn't get to the table for lunch until 2:30 PM.

The "old Marchese" who died was Antonio Litta Visconti Arese, who had been married to Paola Visconti Borromeo; he owned the Palazzo Vercellana (Corso Magenta #24). Palazzo Litta, begun in 1648 by F. Ricchino belonged to the various Dukes Litta Visconti Arese; the facade, from 1752 to 1763, is the work of B. Bolli. The facade features two giants, and large grotesque masks. Inside, there is a monumental staircase by C. Merlo (1740); original tapestries, and the eighteenth-century stucco and painting by Martin Knoller and the Gerli brothers, provide an idea of the opulence of the Melzi palace, which was destroyed in WW II.[10] Today, in the palace, there are the offices of the State Railroad; two or three rooms can be visited by asking permission Monday–Friday 4–5 PM.

[★ ★ CHURCHES OF MILAN]. Although Charles Burney was enthusiastic in describing the church music in Milan during his visit in 1770, Leopold was decidedly not; on 10 February 1770 he wrote to his wife:

You must not expect me to give you a description of the native religious services here; I couldn't do it out of sheer exasperation. Everything imaginable is in the music, and it is ornamented in the church; the remainder is, by the way, the most abominable wantonness.

Aside from the churches which have a decided association with Mozart (**Duomo, S. Marco,** and **S. Antonio**), there are numerous churches which were important in the period of Mozart's visits, which can still be seen today.[11] These include S. Maria del Carmine (where Dr. Burney heard Sammartini); S. Maria della Grazie (with the *refettorio* which has "The Last Supper" of Leonardo da Vinci); the massive basilica of the patron saint of Milan, S. Ambrogio; S. Fedele (near La Scala); S. Maria della Passione (near the Conservatorio G. Verdi); S. Alessandro near **Palazzo Trivulzio** (which had a college for noblemen that was an important center of music); and S. Gottardo in Corte (the court chapel), in the back of the **Palazzo Reale.**

[★ ★ CHARACTERISTIC PALACES OF MILAN]. Despite Milan's unchecked growth in the past fifty years, without aesthetic direction, numerous monumental palaces remain from the time of Mozart in Milan. Of interest are the seventeenth-century **Palazzo Trivulzio** (redone in the early eighteenth century), at #6, Piazza S. Alessandro; at #5, via Clerici is found the early eighteenth-century **Palazzo Clerici,** with a gallery of tapestries, and a fresco by Tiepolo inside (*closed to the public*); opposite from La Scala is the monumental **Palazzo Marino,** begun in 1578; and, the seventeenth-century **Palazzo Brera** (which was a Jesuit college in the time of Mozart) today houses the exceptional Brera Gallery; nearby, at #15 is the fine **Palazzo Cusani** (1719).[12] Finally, at #12–14, via Manzoni are the two **Palazzi Poldi Pezzoli,** the first of which was begun in the seventeenth century (later reconstructed); it houses a remarkable collection of furniture, *objets d'art*, and paintings.

[★ ★ EXCURSION TO LAGO MAGGIORE]. On 8 September 1770, Leopold wrote to his wife about his intention to visit the Borromean Islands, "which are not far away and are noteworthy sights."[13] The islands are usually reached from Stresa, which is about an hour from Milan. **Isola bella,** shaped like a huge boat, has numerous gardens, terraces, and a remarkable view; the numerous rooms of the villa can be visited. **Isola Madre** has fine sixteenth-century gardens in which white peacocks roam, and a marionette museum of the Borromeo family, executed by the set designers of La Scala. The **Isola dei Pescatori** is a more natural setting, with its port and characteristic village.

N o t e s

1 Barille, *Inventari quattrocentesche della biblioteca*; it is published here for the first time in the Mozart literature.
2 Touring Club Italiano, *Milano*, 247.
3 Sadie, footnotes to E. Anderson, *Letters of Mozart* (3rd ed.), 118.

4 Touring Club Italiano, op. cit., 130–33.
5 "From 1878, the Via dei Tre Re was changed into Via Tre Alberghi, as seen in the 'Pianta della Cittá di Milano,' edizione di Antonio Vallardi. Today, after the urban renewal of the first part of the twentieth century, the street disappeared and today it can be individuated, more or less, in the small Via Giardino near piazza Diaz." Communicated by Dott. ssa Gabriella Cagliari Poli, Direttore, Archivio di Stato di Milano in response to my queries and published here for the first time in the Mozart literature.
6 The identity of this church, which today exists intact, is another surprising oversight in the Mozart literature. It was located, in response to my queries, by both Prof. Giulia Bologna of the Archivio Storico Civico e Biblioteca Trivulziana, and Don Bruno Bosatra of the Curia Archivescovile di Milano.
7 Touring Club Italiano, op. cit., 194.
8 Doná', "Milan," *Groves*, 294.
9 Michelin, *Italia*, 139.
10 Touring Club, op. cit., 423–24.
11 A good criterion for understanding which churches were important in the period of Mozart's sojourns is the list of churches for which Sammartini (the most important Milanese *maestro di capella* of the period) furnished musical works, in 1775, at the end of his life. Cf. Churgin/Jenkins, *Thematic Catalogue of the Works of G. B. Sammartini*, 9.
12 Touring Club, op. cit., 194.
13 However, Joseph Heinz Eibl, in an article dealing specifically with the question of whether Mozart and his father could have visited Lago Maggiore, concluded that it would not have been possible; the day-by-day chronicle indicates that time was too short, and Mozart was too engaged in writing *Mitridate*.

*M*ozart in Naples

D a t e s

14 May–25 June 1770

*D*uring their first Italian trip, Mozart and his father departed from Milan, toward Rome and Naples, as part of a great "Italian" trip, which every educated eighteenth-century German speaker desired as part of the fundamental cultural experience. Thanks to letters of recommendation, Mozart was received by the highest society in Naples, including Minister Marchese Bernardo Tanucci, English Ambassador William Hamilton, and the Imperial Ambassador Count Ernst Christoph Kaunitz-Rietberg. In addition to meeting Paisiello, Mozart and his father managed to make the most renowned excursion from Naples, which included Pozzuoli, Baia, Vesuvius, Pompeii, Herculaneum, Caserta and Capodimonte.

In addition, Mozart was amply encouraged by numerous women in Naples, including Countess Kaunitz-Rietberg, Mrs. Hamilton, Princess Belmonte, Princess Francavilla and Duchess Calabritta, who jointly sponsored an academy in the home of the Imperial Ambassador, Kaunitz-Rietberg.

Naples Sites

★ ★ SAN GIOVANNI A CARBONARA. via San Giovanni a Carbonara (near the Central Train Station). When Leopold and Wolfgang arrived in Naples on 14 May 1770, they lodged in a house belonging to the Augustinian Monastery, and were invited to the monastery for lunch on 10 June 1770, where a "great feast" was held. Although the monastery was transformed into a barracks, the church (founded in 1343, and renovated at the beginning of the fifteenth century, and again in the eighteenth century) can be seen; it is renowned for the sculpture found inside. Above the eighteenth-century staircase, there is a fine Gothic portal; inside, the fifteenth-century frescoes and maiolica pavement in the circular chapel of Caracciolo del Sole are noteworthy, as is the monument to the fifteenth-century King of Naples, Ladislaw.[1] The church was severely damaged in 1943, and is slowly undergoing restoration.

★ SITE OF THE CONSERVATORY "DELLA PIETÁ DEI TURCHINI." via Medina, next to #24 (which is Palazzo Fondi). In April 1792, Nannerl wrote that during Mozart's concert at this conservatory, a rumor was circulated that his playing was produced by a magic ring, and that his removal of the ring created great excitement. The conservatory was founded in 1583, and had among its illustrious pupils Niccoló Jommelli, whom Mozart and his father met in Naples. The name "Turchini" derives from the color turquoise, which the orphans in the conservatory wore. The conservatory combined with other Neapolitan musical institutions in 1806, under the direction of Giovanni Paisiello and others; in 1808, the conservatory moved to the former convent of San Sebastiano, and in 1826, relocated to the present site, at San Pietro di Maiella. The church "della Pietá dei Turchini" still exists; it was founded in 1592, and was remodeled around the middle of the seventeenth century. Inside, there are numerous art works in the various chapels. Nearby there is the eighteenth-century Palazzo Fondi, rebuilt to designs of Vanvitelli, with frescoes by F. Fischetti on the first floor (American: Second floor).[2]

Naples. Teatro San Carlo (San Carlo Theater). Unsigned engraving.

★ ★ SAN CARLO THEATER. via S. Carlo. On 30 May 1770, Mozart and his father heard *Armida abbandonata* by Jommelli here, which Mozart described as "beautiful, but too serious and old-fashioned for the theater." The impresario Amadori later made Mozart an offer to write an opera here, which was not possible because of Mozart's contract with Milan. Years later, in 1777, Mozart wrote about his offer from Myslivíček in Munich, to write an opera for this theater during Carnival, an offer which never came to fruition. The grey-and-white theater, which Mozart described as "beautiful," was built in 1737 and reconstructed in neoclassical style in 1816.[3] Open 10 AM–Noon; closed Monday and during August.

★ ★ CERTOSA OF SAINT MARTIN (CERTOSA DI SAN MARTINO). On 16 June 1770, Leopold and Wolfgang ate at this splendid monastery, one of the finest examples of Neapolitan Baroque style. They "visited all the sights and rarities of the place and admired the view" of the Gulf of Naples (the "Belvedere," which can be seen from Room 25). This enormous monastery, renovated in the sixteenth to seventeenth centuries, overhangs the Sant Elmo Fortress. The white cloister of Fanzago and the lavish Baroque church with their multicolored marble, stucco, and paintings are impressive. In addition, the monks' choir, the paintings by Reni and Ribera, and the inlaid sacristy are exceptional.[4] Open 9 AM–2 PM (–1 PM on Sundays and holidays); closed Monday and holidays; admission charge.

★ ★ CAPODIMONTE. via Capodimonte. Leopold mentioned visiting this Royal Palace in his letter of 16 June 1770. It was begun in 1738, and in the time of the Mozarts' visit it housed the Farnese painting and coin collection.[5] In 1743 the porcelain factory was founded, renowned for a porcelain of fine translucence. The park with the "Queen's Casina," modeled after the Trianon of Versailles, is of interest, as are the furnished royal apartments. Open 9 AM–2 PM (–1 PM Sundays and holidays); closed Mondays and holidays; admission charge.

[★ ★ CHARACTERISTIC SIGHTS OF NAPLES]. Leopold wrote on 22 May 1770 that Marchesa Tanucci, the Prime Minister's wife, sent her steward to take them to see "all the rare sights of Naples." In 1770, these sights would have included the Gothic Cathedral (**Duomo**) from the fourteenth century and much renovated afterward; inside, the sixteenth-century tomb of Charles I d'Anjou, the opulent Baroque chapel of San Gennaro, and the Basilica di Santa Restituta, with parts remaining from the fourth century, are noteworthy. The imposing **Castel Nuovo**, built in 1282, has a triumphal arch at the entrance, which is a masterpiece from 1467. The seventeenth-century **Palazzo Reale**, inhabited by kings only from 1734, has interesting royal apartments.

Excursions from Naples

★ ★ ROYAL PALACE OF CASERTA. On 18–19 June 1770, Leopold and Wolfgang made an excursion which included Vesuvius, Pompeii, Herculaneum, Capodimonte, and Caserta. The palace of Caserta (the Versailles of Naples) was begun by Vanvitelli in 1752 for Charles III of Bourbon, and was finished in 1774. The palace has 1,200 rooms and 34 staircases, with opulent apartments decorated with gold leaf, stucco and marble.[6] The park, designed by Vanvitelli, has a great waterfall, with a basin with sculpture groups. The palace is about 19 miles from Naples; open 9 AM–1:30 PM daily except Monday; admission charge.

★ ★ POZZUOLI AND BAIA. On 13 June 1770, Leopold and Wolfgang left at 5 AM for Pozzuoli, and took a boat to Baia. From there they visited the baths of Nero, the grotto of Sibylla Cumana, the crater Lake of Averno, the "Temple" of Venus, the "Temple" of Diana, the supposed tomb of Agrippina (who was ordered killed by her son Nero), the Elysian Fields (**Campi Flegrei**), the Dead Sea (**Mare Morto**), **Piscina Mirabile**, and the **Cento Camerelle** (a water holder from Republican Rome). Returning to Naples, they visited **Monte Nuovo, Monte Gauro** (now **Monte Barbaro**), the "Molo" of Pozzuoli, and the splendid Colosseum (which can hold 40,000 spectators; here Saint Gennaro was thrown to the wild animals in 305 AD, only to leave unharmed), Solfatara (an active volcanic crater), the Astroni crater (**gli astroni**), the grotto of the dog (**Grotto del Cane**), the Lake of Agnano, and particularly the "Grotto" of Pozzuoli and the grave of Virgil.

★ ROYAL SUMMER RESIDENCE AT PORTICI. Between Naples and Herculaneum. Here, in the summer residence built by Charles III in 1738, Leopold and Wolfgang were received by the powerful minister Marchese Bernardo Tanucci on 20 May 1770. Tanucci, famous for his power struggle with the Vatican and for his influence in dissolving the Jesuit Order in 1773, was deprived of his office in 1776.[7] Portici has a renowned park, in addition to the residence of the Bourbons of Naples. On 19 May 1770, Mozart also wrote to his sister, concerning the Court Chapel at Portici, "We saw the King and Queen at Mass in the Court Chapel at Portici."

★ ★ ★ VESUVIUS, POMPEII AND HERCULANEUM. On their excursion of 18 and 19 June 1770, Leopold and Wolfgang made an trip to this famous volcano, which Mozart had described in Naples as, "smoking furiously today. Thunder and lightning and all the rest." They also visited the excavations of these two ancient cities.

Puerta Capua, on route to Naples. Lithograph after a drawing by F. Wenzel, ca. 1825. Museo Correale, Sorrento.

N o t e s

1 Michelin, *Italia*, 157. Despite my letters to the archives and Biblioteca Nazionale, many questions have been left unresolved. The situation of the archives in Naples is chaotic. Questions about the location of the villa of Ambassador William Hamilton, the residence of the Imperial Ambassador, Count Ernst Kaunitz-Rietberg, the Teatro Fiorentini (which no longer exists), and the Teatro Nuovo, are not discussed, as I have received no communications from the various institutions in Naples.
2 Touring Club Italiano, *Napoli*, 140.
3 Michelin, op. cit., 152.
4 Ibid., 155.
5 Bauer/Deutsch/Eibl, *Mozart Briefe*, V, zu 191/28.
6 Michelin, op. cit., 72.
7 Anderson, *Letters of Mozart*, I, 199.

Mozart in Padua

Dates

About 10 February 1771 ▪ 12–14 March 1771

When Mozart and his father traveled from Milan, through Canonica, Brescia, Verona, Vicenza and Padua, Leopold described the route as "the most dangerous place in all of Italy." During their return trip to Salzburg, they again stopped in Padua, where they stayed in the Palazzo Pesaro, and visited Padre Francesco Antonio Valotti and Giovanni Ferrandini. In addition, Mozart performed on the organ in San Giustina.

Music

The most significant aspect of the Mozarts' visits to Padua was the commission to write an oratorio on a text of Metastasio. The composition (which was probably never performed in Padua in Mozart's lifetime), is the compelling work, "La betulia liberata," K. 118/74c.

Padua Sites

★ ★ BASILICA SANTA GIUSTINA. via Cavazzana. Mozart played "on the very good organ in the incomparable church of Santa Giustina" on 13 March 1771. This remarkable church from the fifth or sixth century was rebuilt after destruction in 1119 and in 1502. The church, which was frequented by Goethe during his stay in Padua, had an epistle organ and a gospel organ, both of which were destroyed almost completely in 1927.[1] In the back of the choir is a splendid work by Veronese, representing the martyrdom of Santa Giustina. Open weekdays 7:30 AM–Noon and 3 PM–7:45 PM; Sundays and holidays 7 AM–1 PM and 3–7:45 PM.

★ ★ ★ ST. ANTHONY BASILICA (BASILICA DEL SANTO). Piazza del Santo. On 13 March 1771, Leopold and Wolfgang went to the Church of Saint Anthony to visit the organ virtuoso Father Antonio Valotti, one of the most important music theorists of his day, and author of the treatise "On theoretical and practical science." The Romanesque-Gothic basilica with eight cupolas (1232 to 1310) is also noted for the renowned "Gattamelata" (1447), the bronze equestrian statue on the square before the church. Inside the church, the major altar by Donatello (1450) and the oratorio of San Giorgio with 21 frescoes are noteworthy.[2] There are two courtyards, from which the cupolas and the ornate bell tower can be seen. In addition to a Tartini monument, there is also a modern brass commemorative plaque with a portrait of Valotti.

Padua. San Giustina. Engraving by Antonio Sandi after Antonio Bellucci.

GENERAL SITE OF THE HOME OF GENTILUOMO PESARO. Corso Vittorio Emmanuele secondo, which opens (from Piazzale S. Croce) into Prato della Valle.[3] When Mozart and his father arrived in Padua on 13 March 1771, they stayed in Palazzo Pesaro, with the "gentleman" Pesaro, perhaps a member of the Venetian Pesaro family, who owned a palace on the Grand Canal (Canal Grande). The Pesaro family, noble Venetians, lived on **borgo Santa Croce.**[4]

★ ★ ★ **BOAT TRIP ON THE BRENTA (BURCHIELLO).** On 12 March 1771, Mozart and his father left Venice accompanied by Johannes Wider, his wife and daughters, and Abbate Ortes, taking their own rented boat to Padua. The trip usually lasted an entire day, and Leopold wrote, "They brought food and drink and everything necessary and we cooked and ate on the boat." Today, from 18 March to 29 October, the *Burchiello* travels from Padua to Venice and back along the banks of the Brenta, past seventeenth-eighteenth-century villas, following the classic itinerary.

★ ★ ★ MISCELLANEOUS SITES OF PADUA. Leopold wrote that "we saw in Padua what it was possible to see in a day." In 1771, that would have perhaps included the fourteenth-century Scrovegni Chapel with the 38 frescoes of Giotto, the Church of the Eremitani, and the Palace "della Ragione" with a single room, decorated with fifteenth-century frescoes. In addition, the **Orto dei Semplici** (the present Botanical Garden, from 1545), the University founded in 1222 (Galileo, Copernicus, and Tasso taught here), and the cathedral, with its Romanesque baptistery containing magnificent fourteenth-century frescoes, were important sights, all of which can be seen today.[5] The splendid park, Prato delle Valle, with statues, water, and bridges, was redone into its present form in 1775 by Memmo, so Mozart and Leopold did not see it as it is today. The "School of the Saint" ("Scuola del Santo"), painted by Titian, and the nearby oratorio of St. Giorgio (**oratorio di S. Giorgio**) with frescoes by Altichiero da Verona, as well as the **Collegio Pratense**, and the **loggia Cornaro del Falconetto** along via Cesarotti, not far from the piazza del Santo.[6]

N o t e s

1 Bauer/Deutsch/Eibl, *Mozart Briefe*, V, zu 236/20
2 Michelin, *Italia*, 168.
3 Communicated by Dott. ssa Raffaella Tursini, Archivio di Stato, Padova.
4 In March 1771, Mozart received the commission for "La betulia liberata" (K. 118/74c) to a text by Pietro Metastasio, from Don Giuseppe Ximenes de Principi d'Aragona. In addition, on 13 March 1771, Mozart and Leopold paid a visit to the former director of chamber music at Munich, Giovanni Ferrandini, in whose house Wolfgang played the cembalo. In regards to the *palazzi* of Don Ximenes, Prince of Aragon, and that of Ferrandini, it can only be determined from the *Cronaca dell 'abate Giuseppe Gennari* that they lived in the area of the Basilica del Santa; while it is presumed that casa Pesaro was located at the end of borgo S. Croce almost as it opens into Prato della Valle (perhaps on the same side as the casa Grimani, which still exists), it is not possible to determine exactly which *palazzo* it was, as several edifices were demolished and many were completely renovated. Communicated by Dott. ssa Raffaella Tursini, Archivio di Stato, Padova.
5 Michelin, op. cit., 166–68.
6 Communicated by Dott. ssa Raffaella Tursini, Archivio di Stato, Padova.

Mozart in Rome

Dates

11 April 1770–8 May 1770 ▪ **26 June 1770–10 August 1770**

Mozart and his father stopped in Rome twice, on the way to and from Naples. However, Mozart's stay in Rome was memorable; Mozart heard the *Miserere* of Allegri (in nine voices) in the Sistine Chapel, and proceeded to write the entire work down from memory. Instead of being excommunicated (as it was forbidden to transcribe the work), Mozart, upon his return to Rome from Naples, was honored with the Order of the Golden Spur from Pope Clement XIV. During the first Roman sojourn, Mozart was received in remarkably important houses, and apparently made a considerable impression.

After Mozart's second sojourn in Rome, there was an unfortunate accident while they were returning to Milan in which Leopold received an injury to his leg in the coach, an injury which was to cause him problems for several weeks afterward.

Music

Mozart wrote, on 16 or 25 August 1770, "When I finish this letter I will finish a symphony of mine." The symphony mentioned by Mozart could be either K. 95/73n (assigned to Rome for reasons which were never stated in the Köchel catalog) or K. 97/73m (also assigned to Rome, by Breitkopf and Härtel for unstated reasons; the manuscript no longer exists); other possibilities would be the symphony K. 81/73l (also attributed to Mozart's father, Leopold), and K. 73. However, as Alan Tyson writes, the symphony No. 10 in G, K. 74, is on the same type of paper used by Mozart for the aria K. 82/73o, composed in Rome in April 1770; this provides more striking documentation that this symphony may have been among those written in Rome during this period.*
On 25 or 26 April 1770, Mozart wrote, "the aria is finished," referring probably to K. 82/73o, "Se ardine, e speranza" (Metastasio: *Demofoonte*); Rome, 25 April 1770. Another aria written during this time was K. 83/73p, "Se tutti i mali miei," on a text from Metastasio's *Demofoonte*; Rome, April–May 1770.
Other works include Menuett, K. 94/73h, written in Bologna or Rome, probably in April 1770; Kyrie, K. 89/73k, and Canon, K. 73i. Contredanses K. 123/73g are believed to date from Mozart's Roman sojourn.

* Zaslaw, *Mozart's Symphonies*, 166–81.

Rome Sites

★ ★ ★ SISTINE CHAPEL. Entrance by way of the Vatican Museum, Viale Vaticano. On their first afternoon after arriving in Rome on 11 April 1770, Mozart and his father went to the Sistine Chapel to hear the *Miserere* of Allegri. After returning to their lodging, Mozart then wrote down the nine-part choral work, the copying of which was not allowed, in its entirety by memory. After their return to the chapel the next day, they made their way to the Cardinals' table, and Mozart talked with the Secretary of State, Cardinal Lazzaro Pallavicini. The spectacular chapel, which has undergone a controversial restoration, was erected by Francesco della Rovere under Pope Sixtus IX from 1473 to 1481; it is decorated with magnificent frescoes by Michelangelo on the ceiling (1508–12) and above the altar (1535–41). It has also been the seat of the conclaves and the theatrical backdrop of solemn ceremonies of the Holy See.[1] Open 9 AM–2 PM; closed Sundays and holidays; open also on the last Sunday of each month; admission charge.

Rome. St. Peter's, in 1785. Engraving by J. Brun, 1785.

★ ★ ★ ST. PETER'S CHURCH. Vatican City. Mozart and his father came to St. Peter's on Easter Sunday, 15 April 1770, where Pope Clemens XIV was presiding, and then again on 29 June 1770, where they heard Vespers. They explored the church thoroughly, and Leopold wrote that there was "certainly nothing that we left unnoticed." Wolfgang wrote to his sister (in Italian) that he "had the honor of kissing the foot of St. Peter," but, because he was so small, he had to be raised up. (The bronze statue from the thirteenth century, attributed to Arnolfo di Cambio, is traditionally venerated in this way by pilgrims.) The massive church, originally planned by Bramante as a Greek cross topped by a cupola, was transformed into a Latin cross in 1606. In 1629, Bernini designed the sumptuous Baroque interior, as well as the bronze *baldacchino* (canopy) in the center. The facade of the church is by Maderno (1614). It looks out on a masterpiece of urban design by Bernini, St. Peter's Square (1656–67), with two hemicircles of columns. The cupola was projected by Michelangelo, and finished in 1593 by Giacomo Della Porta and Fontana.[2]

Rome. Engraving, published by Carel Allard, ca. 1700.

★ ★ CHURCH OF SAN LORENZO IN DAMASO. Piazza della Cancelleria. On 23 April 1770, Leopold wrote, "Yesterday we went to S. Lorenzo, and we heard the Vespers. Today in the morning we heard Mass sung, and in the evening we heard the second Vespers, because it was the Feast of the Virgin of Good Council." In this church, festivities surrounding the miraculous painting of the Virgin took place. The church was erected (380) in honor of Saint Lorenzo, and was later redone by Bramante, who changed the form, but included the antique columns of the basilica in the courtyard. The interior maintains the plan by Bramante of three naves, divided by six arcades, and is particularly ornate, with a ceiling in gold leaf, frescoes, stucco, and marble.[3] The altar painting of the Virgin with St. Philipp Neri and St. Nicola is by Sebastian Conca. Open 7 AM– Noon and 4:30–8 PM (Winter); 5–8:30 PM (Summer).

Rome. Church of San Apollinare & Collegium Germanicum. Engraving by Giuseppe Vasi, 1769.

★ **COLLEGIUM GERMANICUM.** Piazza S. Apollonaire, 49. On their first afternoon in Rome, 11 April 1770, Mozart and his father went immediately to the German College, to meet the son of the Salzburg court chancellor, Albert von Mölk, who was staying there. Later, on 2 May 1770, Mozart's last performance in Rome took place here, with the participation of the Salzburg bass Meissner. The diary of Biringucci describes the young boy who improvised on the harpsichord on melodies given to him on the spot, to everyone's astonishment, at which point everyone went to the church to hear him play organ. The unimposing facade, with a huge cornice and a coat-of-arms over the entrance, is the work of Camporere V from the second half of the eighteenth century. Today the building houses an institute of Arab studies (**Ponteficio Istituto di Studi Arabi**); the nearby residence for priests at via della Scroffa, 70, was also part of the Collegium. *Closed to the public.*

★ ★ **ALTEMPS PALACE.** via S. Apollinare, 8. This massive *palazzo* was the site of a reception by the learned connoisseur of art, Baldassare Odescalchi, Duke of Bracciano and Geri. Since this palace of Duke Giuseppe Altemps had a small theater, Duke Odescalchi invited Mozart and his father here on 29 April 1770. Today the building, which houses the offices of the Ministry of Italy's art treasures (**Ministero Beni Culturali**), is beautifully restored. The building in classical style has a sculpted cornice and obelisks; adjacent is an ornate medieval tower, the **Tor Sanguigna**. Inside there is a harmonious courtyard with elegant loggias, as well as a chapel, the theater mentioned, and a library.[4]

★ ★ ST. AUGUSTINE CHURCH (S. AGOSTINO). Piazza S. Agostino. After he improvised on the harpsichord at the Collegium Germanicum, Mozart and his audience all moved to the church, where he continued his performance on the organ. The description from the diary of Biringucci suggests that they moved nearby either to S. Apollinare (1742–48), or to S. Agostino Church, adjacent to the Augustinian Monastery, both very close to the Palazzo Altemps and the Collegium Germanicum.[5] The fifteenth-century church has a massive staircase leading to a sober facade, one of the first Renaissance facades of Rome. The interior, redone in the eighteenth-nineteenth centuries, has, in addition to many frescoed altars and a multicolored marble pulpit, a fresco by Raphael of the prophet Isaiah (1512), and the "Virgin of the Pilgrims" by Caravaggio (1605) in the first chapel to the left.[6] Open 7:45 AM–Noon and 4:30–7:30 PM.

[★ ★ LIBRARY OF THE AUGUSTINE MONASTERY]. Piazza S. Agostino. The present Angelica Library, once part of the monastery visited by the Mozarts, has more than 20 tiers of leather books, comprising thousands of volumes. Leopold's love of books and his interest in scholarly subjects suggests that their visit to the monastery would have included this library. Open Monday/Wednesday/Friday 8:30 AM–7:30 PM; Tuesday/Thursday/Saturday 8:30 AM–2 PM; no admission charge.

★ ★ AUGUSTINIAN MONASTERY. via del Portoghesi, 12. On Monday, 30 April 1770, Mozart and his father dined in this monastery, with Father Vasquez, the general of the order. The monastery is remarkably intact, restored, and presently the seat of the lawyers of the state (**Avvocatura General dello Stato**); however, *it is closed to the public*. The beautiful entrance with a shell above leads to a portico courtyard with Renaissance funeral monuments incorporated into the walls on the left. Mozart and his father most probably dined with the monks in the present "Vanvitelli Room" (which was the refectory); it is a masterpiece of fresco depicting Jesus multiplying the loaves and fishes. Special permission to view the Vanvitelli room may be requested in writing from the Avvocatura Generale at the above address (or occasionally by asking in person, in the morning).

★ SITE OF THE SCATIZZI PALACE. 20, Piazza Nicosia. After four uncomfortable days in a room with a double bed in a private house, Mozart and his father moved on 14 April 1770 into an apartment in the Palazzo Scatizzi, a side wing of the Collegium Clementinum. The spacious apartment, with a clavier at Mozart's disposal, belonged to the Papal Courier Steffano Uslenghi, who was absent, and his young wife refused to accept payment from Leopold, who was treated like the master of the house by the servants. Returning from Naples, after the accident which injured Leopold's leg, Mozart and his father again stayed here from 26 June 1770 until their departure, and invited Sartorino, the singer, here on 29 July. Although the building no longer exists, there is a commemorative plaque indicating where the Collegium Clementinum was located. The little fountain in the square is by Giacomo Della Porta (1573).

★ ★ CHIGI PALACE (PALAZZO CHIGI). Piazza Colonna. Tradition claims that the performance of Mozart for Princess Chigi and her guests on 20 April 1770, was in the "Golden Room" (**Sala d'oro**), constructed in 1765–67 for the marriage of Don Sigismondo Chigi to Princess Maria Flaminia Odescalchi.[7] Among the invited guests were the Secretary of State, Cardinal Lazzaro Pallavicini, Baron Saint-Odile, and the English pretender to the throne Charles Edward Stuart. The sixteenth-seventeenth-century palace, under tight security, is the office of the President of the Council of Ministers. The splendidly restored facade was begun in 1580 by Matteo di Cittá di Castello with the probable consultation of Giacomo Della Porta. It dominates Piazza Colonna, which has a massive column depicting the war of Marcus Aurelius, a masterpiece from the second century. *The palace, including the Golden Room, is closed to the public.* The Golden Room is a unique jewel decorated by Giovanni Stern, with a ceiling fresco of Diana and Endimione by Baciccia (1668); it is an ensemble of many diverse media including stucco, painted marble, sculpture, and painting.[8]

★ PALAZZO MONTECITORIO. Piazza di Montecitorio. In his travel notes, Leopold noted "Monte Citorio" among the names and addresses, which most likely indicates this palace, with a facade begun in 1650 by Bernini and finished in 1697 by C. Fontana. Bernini's grandiose facade has a balcony supported by four Doric columns, an attic with a clock, and a bell tower. The characteristic square has an Egyptian obelisk from the sixth century BC, brought by Augustus to Rome, and erected here in 1792. Since 1871, the palace has been the seat of Parliament (Chamber of Deputies), and is *closed to the public.*

★ FORMER EMBASSY OF THE MALTA ORDER. via Condotta 68. Mozart performed at the palatial home of the Ambassador of the Order of the Knights of Malta (probably Cavaliere Giuseppe Santarelli) on 28 April 1770. Here Mozart and his father met the Swedish Ambassador, whom they had met in London, and Count Kraft Ernst zu Öttingen-Wallerstein. This edifice, the **Palazzo del Gran Magistero dell ' Ordine di Malta**, dates back to the seventeenth century.[9] Nearby, at #86 is the renowned **Caffé Greco**, founded in 1760; famous foreign guests have included Goethe, Mendelssohn, Berlioz, Stendhal, Wagner and Liszt.[10]

★ ★ PARK OF VILLA MEDICI. Viale Trinitá dei Monti, 1. Leopold and Wolfgang went walking in the garden of the Villa Medici on the morning of 21 April 1770 with several Englishmen, including Peter Beckford, whom the Mozarts had met in London. The villa was erected in 1544 for Cardinal Ricci de Montepulciano, and later became property of the Grand Dukes of Tuscany and France, the Medici family. In 1803, the villa was bought by Napoleon, and became the center for the Academy of France (founded in 1666 by Louis XIV), where young French artists have the opportunity to study in Rome for three years. The vast park has rich vegetation, numerous antique statues, and a spectacular view from the Belvedere.[11] It is open to the public on Sundays 10 AM–Noon (guided visits).

★ ★ BARBERINI PALACE. via Quattro Fontane, 13. Around 26 April 1770, Mozart performed at the Palazzo Barberini for the Princess Barberini-Colonna and her guests, including Cardinal Pallavicini, the pretender to the English throne, and the young Prince Franz Xavier August von Sachsen, who was traveling incognito. The massive palace, in need of restoration, is the work of the most celebrated Italian Baroque architects, Maderno (1625), Borromini (1629), and Bernini (1633). The right wing is a private club for Army Officers (*not open to the public*); however, a monumental marble staircase by Bernini leads to a fascinating art museum in the left wing, containing the Holbein portrait of Henry VIII, a *trittico* by Fra Angelico, "la Fornarina" of Raffael, and the portrait of Erasmus by Metsys. It is possible that Mozart performed in the last room in the present museum, the *salone*, with a frescoed vault of Pietro da Cortona (1633–39), depicting the triumph of the Barberini family. Throughout the palace, the three bees of the Barberini coat-of-arms are a recurrent theme. The museum is open Monday–Saturday, 9 AM–2 PM; 9 AM–1 PM Sundays and holidays; admission charge.

★ ★ PIAZZA DEL QUIRINALE. Before Mozart and his father entered the Quirinale, they passed through one of the most renowned squares of Rome, with a panorama of the cupola of St. Peter's. The splendid sculptures of Castor and Pollux, with their horses, are a Roman version of a Greek original from the fifth century BC, originally located at the Baths of Constantine. In 1588 Sixtus V restored them and moved them facing Via Pia, which was the location in which Mozart and his father would have seen them. After Mozart's Roman sojourn, under Pius VI (1783–86), the sculptures were moved to the present direction, facing the Quirinale Palace, to make room for the Obelisk from the Mausoleum of Augustus, which was added at that time.[12]

★ ★ PALACE OF THE QUIRINALE. Piazza del Quirinale. The highest class of the Order of the Golden Spur was conferred on Mozart by Pope Clement XIV; Cardinal Pallavicini personally decorated him here on 5 July 1770, in what was the summer residence of the popes. The only previous musician upon whom this unique honor had been conferred before Mozart was Orlando di Lasso. Mozart became *eques auratae militiae*, giving him protection by the Apostolic See and the privilege of entering the papal chambers at any time. The palace is the work of the most renowned Roman architects from the sixteenth to eighteenth centuries, Longhi V, Fontana, Ponzio, Maderno, Bernini, and Fuga. Popes lived in the palace from 1592 (Clement VII) until 1870. The marble portal faces one of the most beautiful squares of Rome. Since 1947 it is the official residence of the President of the Republic, and *it can be visited by presenting or sending a request eight days prior* to the Secretary General of the President at the Office of the *Intendenza* (except Saturday and Sunday, or during August).

★ ★ CHURCH OF THE APOSTLES (SS APOSTOLI FILIPPO E GIACOMO). Piazza SS. Apostoli, 51. Leopold (and presumably Mozart) were attending Mass in this church on the feast day of these saints when Leopold saw a well-dressed "familiar face," their former servant Porta, who offered his services. Leopold, who later called him "an adventurer" in his letter, declined, thanked him and "closed his ears" to the man. The basilica, erected in the sixth century, after the Goths were driven out, was redone 1702–14 by Francesco Fontana and his father Carlo. The simple neoclassic facade by Valadier (1827) is preceded by a large portico with nine arcades (fifteenth century), and an added balustrade with statues of Christ and the twelve Apostles (1681).[13] In the left nave at the back is the first Roman work by Antonio Canova (1789), the monument to Clement XIV, the Pope who awarded Mozart the Order of the Golden Spur.

[★ PALAZZO ODESCALCHI]. Piazza SS. Apostoli, 80. Although it is not known if the Mozarts were invited to this imposing palace, across from the Church of the Apostles, Duke Odescalchi did invite them to a reception in the Palazzo Althem, which had a theater.[14] The facade of the Palazzo Odescalchi was designed by Bernini (1664), surmounted by a balcony with the Odescalchi coat-of-arms, facing a courtyard by Maderno (about 1623) with sculpture.[15] Today the palace is private residences, *which are closed to the public.*

★ PALAZZO DORIA. via del Corso; entrance to Museum at piazza del Collegio Romano, 1. In this massive palace of Princess Doria, Mozart performed on 3 May 1770, with Count Kraft Ernst zu Öttingen-Wallerstein as one of the guests. The elegant Rococo facade by Valvassori (about 1734), which faces the Corso side of this fifteenth-century palace, has a large portal, topped by a balcony and fine windows. The sixteenth-century courtyard, inspired by Bramante, has a portico with Doric columns. Behind the building, there is a collection of painting from the sixteenth to eighteenth centuries in the **Galleria Doria Pamphili**, fine private apartments, and a ballroom from the seventeenth century (redone in the nineteenth century).[16] Open Tuesday/Friday/Saturday/Sunday 10 AM–1 PM; admission charge.

★ ★ ★ CAPITOLINE MUSEUM. Campidolio. Mozart wrote to his sister (around 25 April 1770), "Recently we were at the Campidolio and we saw various beautiful things; if I wanted to write to you about everything that I saw, these pages would not be enough." This suggests the collections in the Capitoline Museum.[17] The famous Campidolio was designed by Michelangelo (1536), and he himself restored and installed the second-century equestrian statue of Marcus Aurelius which was in the center of the square (today in the museum). The Capitolinum Museum is located in the New Palace (**Palazzo Nuovo**), built in 1655 by Rainaldi, which contains the Roman sculpture, "The

Dying Gaul," a copy of a third- to second-century BC bronze from the school of Pergamon, a copy of Praxiteles' "Venus," and the "Dove Mosaic" from Villa Adriana in Tivoli. In the museum inside the fifteenth-century Conservatori Palace, the famous sixth-fifth century Etruscan wolf can be found (with the later additions of Romulus and Remus).[18] Open 9 AM–2 PM as well as 5–8 PM Tuesday and Thursday; closed Mondays and holidays.

★ ★ SANTA MARIA MAGGIORE CHURCH, AND PALACE. Piazza S. Maria Maggiore. After his remarkable feat of writing the *Miserere* of Allegri from memory (the copying of which was not permitted), Mozart was not excommunicated, but instead made a Knight of the Golden Spur, in the Quirinale Palace, officially for his excellence as a harpsichord player. Two days later, on 8 July 1770, wearing the golden cross of the order, Mozart was given an audience with Pope Clement XIV in the summer residence of the popes, the Palace Santa Maria Maggiore (perhaps with the later Salzburg Archbishop Hieronymus Colloredo as a required witness). Facing the church, the palace is behind, to the right, and in the **Canonica Paolina**, there are different rooms where important papal documents were signed (*closed to the public*). The church, begun by Sixtus III in 432–40, is one of the four major basilicas in Rome, with a facade by Ferdinando Fuga (1743–50) which unites two twin buildings. Inside, an ensemble of many of the oldest mosaics in Christian art are found, dating from the fifth century. The caisson ceiling is said to have been leafed with the first gold from Peru.[19]

N o t e s

1 Michelin, *Italia*, 209.
2 Ibid., 207.
3 Touring Club, *Italia*, 228–29.
4 Ibid., 204.
5 Since I received no response from archives and libraries in Rome, it was difficult to confirm in which church Mozart played the organ.
6 Michelin, op. cit., 203.
7 Bauer/Deutsch/Eibl, *Mozart Briefe*, V, zu 177/43.
8 Touring Club, op. cit., 163–64.
9 Although I received no response from the archives to confirm my conclusion that this was the palace in which Mozart performed, it is nevertheless extremely probable; it is presented here for the first time in the Mozart literature.
10 Touring Club, op. cit., 269.
11 Ibid., 272.
12 Ibid., 303–04.
13 Ibid., 259–61.
14 Since I received no response from the archives in Rome, it was not possible to determine who owned and lived in the palace in the time of Mozart's visit.
15 Touring Club, op. cit., 261.
16 Ibid., 151–55.
17 Bauer/Deutsch/Eibl, op. cit., 179/6.
18 Michelin, op. cit., 201.
19 Touring Club, op. cit., 363–68.

Mozart in Rovereto

Dates

24–27 December 1769 ▪ **About 20 March 1771** ▪ **17 August 1771** ▪ **29/30 October 1772**

During the first Italian trip, *en route* to Milan, Mozart and his father stopped in Rovereto. Mozart performed a concert at the home of Baron Todeschi; later, when word spread that Mozart would perform on the organ of San Marco, there were such crowds that it was difficult for them to enter the church. At the end of the first Italian sojourn, they returned by way of Rovereto.

In August 1771, on the way to Milan from Salzburg, at the beginning of the second Italian trip, Mozart and his father again stopped here. Finally, while returning to Milan during the third Italian trip, Mozart and his father again stopped in Rovereto, where they made a visit to Baron Pizzini and Dr. Bridi.

Rovereto Sites

★ ★ SAINT MARK'S CHURCH (CHIESA SAN MARCO). Piazza San Marco. When Mozart played a concert on the organ here on 27 December 1769, during his first visit to the city, "the entire population of Rovereto" came to hear him, and several robust young men had to clear a path through the crowd for Mozart to reach the church. The interior of the church, with a splendid ceiling ornamented by stucco and painting, has nine side altars, each one different, with marble pillars, paintings and sculpture. The organ played by Mozart was replaced in 1922 by the present one by Mascioni, in a case with refined classic lines. Outside, the winged lion of Venice was added in 1950 to the facade, which, however, preserves the previous door and windows.[1] Occasional organ concerts and chamber music concerts are given here. Open daily 7:30 AM–Noon and 1:30–8 PM.

★ HOME OF THE COSMI FAMILY. via Rialto, 49.[2] Mozart and his father were invited by the noble, Giovanni Battista de Cosmi, on the day of Wolfgang's first private academy in Italy, which took place in the house of Baron Todeschi. Only the ornate wooden carved bay windows remain; the remainder of the building has been extensively remodeled. Over the portal, the marble coat of arms can be seen. *The apartments are privately owned.*

GENERAL SITE OF THE "GOLDEN ROSE" INN ("L'ALBERGO DELLA 'ROSA D'ORO' "). During their first stay in Rovereto, from 24–27 December 1769, Mozart and his father stayed in this "Imperial" hotel, where later guests included Peter Leopold, Grand Duke of Tuscany, and his wife Maria Lodovica, as well as Maximilian Saverio, Archduke of Austria, Ferdinand Charles, Archduke of Austria, and even Goethe (who was *en route* to **Lago di Garda**).[3] The hotel no longer exists; until about 1873 it was located "in the area adjacent to the large house at the entrance of the present Corso Bettini toward the hill, which forms the eastern side of the bottleneck that opens into Piazza Rosmini."[4]

★ PALAZZO TODESCHI. via Mercerie, 14. After Mozart played his first Italian concert here on 26 December 1769, to guests invited by Baron Giovanni Battista Todeschi, Leopold wrote, "It is not necessary to write to you how much honor Wolfgang brought us." The facade is preserved, including the marble balcony and the portal decoration; inside there are noteworthy arches and pink marble steps. The large room where Mozart would have played on the first floor (American: second floor) still remains, although it has been remodeled. *The apartment is private property.* A commemorative plaque outside cites Mozart's first Italian concert.

★ ★ PALAZZO PIZZINI. Piazza Malfatti, 19–24.[5] Leopold Mozart had letters of recommendation for Baron Gian Giulio Pizzini during their first stay in Rovereto in 1769; later, during their third stop in the city, they visited him, on 17 August 1771. Today, in the palace, the main room remains much as it was in the time of Mozart's visit, with stucco and a frescoed ceiling. The outside has an austere, unrestored facade, with a massive cornice. It is privately owned, with shops on the ground level. The large salon, lighted at night, can be seen from outside, and it can occasionally be visited during the day by requesting permission.

[★ MOZART MONUMENT IN VILLA DE PROBIZER]. Viale Trento, 42.[6] During his Vienna years, Mozart had close contacts with Giuseppe Antonio Bridi, who sang the role of the protagonist in *Idomeneo*, for the performance in 1786 in the Auersperg Palais in Vienna. In 1825, after Mozart's death, Bridi, a successful banker as well as amateur musician, erected a splendid Temple of Harmony (**Tempietto dell 'Armonia**) in the extensive parks. Bridi, who was cited in Nissen's biography for having contributed to the book, had the fine temple built, with ceiling frescoes by Craffonara; later, in 1831, he built a fine sepulchral monument to Mozart. The complex was severely damaged during bombing attacks from 1940 to 1945, but many structures were rebuilt. It has been called the oldest (existing) monument built to honor Mozart after his death.[7] Mozart concerts, during Mozart festivals, are also held here.

[★ ★ ZANDONAI THEATER (TEATRO ZANDONAI)]. Although it was built after the visit of Mozart and his father, this theater is a fine example of eighteenth-century architecture. The theater, designed by the Bolognese architect F. Maccani, and by F. Marcora, has three orders of boxes and delicate frescoes, and was praised by Gustave III of Sweden and by Emperor Joseph II, who saw it in 1783, before the inauguration in 1784. In 1923 the theater was renamed Zandonai; the elegant facade of the theater is a product of the extensive restoration of 1870.[8] Mozart concerts are held here.

Concerts in Rovereto

Numerous Mozart concerts have been organized in **Palazzo de Pizzini, San Marco, Teatro Zandonai,** and in **Villa Lodron** in Nogoredo.[9] For information contact the Assessorato al Turismo del Comune di Rovereto, Piazza Podesta.

N o t e s

1 Tranquillini, *Rovereto*, 121.
2 Located in response to my queries by Leoni Walter, Biblioteca Comunale, Rovereto, document Ar. C. 15. 20; it is presented here for the first time. It was not possible to locate the home of Giuseppe Nicoló Cristani, where the Mozarts were invited on 25 December 1769.
3 C. Antonelli, "I soggiorni di Wolfgang Amadeus Mozart a Rovereto," 28.
4 Fiorio, "Rovereto ricorda W. A. Mozart," 10. The location of this inn was not cited in the Bauer/ Deutsch/Eibl notes to the Mozart letters.
5 This palace is another example of an existent Mozart site which was not cited in the Bauer/Deutsch/Eibl notes to the Mozart letters.
6 Communicated by Dott. Gianmario Baldi, Direttore, Biblioteca Civica Rovereto.
7 Barblan/Lunetti, *Mozart in Italia*, 180–82.
8 "W. A. Mozart a Rovereto," np.
9 Leopold Mozart also had a letter of recommendation for Count Settimo (Maximilian) Lodron, and perhaps visited him at his villa, with Mozart, as was his habit. Count Lodron was dean of the beautiful church at Villa Lagarina, which can be seen today, including the chapel of Saint Ruperto, painted by the Florentine, Mascagni. Count Settimo Lodron and his illustrious predecessor, Paris Lodron (the renowned Archbishop of Salzburg), were responsible for the remarkable beauty of this church near Rovereto. Cf. Barblan/Lunelli, *Mozart in Italia*, 42–43.

$\mathcal{M}$ozart in Turin

Dates

14–31 January 1771

$\mathcal{I}$n the eighteenth century, Turin was the capital of the Kingdom of Sardinia. Since it was so close to Milan, Leopold had been planning to take a brief trip to Turin for some time, but it had to be postponed so that they would be able to arrive in Rome for Holy Week. We have almost no documentation about this visit. The likely explanation is that Leopold and Wolfgang were so busy they did not have time to write; however, they decided to extend their stay to about sixteen days.

In addition to noting several of the great names of Turinese nobility, such as Lascaris and Caron (Carron), Leopold cited numerous musicians, including Giovanni Paisiello, Abbate Quirino Gasparini (the *maestro* of the cathedral), and Alessandro and Gerolamo Besozzi, one of whom was a basoonist. They probably heard the listed musicians perform, and performed with them, as they usually performed for members of the nobility who wished to hear them. Likely candidates for an academy (concert) would have been Count Lascaris, Count Carron, and the Spanish Ambassador, Count d'Aguilar.

The numerous musicians associated with the Royal Chapel cited in Leopold's notes, such as Giai, Pugnani and Gasparini, indicate that the Mozarts were in close contact with music in the cathedral. The mention of Gasparini is somewhat ironic, as Leopold's letter to Padre Martini several weeks before described one of the intrigues during the rehearsal of Mozart's opera *Mitridate* in Milan:

Someone had the cunning to bring all his arias to the Prima Donna . . . all the composition of Abbate Gasparini of Turin . . . to persuade her to substitute these arias and to not accept anything from the boy [Mozart], who would not be capable of writing a single good aria. However . . . having seen them she was content, in fact, extremely content.

Turin Sites

★ "OLD CUSTOMS" HOTEL ("DOGANA VECCHIA"). Corso Corte d'Appello 4. Leopold wrote in his travel notes, concerning their stay in Turin from 14 to 30 January 1771, that they lodged "alla Dogana Nova," most likely the present Hotel "Dogana Vecchia" (which in 1771 would have been the "New Customs").[1] In 1719, the building was initiated as a hotel for important visitors. Today the "Dogana Vecchia" is a two-star hotel which features vaulted ceilings, stucco ornament in the salon, and an antique staircase. Architectural features of the former stables can be seen in the courtyard.

★ ★ PALAZZO LASCARIS. via Alfieri 15. Although little is known about their stay in Turin, Leopold cited the names of Count Caron (Carron) and Count Lascaris in his travel notes. As Mozart frequently gave concerts for noble families cited in the travel notes, Palazzo Lascaris is the most probable site of an academy in Turin.[2] In the eighteenth century, the palace was named after the Carron family, who were also cited in Leopold's notes. The edifice, dating from the seventeenth century, is attributed to Amedeo di Castellamonte. The main entrance has a massive door in wood, with columns *a manicotti*. The palace is presently the seat of the regional government (**Consiglio Regionale Piemontese**), and is *not open to the public*, although the seventeenth-century courtyard, with stucco and sculpture in niches, can be seen 9 AM–8 PM, by asking at the door.

★ ROYAL THEATER (TEATRO REGIO). Piazza Castello 215. Mozart and his father saw an opera which Leopold described as "truly splendid" (most likely *Annibale in Torino* by Paisiello) in the Teatro Regio during their stay in Turin (14–30 January 1771). In 1936 the theater burned, leaving only the facade intact from the time of the Mozarts' visit. It is today the major opera house in Turin; the interior is completely renovated.

★ ★ ROYAL PALACE (PALAZZO REALE). Piazza Castello. In 1770, the court of Savoy, the goal of the visit of Mozart, resided in Palazzo Reale,[3] an austere building from the seventeenth-eighteenth century. It was the court of King Carl Emmanuel I, King of Sardinia from 1730 to 1773. Today, the edifice is in a perfect state of preservation in respect to the eighteenth century; it hosts a military museum, with an extensive collection of arms. Open weekdays 9 AM–2 PM; Sundays and holidays 9 AM–1:30 PM; closed Mondays.

[★ ★ PALAZZO MADAMA]. Piazza Castello. Leopold and Wolfgang undoubtedly saw the varied facades of Palazzo Madama, which had been the home of the two "royal madames," Christine of France and Joan of Savoy-Nemours, in preceding periods, as late as 1724. The earliest layer of the palace is the Decumana Gate of the ancient wall of Augustus. The eastern facade in brick dates from the fifteenth century, while the classic western facade, in cut stone, was designed in 1718 by Juvara. A monumental staircase, also by Juvara, is found inside.[4] The palace and the Museum of Ancient Art are open weekdays 9 AM–7 PM; Sundays and holidays 10 AM–12:30 PM and 2–6:30 PM; closed Mondays and holidays.

★ ★ COURT CHAPEL IN ST. JOHN'S CATHEDRAL. Piazza S. Giovanni. Leopold and Wolfgang undoubtedly visited the fifteenth-century cathedral, and Leopold cited many musicians associated with the chapel, such as the conductor, Francesco Saverio Giay, and Abbate Quirino Gasparini. The Shroud of Turin has attracted pilgrims for centuries. The facade of the cathedral is by del Caprino, and the bell tower was completed by Juvara in 1720. Guarini designed the Chapel of the Holy Shroud, as well as the expansive cupola, in the seventeenth century.[5] Open Monday–Saturday 7:30 AM–4 PM; Sundays 8 AM–4 PM.

N o t e s

1 Bauer/Deutsch/Eibl, *Mozart Briefe*, V, zu 229/2; communicated by E. Bottasso, Biblioteche Civiche Torino.
2 Before the publication of this book, Palazzo Lascaris, which is in a remarkable state of preservation, had been overlooked in the Mozart literature. Mozart's stay in Turin has been neglected as well, and merits a detailed investigation.
3 Communicated by Dottoressa Marina Spini, Biblioteche Civiche, Torino.
4 Michelin, *Italia*, 242.
5 Michelin, op. cit., 241–42.

Mozart in Venice

Dates

11 February–12 March 1771

During their month in Venice during the first Italian trip, Mozart and his father found the city in the height of Carnival festivities, prompting Mozart to write, "I really like Venice." Mozart seems to have been attracted to the daughters (whom he called "pearls") of the Wider family, friends of their landlord, Lorenz Hagenauer, in Salzburg. In general, they found a great hospitality in Venice; Leopold wrote that the "gondolas of the nobility are constantly in front of our house . . . at every opportunity they heap such honors on us, that we are not only picked up and taken home in gondolas with the secretaries, but often the noble himself accompanies us home, and this is even true of the greatest of them."

Music

Mozart never wrote an opera for Venice. Despite a contract to write an opera for the Theater San Benedetto in 1773, the theater burned in 1772. However, the opera *Mitridate* had just been performed in Milan, and the oratorio, *La betulia liberata*, was written later, as a result of a commission which he received in Padua during this first Italian sojourn.

Venice Sites

★ ★ ★ GRAND CANAL (CANAL GRANDE). Wolfgang and his father were impressed by the view of the Grand Canal from a gondola, and Leopold wrote enthusiastically, ". . . the gondolas of the nobility are constantly in front of our house, and we ride on the Canal Grande every day."

[★ ★ ★ RIDOTTO VENIER]. The entrance is near the **Ponte dei Barretteri**, at #4939, in the **Mercerie**; today it houses the **Alliance Française**. Inside this elegant eighteenth-century meeting-place, original stucco works, paintings, mirrors, carved doors and mantlepieces can be seen, offering an intimate view into the *ridotti* of aristocratic Venice.[1] Accessible Monday–Friday from 4–7 PM; request permission in the office.

★ ★ CASA CESELETTI. At the bridge of Rio dei Barcaroli in the Parish di San Fantino; commemorative plaque. The private home in which the Mozarts stayed in Venice, from 11 February to 12 March 1771, was that of the Ceselettis (called Cavalletti by Leopold).[2] It is a short distance from San Marco, on a corner near the **Ponte dei Barcaroli Cuoridoro.** The location is picturesque, with stone and wrought-iron balconies characteristic of Venice. *Only the facade can be seen*, as the building today houses the offices of a charitable organization, the **Opera Santa Maria della Caritá.**

Venice. Engraving, published by Carel Allard, ca. 1700.

★ ★ THE "RIDOTTO." 1362 Calle del Ridotti near St. Mark's Square. Mozart visited and perhaps performed in some of Venice's famous gambling casinos, or "*ridotti.*" Young Wolfgang wrote, "between 11 and 12 o'clock at night we were in St. Mark's Square, in order to go to the ridotto." The *ridotto* visited by Mozart was most likely this edifice, the first Venetian public gambling house, which was opened in the palace Dandolo in 1638, and became famous as a gathering place for the Venetian nobility, who were required to enter with masks. Later it was decorated with frescoes depicting the "Triumph of Bacchus," and in 1774, it was closed by the Signoria because of the exorbitant fortunes lost by gambling.[3] To visit this renowned *ridotto*, presently **Teatro del Ridotto,** ask permission from 30 April to 1 September between 9 AM–1 PM at the box-office, or attend a theater performance during the other months.

★ PALAZZO BARBARIGO. Facade on the Canal Grande, between rio di S. Maurizio and rio di S. Maria Zobenigo. Leopold mentioned Catherina Sagredo, wife of the Senator Piero Barbarigo, in his travel notes, and also wrote, "in the coming week we will dine mostly with nobles." The Barbarigo Palace in 1771, where the Mozarts would have been invited, was most likely this double structure, with characteristic Gothic windows in one part, and balconies with arched windows in the other.[4] Today the palace is private apartments, and it is difficult to see from outside, except when riding on the Grand Canal; *the palace is not open to the public.*

★ ★ PALAZZO MOCENIGO. Four adjacent palaces at S. Samuele on the Grand Canal.[5] Leopold wrote that the greatest families, including the Mocenigo, accompanied them home in the gondolas. The Mocenigo Palace of the period was this complex from the sixteenth to seventeenth centuries. Today they are individually owned and are *closed to the public.* The post-Palladian classic facades are difficult to see, except when riding on the Grand Canal.

[★ ★ PALAZZO CAVALLI FRANCHETTI]. San Vidal, at the base of the bridge of the **Accademia**.[6] One of the most splendid buildings of Venice, with a beautiful garden that can be seen from the Bridge of the Accademia, the palace today houses the Federal Savings Bank. It was been speculated in the musicological literature that Mozart played in the *ridotto* here.[7] Since it houses bank offices, *the building is closed to the public*; special permission to see it may be requested.

★ OSPEDALE DEGLI INCURABILI. Dorso Duro, located at the bridge **degli Incurabili** on the **Zattere**. In his travel notes, Leopold cited the "hospitals," which were originally charitable organizations to accommodate sick people, orphans, and the poor. Music instruction as part of the education of children was added in the late sixteenth century, and the **Ospedali** became renowned for the quality of musical life. Founded in 1522, this was one of the most famous of the **Ospedali**; Hasse, Galuppi and Jommelli all taught here. The building, reflecting a classical facade from the sixteenth century, is today a home for juvenile delinquents; *it cannot be visited.* However, the enormous facade is intact, with a doorway in classical style originally made for a room in the Ducal Palace.

★ ★ PALAZZO CORNER. 2128 Campo San Polo.[8] Here at the Palazzo Corner (later called Palazzo Corner-Mogenigo), the Mozarts were entertained on 21 February and 11 March 1771. It was the residence of Catarina Corner, a member of the Venetian patrician family Cornaro; she presented the Mozarts with a "beautiful snuff-box and two pairs of lace cuffs" as travel gifts. The palace, which was designed by Sanmicheli in the mid-sixteenth century is today the **Comando di Legione**. The main facade on the water reflects a bold classical style with tiers of balconies, arches and pillars. Inside, there are numerous splendid rooms with frescoes and decoration maintained from the eighteenth century; *not open to the public.*

★ PALAZZO TIEPOLO. 1957 Campo San Polo. Mozart performed on 5 March 1771 at the Maffetti Palace, which is presently the Tiepolo Palace; today there are private apartments in the palace, which are *not open to the public.* Although the *piano nobile*, where Mozart's academy would most likely have been held, is private, the eighteenth-century Baroque facade, attributed to Dominico Rossi, can be seen.[9]

★ ★ OSPEDALE DEI MENDICANTI (HOSPITAL OF THE BEGGARS) AND CHURCH OF SAN LAZZARO DEI MENDICANTI. Fondamenta dei Mendicanti. Galuppi taught here from 1740 to 1751. The classical-style church, built between 1601 and 1631, contains numerous art treasures. The hospital entrance is a unique work of carved marble and colored stone. Fascinating features from the eighteenth century include staircases, courtyards, and the private library. Open 8 AM–1 PM.

★ ★ PATRIARCH'S PALACE. Campo S. Pietro di Castello.[10] The Mozarts lunched here with Giovanni Bragadino, the Patriarch of Venice, on 24 February 1771. The building, which had been a barracks since 1807, is presently apartments, with an original courtyard in need of restoration. Inside the building, nothing remains of the former splendor. The main entrance is distinguished by the coat-of-arms from the sixteenth century. The church, with its altar and frescoes, and the massive leaning bell tower, are worthy of note.

★ SITE OF THE OSPEDALE DELLA PIETÁ. Sestier di Castello. The church associated with this *ospedale*, where Vivaldi taught and performed, remains; inside the church there is a ceiling by Tiepolo. Open for Mass 5:30 PM on Saturdays, Sundays and holidays. In addition, the edifice of the *ospedale* still exists, on the side of the church; today it is the seat of the **Istituto Provinciale per l'Infanzia S. Maria della Pietá**, Castello 3701; it can be visited by asking the administration for permission.[11]

★ ★ ★ OTHER VENETIAN SITES. Like all first-time visitors to Venice during Carnival season, Mozart and his father were swept up in the excitement of the city. Between 11 and 12 o'clock at night, they were already on ★ ★ ★ **St. Mark's Square**, amid the masks and costumes. The visitor of today is fortunate, inasmuch as much of Venice, the "Serenissima," has remained from the eighteenth century. Leopold cited the ★ ★ ★ **churches of Venice** in a letter, which most likely included such renowned churches as **Redentore, Salute,** and **San Rocco.** In addition, he cited the ★ ★ **Arsenal (Darsena Grande)**, meaning "the great shipyard," located at the Fondamenta dell'Arsenale. It was constructed in the twelfth century, and was once the supreme shipyard of the world. There are numerous fascinating architectural features remaining, as well as an Historical Naval Museum.

N o t e s

1 These exquisitely decorated gambling houses, found in Venice as well as other Italian cities, supplied the resources for the extremely expensive opera performances.
2 Barblan/Brenzoni, *Mozart in Italia*, 138.
3 Lorenzetti, *Venice*, 524. This edifice was overlooked in Bauer/Deutsch/Eibl and in Barblan/Brenzoni.
4 Communicated by Dottoressa Maria Francesca Tiepolo, Archivio di Stato, Venice, who located numerous palaces of families mentioned by Leopold. As the names of Venetian palaces have often changed throughout history, finding the correct palace in 1771 presented some difficulties. It was not possible to identify the Palazzo Dolfin where Mozart was invited (it was not the Palazzo Dolfin-Manin on the Canal Grande), or Palazzo Grimani and Palazzo Valier.
5 It is not possible to establish exactly in which of the four palaces the Mozarts were hosted; communicated by Dottoressa Maria Francesca Tiepolo, Archivio di Stato, Venice.
6 Communicated by Dottoressa Maria Francesca Tiepolo, Archivio di Stato, Venice.
7 Barblan/Brenzoni, op. cit., 140.
8 Communicated by Dottoressa Francesca Maria Tiepolo, Archivio di Stato, Venice.
9 Ibid.
10 Ibid.
11 Ibid.

$\mathcal{M}$ozart in Verona

Dates

27 December 1769–10 January 1770 · between 4 and 11 February 1771 · 16–20 March 1771 · 18–20 August 1771 · 7/8 December 1771 · 1–3 November 1772 · About 6–7 March 1773

During Mozart's first stay in Verona, during the first trip to Italy, he performed a concert for the Accademia Filarmonica and performed on the organ to a enthusiastic throng in the Church of St. Thomas. Before continuing on to Milan, via Mantua, Mozart and his father were invited by the Carlotti and Emilei families, as well as by Conte Francesco del Giardino at his renowned palazzo, with cypresses and sculpture. In addition, the highly refined Mozart portrait by Saverio dalla Rosa dates from this period.

On the way to Venice, Mozart and his father again stopped in Verona. Returning from Venice, en route to Salzburg, they again stopped in Verona, where Mozart played before the invited guests of their host Pietro Lugiati.

Returning to Italy for the second Italian trip, in August 1771, they again stopped in Verona, lodging again at Pietro Lugiati's. Returning from Milan, en route to Salzburg, again they interrupted their journey in Verona.

On the final trip to Italy, Mozart and his father again stopped in Verona, and saw an opera on the next day. Finally, returning to Salzburg, they stopped for a last time in this unique art city, with its splendid Roman amphitheater.

Music

On the way to Milan, during the third Italian trip, Mozart wrote the first of a series of string quartets, K. 155/134a, in "sad Bolzano," before arriving in Verona.

Verona Sites

★ ★ **THEATER OF THE PHILHARMONIC ACADEMY (TEATRO DELL'AC-CADEMIA VECCHIA).** Via Mutilati 4/1. Mozart and his father attended the opera *Ruggiero* by Guglielmi here at the beginning of January 1770. Although Wolfgang humorously criticized the singers, the novelty of his wearing a Carnival mask delighted him. The theater was inaugurated in 1732, destroyed by fire in 1749, and reopened in 1754. Again in 1945, it was completely destroyed during an air raid. When construction began in 1961, the architects looked to eighteenth-century ornamentation, to mirror the decoration of the old theater.[1] Today, the left half of the loggia of the facade on via Roma looks as it did in the time of Mozart's visit; the other half has been extended in the same style.

★ ★ RIDOTTO OF THE THEATER OF THE PHILHARMONIC ACADEMY (ACCADEMIA FILARMONICA). via dei Mutilati, 4/1. The first concert of Mozart in Italy took place here on 5 January 1770 for the **Accademia Filarmonica**, founded in 1543. Wolfgang performed "before a select circle of competent professionals" including reading a concerto, sonatas, and a trio by Boccherini at sight, composing and singing an aria, combining a theme and finale at sight, and writing a full score for a theme that was given to him on the violin. From the large room where Mozart performed these tests, which is the present *ridotto* outside the theater hall, the original structure is preserved, although the wall paintings have been redone. *It is not open to public*, but is used for marriages and private functions; permission to see it may be requested at the Administrator's office.

★ PALAZZO CARLOTTI. Corso Cavour 2.[2] Leopold wrote on 7 January 1770, "We have standing invitations here from Marchese Carlotti and also from Signor Locatelli . . . We have lunched twice with Marchese Carlotti." Marchese Alessandro Francesco Carlotti was the censor of the Philharmonic Academy. The austere edifice, with varying window ornamentation on each floor, is presently property of Marchese Claudio Carlotti; *it cannot be visited.*

★ ARCHBISHOP'S RESIDENCE (PALAZZO VESCOVILE). Piazza Vescovado.[3] On 7 January 1770, Mozart and his father were invited by Archbishop Nicoló Antonio Giustiniani, known for his love of art, music and literature. However, since Mozart had to sit for his portrait, they only had time for a brief audience after Mass (Mass was presumably said next door in the cathedral). The facade of the Palazzo Vescovile is in Renaissance style, crowned by Venetian lace in stone. The large portal in white and blue marble is formed by two pairs of columns which support the large round timpanum.[4] The entire *canonici* quarter, including the canonic houses, and the baptistery of San Giovanni in Fonte, is of interest.[5] *The palace of the Archbishop cannot be visited.*

★ ★ PALAZZO EMILEI. Via Francesco Emilei 1.[6] Leopold wrote on 7 January 1770, "We have dined twice with Marchese Carlotti and also with Count Carlo Emilei . . ." Count Giovanni Carlo Emilei was the secretary of the Academy, and a member of one of the oldest noble Veronese families. Today the palace

(**Palazzo Emilei-Forti**), with a facade by Francesco Zoppi including niches with statues, houses the gallery of modern art (**Galleria d'Arte Moderna**) and the Museum of the **Risorgimento**.

★ ★ "TWO TOWERS" HOTEL (ALBERGO DUE TORRI). Piazza S. Anastasia, 2. When Leopold and Wolfgang arrived in Verona on 27 December 1769, they stayed in this inn. The present hotel, spectacularly rebuilt in 1958 on the site of the previous inn that had been closed since 1882, has 100 rooms today, furnished with authentic eighteenth-nineteenth-century pieces. The old building, belonging to the della Scala family, Lords of Verona, had been used during the fourteenth century as their official guesthouse. After the fall of the family, the building became an inn, with Mozart, Goethe, Heine, Franz Joseph I and Maria Theresa among its guests. In the lobby, a commemorative plaque cites the visit of the 13-year-old Mozart.

SITE OF THE LUGIATI HOME. Piazza Viviani 7. Here, where the present post office is located, was the home of Pietro Lugiati, of the established wealthy merchant family Lugiati; he was the host of the Mozarts during numerous visits to Verona. From January 6 to 9 1770, after Mozart's concert at the **Accademia Filarmonica**, the Lugiatis had the splendid portrait of Mozart by Saverio della Rosa painted. Their third time in Verona, arriving on 16 March 1771, Mozart and his father lived here as guests of Lugiati, and on 17 March 1771, Mozart played at Lugiati's before invited guests. Again, in August 1771, they lodged here, as well as in November 1771, and they visited him again in March 1773, passing through Verona. There is no longer a commemorative plaque noting Mozart's visits to the Lugiati home.

★ ★ SAINT THOMAS CHURCH (SAN TOMMASO). Stradone S. Tomaso. On the afternoon of 7 January 1770, Mozart played the Gospel and Epistle organs of this fifteenth-century church, named after Thomas Becket, the murdered Archbishop of Canterbury. Leopold wrote that "such a crowd was . . . at the church when we arrived that we scarcely had room to step down from the coach. . . . When we were done, the tumult was even greater, for everyone wanted to see the little organist." The organ (1716), the finest work by Bonatti that now exists in its original form, is undergoing restoration. The Baroque case is splendid, and on the left side there is an inscription—W. S. M.—strongly believed to signify Wolfgang (Salzburger) Mozart.[7] The exterior in terra-cotta and stone is a mix between traditional Veronese Romanesque and Gothic. The interior (about 1546) by Sammicheli has numerous fine altars and paintings, and a precious cameo relief of San Rocco.[8] Open 8:30 AM–Noon and 3:30–6 PM.

[★ PALAZZO ALLEGRI]. via S. Vitale 29.[9] In his list of cavaliers to whom he had been recommended, as cited in his letter of 7 January 1770, Leopold included Count Giovanbattista Allegri. It is very possible that he and Mozart were invited here to the home of Count Allegri, who lived in this imposing palace, with graceful, Venetian Gothic windows on the *piano nobile*; the palace today is in a fine state of preservation.[10]

★ ★ ★ PALACE AND GARDENS OF COUNT DEL GIARDINO. via Giardino Giusti, 2. Leopold and Wolfgang dined twice with Count Francesco Guisti del Giardino, who had "a beautiful garden and picture-gallery." The gardens of the palace, from the fifteenth century, are renowned for the avenue of cypresses, the numerous statues and fountains, the spectacular view of Verona, and the stalactite grotto under the great carved mask (*mascherone*) which was built to spew flames from its mouth. The eighteenth-century features seen by Mozart, as well as Joseph II, de Brosses, and Goethe, are intact. The gardens and the adjoining sixteenth-century palace are today the property of Count Guisti; gardens open daily 9 AM–8 PM; admission charge.

★ ★ ★ CHARACTERISTIC SIGHTS OF VERONA.
Arena. On 8 January 1770, with Signor Michelangelo Locatelli,[11] Leopold and Wolfgang visited this remarkably preserved Roman amphitheater from the first century, built from pink marble. Today, during the summer months, spectacular opera performances are held here. Open 9 AM–12 Noon and 2:30 PM–6 PM (–5:30 PM in Winter); during the opera season 8 AM–1:30 PM; closed Mondays; admission charge.
Museum Lapidarium (**Museo Lapidario Maffeiano**). Piazza Bra 28. Leopold was particularly interested in the antiquities found in this part of the **Accademia Filarmonica**. These included altars, bas-reliefs, and inscriptions. The collection may be visited 8 AM–6:45 PM Tuesday–Sunday; admission charge.
"Other rarities of the city." Numerous sights of Verona remaining from the time of the Mozarts' visit include: **Piazza delle Erbe, Piazza dei Signori**, the "della Scala" arches (**Tombe scaligere**), the marble Gothic Staircase of Reason (**Scala della Ragione**) in the courtyard of the City Hall, **Castelvecchio** and the **Scaligero Bridge**, the important Romanesque church, **San Zeno**, the cathedral (**Duomo**) dating partly from the twelfth century, the Gothic **Sant'Anastasia Church** (near the Two Towers hotel), the **Roman Theater** from the time of Augustus, the spectacular view of Verona from **Castel S. Pietro**, the Roman Tax-Collectors' Gate (**Porta dei Borsari**) and the Roman **Gavi Arch**.

N o t e s

1 Paganuzzi, *L'Accademia Filarmonica*, 190.
2 Angela Miciluzzo and the Director of the Verona Archives, Dr.ssa Laura Castellazzi, have communicated to me that Marchese Alessandro Carlotti, in 1770, lived in this *palazzo*; the address at that time was contrada S. Michele alla Porta (old number 2759).
3 Angela Miciluzzo and the Director of the Verona Archives, Dr.ssa Laura Castellazzi have communicated to me that Bishop Nicoló Antonio Giustiniani lived in the Palazzo Vescovile.
4 Communicated by Prof. Piero Nichele, Presidente, Azienda di Promozione Turistica, Verona.
5 Michelin, *Italia*, 262.
6 Angela Miciluzzo and the Director of the Verona Archives, Dr.ssa Laura Castellazzi have communicated to me that Count Giovanni Carlo degli Emilei lived in this palace in 1770.

7 Barblan/Schenk, *Mozart in Italia*, 49.

8 Segala, *San Tomaso*, 17–23.

9 Communicated by Angela Miciluzzo and the Director of the Verona Archives, Dr.ssa Laura
Castellazzi.

10 Bauer/Deutsch/Eibl, *Mozart Letters*, V, zu 152/58 (N).

11 Leopold wrote 7 January 1770, "We have standing invitations here from Marchese Carlotti and also
from Signor Locatelli." They dined at Locatelli's home on 6 January 1770, and again on 8 January
1770, after their visit to the Arena and the Lapidarium with Signor Locatelli, they were invited here for
lunch. Angela Miciluzzo and the Director of the Verona Archives, Dr.ssa Laura Castellazzi, in response
to my queries, have located where Locatelli lived: contrada S. Andrea (in the house designated with the
old number 1416), which today corresponds to Corte Nogara. In addition, they located the
approximate site of the home of Francesco Maria Regazzoni, in the area of the present via Enrico
Noris (which was in the central *contrada di S. Quirico*); in Leopold's letter of 7 January 1770, he
wrote, "We were invited to the house of a certain honest fellow, Signor Ragazzoni."

Mozart in Vicenza

Dates

Between 4 and 11 February 1771 • 14 and 15 March 1771

During their first Italian trip, Mozart and his father took an excursion to Venice, during which they stopped in Vicenza, the city of Palladio. On the return to Salzburg from Venice, they traveled to Vicenza with the Wider family and Abbate Ortes; here Mozart and his father were guests of Bishop Marco Giuseppe Cornaro.

Vicenza Sites

★ ★ ARCHIBISHOPS' RESIDENCE (PALAZZO ARCIVESCOVADO).[1] Piazza Duomo, at Contrà Arcivescovado. During their second brief stopover in Vicenza, on 14 and 15 March 1771, Mozart and his father were the guests of Bishop Marco Giuseppe Cornaro. They were on their way back to Salzburg at the end of their first trip to Italy, and shortly thereafter, in Verona, Mozart received the commission to return to Milan and write the 1772 Carnival opera (*Lucio Silla*). Bishops of Vicenza lived in this imposing residence near the cathedral, and it was undoubtedly the scene of a musical performance by Mozart. The original *palazzo*, with columns which alternate with windows, was once dominated by a large tower. The edifice was redone in 1819, but was destroyed during an aerial bombing in 1944; it has been rebuilt in the original form, with the addition of an attic and two lateral doors on the ground floor.[2] However, the courtyard, which is laid out with the outlines of a monastery garden, contains the splendid **Loggia Zeno**, built by Bernadino da Milano in 1494. It consists of a portico of four arcades, with octagonal pilasters; the parapet is decorated with exquisitely detailed bas-reliefs of foliage.[3] Open 9 AM–12:30 PM and 1:30–5 PM (or 6 PM) daily except Sundays; ring the bell at the Arcivescovado to ask permission.

Vicenza. Loggia in the Courtyard of the Archbishop's Residence.

[★ PIAZZA DUOMO]. Mozart and his father, during their time spent in Vicenza, certainly managed to see some of the refined architecture of the edifices which surround the *arcivescovado* (archbishop's residence), such as that of the elegant **Oratorio del Gonfalone** (1596), attributed to Albanese. Other *palazzi* include the imposing **Palazzo Roma** (**Proti**) from 1599, and the cathedral (**Duomo**), with a Renaissance apse and a Gothic nave and facade, and, inside, a polytych by Veneziano from 1356.[4] The statue in the center did not exist during the Mozarts' visits in 1771; it dates from 1880, and represents Vittorio Emmanuele II.

[★ ★ ★ CHARACTERISTIC SIGHTS OF VICENZA]. Vicenza, the city of the last great Renaissance architect, Andrea Palladio (who died here in 1580), is rich in architectural monuments. During their two brief visits to Vicenza (sometime between 4 and 11 February 1771, and 14 and 15 March 1771), Mozart and his father certainly did not fail to walk from the *arcivescovado* to see the interesting sights, as was their habit. These included the **Piazza dei Signori**, which has a twelfth-century tower (**Torre Bissara**), as well as a sixteenth-century **Basilica** by Palladio, a fifteenth-sixteenth-century frescoed facade (**Monte di Pietá**), and a Baroque facade (**Chiesa di San Vincenzo**); the *piazza* is also noteworthy for the unfinished sixteenth-century **loggia del Capitanio.**[5] The spectacular sixteenth-century theater (**Teatro Olimpico**) by Palladio and the noble facades of the **Corso Andrea Palladio** were other likely sites visited by Mozart and his father in 1771.

Other Sites of Interest: Civita Castellana

★ ★ CATHEDRAL. This Romanesque cathedral, from the twelfth century, has a splendid portico (1210) with Ionic columns. After the Mass, Mozart played the organ here. The timpanum of the portal has a mosaic of Christ by Cosma. Inside, there are two splendid marble and mosaic pulpits from the thirteenth century.

[FORTIFICATIONS]. This **Rocca,** or fortress, inevitably seen by Leopold and Wolfgang, was erected by Sangallo the Elder from 1494 to 1500, under Pope Alexander VI.

Other Sites of Interest: Loreto

Dates

16 to about 17 July 1770

Music

After returning to Salzburg from the first Italian trip (and a visit to the shrine of Loreto), Mozart wrote a litany in honor of the Blessed Virgin, the Litaniae Lauretanae (Litany of Loreto), K. 109/74e (May 1771) Several years later, in 1774, Mozart wrote a second, and larger, setting, K. 195/186d.

The name of the city of Loreto is derived from **lauretum,** the Latin name for laurel. According to tradition, the House of Mary (Santa Casa) was miraculously carried by angels in 1291, from Nazareth to Dalmatia (in present-day

Yugoslavia), and placed on a hill near Fiume. It was then carried over the Adriatic in 1294 to Italy, where the angels deposited it in a wood of laurel.

During the first trip to Italy, en route from Naples and Rome to Bologna, Mozart and his father stopped in the world-renowned *Sanctuary of Loreto.* The city, with its basilica, was the frequent site of pilgrimages, and as a practicing Catholic, Leopold was eager to visit the sanctuary.

The city of Loreto is approximately three miles from the Adriatic, surrounded by sixteenth-century walls. The Sanctuary of the Holy House of Mary dominates the city; of interest, also, is the Square of the Madonna (**Piazza della Madonna**) with a fountain from the seventeenth century, and the porticos of the apostolic palace (unfinished) by Bramante and Sansovino.[6]

N o t e s

1 This edifice is another example of a site which has been overlooked in the Mozart literature.
2 Touring Club Italiano, *Veneto*, 238.
3 Touring Club Italiano, op. cit., 239.
4 Michelin, *Italia*, 262.
5 Ibid., 262.
6 Michelin, *Italia*, 130.

Other Sites of Interest:
Parma

Dates

Between 16 and 24 March 1770 ▪ About 14 October 1770

★ GENERAL SITE OF THE HOME OF LUCREZIA AGUJARI. via F. Caval-lotti.[1] During the first trip to Italy, sometime between 16 and 24 March 1770, en route to Bologna, Mozart and his father were dinner guests of the exceptional singer Lucrezia Agujari, who was called "la Bastardella," as she was born out of wedlock to a nobleman. Mozart wrote to his sister, "In Parma we got to know a singer and heard her perform very beautifully in her own house—the famous Bastardella who has, 1) a beautiful voice, 2) a gallant trill, and 3) an unbelievable upper range." In the postscript to his sister, Mozart wrote down some of the musical passages from the three arias which she sang. Leopold described her as: ". . . not beautiful, and yet not ugly, but occasionally she has a wild look in her eyes, like that of people who are subject to epilepsy, and she limps with one foot. Otherwise she has a good presence, a good character and a good reputation." Returning to Milan from Bologna, Mozart and his father again passed through Parma.

[★ ★ CHARACTERISTIC SIGHTS OF PARMA]. Many of the splendid monu-ments of Parma can still be seen since the time of the two visits of Mozart and his father in 1770, during their first trip to Italy. The spectacular ensemble of the Cathedral (**Duomo**), the Baptistry (**battistero**), and the Church of St. John (**chiesa di San Giovanni**) create a unique monumental complex in rose marble.[2]

Notes

1 Communicated by S. Martani, Parma, in response to my queries.
2 Michelin, *Italia*, 170.

Netherlands

Amsterdam, Haarlem,

The Hague, Rotterdam,

Utrecht

Mozart in Amsterdam

Dates

About 27 January 1766 to the beginning of March 1766
About the middle of April to 18 April 1766.

Mozart and his sister gave three concerts in Amsterdam during their two visits to the city. The first sojourn, after a journey during winter (without their furs which had been packed and sent to Paris), lasted about five weeks. Since it was "fasting time," all public concerts were prohibited, yet Mozart was able to perform, as this "wonder" "served God's praise"; the concert consisted entirely of his orchestral music, conducted by the ten-year-old Mozart for the first time. After a stay in The Hague, the Mozart family returned for a third concert in April.

Music

7 Solo variations for keyboard, K. 25, on the Dutch national song "Willem van Nassau"; February 1766
Symphony in B flat, K. 22, written in The Hague in December 1765, was probably performed, with Mozart directing, on 29 January 1766.
While the Köchel Catalog notes that the 6 Sonatas for keyboard and violin, K. 26 to 31 were composed in The Hague in February 1766, it should be noted that Mozart was in Amsterdam, and not in The Hague, during that period.

Amsterdam Sites

GENERAL SITE OF THE "GOLDEN LION" INN ("DE GOUDEN LEEUW"). Warmoesstraat.[1] The Mozarts arrived in Amsterdam on 28 January 1766, after a winter ride through Holland without their furs, which had been shipped to Paris. When they returned to Amsterdam in mid-April 1766, they again stayed in this inn, which has since been demolished. Leopold also cited Jacob Reynaud (which suggests the possibility that the Mozarts were invited to his home); Reynaud lived on Warmoestraat in the second house on St. Jansstraat (both streets which still exist)[2]; the present numbers of the houses on the corners of the St. Jansstraat are #165 and #167, so that the home in which Reynaud lived could have been at #161 or #163 (northside), or #169 or #171 (southside), depending on whether they are counted inclusively or exclusively.[3] The present street, near the Central Station, despite occasional architectural interest, is part of a red-light district.

[★ OUDE KERK]. Oude Kerksplein 23. This Gothic church, consecrated in 1306, is a few minutes away from the inn in which the Mozarts are believed to have stayed; despite the red-light district which surrounds the church, the area provides a glimpse of the Amsterdam which the Mozarts saw in the eighteenth century. Sweelinck was organist here 1577–1621, and a great organ from the eighteenth century still remains. Although the Mozarts were Catholics (and were able to attend Mass in Protestant Holland only with great difficulty), they were perhaps tempted to see the church, which became Protestant in 1578, because of the fine organs which were located there. Although the interior has been damaged, the sixteenth-century stained glass is of interest, as is the carillon (partly by Hemony) in the bell-tower. Open 11 AM–5 PM in Summer; 1–3 PM in Winter (caretaker lives at #23).

★ ★ ★ ROYAL PALACE (FORMER CITY HALL). Dam. The splendid City Hall, called "the eighth wonder of the world" by the seventeenth-century poet Huygens, was cited by both Leopold and Nannerl in their travel notes. It was built by Jacob von Campen (1595–1657) as a city hall from 1648 to 1662, and in 1808, under Louis Napoleon, it became the Royal Palace. The triangular

Amsterdam. Engraving, published by Carel Allard, ca. 1700.

pediment, with a sculpture group of Amsterdam surrounded by Neptune, nymphs and tritons, is by Artus Quellijn, as are the remarkable marble sculptures in the "Vierschaar" (High Court of Justice), where the death sentence was pronounced. The facade has four orders of windows and pilasters of various orders, as well as an octagonal tower and cupola. During the summer open daily 12:30–4 PM.

[★ ★ NIEUWE KERK]. Gravenstraat 17. Although Leopold did not mention this church, adjacent to the City Hall, the Mozarts' itinerary usually included several important churches in the cities they visited. The Baroque wood pulpit by Vinckenbrinck and the monumental marble tomb of Admiral de Ruyter (1681) are noteworthy. Many concerts are given here on the two organs. Open Monday–Saturday 11 AM–5 PM; Sundays 11 AM–3 PM.

GENERAL SITE OF THE PUBLISHING FIRM OF JOHANN JULIUS HUMMEL. On the former Vijgendam, a street which was south of the **Vismarkt** (fishmarket); the Vismarkt was, until 1841, on the east side of the present Dam Square. The topography was drastically changed in the twentieth century.[4] During their two trips to Amsterdam in March and April 1766 (during the "Great Western" trip of 1763–66), Leopold was in close contact with the publisher Hummel, who sold tickets for the Mozart concerts, and with whom Leopold left copper etchings and sonatas to sell. In the first part of the eighteenth century, the name Vijgendam referred to a street (called Middeldam, or usually Vijgendam) which ran from the southern side of the present Dam Square. Vijgendam also referred (as it does today, unofficially) to the southern side of the eastern part of the Dam Square.[5]

★ GENERAL SITE OF THE SALLE DU MANEGE. Leidschegracht and Linjbaansgract, at the site of the present modern bridge over the Leidschegracht. Here in the fashionable **Salle du Manège** (which was in the upper hall of the house of the riding master of the Manège, near the complex of the Manège between Lijnbaansgracht and Raamplein[6]), where many foreign virtuosos had appeared, Mozart and his sister Nannerl gave two concerts, on 29 January 1766 and 26 February 1766. At the first concert, Mozart's Symphony K. 22 (written at the Hague in December) was most likely performed, with the 10-year-old Mozart conducting for the first time. At the second concert, the two prodigies played concertos on different pianos, as well as one for four hands on the same piano, and Wolfgang performed organ capriccios[7] and fugues. When the Mozarts returned, the children were permitted to give another concert on 16 April 1766, at which time only Wolfgang's instrumental music was performed, and they played four-hands and individually. The Leidschegracht, where the concert room was located, was begun after 1658, and is one of the many canals crossing the Singelgracht; it is one of the characteristic areas of Amsterdam.

SITE OF THE AMSTERDAM OPERA (GROOTEN SCHOUWBURG). Behind #384 Keizersgracht. Leopold, in his travel notes, mentioned Pietro Nieri (dancer and ballet composer) who was married to the dancer Giromama Monti, both of whom were engaged at the Amsterdam opera.[8] Before the fire in 1772, at which time the Schouwburg moved to Leidseplein, it was located where the present courtyard (behind #384 Keizersgracht) is found; today it is surrounded by buildings that were used by the Roman Catholic church as residences for older persons without means (installed in the house of the innkeeper of the Schouwburg).[9]

★ ★ PORTUGUESE SYNAGOGUE. Mr. Visserplein 3. Mozart's sister mentioned the German and Portuguese Synagogues in her travel notes. Charles V granted to the Jews the right to settle in the Netherlands, where they were able to benefit from the great tolerance, despite a brief period of persecution. The German Synagogue no longer exists, while the Portuguese Synagogue, built by Bouman from 1671 to 1675 can still be seen. The interior is a single large hall with large carved wood pieces, and four massive Ionic columns. Open Sunday–Friday 10 AM–12:15 PM and 1–4 PM; admission charge.

★ ★ ARSENAL. Kattenburgerplein 1. Leopold's impressions of Amsterdam included the Arsenal and the ships. Today, in this building, which has an elegant facade that is much like the facade of 1766, there is an extensive Maritime Museum, the **Nederlands Scheepvaart Museum.** In addition to paintings, engravings, and ship memorabilia from the eighteenth century, there is an actual *trekschuit* (small boat), like the one in which the Mozarts traveled to The Hague. Open Tuesday–Saturday 10 AM–5 PM; Sundays and holidays 1–5 PM; admission charge.

★ EAST-WEST INDIA COMPANY. Oostenburgergracht 77. The palace of the East-West India Company, mentioned in Leopold's travel notes, still stands today. Numerous trading companies were combined into the United East India Company in 1602, and in 1621, the Chartered West India Company was created. Trading colonies were founded in the West Indies, and in 1625 Manhattan was acquired (the city founded was Nieuw Amsterdam, now New York). On the pediment of the East India Company facade, the coast-of-arms with VOC (Vereenigde Oostindische Compagnie) can be seen. The other building, completed in 1642, is less monumental. Inside the private building there are beautifully restored rooms with painting, prints and historical artifacts. Only the facade can be seen; *the inside is closed to the public.* The Werkspoor Museum can be seen by appointment.

N o t e s

1 The Bauer/Deutsch/Eibl notes to the Mozart letters cite this as the address of the Mozarts' inn; however, the Amsterdam archives were not able to find any record of a "Golden Lion" inn on

Warmoesstraat around 1766. Communicated by Dr. W. Chr. Pieterse, Director of the Municipal Archives.

2 Bauer/Deutsch/Eibl, *Mozart Briefe*, V, zu 105/71–72.

3 Communicated by Dr. W. Chr. Pieterse, Director of the Municipal Archives, in response to my queries. He notes, "Reynaud was not an owner, and, prior to 1805, generally speaking, only the owners of houses and not the inhabitants are documented through tax registers; as a result, the exact address could not be located." Other sites not located by Dr. Pieterse, because of the involved research which would have been required, include the homes of de Suasso and Capadocci, and the site of the Banquiers, Mr. Neel and son.

4 Communicated by Dr. W. Chr. Pieterse, Director of the Municipal Archives, Amsterdam, and published here for the first time the Mozart literature. "In Amsterdam, generally speaking, only the owners of houses and not the inhabitants are documented through tax registers, prior to 1805. According to the archives, Hummel was not an owner; as a result, the exact address could not be located."

5 The present situation of the Vijgendam is rather different from that during the eighteenth century. Only a close reading of the various maps can make this clear; it is very difficult to explain these topographical changes in writing. Communicated by Dr. W. Chr. Pieterse, Director of the Municipal Archives, Amsterdam. This applies also to the site of the Exchange (Boerse); Leopold mentioned the widow Menanteau, who lived near the Exchange, indicating that the Mozarts saw it, and perhaps visited it, as they did in numerous other cities. The Exchange, an edifice with five arched vaults of which the middle one served as a passage for boats, was built by Hendrick de Keyser; it was located, from 1611 to 1838, on the sluice (Beurssluis, an extension of Damsluis) behind the houses of the former Vijgendam. The river was the Amstel, which can no longer be seen near the Dam, as it presently flows underground. Communicated by Dr. W. Chr. Pieterse, Director of the Municipal Archives, Amsterdam.

6 Communicated by Dr. W. Chr. Pieterse, Director of the Municipal Archives, Amsterdam.

7 Perhaps the Capricci from the *Sketch Book* K. 32a. Bauer/Deutsch/Eibl, op. cit., 103/173–74.

8 Scheurleer, *Het Muziekleven in Nederland*, 324–25.

9 Communicated by Dr. W. Chr. Pieterse, Director of the Municipal Archives, Amsterdam.

Mozart in Haarlem

Dates

From the beginning of April to the middle of April 1766

During the "Great Western" trip of 1763–66, the Mozart family left The Hague, on the way to Amsterdam for the second time, and stopped in Haarlem. Here, Mozart played on the great organ in Haarlem. The publisher Joannes Enschedé gave Mozart's father the Dutch edition of Leopold's treatise for playing the violin, as well.

Haarlem Sites

SITE OF THE "GOLDEN FLEECE" INN ("HET GULDEN VLIES"). Grote Markt 25.[1] For a brief period in the beginning of April 1766, Leopold Mozart and his family stayed in this inn while visiting Holland during their "Great Western" trip of 1763–66. The publisher Johannes Enschedé "came to them," with the organist of Haarlem, and Enschedé presented Leopold with his beautiful edition of the Dutch translation of Leopold's *Violin School*. At that time, the organist invited Wolfgang to play the famous great organ in the St. Bavo church. The inn originally consisted of two narrow buildings, each with a step-gable; today on the site there is a cinema ("Studio"); it is possible that parts of the building (which dates from the seventeenth century) are original.[2]

★ ★ GREAT CHURCH OF SAINT BAVO (GROTE OF ST.-BAVOKERK). Grote Markt (not the Catholic St. Bavo Cathedral). During their visit to Haarlem in the beginning to mid-April 1766, the organist of Haarlem, in the company of the publisher Enschedé, invited Wolfgang to play the remarkable organ in the **Grote of St.-Bavokerk.** Mozart played the instrument, regarded by some as the finest in the Netherlands, from 10 to 11 AM. The organ, which was finished by Christian Müller in 1738, with three manuals, 68 registers, and 5,000 pipes,[3] was described by Leopold as "an excellent, beautiful work ...

*Haarlem. Organ in
the Bavokerk.*

[with pipes] made completely of tin, as wood does not last long in this damp country." The fifteenth-century church has a fine cedar ribbed vault, a seventeenth-century pulpit and Gothic sounding board, a sixteenth-century pelican-shaped lectern, a sixteenth-century chancel screen of brass filigree, and carved choir stalls employing humorous designs (1512).[4] The organ was completely restored in 1868; every two years international organ competitions are organized in Haarlem. Open every day except Sundays, 30 April, and religious holidays; admission charge. Free organ concerts, lasting a hour, are performed mid-May to mid-October 8:15 PM; late June to late August also Thursdays, 3 PM.

★ ★ GROTE MARKT (GREAT MARKET). Most of the Mozarts' activities in Haarlem centered around this square. The Town Hall (**Stadhuis**), one of finest of the approximately 1,200 monuments preserved in Haarlem, is a fourteenth-century Gothic building with a Renaissance loggia; the Counts' Hall (**Graven-zaal**) is restored in earlier style.[5] The fine Renaissance-style Meat Market (**Vleeshal**), was built in 1603 by Lieven de Key. In the **Grote Markt** is a statue of Laurens Coster (Laurens Janszoon), who is believed to have invented printing

Haarlem. The Great Market with the Golden Fleece Inn. Engraving by Hendrik Spilmann, 1740.

with movable type about 1430, about ten years before Gutenberg. Tours of the Town Hall are possible, by applying to the mayor. The Meat Market is open 11 AM–5 PM (1–5 PM Sundays and holidays).

★ **PUBLISHING FIRM OF JOHANNES ENSCHEDÉ.** 3–7 Klokhuisplein.[6] When the Mozarts visited Haarlem, Johannes Enschedé presented Leopold with the Dutch translation of his *Violin School*, which Leopold called "unbelievably beautiful; even more beautiful than my own." The Enschedé publishing business was located behind the Church of St. Bavo; the office still exists (at 5 Klokhuisplein) and part of the business is still located there. The edifice is found in the square with the bell tower (the "Klokhuisplein"), just to the right of the bell tower.

[★ ★ ★ **FRANS HALS MUSEUM**]. This edifice from 1608 by Lieven de Key, which was formerly an almshouse for old men, today houses a fine collection of paintings (eight by Hals) and furniture. Open Monday to Saturday 11 AM–5 PM; Sundays and holidays 1–5 PM; admission charge.

N o t e s

1 Frans Tames, Conservator of the Stedelijke Atlas van Haarlem, in response to my queries, identified the site of this inn; it is presented here for the first time in the Mozart literature.
2 Communicated by Frans Tames, Conservator of the Stedelijke Atlas van Haarlem (Gemeentearchief Haarlem).
3 Bauer/Deutsch/Eibl, *Mozart Briefe*, V, zu 105/64.
4 Michelin, *Netherlands*, 109.
5 Ibid., 109–110.
6 Communicated by Frans Tames, Conservator of the Stedelijke Atlas van Haarlem (Gemeentearchief Haarlem). Before the publication of this book, this edifice had been overlooked in the Mozart literature.

ozart in The Hague

Dates

10 September 1765–about 27 January 1766 ▪ Beginning of March–end of March 1766

The Mozart family, during their "Great Western" trip of 1763–66 to London and Paris, stayed twice in the Hague. Soon after their first arrival, Nannerl became very sick (probably abdominal typhus), and received the last rites; Leopold's knowledge of Latin may have contributed to her recovery, as he was able to correct a doctor's diagnosis based on erroneous symptoms. In September, Mozart performed concerts for the Princess Caroline von Nassau-Weilburg and for Prince Willem V of Orange; in November, he also took sick, and was reduced to "skin and bones." In January 1766, the children, both recovered, played a concert in the "Oude Doulen," before leaving for Amsterdam.

The family returned from Amsterdam for the celebration of Willem V's attaining of the legal age required to rule. Mozart, his sister, and his father were very much involved in the musical festivities surrounding this occasion, as the amount of music composed by Mozart suggests. The celebration lasted from 7 to 12 March 1766.

Music

Symphony in D, K. 19, composed in London, beginning 1765, and perhaps performed at one of the concerts given by Mozart and his father in September 1765 and January 1766.
Symphony in F, K. Anh. 223/19a, parts of which in Leopold's hand were rediscovered in 1981; composed in London, beginning 1765, or perhaps written for The Hague concerts.
Symphonie in B flat, K. 22; composed in The Hague, end of December 1765, probably for Mozart's concert on 22 January 1766.
Symphony in G, K. Anh. 221/45a, "Alte Lambacher," the original parts of which were discovered in 1982, with "The Hague 1766" in Leopold's hand; probably composed for the festivities of the investiture of Willem V.

Aria, "Conservati fedele," K. 23 to a text by Metastasio (*Artaserse*); composed in The Hague, October 1765.

Eight solo keyboard variations on "Laat ons Juichen" (Dutch song), K. Anh. 208/24; composed in The Hague in January 1766.

Seven solo keyboard variations on "Willem van Nassau" (Dutch national song), K. 25; written in February 1766 in Amsterdam, probably for the festivities in The Hague from 7 to 12 March 1766.

Six keyboard and violin sonatas, K. 26 to K. 31; dedicated to Princess Caroline of Nassau-Weilburg as op. 4; composed in The Hague, February 1766 (probably also partly in Amsterdam 1766).

"Gallimathias musicum" (Quodlibet), K. 32, for keyboard, 2 oboes, 2 horns, bassoon, and strings; composed in The Hague, March 1766, performed during the festivities of Willem V's reaching the legal age to rule; the closing fugue uses "Willem van Nassau" as the theme.

The Hague Sites

★ ★ SITE OF THE PALACE OF THE PRINCESS OF NASSAU-WEILBURG. Korte Voorhout 3. Although it has been published that Mozart played in this splendid palace which today houses the Royal Theater (**Koninklijke Schouwburg**),[1] the present splendidly restored facade belongs to a palace of Princess Caroline von Nassau-Weilburg which was constructed from 1766 to 1774; it was therefore begun after Mozart had performed for her. Between 12 September and 19 September 1765, Mozart played twice for the Princess, who was the person most eager to bring the Mozarts to The Hague. Mozart dedicated six sonatas for keyboard and violin, K. 26 to K. 31, to the princess, who sang and was an excellent pianist. The present palace on the site, of which only the facade is original, is a superb example of ornate yet refined eighteenth-century style, with elaborate wrought-iron balconies.

★ "OUDE DOULEN." Tournooiveld 5, near the Royal Theater. The scheduled concert of the Mozart children on 30 September 1765 was cancelled because of their successive illnesses, but it was later given on 22 January 1766. Music lovers were encouraged to place any music of their choice before Mozart, who would then play it at sight. Today little remains of the original building except for the unimposing brick facade with "Oude of St. Jovis Doehlen, Anno 1695" over the door, with a ceramic ornament of St. George and the dragon. The three-story brick building is today owned by the adjacent **Staal Bankiers**.

★ VOORHOUT. This historic L-shaped area of The Hague was regarded as one of the most picturesque corners of Europe in the eighteenth century. Leopold cited "General Major de Cavallerie, Mr. Bigot": Jacques Bigot, a cavalry general

The Hague. Unsigned engraving, ca. 1760.

and *opperschenker* (who was responsible for paying musical performers such as the Mozarts), lived on the southern side of the Large Voorhout, #19 or #21.[2] Most of the elegant patrician palaces were redone in the nineteenth century, and only a few buildings remain in the state in which they were in 1765. These include the Convent Church **Kloosterkerk** (1540) at Lange Voorhout 2, the palace at Lange Voorhout 74 (1760–64), which is today the property of the Dutch royal family, and the **Huguetan** house (1734–36) at Lange Voorhout 32a–34–36, which presently houses the Supreme Court of Appeal; also of interest are the **Pageshuis** (1618) at Lange Voorhout 6, and the present American embassy (1764) at Lange Voorhout 102.[3]

★ ★ BINNENHOF.[4] The **Binnenhof**, perhaps the most historic area of The Hague, is a large courtyard surrounded by buildings of different periods. The Prince of Orange, *Stadtholder* Willem V, lived here at the *Binnenhof* in his official residence (the **Hof**, or **Stadhouderlijk Kwartier**), which had views on the *Binnenhof*.[5] Many of Mozart's activities related to the court must have taken place in the quarters of the *Stadtholder*: for example, Mozart's reception at court and performance for the prince, sometime between 12–19 September 1765 (during Nannerl's serious illness). In the period of Mozart's visit, the quarters of the *Stadtholder* occupied the north wing (approximately as far as the doors of the Knights' Hall), the west wing, and then extended from the southwestern corner (in a part now demolished) over the **Hofweg**.[6] Today the north wing is occupied by the Upper House, or Senate; the west wing houses part of the State Council.[7] In his travel notes, Leopold cited the "Room of the States

General," which refers to the seventeenth-century "First Chamber of the States General," where the Holland and West Friesland States met; the room can still be visited today. In addition, the thirteenth-century Knights' Hall (**Ridderzaal**), with its Gothic vault and wooden beams, is of interest; it has been restored, and the States General meet here for the opening session each year.[8] The Truce Hall (**Trêveszaal**), redone in Louis XIV style in 1697, and the fourteenth-fifteenth-century former prison of the States of Holland (**Gevangenpoort**) at Buitenhof 33 are also of interest. Nearby, the neoclassic **Mauritshuis** (1633–44) at Plein 29/Korte Vijverberg 8 today houses a fine art collection.

★ ★ ROUTE OF THE PROCESSION FOR THE INSTALLATION OF PRINCE WILLEM OF ORANGE. The extraordinary festivities surrounding this ceremony, which lasted from 7 to 12 March 1766, included a procession of 34 gilded carriages and their retinue, as well as a splendid "illumination." Poems, portraits, commemorative coins, and cannon salutes (as well as Mozart's music, and the Dutch translation of Leopold's treatise on violin playing) were commissioned. Many of the most interesting and characteristic parts of The Hague can be seen by following the route of the *cortège*, from the **Binnenhof** to the **Oude Hof** (**Paleis Noordeinde**). It took the following route: from the *Binnenhof*, left through the Prins Maurits Poort, Plein at the north side, Houtstraat, Tournooiveld, Lange Vijverberg, Plaats, Noordeinde until the *Oude Hof*.[9] In the seventeenth century, "Fire Theaters" were constructed in the large court pond, the Hofvijver, with spectacular fireworks; during Willem V's installation, the city was illuminated on 8 March, after the prince had taken a brief rest.[10]

★ ★ "OLD COURT" PALACE (OUDE HOF OR PALEIS NOORDEINDE). Noordeinde 68. The *cortège* during the installation of Willem V in March 1766 ended at this palace, where the prince had dinner with his guests. The prince did not live here at the time, as the palace was in a bad state of repair, and was used only as guest quarters, or for special festivities like the wedding of Princess Caroline von Nassau-Weilburg in 1760.[11] Wolfgang contributed numerous pieces during this time, including two sets of variations for clavier, K. 24 and K. 25, and the "Gallimathias musicum," K. 32. Mozart's concert at the court was 11 March 1766; while it is not known exactly when Mozart's "Gallimathias musicum" (with a closing fugue based on the present Dutch national anthem, "Willem van Nassau") was performed in connection with these festivities, it is very possible that it was here on 11 March 1766, perhaps as dinner music.[12] This impressive edifice is today the work palace of the queen of the Netherlands. *It is closed to the public*, although the fine facade and wrought-iron gate can be seen. A simple nineteenth-century park with a duck pond behind the palace is open from sunrise to sundown every day.

SITE OF THE HOME OF THE CLOCKMAKER ESKES. Spui #34. After a brief stay at the "very bad inn," "La Ville de Paris," the Mozarts moved to the home of the clockmaker Eskes, which must have been between 27 September 1765 and 17 January 1766. It was here that first Nannerl, and then Wolfgang, became seriously ill with *typhus abdominalis*, to the extent that Nannerl received the sacrament of Extreme Unction. Fortunately, Leopold, who could understand Latin, was able to dispute Dr. Haymans's diagnosis, based on symptoms which Nannerl did not have, so that Dr. Schwenke (sent by the Princess of Nassau-Weilburg) could properly treat her. In the beginning of March 1766, after returning from Amsterdam, the Mozarts again lodged here, on what was the river port (*Spui*) of The Hague in this period. Although nothing remains of the building or of the previous street number (#44), there is a bronze portrait relief of Mozart by Gobius on the site, where the department store MARCA is found.

★ ★ THE "BUSCH" (PARK).[13] Both Leopold and Nannerl cited the "*busch*" or park, and Leopold noted the many **Spaziergänger**, or walks. The park of the **Huis Ten Bosch**, the residence (1645) in the Haagse Bos, is of interest; in the summer, Willem V lived in the palace, which was enlarged from 1734 to 1739 with two large wings. The huge paintings in the domed hall (**Oranjezaal**) are noteworthy.

[★ ★ CHARACTERISTIC SIGHTS OF THE HAGUE]. Other places which the Mozarts might have seen during their visits to The Hague include the fifteenth-sixteenth-century Church of St. John (**De Grote of St. Jacobskerk**), the Van Schuylenburch house (1715) at Lange Vijverberg 8, the **Sint Sebastiaansdoelen** (1636) at Korte Vijverberg 7, the Queen's Cabinet (1725) at Korte Vijverberg 3, the **Johan de Witthuis** (1655) at Kneuterdijk 6, the van Wassenaar van Duivenvoorde house (1624) at Kneuterdijk 13, the van Wassenaar-Obdam house (1716) at Kneuterdijk 20, the Johan van Oldenbarnevelt house (1600) at Kneuterdijk 22, the **Rijksdienst voor de Beeldende Kunsten** (1740) at Plein 23, and the former Portuguese Synagogue (1725) at Jan Evertstraat 7a/ Prinsessegracht 26.[14]

N o t e s

1 Lievense, *De familie Mozart*, 16.
2 Located by Peter Wander, author of *Haagse Huizen van Oranje*, in response to my queries. He notes that these houses have been renovated in a nineteenth-century style since 1765–66. Mr. Wander and the archives of The Hague also individually located for me the embassies of numerous ambassadors cited in Leopold's travel notes in 1765: the Ambassador to Spain lived at the still-existent "Spanish Hof" on Westeinde, which is today Glerum Auctioneers (Wander) at Westeinde 12–14 (Archives); the embassy of Portugal was at Lange Houtstraat 11, which no longer exists (Wander); the embassy of Great Britain was at Kneuterdijk at the corner of Heulstraat (Wander), now probably #18–18a, where the famous Indonesian restaurant Garuda is located today (Archives); the Ambassador to the Emperor lived on Assendelftstraat until 1765, and at Lange Houtstraat, now probably #28–30, from 1766 (Archives), which is today a modern bank building about opposite to the Ambassador of Portugal (Wander).
3 Communicated by Peter Wander, The Hague.
4 A surprising gap in the Mozart literature has been the question of where the many court events concerning Mozart's activities in The Hague took place. The separate research provided by Peter Wander, and by the Archives in The Hague, leads me to believe that, as a general rule-of-thumb, the court events related to Mozart's first visit to The Hague (10 September 1765–about 27 January 1766)

took place in the Stadtholder's Quarters in the Binnenhof, while the many activities related to his second visit (beginning to the end of March 1766) transpired in the Oude Hof (the present Paleis Noordeinde), which was in a bad state, and was used only for special festivities.

5 Communicated by Peter Wander, The Hague, in response to my queries. Anna van Hannover lived in the House of Albemarle, with her son Willem. After her death Willem lived there under guidance of the Duke of Brunswijk-Wolfenbüttel. This house of Albemarle does not exist any more. It was situated on the Buitenhof, right now where the Hofweg lies. Communicated by the Gemeentearchief van 's-Gravenhage.

6 Map research provided by Peter Wander, The Hague.

7 Michelin, *Netherlands*, 113.

8 Ibid.

9 This interesting aspect of Mozart's visit, previously overlooked in the Mozart literature, was researched and communicated by the archives of The Hague, in response to my queries.

10 Communicated by the Gemeentearchief van 's-Gravenhage.

11 Communicated by Peter Wander, The Hague.

12 Schenk, *Mozart and his Times*, 87.

13 During the period of the Mozarts' visit, their walks did not include the present park area, Scheveningse Bosjes, as it was predominantly waste dunes, with thicket and underwood, at the time. Communicated by Peter Wander, The Hague, in response to my queries.

14 Communicated by Peter Wander, The Hague, in response to my queries.

Mozart in Rotterdam

Dates

9/10 September 1765 ▪ End of April 1766

During the "Great Western" trip of the Mozart family, 1763–66, and after their sojourns in Paris and London, they visited Holland, traveling from Antwerp to Rotterdam, before continuing on to The Hague. In April 1766, on the way back to Paris from Holland, the family again passed through Rotterdam.

Rotterdam Sites

[★ SITE OF THE "NEW CITY HOSTELRY" ("NIEUWE STADSHER-BERG")]. Westplein 1–3.[1] On 17 September 1765, Leopold wrote, "From [Moerdyk] we traveled over a little arm of the sea, and on the other side there were coaches already prepared for Rotterdam, where one then sat in a little boat, and was taken to the respective inn." Since they only had the next half day in Rotterdam, before traveling to The Hague, this inn, frequented by foreigners, was conveniently located near the water, and was therefore a likely lodging of the Mozarts. The house was built in 1714, and no longer exists. The harbor, in fact, was shortened about 1850, and the hotel was then no longer near the water. Today there is a large building, "Atlantic House," on the site, in a peaceful corner of Rotterdam called Westplein. The present Museum of Folk History and Culture is in close proximity to the site.[2]

★ STATUE OF ERASMUS. Parvis of St. Lawrence; adjacent to St. Lawrence Church. Leopold wrote that he "looked with pleasure at the statue of the famous Erasmus Rottersdami . . . on the square." This fine bronze statue, the work of Hendrick de Keyser, was erected on the Great Market Square in 1622; it has since been relocated to this square.

[★ ST. LAWRENCE CHURCH (GROTE- OF ST.-LAURENSKERK)].
The old town of Rotterdam was almost completely destroyed on 14 May 1940
by the Germans, leaving little from the time of the Mozarts' visits. However, this
massive Gothic church (finished 1646) near the present location of the Erasmus
statue, has been rebuilt, and is one of the few remaining monuments which
would have been familiar to the Mozarts. The interior is in Gothic Brabant style,
with numerous copper chandeliers and eighteenth-century gilded wrought-iron
work. A sixteenth-century organ case is found in the transept, while the organ
case in the chancel is from 1725.[3]

Rotterdam. Engraving, published by Carel Allard, ca. 1700.

N o t e s

1   In response to my queries, A. Gordijn has suggested this inn as the likely lodging of the Mozarts; it is
presented here for the first time in the Mozart literature. Likewise, Gordijn recreated the route of the
Mozarts on maps of the period, based on Leopold's description. Although Leopold mentions only one
"little arm of the sea," there must have been, in fact, two. Gordijn has communicated, "Since there has
been no other route than passing two islands from Moerdyk to Rotterdam (Beyerland and Ysselmonde),
there must have been another stretch of water to cross, which was the Old Meuse (Oude Maas) between
Heinenoord and Barendrecht (a tunnel at present), but it was not of any significance in comparison with
the Hollands Diep between Moerdyk and Stryen, or even with the New Meuse (Nieuwe Maas) between
Katendrecht and Rotterdam." A. Gordijn, dept Topogr. Hist. Atlas, Archiefdienst, Gemeente
Rotterdam.
2   Michelin, *Netherlands*, 159–60.
3   Ibid.

Mozart in
Utrecht

Dates

18 April 1766 to the end of April 1766

The trip of the Mozart family through the Netherlands, as part of their "Great Western" trip to Paris and London, 1763–66, included a brief stay in Utrecht, where a concert including symphonies by Mozart was given on 21 April 1766.

Music

At the concert on 21 April 1766 in the Guild Hall on the Vreeburg, in addition to sonatas and concertos played on the keyboard by Mozart and his sister, symphonies entirely by Wolfgang were played. A sonata for keyboard duet, K. 19d (written in London in 1765), was presumably also in their repertoire at this time. Symphonies from this period which might have been performed include Symphony in D, K. 19; Symphony in F, K. Anh. 223/19a; Symphony in B flat, K. 22 (written in The Hague) and, of course, Symphony in E flat, K. 16, which Leopold would have brought from London.

Utrecht Sites

SITE OF THE MUSIC ROOM ON THE VREEBURG. 5 Vredenburg.[1] Nothing remains from the eighteenth century on the site of the concert room in the carpenters Guild House (**Bijlhouwers**), where Mozart and Nannerl played concertos and sonatas on the harpsichord at the afternoon concert of 21 April 1766. The Collegium Musicum of Utrecht participated, performing symphonies entirely by Mozart. On the site today is **Haut-Brox**, a clothing store in a area of modern shops.

[★ ★ OLD CATHEDRAL (DOMKERK)]. Domplein. Because of the habit of the Mozarts of visiting the important sites of a city, it is almost certain that they visited the cathedral, and the separate bell tower. It has traditionally been one of the major sights of Utrecht and is situated very close to where the Mozarts lodged. The church, built from 1254 to 1517, has a famous organ (still in use today) with a nineteenth-century case (1831) using sixteenth-nineteenth-century pipes. Concerts of the Holland Festival of Old Music are held here. Open Monday to Saturday (May–September) 10 AM–5 PM; (October–April) 11 AM–4 PM, and Sunday 2–4 PM.

Utrecht. Hotel Plaets-Royal. Unsigned drawing. Gemeente-Archief, Utrecht.

[★ ★ DOM TOWER (DOMTOREN)]. The Mozarts often climbed the renowned towers in a city they visited, such as in Ghent. This tower (built 1321–82), was connected to the cathedral until a hurricane in 1674 and is the highest in Holland. It has two chapels, as well as 13 bells and a carillon with 50 small bells (mostly cast by the famous Hemony brothers). Open Saturday and Sunday Noon–5 PM (1 January–31 December); Monday to Friday 10 AM–5 PM (1 April–1 November); public holidays Noon–5 PM; admission charge.

SITE OF THE HOTEL PLAETS ROYAL. Minrebroederstraat 21.[2] Nothing remains of the hotel, home of Mr. Mos, where the Mozarts stayed. It became an orphanage, and was demolished about 1875. In 1877, a Catholic church, **St. Willebrorduskerk,** was built on the site.[3] Although it has been published that the Mozarts gave a concert in the hotel,[4] the concert actually took place in the Music Room of the Guild Hall on the Vreeburg.[5]

[★ JANS CHURCH]. Janskerkhof. This church, so near to the Hotel Plaets Royal, was a likely visit for Leopold Mozart and his family during their five days spent in Utrecht, particularly since it contained the library of the University.[6] It was founded in the eleventh century, and the choir was rebuilt in 1539 in late-Gothic style. The present facade dates from the seventeenth century; the nave has a thirteenth-century wooden barrel-vaulted roof with the original decoration. Nearby, several elegant facades from the seventeenth-eighteenth century are found, such as #13 **Janskerkhof.**[7] Open Monday to Friday 9 AM–5 PM.

[★ ★ CHARACTERISTIC STREETS OF UTRECHT]. Utrecht is a splendidly preserved city, with numerous areas near the cathedral which give a clear idea of the city as the Mozarts saw it in the eighteenth century. Near the **Pausdam,** where the **Kromme Nieuwegracht** and the **Nieuwegracht** meet, is an elegant residential area with seventeenth-, eighteenth-, and nineteenth-century facades, often constructed in front of medieval houses. The Academy Building of the

Utrecht. Cathedral, courtyard.

University at Domplein 29 has a meeting room dating from 1495, and an organ above the entrance from 1739, which can be visited by appointment. In the eleventh-century **Pieterskerk**, there are frequent concerts of the Schola Cantorum Amsterdam during the Holland Festival (Oude Muziek). The Maria Church and the **Maliebaan (Pall Mall)** were also of interest in 1766.[8]

N o t e s

1 Located for me by A. B. R. du Croo de Vries, Utrecht Archives; published here for the first time in the Mozart literature.
2 Ibid.
3 Communicated by A. B. R. du Croo de Vries, Utrecht Archives.
4 Bauer/Deutsch/Eibl, *Mozart Briefe*, V, zu 105/94.
5 Lievense, *De Familie Mozart op Bezoek in Nederlands een Reisverslag*, 37.
6 Communicated by C. J. van de Peet, Utrecht.
7 Michelin, *Netherlands*, 175.
8 Communicated by C. J. van de Peet, Utrecht.

Switzerland

Bern, Geneva, Lausanne, Schaffhausen, Zurich

Other Sites of Interest:

Winterthur

*M*ozart in Bern

D a t e s

18 to about 26 September 1766

*L*eopold's precise notes about the "Great Western" trip of 1763–66 stopped with Dijon, so almost nothing is known about the Mozarts' stay in Bern. However, it can be assumed that they played at least one concert in Bern during their eight days in the city.

M u s i c

In a letter of 26 January 1778, a bitter and ironic Leopold remarked in a letter to Wolfgang about the fact that he had left sonatas and engravings in various cities, including Bern, indicating that he had never received the revenue from them. The sonatas may have been the works of Mozart which had been engraved in this period, including those for clavier and violin, K. 6 to K. 9, which were engraved in Paris; the sonatas for clavier and violin, K. 10 to K. 15 (dedicated to the English Queen Charlotte); and the 6 sonatas for clavier and violin, K. 26 to 31, as well as the solo clavier variations, K. Anh. 208/24 and 25.*

Bern Sites

[★ **CHURCH OF THE HOLY SPIRIT (HEILIGGEIST-KIRCHE)**]. Spitalgasse. This fine Baroque church, built 1726–29, would have been one of the likely sights visited by the Mozarts during their itinerary in Bern.

[★ ★ **PRISON TOWER (KÄFIGTURM)**]. Built on the site of the western gate of Bern from 1641–43, this tower (in use as a prison until 1897) underwent a fine restoration in the eighteenth century; the clock dates from 1690–91.

[**SITE OF THE "FALCON" INN ("FALKEN")**].[1] Amthausgasse 6/Markt-gasse 11. This was one of the most likely inns where the Mozarts would have

*Staehelin, *Die Reise der Familie Mozart*, 51.

lodged in 1766[2]; from 1722 to 1905, it was the most renowned and elegant hotel in Bern. The "Falcon," which dates from the beginning of the sixteenth century, was the inn of the Bishops of Lausanne, and was under the ownership of the city from 1536 to 1546; from 1722 it was privately owned, and was later owned by a partnership society.[3] The inn disappeared in 1904; today the clothing store C & A is located on the site. The present elegant facade of the upper floors has delicate wrought-iron balconies and a large cornice; there is an old handworked shield of a horse in red and gold. In addition, on Marktgasse there are many interesting seventeenth-eighteenth-century facades with arcades.

[★ ★ CHOIR OF THE FRENCH CHURCH]. Zeughausgasse 8. Since nothing is known about the visit of the Mozarts to Bern in 1766 (except the approximate dates), this church has been suggested in the context of the concert life of Bern in 1766; there was a music room (1702) with an organ on the upper floor for the Collegium musicum.[4] The church (originally named after Saints Peter and Paul) was built in the last two decades of the thirteenth century, and belonged to the preaching order of the Dominicans, which had a seat in Bern since 1269. The choir and altar room had been turned into a granary since 1534; it was reno-vated 1723–24 on plans of N. Schildknecht.[5] Today, the choir has fine frescoes below the painted columns and a wood ceiling; during the recent spectacular restoration, the floor, which had separated the two floors of the choir during the time of the Mozarts' visit, was removed.

[★ TOWN HALL OF THE EXTERIOR (ÄUSSERER STAND)]. Zeughausgasse 17. In 1728–30, this fine edifice was built as the mock parliament (*Jugendparlia-ment*) by which young patricians could prepare themselves for a political career. A feature of the Mozarts' trip in Switzerland was the fact that the children were presented in concert in town halls (at least once in Lausanne and at least twice in Geneva). In an attempt to fill in the historical gaps of the Mozarts' eight days in Bern, this historic edifice, near the music room of the Collegium Musicum in the French church, suggests itself as a possible site for a concert.[6] Much later, in 1831, the first Bern constitution was drawn up, and the first federal constitution of Switzerland was accepted here in 1848. The interior underwent a consider-able reconstruction in 1817, including the building of the large **Empire Room**; the facade was radically altered 1904–05, after the building went into private ownership.[7] A café restaurant is located in the edifice today.

[★ ★ CLOCK TOWER (ZYTGLOGGETURM)]. Located at the midpoint of Marktgasse and Kramgasse. Leopold Mozart, with his pedagogic nature, would not have failed to bring his children to this renowned calendar clock, con-structed on what was the west gate of Bern from 1191 to 1250; the painted figures, including the sixteenth-century Jack and bear cubs, create a procession to the accompaniment of the chimes, which begin four minutes before each hour.[8] The inner complexities of the clock can also be seen during the tour of the tower.

[★ ★ TOWN HALL (RATHAUS)]. Rathausplatz 2. Despite all attempts to find documentation, the place where the Mozart children would have played a concert during their approximately eight days in Bern is not known. However, although the Mozarts undoubtedly saw this fine edifice, in the eighteenth century the fine music room (with massive pillars and a wooden slat ceiling) was not in the present condition; it was divided into two floors, and housed the city archives.[9] The Town Hall is today the seat of the legislative assembly of the city of Bern, and of the legislative assembly of the province. It was built 1406–17, and has undergone many changes and restorations, including a neo-Gothic rebuilding 1865–68; however, in 1940–42, the facade and the main hall were restored to their original condition. The square (**Rathausplatz**) has a fountain (**Vennerbrunnen**) from 1542.

[★ ★ CATHEDRAL OF ST. VINCENT (MÜNSTER)]. Münsterplatz. The Mozarts, with their habit of seeing the most renowned monuments in each city, undoubtedly visited this late-Gothic edifice, built 1421–1573 (with the exception of the tower, which was only finished in 1893). The spectacular tympanum

Berne. Town Hall (Rathaus).

of the main portal, by Master Erhard Küng, has 234 figures carved in stone; the chancel has large stained-glass windows dating from the fifteenth century.[10]

[THE "CROWN" INN (DIE KRONE)]. Gerechtigkeitsgasse 64/Postgasse 57. The habit of the Mozarts during their "Great Western" trip was to lodge in the finest inn. In 1766, the finest inns in Bern included the "Crown" Inn, which was erected before 1470; in the first half of the seventeenth century it became the first inn in Bern. The facade on Postgasse dates from 1630.[11] Today, near the site at #66, there is a restaurant, opened in the twentieth century with the same name as the historic inn.

[★ CHURCH OF THE NYDEGG (NYDEGGKIRCHE)]. This fourteenth-century church was built on the foundations of a fortress which was destroyed in 1270.

[BEAR PITS (BÄRENGRABEN)]. At the Nydeggbrücke. A sight that would have been unlikely for the Mozart to miss was that of the famous Bern "bears" which were enclosed in the moats of the city since the fifteenth century; in fact, the name of the city itself is believed to derive from the word "bear" ("Bär," in German). These bear pits have been a popular part of Bern tradition; the present enclosure dates from 1856 to 1857.

[★ ★ ★ CHARACTERISTIC SIGHTS OF BERN].[12] A remarkable number of monuments, well preserved and restored, remain from the time of the Mozarts' visit in September 1766, providing an excellent historical glimpse of what they would have seen.
Citizens' Home (Burgerspital) (1734–42) at Bubenbergplatz 4.
[Boys' Orphanage (Waisenhaus)] (1782–86) at Waisenhausplatz 32; although this edifice was finished after the Mozarts' visit, it is a fine example of eighteenth-century architecture.
[Guard House (Hauptwache)] (1766–68) at Theaterplatz 13; another fine eighteenth-century structure built after the Mozarts' visit.
Granary (Kornhaus) (1711–18; rebuilt 1894–98) at Kornhausplatz 18.
[Hôtel de musique] (1767–70) at Theaterplatz 7; this fine concert hall and theater was begun a year after the visit of the Mozarts, yet is a noteworthy example of eighteenth-century architecture.
May House (1515; addition of upper balcony floors after 1895) at Münster-gasse 62.
City and University Library at Münstergasse 61; originally built as a granary (1755–60), the upper floor was converted into a library (1787–94), with additional wings added (1861–63).
Chapter House (1745–55) at Münsterplatz 3; this structure was constructed on the site of the second Teutonic Order house. The Mozarts visited the Teutonic Order in Frankfurt in 1763, and Mozart related that he was thrown out of the

Teutonic Order house in Vienna (where Colloredo, the Archbishop of Salzburg, had been staying in 1781), "with a kick in my ass."

Béatrice von Wattenwyl House (facade and arcade 1446–49; upper floor 1560 and 1705) at Junkerngasse 59; this fine structure, which was in the possession of the von Wattenwyl family from 1838 to 1934, has since been property of the confederation.

Erlacherhof (about 1746–1752) at Junkerngasse 47; this edifice, begun for Mayor Hieronymus von Erlach, became the seat of the municipal government in 1832, and the seat of the Federal Council from 1848 to 1858.

Antonite House (**Antonierhaus**) (1492–1505) at Postgasse 62; this church of the hospital order of the Antonites, which became a granary and a postal coach house through the years, was renovated and rebuilt 1939–40.

Felsenburg (about 1260–70) near the **Untertorbrücke**; it was originally the east bridge on the right bank but was walled up in the first part of the seventeenth century and converted into a residence 1862–64.

N o t e s

1   It has been suggested by L. Staehelin that the Mozarts stayed at the home of Johann Andreas Seul, a musician, music educator, and local music distributor for Bern (as there were no music shops in Bern at the time); later, Leopold wrote that he received nothing from the engraved music scores and copper engravings that he left behind in Berne with Seul. However, the Stätsarchiv of Bern has been unable to find any information about where Johann Andreas Seul lived; he was primarily a vocal musician and educator.

2   Although the possible lodgings of the Mozarts have been cited for almost every city they visited, neither the Bauer/Deutsch/Eibl notes (nor the literature they surveyed), nor L. Staehelin have suggested the most important eighteenth-century inns of Bern; the "Crown" Inn and the "Golden Falcon," which are included in the present publication.

3   Weber, *Historisch-Topographischen Lexikon der Stadt Bern*, 75–76.

4   Staehelin, *Die Reise der Familie Mozart durch die Schweiz*, 50–51.

5   Weber, op. cit., 80.

6   It is cited here for the first time in the Mozart literature. In regards to the suggestion of a concert in the Rathaus des Äusseren Standes, "It is possible that the festive room (festliche Saal) in the Rathaus des Äusseren Standes was used for a Mozart concert. Unfortunately, there is no documentation for it; until now, no one has been able to find a source which indicates where the young Mozart appeared in Bern." Communicated by Dr. Karl F. Wälchli, Staatsarchivar, Statsarchiv des Kantons Bern.

7   Weber, op. cit., 198.

8   Michelin, *Switzerland*, 51.

9   Communicated by Dr. Karl F. Wälchli, Staatsarchivar, Staatsarchiv des Kantons Bern. Proceeding from L. Staehelin's work, in speculating about concert sites in Bern, I explored the possibility of a town hall concert as in Lausanne and Geneva; however, while "a room often used for concerts today exists in the Bern Town Hall (the so-called Rathaus-Halle), in 1766 it was completely built over with dividing floors and other construction, and contained the documents of the archives (Staatsarchiv)." Communicated by Dr. Karl F. Wälchli, Staatsarchivar, Staatsarchiv des Kantons Bern.

10   Michelin, op. cit., 51.

11   Weber, op. cit., 140.

12   Stadt Bern, "Einige historische Bauten."

$\mathcal{M}$ozart in Geneva

Dates

20 August to about 10 September 1766

lthough it seems that Leopold had intentions of visiting Voltaire in his villa outside of the city (as Leopold was in the habit of looking up the most notable personalities of the time), he was not successful. Leopold, from later letters to Mozart, seems to have been somewhat bitter about this disappointment; Voltaire, however, protested in letters to friends in Paris that he and his partner, Madame Denis, were not well at the time, and that he was disappointed to have missed Mozart. From the French diplomat, Pierre Michel Hennin, we learn that the Mozart children gave two concerts in the City Hall, which were successful, despite the poor time of year. From André Grétry, the renowned eighteenth-century composer, we learn that Mozart played a difficult piece by the older composer (in E-flat minor) at sight. However, as Mozart substituted passages of his own while he performed, Grétry remained unimpressed; he wrote that everyone (except himself) cried out, "What a miracle!"[1]

Geneva Sites

[★ HOME OF JEAN-JACQUES ROUSSEAU]. 40 Grand Rue. The twelve-year-old Mozart set Rousseau's *Le Devin du Village* in a German Singspiel version, as *Bastien und Bastienne* in 1768. With Leopold's admiration of Englightenment culture, it is likely that they noted Rousseau's birthplace, on this characteristic street which is one of the finest, and best preserved, in Geneva today. Commemorative plaque concerning Rousseau.

[★ HOME OF ANDRÉ GRÉTRY]. 29/31 Grand Rue. André Grétry, the innovator of French *opéra comique*, wrote about an event which is most certainly a concert of the Mozart children.[2] Leopold is described as having suggested to him during a concert that he write a new piece, the most difficult possible, to test Mozart's sightreading abilities. For the next performance, Grétry wrote a piece in E-flat minor, which Mozart played superbly, substituting occasional passages of his own; Grétry therefore wrote ironically about the enthusiasm of the public, which he claimed he did not share. In 1766, Grétry lived in this house, which has a charming, characteristic facade; the apartments are privately owned today. Commemorative plaque concerning Grétry.

Geneva. City Hall, Interior, with Carved Marble Portal.

★ ★ ★ HOME OF THE FRENCH "RESIDENT" (MAISON DU RÉSIDENT DE FRANCE).[3] 11 Grand Rue. When the Mozarts arrived in Geneva, Leopold had a letter from Melchior Grimm in Paris addressed to Pierre Michel Hennin, which he delivered personally. Hennin was the French "Resident," not an ambassador but a representative of the French monarchy to scrutinize and report on political actions in Geneva. It is likely that Mozart demonstrated his abilities here to the "Resident" during their visit. This elaborate town house in Louis XIV style, which was one of the earliest museums in Europe, is today the "Société de Lecteur," a private reading club, which has 300,000 volumes, including numerous tiers of antique leather-bound volumes. In addition to the exquisite facade, there is a courtyard where both concerts and plays are given. Inside there are four large salons, completely restored to their eighteenth-century splendor, with period furniture. The mansion, constructed in 1743 by the architect Jean-Michel Billon, was also the site where Napoleon gave an audience before the battle of Marengo.[4] Although it is a private library, permission to visit can be obtained by writing to the Société de Lecture or, occasionally, by inquiring directly at the Society.

★ ★ CITY HALL (HÔTEL DE VILLE). 2 and 4, rue de l'Hôtel-de-Ville. This remarkable fifteenth-sixteenth-century edifice, where Wolfgang and Nannerl gave two concerts during the period approximately from 20 August 1766 to 10 September 1766, is in a fine state of preservation. It features thirteen Tuscan columns which support vaulted ceilings, and an extraordinary Renaissance ramp with a unique square design, which leads up several floors to council chambers.[5] Many other beautiful features remain, such as a splendidly carved arched gate, a spacious courtyard where outdoor concerts are given, and the fifteenth-century fortified Baudet Tower. It is likely that Mozart's concerts were held in the room which is the present office of the Secretary General of the Department of the Interior and Agriculture, on the second floor[6] (American: third floor). The City Hall is open Monday to Friday 7:30 AM–6 PM; closed Saturday and Sunday.

★ HOME OF JEAN HUBER.[7] 5 de la Taconnerie. Leopold Mozart cited "chez M. Huber" as his address in Geneva, suggesting that the family stayed here in Huber's home instead of at the Hôtel de la Balance. Goethe called Huber "the complete man," as he was a "literate man-of-the-world, soldier, linguist, artist, ornithologist, naturalist, poet and musician"; in addition, Jean Huber was known for the artistic silhouettes he created.[8] The building, in the shadow of the cathedral, has an austere original facade which has been remarkably restored; the interior has been renovated as offices and apartments.

★ ★ ST. PETER'S CATHEDRAL (CATHEDRAL DE SAINT PIERRE). Place de la Cathédral. It has been speculated that Mozart played the organ in this cathedral from the twelfth-thirteenth centuries, which had been given an impressive neo-Grecian facade about twenty years prior to his visit.[9] The monumental edifice presents a variety of styles, including the original Romanesque core and ornament, Gothic walls with a copper spire, and the Greco-Roman west facade of pillars with Corinthian capitals and dome, inspired in the 1750s by the excavation of Pompeii and by the Pantheon in Rome.[10] Open daily 9 AM–7 PM; Sunday service (no sight-seeing visits allowed) 10 AM.

★ HOTEL DE LA BALANCE. Place Longemalle. During their stay in Geneva, from 20 August to about 10 September 1766, the Mozarts perhaps stayed in this hotel,[11] today called Hôtel Touring Balance. It was Leopold's habit to choose the finest hotels, close to the center of cultural life in the city, and the Hôtel de la Balance is only a short distance away from the **Vieille Ville** (Old City). Although the interior was completely renovated in 1986, the remarkable facade, a colorful Renaissance fantasy in brick and stone, remains intact.

N o t e s

1 Staehelin, *Die Reise der Familie Mozart*, 90.
2 Staehelin, *Die Reise der Familie Mozart*, 90.
3 Before the publication of this book, this remarkable edifice, in a perfect state of restoration, was completely ignored in the Mozart literature. The letter from Grimm to Hennin, which revealed that Mozart had played twice in Geneva in the City Hall, was discovered by Jean-Daniel Candaux, and published in "Journal de Genève," 5–6 November 1966.
4 Charles, *All About Geneva*, 83.
5 Ibid., 93.
6 Communicated by Jean-Etienne Genequand, Archiviste d'Etat, Geneva.
7 Lucas Staehelin, who was unable to find a residence of Jean Huber within the city limits, suggested that the Mozarts stayed in a hotel. However, this building, which was unquestionably Huber's home in 1766, has been ignored by the Mozart literature until now. (Confirmed by Jean-Etienne Genequand, Archives d'Etat, Geneva.)
8 Staehelin, op. cit., 64.
9 Ibid., 28.
10 Charles, *All About Geneva*, 72.
11 Staehelin, op. cit., 21. cf. footnote #6.

Mozart in Lausanne

11–18 September 1766

*E*n route back to Salzburg, after their "Great Western" trip of 1763–66, Mozart and his family stopped in Lausanne for the afternoon. They were, however, met by the servants of the most important nobility of Lausanne, who succeeded in talking Leopold into staying longer. Mozart gave a concert in the City Hall, and at least another concert during their stay in Lausanne.

Music

Leopold wrote in his catalog of Mozart's works, "Various solo pieces for the traverse flute for Duke Louis v. Württemberg, [composed] in Lausanne in the presence of these gentlemen." These solos, K. 33a, written in September 1766, have been lost.

Lausanne Sites

SITE OF THE VILLA AT GRAND MONTRIOND. In the courtyard of 9, 13, and 15 de l'avenue Dapples,[1] near the hill Montriond between Lausanne and Ouchy. The Mozart family, planning to stay only the afternoon in Lausanne on their way to Bern on 11 September 1766, were met upon their arrival by the servants of Prince Ludwig von Württemberg, and of other noble families, who convinced them to stay longer in Lausanne (until about 16 September). Most likely, they were taken to the Villa Monrion of the Prince, later named Grand Montriond, that had been built in the beginning of the eighteenth century on a hill surrounded by vineyards. Voltaire had lived there earlier, and after the visit of the Mozarts, the world-renowned doctor Tissot moved into this splendid, horseshoe-shaped villa.[2] The villa was destroyed in 1955, but the hill of the same name offers parks and a botanical garden which is open March, April and

October from 10–Noon and 1:30–5:30 PM, and May to September from 10–Noon and 1:30–8 PM (Monday and Friday, it closes at 5:30 PM.) The hill Montriond, which offers a beautiful view of the lake and the mountains, is easily reached by the Metro. On top of the hill, there is an unimposing modern shell for concerts.

★ ★ HOTEL-DE-VILLE. Place de la Palud. Wolfgang and Nannerl gave at least two concerts in Lausanne, one of which was in this splendid City Hall. Two dates cited in a household book indicate 15 September 1766 and 18 September 1766. Jean-Henri Polier wrote in his private diary that, for one concert in the Hôtel-de-Ville, "[Mozart] plays with great facility and composes to the great astonishment of all; there were 70 people."[3] It is equally probable that the second concert was also in the City Hall. The room in which Mozart and Nannerl probably played is the **Salle du conseil communal**, overlooking the exquisite square, Place de Hôtel-de-Ville. The present structure was built from 1673 to 1675 according to the plans of Abraham de Crousaz, incorporating a large part of an earlier city hall from the middle of the fifteenth century.[4] Arched windows on the ground level with pairs of rectangular windows on the upper two floors are mounted by a clock tower spire, with four small spires, topped by a bell tower and an onion dome. Inside, carved portals, medieval doors and locks, paintings, Roman inscriptions, and vaulted ceilings provide architectural interest. The room where the Mozarts probably played is restored, yet maintains

Lausanne. Ancien Académie.

the original style. Carved wooden benches, a blue-white porcelain stove, and wooden slat ceilings are intact from the time of the Mozarts' visits. Open Monday to Friday 8 AM–6 PM.

[★ ★ ANCIEN ACADEMIE]. rue Cite-Devant 3. Dr. Auguste Tissot, a physician in Lausanne who was world-famous for his books on health (which were translated into many languages), studied Mozart's abilities, and then wrote the artistic and psychological "Discours" which appeared in *Aristide ou Le Citoyen* of 11 October 1766 which proclaims, "One can say with confidence, that he will one day be one of the greatest Masters in his Art."[5] In 1766, Tissot was named honorary Professor of Medicine at the renowned Academy of Lausanne. Staehelin suggests that Mozart met him at the home of the Prince, with whom Tissot was friends; it is equally possible that he asked Mozart to visit him at the **Ancien Académie,** or at his residence south of the Academy.[6] The austere, yet dramatic structure of the academy, with a copper-roofed, painted clock tower, was constructed from 1579 to 1587, along the walls of the city. Today it is the **Gymnase cantonal de la Cité.** Although the facade is original, the interior has been completely renovated.

[★ ★ CATHEDRAL NOTRE-DAME]. Place de la Cathédral. The monumental Cathedral was undoubtedly one of the places visited by the Mozart family during their sight seeing in Lausanne. It was constructed on the previous location of two earlier sanctuaries from the eighth to eleventh centuries. The present structure was begun near the middle of the twelfth century under the leadership of Saint Amédée, Mozart's namesake. It was consecrated in 1275, on the occasion of the meeting in Lausanne of Pope Gregory X and the Emperor Rudolf of Habsburg.[7] The walk from the Cathedral to the Hôtel-de-Ville by way of the present University is particularly characteristic and beautiful.

N o t e s

1 In response to my queries, Catherine Girardin, of the Bibliothèque Cantonale et Universitaire, Lausanne, located the site of Grand-Montriond. In addition, she located information about the residences of other nobles associated with the Mozart visit to Lausanne in 1766. In regard to Madame Louise-Honorée-Françoise d'Aubonne (born de Saussure, and married to the captain in the Netherlands service, Etienne-Louis d'Aubonne), she communicated that "the d'Aubonnes had lived on rue de Bourg in the seventeenth-eighteenth centuries." (Bridel, *Lausanne: promenades historiques et archéologiques,* 58); concerning Madame Anne-Louise-Jeanne-Françoise d'Hermenche (born de Seigneur and married to David-Louis de Constant d'Hermenches, an officer in the Dutch service), she notes, "according to Mottaz, *Dictionnaire Historique,* who cites David Constant, professor at the Academy of Lausanne, the family Constant owned the seigneurerie d'Hermenches until the Revolution; concerning Salomon Cherrière de Sévery, private tutor to the Count of Hessen-Kassel, she notes that he "became Seigneur de Sévery et Coseigneur de Mex. He restored the *château* de Sévery in 1768 (Mottaz, 659, 199); of Louis-Eugène de Württemberg (the brother of Prince Carl Eugen von Württemberg, and Schwabian field marshal), she wrote that he "lived at that time at Chablière (country house, northeast of the city, near the end of the avenue Bergières) around 1764, then moved to Montriond (Mottaz, *Dictionnaire Historique,* 259, 334).
2 Staehelin, *Die Reise der Familie Mozart durch die Schweiz,* 31.
3 Ibid., 32.

4 Hugli, *Lausanne*, 23.

5 Staehelin, op. cit., 34, 40.

6 In response to my queries about the location of Dr. Tissot's practice (where he perhaps examined Mozart), Catherine Girardin of the Bibliothèque Cantonale et Universitaire, Lausanne, has written, "Tissot established himself from 1755, the year of his marriage to Charlotte née Dapples, in the house of his in-laws, a building located in the city, to the south of the courtyard of the Academy, and today demolished. The authorities conferred upon him the title of honorary professor of the Academy and created, on 30 January 1766, a chair of medicine. Tissot gave only an inaugural lesson. We have not, unfortunately, found any information concerning his office, or the place where he examined Mozart."

7 Hugli, *Lausanne*, 16.

Mozart in Schaffhausen

Dates

14–19 October 1766

The Mozart family stayed in Schaffhausen for about four days, on the last leg of their journey home to Salzburg, at the end of the "Great Western" trip of 1763–66. It is possible that they performed a concert in the city, as their arrival had been prepared by a local newspaper.*

Schaffhausen Sites

[★ "CROWN" INN ("DIE KRONE")]. Kirchhofplatz 7. While it has never been speculated where the Mozarts stayed during their four days in Schaffhausen, they generally stayed in the best inn in each city during their "Great Western" trip; "Die Krone" was the best inn in Schaffhausen in 1766.[1] Today the edifice is the **Kronenhof**, a three-star hotel; the interior and exterior have been completely modernized. The hotel faces a characteristic square of Schaffhausen.

[★ CITY HALL (RATHAUSLAUBE)]. Rathausbogen 10. The Mozart family stayed in Schaffhausen four days, about 14–19 October 1766, and most likely they performed a concert in the city, which had been prepared for their visit by a local newspaper.[2] As the Mozarts performed concerts in the City Hall in Dijon, Geneva, and Lausanne on this final leg of their "Great Western" trip, it is quite possible that they also performed in the City Hall in Schaffhausen.[3] The City Hall during that period was located in this fifteenth-century edifice, which has a magnificent Renaissance caisson ceiling dating from 1586. Two rooms of the City Hall can be visited. Open Monday–Friday 8:30 AM–6 PM.

*Staehelin, *Die Reise der Familie Mozart durch die Schweiz*, 75.

★ ★ CHARACTERISTIC SIGHTS OF SCHAFFHAUSEN. Despite the fact that Leopold, and later his son, Wolfgang, each expressed distaste for medieval architecture, Schaffhausen is a fascinating medieval city, with numerous Renaissance and classical buildings. The Old Town has the remnants of the ramparts of the city, topped by the sixteenth-century keep (**Munot**). Numerous characteristic streets, such as the fine **Vordergasse**, have oriel windows, and houses decorated by stucco and carving. Noteworthy is the splendidly painted Knight's House (**Haus zum Ritter**). The recently-restored eleventh-century Romanesque All Saints' Church (**Münster**), with a massive fifteenth-century bell, and the adjacent monastery cloister are also of interest. The former Abbey of All Saints today houses the All Saints' Museum (**Museum zu Allerheiligen**), with many manuscripts and historical exhibits.[4]

Excursion to the Rheinfalls

[★ ★ WATERFALL (RHEINFALLS)]. The Mozarts would not have missed the opportunity to visit this renowned 70-foot waterfall,[5] the most powerful in Europe; in 1766, three miles were less than an hour away from the city.

Notes

1 Communicated by Olga Waldvogel, Staatsarchiv, Schaffhausen, in response to my queries, and published here for the first time in the Mozart literature.
2 Staehelin, *Die Reise der Familie Mozart durch die Schweiz*, 75.
3 Published for the first time in the Mozart literature.
4 Michelin, *Switzerland*, 164.
5 Staehelin, op. cit., 76.

$\mathcal{M}$ozart in Zurich

Dates

About 28 September–12 October 1766

On the last leg of their extensive "Great Western" trip of 1763–66, the Mozart family stopped in Zurich for two weeks. Here the Mozart children gave concerts in the music room of the Collegium Musicum in Zurich. In addition, the family met the Gessner brothers, Johannes and Salomon.

Zurich Sites

[★ GASTHOF "ZUM SCHWERT"]. Weinplatz 10; at the Rathaus Bridge. While it is not known where the Mozart family lodged about 28 September–13 October 1766, during their stay in Zurich, the most likely possibility is the historic "Red Sword" Inn ("**Zum roten Schwert**"). Leopold usually chose the finest hotels during his "Great Western" trip through Europe from 1763 to 1766; usually the inn was in a location convenient to the artistic life of the city. Today the inn has been converted into a garden shop with numerous offices above. Only the facade remains from the eighteenth century, as the interior has been completely remodeled. The location, however, provides a splendid view of the **Münster Bridge**, St. Peter's and the City Hall (**Rathaus**). This **Gasthaus** was also in close proximity to the Music Room near the **Fraumünster Church**, where the Mozart children performed. Today the restored facades of the area provide a glimpse of eighteenth-century Zurich. The building, which is today owned by the Schweizer Rückversicherungs-Gesellschaft, has a commemorative plaque citing the stay of Emperor Joseph II, Czar Alexander I, Friedrich Wilhelm III, Louis Philippe, Louis Napoleon, Gustav Adolf IV, Volta, Goethe, Madame de Staëhl, Victor Hugo, Alexander Dumas, Carl Maria von Weber, Liszt, Brahms, and, of course, Mozart.

[★ ★ RATHAUS]. Corner of the City Hall (**Rathaus**) Bridge. Near the "Red Sword" Inn is this splendid Italian Renaissance-style City Hall, built 1698, which the Mozarts undoubtedly visited during their cultural tour of the city. The ground floor offers a beautiful entry with carved doors and portals. The

Zurich. Wein-Platz with The Red Sword Inn. Engraving by J. B. Buttig.

wrought-iron staircase, completely hammered by hand, was the outside gate of the previous City Hall. Inside the rooms can be found several series of extraordinary portraits. The **Regierungsratsaal** on the floor above is noteworthy for the walls, inlaid with fine wood, and for a unique multicolored Delft stove. The City Hall can be visited Tuesday/Thursday/Friday from 10–11:30 AM; no admission charge. The nearby fifteenth-century **Wasserkirche**, which has recently been restored, is also of note.[1]

★ ★ "SWAN" HOUSE (HAUS "ZUM SCHWANEN"). 9 Münstergasse. The Mozarts were undoubtedly frequent guests (their first visit was 3 October 1766) of the artist and poet, Salomon Gessner, who attained world renown for his *Idyllen* (1756), which was translated into numerous languages.[2] Today the ground floor of Gessner's home has been transformed into the Café Salomon, and into offices. There is a carved inscription in gold over the entrance which reads: 1736 "Zum Schwanen," leading to a courtyard. "The immortal Gessner," as his contemporaries called him, was at the focus of cultural life in Zurich in 1766. The edifice is today in the possession of the *Goethe-Stiftung*; it was built over Roman ruins, with a shell from the late Middle Ages. On the street side, the facade has been maintained, and in the small garden of the Café Salomon, original architectural features can be seen. In the offices above the café, many details remain from the eighteenth century and before, including restored rustic wall painting, leaded glass, and reliefs in stucco. Three commemorative plaques can be found, including one which notes the visits of Ewald von Kleist, Christoph Martin Weiland, Johann Wolfgang von Goethe, and Mozart.

[★ ★ CATHEDRAL (GROSSMÜNSTER)]. Zwingliplatz. The usual habit of the Mozarts was to visit the most important religious edifices of each city. This imposing eleventh-thirteenth-century church, where Zwingli began his Reformation preaching in 1519, has a gigantic statue of Charlemagne on the south tower.[3]

★ ★ MUSIKSAAL BEIM FRAUMÜNSTER. In the City Hall (**Stadthaus**), Stadthausquai 17. The Mozarts were given permission to give two concerts in Zurich, which took place on 7 and 9 October 1766 in the music room which belonged to the **Kornhaus** Music Collegium. Today part of the music room has been incorporated into the music room of the *Stadthaus*. Although the organ which Mozart would have played was removed in 1813, certain features remain from the period, such as the stucco ceiling with a fresco from 1729 by Johannes Brandenberg.[4] The room was renovated in 1957 with wood parquet, wainscoting, and large wrought-iron chandeliers. The surrounding area, the **Münsterhof**, with its restored facades, is of interest. The *Stadthaus* is open Monday to Friday 8:30 AM–6 PM.

Zurich. Music Room near the Kornhaus. Engraving by Melchior Füssli, 1718.

[★ ★ ★ GUILDHALL "ZUR MEISEN"]. Münsterhof 20. A fascinating glimpse into eighteenth-century Zurich can be seen in this 1752–57 building by David Morf, in the immediate area where the Mozart children gave two concerts. The edifice features staircases of wrought-iron and gold leaf, and a splendid eighteenth century interior. Painted porcelains by Salomon Gessner, the host of the Mozarts; in addition, there are portraits of Gessner and his wife, and a small bust of Gessner from around 1775–80. The ceiling is original ornate stucco, with fresco painting and large Delft stoves. In addition, there are clocks, antique furniture and parquet floors. The building is presently the **Schweizerisches Landesmuseum.** It is open Tuesday–Friday and Sunday 10 AM–Noon and 2–5 PM; Saturday 10 AM–Noon and 2–4 PM; no admission charge.

Other Sites of Interest:
Winterhur

★ FORMER STADTKANZLEI. Unt. Graben 35, corner of Marktgasse. There are two likely possibilities for where the Mozarts stayed on their overnight stop in Winterthur. The first is the living quarters in the city chancellery furnished by the city to the town clerk, Wolfgang Dietrich Sulzer, who was close friends with the Mozarts' host in Zurich, Salomon Gessner.[5] The large building, known as **Hinwilerhaus**, had an important library with many volumes collected by Sulzer and his father (in German, English, and French), including theology, seventeenth-century history, and natural sciences and philosophy from the Enlightenment.[6] The well-educated city notary was interested in the fine arts as well, and the business-minded Leopold left copper engravings and sonatas with him to sell. The stark gray building with a statue of an apothecary on the corner was restored in 1777; the inside has been completely renovated, leaving nothing from the time of the Mozarts' visit. It is today the site of a drug store (**Rathaus Apotheke**), doctors' offices, and a laboratory.

★ "WILD MAN" INN ("ZUM WILDENMANN"). 3 Obertor. Whether the Mozarts stayed in the Gasthof "Zum Wildenmann" or in the living quarters of the city clerk, Sulzer, is a question that has not been resolved.[7] Today, the former guest house hosts a restaurant on the ground floor, with private apartments above. Although the interior has been renovated in a rustic style, the facade remains, suggesting how the *gasthof* looked in the eighteenth century. The edifice is charming and unpretentious, with a cornice in the original style, arched windows, and smaller rectangular windows characteristic of the period when the Mozarts visited Winterthur. The hanging sign of a wild man has been restored; a commemorative plaque reads that it was the **Gasthof Zum Wilden-**

mann from 1628–1948. The fine street, **Obertor**, is in a remarkable state of preservation, and provides a suggestion of the city the Mozarts saw it in 1766.

N o t e s

1 Michelin, *Switzerland*, 198.
2 Staehelin, *Die Reise der Familie Mozart durch die Schweiz*, 59
3 Michelin, op. cit., 198.
4 Widmer, *Das Stadthaus in Zürich*, 10.
5 Staehelin, *Die Reise der Familie Mozart durch die Schweiz*, 74.
6 Ganz, *Winterthur*, 218–19.
7 Staehelin, op. cit., 74.

Chronology of Mozart's Travels

SALZBURG
27 January 1756–12 January 1762

FIRST TRIP TO MUNICH
(12 January 1762–Beginning February 1762)

MUNICH
*About 14 January to
mid-February 1762*

SALZBURG
Beginning of February 1762–18 September 1762

FIRST TRIP TO VIENNA
(18 September 1762–5 January 1763)

PASSAU
20–26 September 1762

LINZ
26 September–4 October 1762

MAUTHAUSEN
*4/5 October 1762
(Overnight stay)*

YBBS
*5 October 1762
(Mozart performs on the organ
in the Franciscan church)*

STEIN
5 October 1762

VIENNA
6 October–11 December 1762

PRESSBURG (BRATISLAVA)
11–24 December 1762

VIENNA
24–31 December 1762

LINZ
2 January 1763

SALZBURG
5 January 1763–9 June 1763

"GREAT WESTERN" TRIP
(9 June 1763–29 November 1766)

WASSERBURG AM INN
10–12 June 1763

MUNICH
12–22 June 1763

AUGSBURG
22 June–6 July 1763

ULM
6/7 July 1763

WESTERSTETTEN
7 July 1763

GEISLINGEN
7 July 1763

GÖPPINGEN
About 8 July 1763

PLOCHINGEN
About 8 July 1763

CANNSTATT
About 8 July 1763

LUDWIGSBURG
9–12 July 1763
(Lodging in the "Golden Horn"
Inn [Gasthof "Zum
goldenen Waldhorn"])

VAIHINGEN/ENZ
12 July 1763

BRUCHSAL
12–about 14 July 1763
(Lodging in the "Giant" Inn
[Gasthof " Zum Riesen"])

SCHWETZINGEN
About 14–about 29 July 1763
(Excursion to Heidelberg:
about 25 July 1763)

MANNHEIM
About 30 July–about 1 August
1763

WORMS
About 1–about 2 August 1763

OPPENHEIM
About 2 August 1763

MAINZ
About 3 August 1763–about
10 August 1763

FRANKFURT
About 10–31 August 1763

MAINZ
31 August–mid-September 1763

BIEBRICH
Excursion during the course
of the first half
of September 1763

WIESBADEN
Excursion during the course
of the first half
of September 1763

KOSTHEIM
Excursion during the course
of the first half
of September 1763

WALLUF
13/14 September 1763

ÖSTRICH
14/15 September 1763

BINGEN
15/16 September 1763

ST. GOAR
  16 September 1763

SALZIG
  16/17 September 1763

COBLENZ
  *17 September 1763–27 September
  1763*

BONN
  27/28 September 1763

BRÜHL
  28 September 1763

COLOGNE
  29/30 September 1763

AACHEN
  30 September–2 October 1763

LIÈGE (LUETTICH)
  *2/3 October 1763
  (Lodging in the "Black Eagle" Inn
  [Gasthof "Zum schwarzen Adler"])*

TIRLEMONT
  *3/4 October 1763
  (Overnight stay)*

LOUVAIN (LÖWEN/LEUVEN)
  *4 October 1763
  (Lodging in the "Wild Man" Inn
  ["Gasthof "Zum wilden Mann"])*

BRUSSELS
  *About 5 October–15 November
  1763*

MONS
  15 November 1763

BONAVIS
  16/17 November 1763

GOURNAY
  17/18 November 1763

PARIS
  *18 November 1763–10 April 1764
  (Trip to Versailles:
  24 December 1763–8 January 1764)*

CALAIS
  19–about 21 April 1764

DOVER
  About 22 April 1764

LONDON
  23 April–6 August 1764

CHELSEA
  6 August–about 25 September 1764

LONDON
  *About 25 September 1764–24 July
  1765*

CANTERBURY
  *24 July–31 July 1765
  (Visit to Bourne Place:
  26–29 July 1765)*

DOVER
  1 August 1765

CALAIS
  1/2 August 1765

DUNKIRK
  3/about 4 August 1765

BERGUES
  About 4 August 1765

LILLE
  About 5 August–4 September 1765

GHENT
  4 and 5 September 1765

ANTWERP
  6–9 September 1765

MÖERDIJK
  6 September 1765

ROTTERDAM
  9/10 September 1765

THE HAGUE
  *10 September 1765–about 27
  January 1766*

AMSTERDAM
*About 27 January–beginning March
1766*

THE HAGUE
Beginning March–end March 1766

HAARLEM
Beginning of April–mid-April 1766

AMSTERDAM
Mid-April–18 April 1766

UTRECHT
18 April–end of April 1766

ROTTERDAM
End of April 1766

MÖERDIJK
Beginning May 1766

ANTWERP
Beginning May 1766

MECHELEN
Beginning May 1766

BRUSSELS
8/9 May 1766

VALENCIENNES
*9 May 1766
(Visit with Madame
Maria-Thérèse Geoffrin)*

CAMBRAI
*10 May 1766
(Visit to the monument of Fénelon)*

PARIS
*10 May–9 July 1766
(Trip to Versailles: 28–30 May
1766)*

DIJON
About 12–about 25 July 1766

LYONS
*About 26 July–about 20 August
1766*

GENEVA
*20 August–about 10 September
1766*

LAUSANNE
11 September–18 September 1766

BERN
*18 September–about 26 September
1766*

BAADEN IM AAARGAU
27 (28) September 1766

ZURICH
*About 28 September–12 October
1766*

WINTERTHUR
13 October 1766

SCHAFFHAUSEN
14–19 October 1766

DONAUESCHINGEN
*19 October–about 1 November
1766*

MESSKIRCH
About 1 November 1766

ULM
About 2 November 1766

GÜNZBURG
About 3 November 1766

DILLINGEN
3–6 November 1766

BIBERBACH (MARKT BIBERBACH)
6 November 1766

AUGSBURG
7 November 1766

MUNICH
8–about 27 November 1766

ALTÖTTING
About 27 November 1766

LAUFEN
About 28 November 1766

SALZBURG
29 November 1766–11 September 1767

SECOND TRIP TO VIENNA
(11 September 1767–5 January 1769)

VÖCKLABRUCK
11 September 1767
(Overnight stay)

LAMBACH ABBEY
12 September 1767

LINZ
12 September 1767
(Overnight stay)

STRENGBERG
13 September 1767
(Overnight stay)

MELK ABBEY
14 September 1767

ST. PÖLTEN
14/15 September 1767
(Overnight stay)

PURKERSDORF
15 September 1767

VIENNA
15 September 1767–23 October 1767

BRÜNN (BRNO)
24 and 25 October 1767

OLMÜTZ (OLOMOUC)
26 October–about 23 December 1767

BRÜNN (BRNO)
24 December 1767–9 January 1768

POYSDORF
9/10 January 1768
(Overnight stay)

VIENNA
10 January–about 27 December 1768

MELK ABBEY
28/29 December 1768
(Overnight stay)

LAMBACH ABBEY
4 January 1769

SALZBURG
5 January 1769–13 December 1769

FIRST ITALIAN TRIP
(13 December 1769–28 March 1771)

KAITL BEI REICHENHALL
13 December 1769

LOFER
13/14 December 1769
(Lodging with Johann Chrysostomus Helmreich)

ST. JOHANN
14 December 1769

WÖRGL
14/15 December 1769

SCHWAZ
15 December 1769

INNSBRUCK
15–19 December 1769

STEINACH
19/20 December 1769
(Overnight stay)

VIPITENO (STERZING)
20 December 1769

BRESSANONE (BRIXEN)
20/21 December 1769
(Overnight stay)

ATZWANG
21 December 1769

BOLZANO (BOZEN)
21–23 December 1769

NEUMARKT (EGNA)
23/24 December 1769
(Overnight stay)

TRENT
24 December 1769

ROVERETO
24–27 December 1769

VERONA
*27 December 1769–10 January
1770*

MANTUA
10–19 January 1770

BOZZOLO
19/20 January 1770
*(Lodging in the "Post" Inn
["Albergo della Posta"])*

CREMONA
20–about 22 January 1770

MILAN
23 January–15 March 1770

LODI
About 16 March 1770

PIACENZA
Between 16 and 24 March 1770

PARMA
Between 16 and 24 March 1770

MODENA
Between 16 and 24 March 1770

BOLOGNA
24–29 March 1770

FLORENCE
30 March–6 April 1770

SIENA
Between 6 and 10 April 1770

ORVIETO
Between 6 and 10 April 1770

VITERBO
About 10 April 1770

ROME
11 April–8 May 1770

MARINO
8 May 1770
*(Visit to the Augustine
Monastery on Lake Albano)*

TERRACINA
About 10 May 1770

SESSA
11/12 May 1770

CAPUA
12–14 May 1770
*(Mozart and his father are invited to
the festivities of the entrance of a
noblewoman into the convent)*

NAPLES
14 May–25 June 1770
*(Excursion to Pozzuoli: 13 June
1770)*
(Excursion to Baia: 13 June 1770)
*(Excursion to the Monastery of San
Martino: 16 June 1770)*
*(Excursion to Vesuvius, Pompeii,
Herculaneum, Caserta and
Capodimonte: 18 and 19 June
1770)*

ROME
  26 June–10 July 1770

CIVITÁ CASTELLANA
  11 July 1770
  *(Mozart performs on the organ in
  the cathedral)*

TERNI
  Between 11 and 16 July 1770

SPOLETO
  Between 12 and 16 July 1770

FOLIGNO
  Between 12 and 16 July 1770

LORETO
  16–about 17 July 1770

ANCONA
  17 July 1770

SENIGÁLLIA
  About 17 July 1770

PÉSARO
  About 18 July 1770

RIMINI
  About 18 July 1770

FORLÍ
  About 19 July 1770

IMOLA
  19 July 1770

BOLOGNA
  20 July–about 13 October 1770

PARMA
  About 14 October 1770

PIACENZA
  About 16 October 1770

MILAN
  *18 October 1770–about 14 January
  1771*
  *(Trip to Turin: 14 January–31
  January 1771)*

CANONICA
  Between 4 and 11 February 1771

BRESCIA
  Between 4 and 11 February 1771

VERONA
  Between 4 and 11 February 1771

VICENZA
  Between 4 and 11 February 1771

PADUA
  About 10 February 1771

VENICE
  11 February–12 March 1771

PADUA
  12–14 March 1771

VICENZA
  14 and 15 March 1771

VERONA
  16–20 March 1771

ROVERETO
  About 20 March 1771

BRESSANONE (BRIXEN)
  About 21 March 1771

INNSBRUCK
  25/26 March 1771

SALZBURG
28 March 1771–13 August 1771

SECOND ITALIAN TRIP
(13 August 1771–15 December 1771)

KAITL
13 August 1771

WAIDRING
13 August 1771

ST. JOHANN
13/14 August 1771
(Overnight stay)

KUNDL
14 August 1771

INNSBRUCK
14/15 August 1771
(Overnight stay)

STEINACH
15 August 1771

BRESSANONE (BRIXEN)
15/16 August 1771
(Overnight stay)

BOLZANO
16 August 1771

TRENT
16/17 August 1771
(Overnight stay)

ROVERETO
17 August 1771

ALA
17/18 August 1771
(Lodging with the Pizzini brothers)

VERONA
18–20 August 1771

BRESCIA
20/21 August 1771
(Overnight stay)

CANONICA
21 August 1771

MILAN
21 August–5 December 1771

BRESCIA
6/7 December 1771

VERONA
7/8 December 1771

ALA
8/9 December 1771

TRENT
9 and 10 December 1771

BRESSANONE (BRIXEN)
11–13 December 1771
(Mozart and his father have a musical session with Count Ignaz Joseph Spaur)

INNSBRUCK
14 December 1771

SALZBURG
15 December 1771–24 October 1772

THIRD ITALIAN TRIP
(24 October 1772—13 March 1773)

ST. JOHANN
24/25 October 1772

INNSBRUCK
25–27 October 1772
(Excursion to Halle: 26 October 1772)

BRESSANONE (BRIXEN)
27/28 October 1772

BOLZANO
28/29 October 1772

TRENT
29 October 1772

ROVERETO
29/30 October 1772

ALA
30 and 31 October 1772
(Lodging with the Pizzini brothers)

VERONA
1–3 November 1772

BRESCIA
3/4 November 1772

MILAN
4 November 1772—about 4 March 1773

BRESCIA
About 5 March 1773

VERONA
About 6—about 7 March 1773

ALA
About 8—about 10 March 1773
(Visit to the Pizzini brothers)

TRENT
About 10 March 1773

BRESSANONE (BRIXEN)
About 11 March 1773

INNSBRUCK
About 12 March 1773

SALZBURG
13 March 1773—14 July 1773

THIRD TRIP TO VIENNA
(14 July 1773—26 September 1773)

VIENNA
16 July—about 24 September 1773
(Excursion to Baden bei Wien: 21–23 August 1773)

SCHWECHAT
22 September 1773
(Visit to the summer residence of Dr. Franz Anton Mesmer)

ST. PÖLTEN
24 September 1773

LINZ
About 24 September 1773

LAMBACH ABBEY
25 September 1773

SALZBURG
26 September 1773–6 December 1774

SECOND TRIP TO MUNICH
(6 December 1774–7 March 1775)

FRABERTSHAM
6 December 1774

WASSERBRUG AM INN
6/7 December 1774
(Overnight stay)

MUNICH
7 December 1774–6 March 1775

WASSERBURG AM INN
6/7 March 1775
(Overnight stay)

SALZBURG
7 March 1775–23 September 1777

TRIP TO PARIS
(23 September 1777–Mid-January 1779)

WAGING
23 September 1777

STEIN
23 September 1777

FRABERTSHAM
23 September 1777

WASSERBURG AM INN
23/24 September 1777
(Overnight stay)

MUNICH
24 September–11 October 1777

AUGSBURG
11–26 October 1777

DONAUWÖRTH
26 October 1777

NÖRDLINGEN
26 October 1777

HOHENALTHEIM
26–28 October 1777

NÖRDLINGEN
28 October 1777

CANNSTATT
About 28 October 1777

AALEN
About 28 October 1777

SCHWÄBISCH GMÜND
About 28 October 1777

BRUCHSAL
29 October 1777

SCHWETZINGEN
29 October 1777

VAIHINGEN/ENZ
About 29 October 1777

MANNHEIM
30 October 1777–14 March 1778
(Excursion to Kirchheimbolanden:
23–29 January 1778)
(Excursion to Worms: 29 January–
2 February 1778)

METZ
About 18 March 1778

CLERMONT
19 March 1778

PARIS
23 March–26 September 1778
(Visit to Saint-Germain: 19–about
28 August 1778)

NANCY
About 3–about 13 October 1778

STRASBOURG
About 14 October–3 November
1778

MANNHEIM
6 November–9 December 1778

HEIDELBERG
9 December 1778

SCHWÄBISCH HALL
About 9 December 1778

CRAILSHEIM
About 10 December 1778

DINKELSBÜHL
About 11 December 1778

WALLERSTEIN
About 11 December 1778

NÖRDLINGEN
About 12 December 1778

KAISHEIM
13–14 December 1778
(Lodging as guests in the
monastery)

NEUBURG/DONAU
About 24 December 1778

INGOLSTADT
About 24 December 1778

MUNICH
25 December 1778–about 13
January 1779

SALZBURG
Mid-January 1779–5 November 1780

TRIP TO MUNICH AND VIENNA
(5 November 1780–16 March 1781)

SEEON MONASTERY
Around 5 November 1780
(Brief visit)

MUNICH
6 November 1780–12 March 1781
(Excursion of Mozart, his father
and sister to Augsburg: 7–10 March
1781)

KEMMELBACH
About 15 March 1781

VIENNA
(Permanent residence of Mozart from 16 March 1781)

LAXENBURG
20 July 1782

TRIP TO SALZBURG
(End of July 1783−end of November 1783)

VÖCKLABRUCK
27/28 October 1783

EBELSBERG
29 October 1783

LAMBACH ABBEY
28 October 1783

LINZ
30 October−end November 1783

VIENNA
(End of November 1783−8 January 1787)

BADEN (BEI WIEN)
Beginning June 1784

LAXENBURG
Beginning June 1784

KLOSTERNEUBURG (NEUBURG MONASTERY)
19 April 1785
(Mozart and his father visit Baroness Martha Elisabeth von Waldstätten)

FIRST TRIP TO PRAGUE
(8 January 1787−Mid-February 1787)

PRAGUE
11 January−8 February 1787

VIENNA
(Mid-February 1787−1 October 1787)

SECOND TRIP TO PRAGUE
(1 October 1787−Mid-November 1787)

PRAGUE
4 October−about 13 November 1787

VIENNA
Mid-November 1787–8 April 1789

TRIP TO BERLIN
(8 April 1789–4 June 1789)

ZNAIM
8 April 1789

BUDWITZ (MÄHRISCH-BUDWITZ)
8/9 April 1789
(Overnight stay)

IGLAU
9 April 1789

ČASLAV
9 April 1789
(Overnight stay)

PRAGUE
10 April 1789

DRESDEN
12–18 April 1789

MEISSEN
18 April 1789

WURZEN
About 19 April 1789

LEIPZIG
20–about 23 April 1789

POTSDAM
About 25 April–about 6 May 1789

LEIPZIG
8–17 May 1789

BERLIN
19–28 May 1789

PRAGUE
31 May–about 2 June 1789

VIENNA
4 June 1789–23 September 1790

SCHWECHAT
Mid-May 1790 (probably 16 May 1790)
(Mozart visits the parents of the musician, Joseph Eybler)

BADEN (BEI WIEN)
June 1790

BADEN (BEI WIEN)
About 15–18 August 1789

TRIP TO FRANKFURT AM MAIN
(Beginning of November 1790–25 August 1791)

EFERDING BEI LINZ
23/24 September 1790

REGENSBURG
25 September 1790
(Lodging in the "White Lamb" Inn [Gasthof "Zum weissen Lamm"])

NÜRNBERG
About 26 September 1790

WÜRZBURG
About 27 September 1790

ASCHAFFENBURG
About 27 September 1790

FRANKFURT AM MAIN
28 September–16 October 1790

MAINZ
16–21 October 1790

MANNHEIM
About 23–25 October 1790
(Excursion to Schwetzingen: 24
October 1790)

BRUCHSAL
End of October 1790

CANNSTATT
End of October 1790

GÖPPINGEN
End of October 1790

ULM
End of October 1790

GÜNZBURG
End of October 1790

AUGSBURG
About 28/29 October 1790

MUNICH
29 October–about 6 November
1790

LINZ
About 8 November 1790

VIENNA
Beginning of November 1790–25 August 1791

BADEN (BEI WIEN)
June 1791 (perhaps as early as 13
June 1791)

THIRD TRIP TO PRAGUE
(25 August 1791–Mid-September 1791)

PRAGUE
28 August–mid-September 1791

VIENNA
Mid-September 1791–5 December 1791

BADEN (BEI WIEN)
16 October 1791

Useful Bibliography

Anderson, Emily, trans. *The Letters of Mozart and his Family*. Edited by S. Sadie and F. Smart. 3rd ed. London: Macmillan, 1989.

Braunbehrens, Volkmar. *Mozart in Vienna*. New York: Grove, Weidenfeld, 1989.

Einstein, Alfred. *Mozart, His Character, His Work*. New York: Oxford University Press, 1945.

Hildesheimer, Wolfgang. *Mozart*. New York: Farrar, Straus, Giroux, 1982.

Landon, H. C. Robbins, ed. *The Mozart Compendium*. New York: Schirmer, 1990.

_____. *Mozart; The Golden Years*. London: Thames and Hudson, 1989.

_____. *1791; Mozart's Last Year*. New York: Schirmer, 1988.

Levey, Michael. *The Life and Death of Mozart*. Great Britain: Weidenfeld & Nicholson Ltd, 1971.

Marshall, Robert. *Mozart Speaks*. New York: Schirmer, 1991.

Sadie, Stanley. *The New Grove Mozart*. First published in *The New Grove Dictionary of Music and Musicians*, edited by Stanley Sadie. Washington, D.C.: Norton, 1980. The brief catalog of Mozart's works at the end is also very helpful.

Zaslaw, Neil. *Mozart's Symphonies: Context, Performance Practice, Reception*. Oxford: Clarendon Press, 1989.

Select Bibliography

(For a more complete Mozart bibliography, see Bauer/Deutsch/Eibl, *Mozart Briefe und Aufzeichnungen*, VII. In addition, Robbins-Landon's *The Mozart Companion* has a recent bibliography)

Agnelli, Giuseppe. "A proposito della lapide mozartiana alla Gatta." *Corriere dell'Adda* (29 December 1956): 21.

Anderson, Emily, trans. *The Letters of Mozart and His Family*. Edited by S. Sadie and F. Smart. 3rd ed. London: Macmillan 1989.

Angermüller, Rudolph. *W.A. Mozarts musikalische Umwelt in Paris*. Munich: Katzbichler, 1982.

Arnold, Karl. "Mozart in Lodi." *Wiener Figaro* (September 1970): 14–17.

Ausserer, Rudolf. "W.A. Mozarts Reisen durch Südtirol-Trentino." (1982): 120–21.

Austria. Middlesex, England: Michelin, 1990.

Barblan, Guglielmo, *et al. Mozart in Italia*. Milan: Ricordi, 1956.

Barille, Francesca. "Gli inventari quattrocentesche della biblioteca conventuale e della sacrestia di San Marco a Milano . . ." Thesis, Catholic University of the Sacred Heart, Milano, 1984.

Bauer, Wilhelm A., Otto Erich Deutsch, and Joseph Heinz Eibl. *Mozart Briefe und Aufzeichnungen*. 7 vol. Kassel: Baerenreiter, 1962.

Beaumont, Jean. "L'enfant Mozart à Lyon en 1766." *Resonances* 142 (June 1966): 7–8.

————. "Mozart et le Musique Lyonnaise en 1766." *Zebo-Liberté* (4 July 1966): 5.

Belgique. Paris: Michelin, 1990.

Biller, Josef H. and Hans-Peter Rasp. *München Kunst und Kultur Lexikon*. Munich: Süddeutscher Verlag, 1985.

Biraghi, Guiliana. *Palazzo Lascaris*. Turin: Edizione EDA, 1982.

Braunbehrens, Volkmar. *Mozart in Vienna*. New York: Grove Weidenfeld, 1989.

Buchner, Alexander, Karel Koval, Karel Mikysa, and Antonin Čubr. *Mozart and Prague*. Prague: Artia, 1957.

Budian, Hans. "Mannheimer Mozartgedenkstätten." In *Das Mannheimer Mozart-Buch*. Wilhelmshaven: Heinrichshofen, 1979.

Caretta, Alessandro. "Le epigrafi sbagliate." *Il Cittadino* (23 October 1987): 11.

Charles, Scott. *All About Geneva*. Geneva: Georg et Cie, 1985.

Corneloup, Gérard. "Quand Lyon recevait Mozart dans la Salle des Concerts de la Place des Cordeliers." *Souvenir Musical* (26 December 1982).

Czeike, Felix. *Das Grosse Groner-Wien-Lexikon*. Vienna: Molden, 1974.

Eibl, Joseph Heinz. *Chronik eines Lebens*. Kassel: Baerenreiter, 1965.

Evertz, Leonhard. *Mozart am Rhein 1763*. Aachen: Rheinische Mozart-forschung, 1977.

Ferrari-Bravo, Anna, ed. *Milano*. 9th ed. Milan: Touring Club Italiano, 1985.

Francia. Milan: Touring Club Italiano, 1984.

Fritsch, J. "Le Thêâtre français à Strasbourg de 1830 à 1870." Unpublished article, [n.d.]: 9–10.

Fyot, M. Eugène. "Mozart à Dijon." *Mémoires de l'Académie de Dijon* (1937): 23–27.

Ganz, Werner. *Winterthur; Einführung in seine Geschichte*. Neujahrsblatt der Stadtbibliothek Winterthur, 1961: 292.

Germany. Middlesex, England: Michelin, 1986.

Giersberg, Hans-Joachim and Harmut Knitter. *Potsdam*. Berlin: VEB Tourist Verlag, 1985.

Graf zu Lynar, E. W. *Schloss Donaueschingen*. Munich/Zurich: Schnell & Steiner, [n. d.].

Haas, Rudolf. "Mozart im Bretzenheimschen Haus zu Mannheim." In *Das Mannheimer Mozart-Buch*. Wilhelmshaven: Heinrichshofen, 1979.

Häuserbuchs der Stadt München. 5 vol. Munich: Stadtarchiv München, 1958–77.

Hillairet, Jacques. *Dictionnaire historique des rues de Paris*. 3rd ed. Paris: Minuit, 1963.

Hugli, Jean. *Lausanne: Destin d'une ville*. Lausanne: Municipalité de Lausanne, 1981.

Italia. Turin: Michelin, 1984.

Kampé de Fériet, M. J. "Le Séjour de la Famille Mozart à Lille en 1765." Communication of the *Société des Sciences de l'Agriculture et des Arts de Lille* (8 March 1957).

Kenyon, Max. *Mozart in Salzburg*. New York: Putnam, 1953.

Klein, Rudolf. "Der Saal des Ignaz Jahn: Eine Wiener Mozart-Beethoven-Stätte." *Acta Mozartiana* 17 (November 1970): 51ff.

Landon, H.C. Robbins, ed. *The Mozart Compendium*. New York: Schirmer, 1990.

_____. *Mozart, The Golden Years*. London: Thames and Hudson, 1989.

_____. *1791, Mozart's Last Year*. New York: Schirmer, 1988.

Layer, Adolf. "Mozart in Dillingen." *Jahrbuch des Historischen Vereins Dillingen* LVII/LVIII (1958).

Leroy, J, ed. *Brussels*. Brussels: Puvrez, 1989.

Levin, Robert D. *Who Wrote the Mozart Four-Wind Concertante?* Stuyvesant, N. Y.: Pendragon Press, 1988.

Lievense, W. *De Familie Mozart op Bezoek in Nederlands een Reisverslag.* Helfenshoen: 1965.

Lorenzetti, Giulio. *Venezia e il suo estuario.* Triest: LINT, 1974.

Mancal, Josef. "Augsburger Mozartstätten."

Marez, G. des. *Guide illustré de Bruxelles.* Brussels: Touring Club, [n. d.].

Massin, Jean and Brigitte Massin. *W.A. Mozart.* Paris: Fayard, 1970.

Mauthe, Ursula. "Wo blieb die Heidelberger 'Mozart-Orgel'?" In *Das Mannheimer Mozart-Buch.* Wilhelmshaven: Heinrichshofen, 1979.

Mossemann, K. "Ortsgeschichtliche Betrachtung über die Gaststätte 'Das rote Haus' in Schwetzingen." Schwetzingen, unpublished article, [n.d.]: 1–6.

Münster, Robert. " 'Ich bin hier sehr beliebt.' " *Acta Mozartiana* 25 (Jan. 25, 1978): 3–18.

———. "Mozart Münchener Aufenthalt 1777 . . ." *Mozart Jahrbuch* (1964): 88ff.

———. "Mozarts Münchener Aufenthalt von 1766." *Acta Mozartiana* 18 (1971): 2–7.

———. "München und Wasserburg am Inn." *Acta Mozartiana* 15 (1968): 32–41.

———. "Zwei verlorene Münchener Mozart-Stätten: Das Haus des Grafen Salern und Alberts Gasthof zum Schwarzen Adler." *Mozarteums-Mitteilungen* 14 (February 1966): 15ff.

Netherlands. Middlesex, England: Michelin, 1990.

Paganuzzi, E. *L'Accademia Filarmonica di Verona e il suo teatro.* Verona, 1982.

Pahlmann, Manfred. "Tiergarten." In *Vom Brandenburger Tor zum Zoo.* Berlin: Historical Commission of Berlin, 1989.

Pohl, C. F. *Mozart und Haydn in London.* Vienna: Carl Gerold's Son, 1867.

Poll, Bernhard. "Mozart in Aachen." In *Zeitschrift des Aachener Geschichtsvereins,* 68 (1956): 360–70.

Pröger Johannes. "Die 'Mozartorgel' in der St. Pauluskirche zu Kirchheimbolanden." *Acta Mozartiana* 15 (1968): 26–31.

Reuter, Fritz. *Worms: Concise City Guide.* Worms: Hermann G. Klein, 1987.

Roma e Dintorni. Milan: Touring Club Italiano, 1977.

Saam, Josef. "Mozart in Passau." *Acta Mozartiana* 13 (1966): 7–15.

Sadie, Stanley. *The New Grove Mozart.* Washington, D. C.: Norton, 1980.

Sartori, Claudio. "Mozart in Brescia." *Music and Letters.* MLXLVII (1966): 141ff.

Schenk, Erich. *Mozart and His Times.* London: Secker & Warburg, 1960.

———. "Mozart in Mantua." In *Studien zur Musikwissenschaft* 22 (1955): 1ff.

Segala, Franco. *La Chiesa di San Tomaso Cantuariense.* Verona, 1988.

Stadtarchiv München. *Häuserbuch der Stadt München.* 5 vol. Munich: Oldenbourg, 1958–77.

Staehelin, Lucas. *Die Reise der Familie Mozart durch die Schweiz.* Bern: Francke Verlag, 1968.

Stief, Werner. "Mozart in Schwetzingen—'Stern-allee' und 'Rotes Haus.' " In *Das Mannheimer Mozart-Buch.* Wilhelmshaven: Heinrichshofen, 1979.

Switzerland. Middlesex, England: Michelin, 1990.

Tyson, Alan. *Mozart: The Autograph Scores*. Cambridge, Mass.: Harvard University Press, 1987.

Veneto. Milan: Touring Club Italiano, 1969.

Vernisy, Edmond de. "Mozart à Dijon." In *La vie française* (11 November 1938).

Wachmeier, Günter. *Paris*. Zurich: Artemis, 1984.

Widmer, Sigmund. *Das Stadthaus in Zürich*. Basel: Birkhäuser AG, 1979.

Würtz, Roland, ed. *Das Mannheimer Mozart-Buch*. Wilhelmshaven: Heinrichshofen, 1977.

Zaslaw, Neil. *Mozart's Symphonies: Context, Performance Practice, Reception*. Oxford: Clarendon Press, 1989.

Acknowledgments

I would like to acknowledge those whose collaboration made this book possible. The many contributions of those who participated are cited in the notes to the individual chapters. In addition, there are many others, without whose help this book could not have been written. My thanks to Dr. Robert Marshall, Mr. Alfredo Mandolini, and the many kind hosts in each country: Mr. Jan Theodor de Vries, Mrs. Ingrid Hesse Peitchev, Dr. Alberto Cervi, Mr. Christian Schoonis, Mr. and Mrs. Michael and Alisa Craxton, Mrs. Monika Scheck, Dr. Florian Scheck, Mr. and Mrs. Stefano and Patrizia Mandolini, Mr. Manfred Pahlmann, Mr. Friedrich Wagner, and Mr. Tullio Mandolini. In addition, a special thanks to Monsieur Paul Doguereau.

AUSTRIA

Mr. Hans Zöttl, Café Centrum; Miss Albine Felber, Salzburg Information; Maria Paula Palma Caetano, Dir. Elfriede Winter, and Renate Walli, Wiener Fremdenverkehrsverband, Vienna.

BELGIUM

Léon Zylbergeld, Archiviste Musées Communaux, Brussels; Annette Onyn, Office de Tourisme, Brussels; O. Guffens, Town Clerk, Leuven.

CZECHOSLAVAKIA

Ing. Helena Holcová, Travel and Hotel Corporation, Prague.

ENGLAND

Sue Williams, London Tourist Board.

FRANCE

Robert Furter, Syndicat d'Initiative de Dijon; Gilles Eboli, Conservateur, Bibliothèque Municipale, Dijon; Vera Dupuis, Office of Tourisme, Lille; G. Tournouer, Bibliothèque Municipale, Lille; Valérie Mesle, Office du Tourisme, Lyons; Christiane Drouin, Manager, Office de Tourisme de Nancy; Marcelle Benoir, Archives Nationales, Paris; J. Y. Mariotte, Directeur Archives, Strasbourg.

GERMANY

Verena Kienzle, Verkehrsverein Bad Aachen; Gerda M. Rutsche, Tourist Office Augsburg; Karl-Heinz Gummich, Reisebüro der Deutschen Demokratischen Republik, Berlin; Dir. Rolf E. Scheid and Uwe Weiland, Tourist Agency Coblenz; Amtsrat Hechler, Frankfurt; Herr Hütte, Verkehrsamt Frankfurt; Landesmusikrat Engelbert Licht, Mainz; Jürgen Schmidt, Verkehrsverein, Mainz; Stadtarchivamtfrau Becker, Mannheim; Dir. Herbert Winkler, Dr. Verena Schaefer, and Elsa Klotz, Tourist Office, Munich; Dr. Heimers, Stadtarchiv München; Dir. Georg Steiner, Fremdenverkehrsverein, Passau; Stadtarchivar Schaffner, Passau; Dr. Eugen Specker, Stadtarchiv Ulm; Hildegard Osswald, Verkehrsverein Ulm.

HOLLAND

J. F. Roentgen, Maritime Museum, Amsterdam; H. Vink, Amsterdam Tourist Office; Dir. Hans van Westreenen, Royal Theater, The Hague; G. Charlier, Dienst Toerisme, Mechelen.

ITALY

Sig.na Maria Antonietta Nuti, Bologna; Consorzio Siat, Bologna; Sig.na Mirka Bolognese, Tourist Office of Parma; Prof. Luigi Samarati, Lodi; Mariangela Doná, Biblioteca del Conservatorio, Milan; Dr. Vito di Cesare, Ente Provinciale per il Turismo, Rome; Dott.ssa Giselda Russo, Biblioteche Civiche, Turin; Dir. Mario Girard, Azienda di Promozione Turistica di Torino; Mario Berti, Accademia Filarmonica, Verona; Prof. Piero Nichele; Azienda di Promozione Turistica, Verona.

SWITZERLAND

Marianne Howard, Staatsarchiv des Kantons Bern, Martine Rey-Lamini, Archives musicales, Lausanne.